WHICH WITCH?

WHICH WITCH?

BEING

A GROUPING OF PHONETICALLY

COMPATIBLE WORDS

BY

JULIAN FRANKLYN

DORSET PRESS

New York

This edition published by Dorset Press,
a division of Marboro Books Corporation,
by arrangement with
Hamish Hamilton Ltd.
1987 Dorset Press

ISBN 0-88029-164-8

Printed in the United States of America

M 9 8 7 6 5 4 3 2 1

DEDICATED TO

The Much Honoured, The Laird Of Gayre

LT.-COL. GAYRE OF GAYRE AND NIGG:

A SCHOLAR

of International renown

AND A

very Christian

GENTLEMAN

Contents

Acknowledgments

The debt of gratitude I owe is largely due to Eric Partridge who has inspired, encouraged and helped me in all my literary endeavours over a period of more than thirty years.

JULIAN FRANKLYN

List of Abbreviations

Am	=	American
(')	=	also possessive case
C	=	extreme cockney
pl	=	plural
ppl	=	participle
pst	=	past
q.v.	=	*quod vide*, 'which see'
sl	=	slang
tns	=	tense
U.S.A.	=	United States of America
v	=	verb

SIGHT, SENSE AND SOUND

*An essay on the appearance, the meanings and
the pronunciation of certain English words*

The Society for Pure English was founded in 1913, and, like all other
cultural movements of the time, was brutally bludgeoned on 4 August
1914. The S.P.E. was, however, a hardy infant: it did not die of the blow,
but met together again after the Armistice and announced October 1919
as the publication date of its *Tract No. 1*.

This Tract, which sets forth the history, constitution and aims of the
Society, is of historical interest only. *Tract No. 2*, undated except for
the insertion of the year, MDCCCCXIX, on the title-page below the
armorial colophon of the Oxford University Press, has, imprinted on the
verso by the British Museum, '29 October 1919'; hence, it seems to
have been issued simultaneously with No. 1: it is entitled *On English
Homophones*, and its author is Robert Bridges.

The Oxford English Dictionary, and higher authority there is none,
tells us that 'homophone [is] applied to words having the same sound
but differing in meaning or derivation'. Seeking further, we discover from
the same source that 'homonym [is] applied to words having the same
sound but differing in meaning'. The addition to the former definition of
the two words 'or derivation' is not significant: they do not indicate a
subtle difference, for under 'homograph' appears, 'a word of the same
spelling as another, but of different origin and meaning'.

It would seem that words qualify as homophones when they have the
same sound as another word, a different meaning, and a different origin
and derivation. This is comforting, for no learned philologist will refer to
this book as a dictionary of (or even as a glossary of) homonyms, which
would be a flattering description; however, it is to be hoped that, on the
other hand, none will brand it as a punster's compendium. Let it not be
hastily concluded at this juncture that punsters and their products are
exceptionable: far from it. The pun is the power-unit that drives, and
that has always driven, the lifeboat of English humour. We shall return
to puns with laudation, but our object just now is to define the nature and
scope of this book.

It is not a dictionary of homonyms: it is not, strictly speaking, a
dictionary. Strangers to our strange English tongue are advised not to
take the gloss given for each word in a group as a full and satisfactory
definition but to consult *The Oxford English Dictionary*, or if that titanic

opus is not available, *The Shorter Oxford English Dictionary*, wherein many nuances of meaning, not given in the following pages, will be found: but let not the Stranger to our strange English tongue grow apprehensive at the foregoing confession of inadequacy, only what is said is meant; the definitions are often too thin and too short, but they are never misleading. We have not been guilty of writing, for example: '*cat*, a canine quadruped', or '*dog*, a felid ditto'.[1]

In the following groups of words, homophones and homographs, whether they be true or false, are stood together in a line, defined accurately and as copiously as space will permit, then compelled to do a sort of figure-dance in which they fit into place but at the same time assert their individualities. In short, having brought a number of words into juxtaposition, we endeavour to employ them all in one exemplifying paragraph. We have not always succeeded in using, in the example, all the words in a group because these paragraphs, if they are to serve a good purpose, must not run into verbosity.

II

Precognition normally (or rather, abnormally) demands the exercise of Extra Sensory Perception, but none is needed to hear ahead the roar of dissenting voices all excitedly asserting that the pair of words on page x, and the triplets on page y, are not only not homophonous, but are wide asunder in the scale of sound, and only a person with a diseased ear could have brought them together; or, if it is not due to auditory degeneracy, it is a symptom of crass ignorance, an error of comparative phonetics that could have been made only by one unaccustomed to speaking 'the Queen's English'.

It is acknowledged by everyone from Aberdeen that there, and only there, is pure, unadulterated, non-distorted Queen's English spoken. The same may be said for Belfast, Dublin, Cardiff, Earby, Wigan and where you will. Nevertheless, standard English, received English, is Southern English, hence, Cockney English: this there is no denying. The spates of infuriated contention pouring in torrents from all points of the compass are occasioned by the supposition that Cockney refers only to the deep dialect of the established Londoner. It does not. The word has wider signification. It includes, as well as the 'shape' of speech, the tone and timbre of the speaker's voice.

The coverage of Cockney is a matter dealt with elsewhere;[2] here, we handle homophones, and to please all speakers of the Queen's English (for all English spoken is Her Majesty's save that section owned by Uncle

---

[1] Perhaps, for the sake of our hypothetical stranger who may, after all, have substance, we had better say at once that the cat is felid and the dog canine. (K9, which is homophonous.)

[2] *The Cockney*, Julian Franklyn, 1st edn. Feb. 1953, 2nd edn, May 1953.

Sam), we would need to produce a separate thesaurus of homophones for circulation in each dialect area. That version for use north of the River Trent will make a pair of 'coil' and 'coal', of 'oil' and 'hole', of 'flow' and 'flaw', 'no' and 'gnaw', 'sow' and 'saw', even of 'ewers' and 'yours'; but no speaker of the Queen's English who does not know the dialects of the districts north of Trent will cognize the homonymity. The basic reason for such non-recognition is that language is made in the market place, not in the cloister, and the average man—for whom this book is produced—judges the speech-form that differs from his own as faulty, and he finds it just the slightest bit irritating.

Women and children are the guardians of the language of the people. The shape of the speech-form in any area is more strongly emphasized in the school playground than in the public house, and when one whose speech, when a child, would have been unintelligible to a Londoner, settles in London, the strong impact of Cockney takes the corners off so that when he goes north again to visit his aged parents, they complain that he has grown 'reet cockney'. His wife, on her homeward excursions, proves to have modified her own speech-form but little. That the homophones in the following groups do not ring true in the shires is, then, both understandable and forgivable, but the loudest and the longest complainings will come from the people who believe dialect to be vulgar speech, and who, should one run into them after dark at the wrong end of the High Street, will explain that their objective is that place where one can get 'sex',[3] where they supply all kinds of oddities including 'race sex'.[4]

These pillars of society, these criteria of good, bad and indifferent verbal delivery, may generously concede a point when we make of 'tail' and 'tale' a pair, but they will not suffer us to extend it to a triplet by the inclusion in the group of 'towel'. However, to the Cockney 'tail', 'tale' and 'towel' are phonetically all one. They are, as far as the Roman alphabet can reveal, just 'taou'. When we go to such extremes in the glossary, we shall indicate, without apologies, our trespass; but of Cockneys there are roughly ten million, all of whom will accept the groups of words following as homophonous, and some may even complain of the omission of 'air' and 'our'. If only ten per cent of them buy a copy of this book, all the 'naicely spooken' people are welcome to refrain.

III

Of course, people who speak correctly[5] (and that category does not include the 'naicely spooken') make a quite audible distinction between the elements of some of the pairs following, but 'life is real and life is

---

[3] Sacks.   [4] Rice sacks.

[5] P.S.P., Public Schools Pronunciation, is correct because it is accepted as correct, but it is, in itself, a sort of acquired dialect.

earnest' and the average person cannot pick a delicate path between perfect elocutionists. Hence, in the ordinary round of one's daily affairs the best delivery that falls upon the ear is at least modified: it is more likely to be mumbled, only half articulated, and utterly sloven. Furthermore, the auditor is often but partly attentive and, in any case, does not possess an ear sensitive to fine shades of difference in any of, or in all of the elements that go together in the making of verbal articulation.

Shorthand-typists, girls leaving school with the essential G.C.E.,[6] and instantly becoming 'secretaries', are productive of phonetical errors which ought to make them famous, but which, as a rule, simply have the effect of angering their employers (if they notice). It is certainly reprehensible, and it is a disgrace to the teaching profession and an indictment against our painfully expensive educational system, that these girls sometimes do not know which witch: but phonetical errors involving a phrase are often in a different case, and sometimes it takes two to produce them.

The employer ought not to dictate with his pipe in his mouth and his chin on his chest: further, if he makes use of a technical, or only semi-technical word or phrase, or even a non-technical expression that he might reasonably assume to be outside his 'secretary's' experience, he ought to give the girl a gloss. That he fails to do so makes him accessory to the error, and he is himself as culpable as he thinks his 'secretary' is.

It must be admitted—in defence of the employer—that a 'secretary's' range of experience is sometimes so very limited that it seems it would have been necessary, if a phonetical error was to be avoided, to have spelt each word out, letter by letter. What employer, dictating 'I am interested in armorial banners' would have expected to read, 'I am interested in our more real banners'?[7]

A writer who dictated an article on that overwhelming Cockney caricaturist of the late nineteenth to early twentieth centuries, Phil May, was shocked to read, each time the name occurred in the typescript, 'Film A'. The cinema fell within the girl's world; to her, the period of King Edward VII was ancient history. How much more remote the Middle Ages were to an uneducated G.C.E. holder appeared when the dictated sentence, 'at that time the work was executed by lay scholars', was rendered on the typed page as, 'at that time the work was executed by lace collars'.

In the foregoing examples both of the employers had a little responsibility for the errors, but very little, because neither Phil May nor lay scholars ought to be unrecognizable to the G.C.E. holder, but when a girl received the sentence 'insurance cover while he is in America' she is wholly to blame for typing 'insurance cover. Wiley is in America'.[8]

(Loud clamour from the River Trent and parts North: 'Eigh! It couldn't 'appen oop 'ere. We sound t' internal aaitch.')

[6] General Certificate of Education.
[7] From a letter received December 1964.
[8] From a letter dictated in Autumn 1964.

The shorthand-typist is not alone: even the Post Office telegraphist can fall into the trap. Dictating a telegram over the 'phone, and being supremely cautious because the addressee was one who objected to a mis-spelt name, the subscriber began, 'Anne—with an "e", Wolfe—with an "e".' Two telegrams were delivered simultaneously to the address. One to 'Ann Witheney', the other to 'Wolf Witheney'. The subscriber ought to have spelt the names out, or, at any rate, have said, 'with a final "e"' but even though he did neither, the telegraphist ought not to have been so stupid.

Enough has been said to indicate the havoc wrought upon the language by a combination of carelessness, sloven articulation, divided attention and crass ignorance, an alliance that is always with us. By comparison, homophones are harmless, although they are often accused of sabotage and are, in consequence, mercilessly condemned to death.

IV

Robert Bridges says, in *S.P.E. Tract No. 2*, 'it is needful to state that homophonous words must be *different*[9] words, else we should include a whole class of words which are not true homophones.' He uses as an example the words 'draft—draught', divergent in both spelling and meaning but ultimately converging on the idea 'to draw' and many different things can be drawn in variety of ways.

Because Robert Bridges was writing for a specializing public he was well advised to exclude false homophones, but this book is directed to the general public: hence, words of the nature of those excluded from the tract are here included because, to the average person, when a word, spelt and spoken in precisely the same way, has two apparently totally unrelated meanings it is two words notwithstanding that scholars insist upon its being but one, and diversity of spelling strengthens the illusion.

To a person who has 'never given the matter a thought' the statement that there are simple, everyday words of four letters, used by everyone at every cultural and educational level, that, standing alone, have no meaning; and that a simple English sentence involving words of three letters cannot be written by even the most learned, comes as a shock.

Such a word, meaningless, in fact unpronounceable, when in isolation is LEAD: give it a companion and the case is altered: 'lead pipe'. It becomes readable because we know that we pronounce it 'led'; it assumes meaning, for we perceive that it is the name of the heavy, grey metal from which water-pipes are customarily made. 'Lead on', and we read 'leed' which we know means go first, act as guide, set an example. 'Lead', the metal, and 'lead', the action, are not homophones, they are homographs, but 'lead', the metal, and 'led' the past tense and participle of 'lead', the action, are homophonous without being homographic, but

[9] His italics.

'led' and 'lead' the action, are neither homographs nor homophones. The pedant may protest that all three cannot be marshalled in one group, but a glance at the appropriate page in the following glossary will reveal that the pedant is wrong: we have unblushingly done it.

Now let us dictate to our typist a simple little statement of domestic facts and see what she will make of it:

   ... he was sowing seed, and she was sewing sheets: both were ...

Ah! what were they both doing? They were certainly not both sowing; only he was so engaged. Equally certainly, they were not both sewing: only she was doing so. 'Sow' and 'sew' are homophonous, therefore we can dictate the statement and bring it to its conclusion, but because 'sow' and 'sew' are not homographs no one on earth using the Roman alphabet can write the sentence.

The foregoing is a pretty example (the reader might be well advised to make a note of it for use at the next children's party he or she attends) because it leads to a grouping that will not simply shock, but will petrify the pedant.

'Sow' and 'sew' are homophonous, and so is 'so': 'sow', to plant seeds, and 'sow', a female pig, are homographs, and the latter is homophonous with 'sough', the wind in the woods. 'Sough' is both homophonous and homographic with 'sough', a muddy or boggy area of ground. 'Sow' and paucine 'sow' have no such affinities with 'so', or with 'sew' or with 'sow': and this essay is not suitable for reading aloud.

V

The Poet Laureate of the period of *S.P.E. Tract No. 2* displayed in his work a strong dislike of homophones and he revealed a sensitiveness to the sounds of words that only a poet may possess. He asserted that 'homophones are a nuisance, they are exceptionally frequent in English, they are self-destructive and tend to become obsolete'.

He confessed that his second assertion was a reckless one, admitting, 'with all our embarrassment of riches, we cannot compete with the Chinese nor pretend to have outbuilt their Babel'. We have no need to go so far as China: before we are half-way there we find Arabic astride the pass, and that language is quite as rich in homophones as English is. Robert Bridges also admits the weakness of the third assertion, and points out that many words other than homophones have equally gone out of use. 'The best evidence of the obsolescence of any word is that it should still be heard in some proverb or phrase, but never out of it ... In deciding whether any obsolete homophone has been lost by its homophony, I should make much of the consideration whether the word has supplied a real need, by naming a conception that no other word so fitly represented; hence, its survival in a proverb is of special value, because the words of proverbs are both apt and popular; so that for the disuse of

such a word there would seem to be no other cause so likely and sufficient
as damage to its signification.'

It is far from our purpose to contend with Robert Bridges, but in 1965
it is more strongly manifest than it was in 1919 that changing social conditions have a heavier impact on the language than do the sounds of the
words that constitute it. For example, all the terms relative to draught-
horses and their harness, and to horse-drawn carts and carriages, are now
gone: homophony was not contributive to their end. In their place has
grown up a motor-vehicle vocabulary, and no one takes the slightest
exception to some of the words being homophones; in fact, no one
notices them. They are not a nuisance, they are employed in their
context and no road-deaths occur because of them.

Many of the words that survive in proverbs but are never used in
general conversation probably never were used in the current speech
of the educated section of the population. They were dialect, or semi-
dialect, and may still be employed in dialect-speaking areas.

In the South of England no one says 'yonder' for 'there', nor 'yon'
for 'that': in the North of England everyone does: 'Are we going up
yonder?', 'Look at yon cat!' 'There', being a homophone ought, if
homophony were lethal, to be obsolescent and, in its place, 'yonder'
should have become standard English. This indicates very firmly that the
sound alone of a word does not affect its survival.

How obsolete does a word get? and by what standards is it judged?
Not by common usage, for there are very many non-technical English
words that the average man demonstrates his ability to dispense with
utterly: this does not include words that have acquired a special meaning
and are familiar only to persons engaged in a profession, or a trade,
where they have currency. For example, the simple, far from obsolete
word 'statutory' is seldom, if ever, heard in ordinary daily conversation:
the word 'legal' serves in its stead.

The average person is word-shy. With a sufficient vocabulary to say,
'I regret having done that', he (or she) will prefer, 'I am sorry I did
that'. He will choose the homely homophone and reject a more literary
construction by which it might have been avoided: he will prefer, 'I like
to see the sea once a year', to, 'I enjoy the sight of the ocean annually'
and in that choice he could be right.

Few speakers of English are aware of the elasticity and flexibility of
the language; fewer still appreciate its expressiveness and its beauty, its
poetic quality. Robert Bridges, being Poet Laureate, and more, a master
of English, was supremely conscious of all the virtues the language
possesses, and was super-sensitive to the sound of words. To him, 'see
the sea' would have been impossible, but to the average speaker, 'see
the ocean', 'the deep' or 'the main' is ostentatious.

This essay does not plead for the preservation of homophones, neither
does it demand their destruction: the glossary following does not exist to
expose the horror of the homophone nor to demonstrate its desirability.

If this book has a purpose it is to present the humour of the homophone and, secondarily, to save the shorthand-typist from anxiously chewing her pencil while she wonders which witch. Nevertheless, in support of one of Robert Bridges' motives of dislike, there is, implicit in this book, an overwhelming demonstration that our golden tongue can become, by way of the pen of the insensitive unskilled writer, a confused and confusing jumble of meaningless repetition.

VI

Homonyms are inherently humorous; and it may be merely a coincidence that the nations speaking the languages that largely harbour them are noted for their high senses of humour. It is acknowledged that we survived the war of 1914–18 because, among our superiorities, was the ability to laugh our way to what passed as Victory. The enemy, aware of this, and secretly planning the second war, employed a ponderous Herr-Doctor to produce a book for use in the future training of Hun-officers, so that they would know exactly when to order the troops to laugh. The Herr-Doctor-Professor employed the works of Bruce Bairnsfather as his raw material.

Sir Richard Burton, in *The Book of a Thousand Nights and a Night*, reveals the risibility of the Arab, and who doubts that Chinese humour is surpassed only by Chinese pottery? Did they not discover gunpowder and employ it in the manufacture of fireworks?

We may be stretching the meaning of the word 'homonym' too far if we ask it to include a specialized form of graphic art: nevertheless, the canting coat of arms and the rebus, leading to the picture-puzzle which, if not so popular as it was in the first decade of the century, is still with us, indicate our appreciation of these pictorial puns.

Heraldry, a military necessity following the innovation of the close-helmet, emerged, to the best of our knowledge, in the last quarter of the twelfth century, and some of the earliest devices were ingenious pictographs: Ermine for Apulderfeld, and fretty for Maltravers were most apt, and it is amazing that their canting quality was lost sight of for centuries and rediscovered comparatively recently.

Ermine, the heraldic fur, consists in silver, dotted all over with black shapes called points, or spots; hence, the arms of Apulderfeld were a powdered field.

Fretty is constructed by a number—eight or ten—of narrow strips crossing the shield diagonally in one direction, and interlaced at each crossing with an equal number of similar strips running diagonally in the opposite direction. One cannot journey from end to end of any one of these strips in comfort: one is compelled either to climb over a hump-back bridge every few yards, or pass through the narrow arch created by one. This inconvenience exists equally on each strip—on every road—it occasions bad travelling, hence, the arms of Maltravers.

That noble name, Plantagenet, is revealed in an armorial device; a double pun, somewhat unrelated in its parts, a genet (civet-cat) between two sprigs of heath, or broom, planta-genesta.

The punning proclivity has not departed from heraldry. Coats-of-arms devised and granted today will often, in the absence of other claims and considerations, parade in as pictographic a guise as did their prototypes in the late twelfth and early thirteenth centuries. Why should they not? A canting coat-of-arms is more personal and is not less dignified than is an achievement innocent of such sly wit, devised for the petitioner by a dull, unimaginative, humourless Herald.

The people who pretend to be offended by a pun are probably poseurs, for it is most unlikely that any one of them would confess to a dislike of the works of Shakespeare, yet, throughout his pages, and not only in the comedies, puns abound. These 'offences' in the serious plays are not confined to the minor characters who provide the comic relief, but are often uttered ponderously in dramatic passages by major characters, thus:

> JOHN O'GAUNT: O how that name befits my composition;
> Old Gaunt indeed, and gaunt in being old.
> *Richard II*, ii. i. 73–6

> Three corrupted men, . . .
> Have for the gilt of France,—O guilt indeed!
> Confirmed conspiracy . . .
> *Henry V*, ii Prologue 22-8.

> GRATIANO: Not on thy sole but on thy soul, harsh Jew,
> Thou maks't thy knife keen.
> *Merchant of Venice*, iv. i. 123–4.

> 2ND COMMONER: Truly, sir, all that I live by is with the awl:
> I meddle with no tradesman's matters, nor
> Women's matters, but with awl.
> *Julius Caesar*, i. i. 23–5.

> SURREY: That lie shall lie so heavy on my sword
> That it shall render vengeance and revenge,
> Till thou, the lie giver and that lie do lie
> In earth as quiet as thy father's skull.
> *Richard II*, iv. i. 66–9.

The anti-pun people will probably argue that the foregoing puns are not puns, or are not what they mean by puns, or are not the kind of puns they abhor, so let us serve them a second course:

FALSTAFF: Indeed I am in the waist two yards about; but I am
           Not about no waste; I am about thrift.
                Merry Wives of Windsor, I. iii. 43–5.

PETRUCHIO: But Kate, the prettiest Kate in Christendom;
            Kate of Kate Hall, my super-dainty Kate
            For dainties are called cates.
                Taming of the Shrew, II. i. 186–90.

SAMSON: Gregory, o' my word, we'll not carry coals.
GREGORY: No, for then we should be colliers.
SAMSON: I mean, an' we be in choler, we'll draw.
GREGORY: Ay, while you live, draw your neck out o' the collar.
                Romeo and Juliet, I. i. 1–6.

We could, without any effort, provide a third, and even a fourth course.
  This leaves the anti-pun people no alternative but to turn the talk onto
Thomas Hood who, it is said, when congratulated on his phenomenally
prolific output of both puns and pictures, replied, 'It takes a lively Hood
to gain a livelihood.'
  If punning is the lowest form of wit, it possesses, at least, the distinction of being classified as wit. Henry Erskine, Lord Advocate, being
challenged by an opponent's use of the hoary cliché, agreed heartily: 'It
is,' and after a pause he added, 'therefore the pun is the foundation of
all wit.' Puns vary in their quality, but the least of them has the power to
induce laughter. 'Men laugh at puns; the wisest and wittiest of our
species have laughed at them; Queen Elizabeth, Cicero and Shakespeare
laughed at them; clowns and children laugh at them and most men, at
one time or other, are inclined to do the same,' said James Beattie, the
Scottish poet, essayist and moral philosopher. He was strongly supported
by Edward William Cox, poet, law-writer and periodical proprietor. 'I
would question the wit or the humour of any man who could not either
make a pun himself or relish it when made by others.'
  Walter Jerrold, in the general commentary upon wit and humour with
which he opens *A Book of Famous Wits*,[10] recounts how Lord Chester-
field, hearing that an inveterate gamester had married a notorious terma-
gant, remarked, 'Cards and brimstone make the best matches.'
  'The pun of that closing word,' Jerrold continues, 'suggests that a few
words should be said on a manifestation of wit and humour which is
widely decried—chiefly it may be believed by those who have not the
faculty of instantly perceiving similarities in things seemingly remote.
People who condemn punning offhand do so with insufficient consideration . . . The true pun needs defence no more than any other work of
art.' Jerrold has himself written a sonnet in defence of the pun, to be read
before a gathering of anti-punsters, and one rather regrets that he took

[10] Methuen, 1912.

his task so seriously: had he put a pun in every line he would have been dispensing poetic justice. Tilting at anti-punsters was not a chronologically local pose adopted as part of Victorianism: it came into our own time through the powerful pen of G. K. Chesterton who says, 'Suppose that Hood, writing a journalistic report of one of the last duels, had written: "Both principals fired in the air: and we cannot too strongly express our hope that those who think it incumbent upon them to use this old form of self-vindication may imitate such a sensible and humane interpretation of it." That is sound enough but it is a little laborious and does not express either the detachment or the decision of such a critic of duelling. Hood, as a fact, did write:

> So each one upward in the air
> His shot he did expend.
> And may all other duels have
> That upshot at the end.

Here the verbal jest, falling so ridiculously right, does express not merely the humanity of the critic, but also his humorous impartiality and unruffled readiness of intellect.'

We judge it unnecessary to quote *Popular Fallacies: IX—That the worst puns are the best*, because, even in this age of the tyranny of television, most people are familiar with *The Essays of Elia*, and if any of those who are not possess this book it is likely to be consulted only as a guide to the comparative spelling of homophonous words. Those who have not read Elia's essay, will not read this essay, either.

However, before leaving Lamb we must succumb to the temptation of suggesting that no one, including the most rabid, sour-visaged anti-punster, could, when of school age, refrain from repeating that hoary pun, 'Lamb's Tails from Wagspear'.

There is no need to blush: the guilt lies wholly on the homophone.

VII

John Entick, born about 1703, was a man of parts: an author, a historian of London, a politician and a journalist as well as being a schoolmaster in Stepney, where he died in 1773. Among his numerous and voluminous works is his *Spelling Dictionary* which was first published in 1764. There was a revised edition in 1773, a re-issue in 1776 and, under the editorship of others, at least five more editions down to 1800, and reprints till as late as 1825. It is said that each reprint was of twenty thousand copies and it is certain that the later issues were stereotyped.

The editor responsible for this vitality was William Crakelt, M.A., Rector of Nursted and Ifield in Kent. In the edition of 1791, perhaps too in earlier editions, there appears, commencing on page ix, 'A Table of

Words That are alike, or nearly alike, in Sound, but differing in Spelling and Signification': in short, a list of homophones.

This list, containing, in round figures, four hundred and fifty groups, is most interesting because more can be read than is printed there. One may see in it a phonetical grouping that would not suggest itself today: 'do' and 'doe', 'coin'd' and 'kind', 'ear' and 'year', 'earth' and 'hearth', to select but a few at random.

The phonetician does not need to enjoy himself reading the novels of two centuries ago in order to discover linguistical sound change: he can stick to the dictionary.

Entick's work, the declared purpose of which was to teach 'To Write and Pronounce the English Tongue with Ease and Propriety', was too popular for the grouping of its homophones to have been idiosyncratic on the part of either John Entick himself or that of a subsequent editor. The great lesson to be learnt is that homophony is local in time as well as in space: the homophones of 1764 are not quite the same as those of 1964 (the date of writing), and we have already stressed that the homophones north of Trent differ from those recognized south of that select boundary.

To the 1964 eye and ear, conditioned to accept the voicing or the dropping of an initial aspirate as the acid test between educated and ignorant delivery, this eighteenth-century list is a shock. 'Ale' and 'hail', 'air' and 'hair' (this group includes 'are'), 'and' and 'hand', 'ill' and 'hill'. Even as late as the publication of the edition of 1791 a dictionary was produced only for educated people (the artisans were still illiterate), it follows, therefore, that the juxtaposition of words having initial aspirates, and words beginning with the vowel following such aspirates, is expected and normal to the reader of the period. The suggestion is that two hundred years ago a great many more initial aspirates were mute than is generally supposed; hence, there was then quite a large body of homophones that are now inadmissible not because of obsolescence, but as a result of sound change.

'H' is fugitive. It is dropped unblushingly by both the Countess and the charwoman; it is the clerk who is so exquisitely careful to give his employer's office address as High Holborn, but he is not quite so 'H'-conscious when directing lorry drivers to the warehouse in Hoxton, and not at all when claiming to possess a sense of 'yeumer'. In the following glossary we have not gone as far as the Rector of Nursted and Ifield did —in mid-twentieth century 'hand' and 'and' would not be tolerated— but we have, here and there, dragged in a word with an 'h' to march in procession with the h-less, and our justification is that there are at least as many people dropping these aitches as there are sounding them. It is an interesting experiment to find out how many of one's friends stay at a hotel, and how many at an 'otel. It is not advisable, though, to search for which of them has a son and heir—quite heavily aspirated.

Another lexicographer who was homonym-conscious was the Rev.

Walter W. Skeat. His etymological dictionary made its appearance in 1881. He was not so naïve as Entick and Crakelt: nevertheless, in the eighty-two years that have blundered their heavy-footed way over life and language since Skeat's dictionary was published, the work has changed from the last word in scholarship to an interesting historical relic, and not quite all his homophones find a sympathetic modern ear.

In eighty-two years' time the true homophones, those against whose grouping none can inveigh, that appear in the following glossary, will be subject to revision, some of them will have fallen by the wayside, and the gaps in the ranks will have been filled by words not today homophonous. What seems most likely is that a number now included that are homophonous only to the Cockney will have risen in the world, and become standard English homophones, the Public Schools Pronunciation having become tinctured: hence, the late George Bernard Shaw was fortuitously right when he said, 'Already the West End and Oxford have acquired more than half this terrible pronunciation, and they will soon acquire it completely.' He continues by giving samples, in his phonetic spelling, of how he thinks 'smart society'[11] speaks, together with his idea of the way in which a Cockney costermonger pronounces the same words. Both are wrong.

In another place[12] he declares: 'The Cockney dialect which so astonishes readers of *Captain Brassbound's Conversion* is so much more scientific in its analysis of London coster lingo than anything that had previously appeared in fiction.'

Authors should have good memories. Five short years later he effectively shattered this modest claim. In the preface that he contributed, in 1937, to *The Miraculous Birth of Language* by Professor Richard Albert Wilson, one may read: 'A well-known actor, when studying one of my Cockney parts had to copy it in ordinary spelling before he could learn it.' It is most likely that the actor had been forced to transliterate before he could read it, because Bernard Shaw's phonetics are even weaker than his Cockney dialect.

Let him stand self-condemned: writing of the year 1879, 'the late James Lecky ... was one of my friends ... through him I got ... [if] not a knowledge of phonetics, at least an interest in it'. This deficiency was never supplemented: he remained ignorant of phonetics: a fact confirmed by his late Will.

He had misunderstood, but had hero-worshipped, Henry Sweet of Oxford and made of him Professor Higgins in *Pygmalion*. Sweet devised the English Phonetic Alphabet, because English long vowels have been, as it were, squeezed through the washerwoman's mangle, and the International Phonetic alphabet will not quite do.

Both of these writing systems are phonetician's tools, and since Sir James Murry used Sweet's alphabet in the O.E.D. its use has become

[11] *The Simplified Spelling Reform*, 1906.
[12] *Bernard Shaw—Playboy and Prophet*, by Archibald Henderson (1932).

the method of indicating pronunciation according to the best lexicographical practice, notwithstanding that the ordinary citizen, who uses the dictionary only for guidance on spelling and pronunciation, cannot read it.

It is ardently to be hoped that a new, ugly, traditionless alphabet is never introduced for if it were it would cut English literary history off short. In a generation no one would be able to read anything that had been printed in the past. If, however, an author feels he must write Cockney dialect in spite of there being no need for him to do so,[13] he must run the risk of writing homophones; for example, 'snow ink tar law fat'.[14]

Language is more than words, it is part of human life, and the evolutionary process is forever creating. Speech-form changes, and so does script, by a slow and natural process part of which seems to be over the stepping-stones of homonyms. The following words were currently so spelt down to the fifteenth century: ansquere (answer), auncyet (ancient), ben (has or have), baenynge (burning), dowghtier (daughter), eyre (heir), fautys (faults), her, or heir (their, or there), pore (poor), qwose (whose), steyne (certain), sufferyn (sovereign), ystis (gifts). It is, perhaps, necessary to emphasize that the foregoing words are English. The change in spelling reflects sound change, not reform. The change in cursive script is as great as the evident spelling change, and the implied sound change. The printing type-face has kept pace: we are a long way from 'Block letter', and these developments in speaking, in writing, and in printing have been facilitated by the nimble homophone which seems to act as a catalyst.

VIII

There are miserable repentant sinners who remain repentant and continue to sin: there are gleeful obdurate sinners who glory in having done it, and who seldom, if ever, do it again.

Your author, being himself included in the latter category, makes no apology for having, in the following grouped glossary, strained phonetics to bending-, if not breaking-point.

Since morality is a matter not of universal norms but of time, place and people, he is satisfied that his iniquities will not be condemned by the word-conscious, laughter-loving Cockney who, in most cases, will not notice the deviations all of which incline in his direction.

The Northern men will notice but in the generosity of their hearts forgive: they do not expect a Southerner to know how to pronounce the mother tongue. It is the pedants (whom we acknowledge to be strictly correct) who will, on recovering from the shock, express their disap-

---

[13] See *The Cockney*, by Julian Franklyn, 2nd edn, May 1953.
[14] It is nothing to laugh at.

proval in unmistakable, though, of course, non-violent terms. We shall not wilter in the fierce flame of their fury nor smother in the smoke of their snorting. To take their trouncing is a normal professional hazard, negligible, because the periodicals that print the learned vituperative outpourings are, as a rule, not in general circulation, and the members of the Society, who receive them, seldom read them.

'Love thyself last: cherish those hearts that hate thee';[15] and in the spirit of the Cardinal's good advice we express our sympathy with the pedant: we do not go so far as to cherish, nor he to hate, but that this book is an irritant to him is undeniable.

The gravest menace, we foresee, will belch forth from the horde of the 'naicely spooken' because, in addition to their complacency concerning their own speech-form, they possess an equally strong (and equally erroneous) belief in their own literary proficiency, and they write letters: very long, dull letters. Some of these masterpieces are sent to the Editors of Newspapers who, often looking for column fill-up, publish them in shortened form.

It is to be regretted that there is not more space to spare in the daily press because if there were, it might absorb all those screeds; as it is, the bulk of them are addressed to the author, who is put to the trouble and expense of answering. It never occurs to these letter-writers that the author is well aware of all the faults they find in him and is unregenerate: is, in fact, made by their approach obstinate enough to rather regret having refrained from providing greater and graver offences for them to inveigh against.

Is that possible?

Yes, that is possible.

We have abstained from including in the glossary homophonous phrases of which samples are displayed on pages xiv–xv. If such atrocities are perpetrated by English people, think of the curious phonetical distortions that can be manufactured by foreigners struggling to learn, without the advantage of university, or any other educational establishment, this very difficult language. To call the Post Office 'day puss tar fizz', and to refer to ironmongery as 'eye on a moon gray' are, as it were, elementary. Perhaps the most delightful hotch-potch of human speech that ever fell on listening ear was the delivery of an Italian waiter who had acquired his English in the hard way while working at an establishment in Yorkshire.

We have further refrained from including assemblies of letters of the alphabet: for example, in the group commencing 'algae' we might have paraded L.G. We could have included emu for M.U. and energy simply to bring up the rear with N.R.G: and it will be observed that we describe the present writing as an essay, not as an S.A. (We plead guilty to the footnote on page xii, but that, we think, is a fairly safe transgression: he

[15] *Henry VIII*, III. ii.

who is foolish enough to make a fuss about it is too foolish to read footnotes.)

Yes, we could certainly have done worse in the estimation of our adverse critics: what distresses us is that we could not, in our own estimation, do better, for we do not flatter ourselves that we have produced a work of perfection.

We invite constructive criticism, and we shall be grateful for all the help and friendly advice we receive either through the press or through the post.

THE GLOSSARY

A

1. **A**: first letter of the alphabet; a; indefinite article.
2. **AYE**: ever; futurity.
3. **AYE** (eye): affirmative; signification of assent (q.v.); formal Parliamentary supporting vote.
4. **EH**: an exclamation of enquiry, or the solicitation of agreement.
5. **EYE**: the optical organ.
6. **I**: the ninth letter of the alphabet; i; personal pronoun, myself.
   Eh? What's that? You don't wish to come for a walk with me? I do not investigate your reason from A to Z—but I have my eye on it: a promise of ice-cream will induce you to change your 'no' to 'aye', eh? or will you sulk for aye?
1. **abate**: to reduce, stop, or prevent.
2. **ABBATE**: the senior priest in an Italian monastery.
3. **ABBOT**: the principal (q.v.) of an abbey.
   The argumentation will not abate till it is decided whether an English Abbot or an Italian Abbate has the superior status.
1. **abattoir**: a slaughter-house.
2. **ABETTOR**: one who assists, or who encourages another in a criminal act, or in any illegal activity.
   When the boy was sentenced for cruelty to animals it is gratifying to note that the foreman of the abattoir, who had been cited as an abettor, was also sentenced.
Abbate, see abate.
1. **Abess**: the Mother Superior of a nunnery.
2. **ABYSS**: a deep pit, or cavity, in the earth; the infernal region; primal chaos.

3. **ABYSS**: an obsolete heraldic term (q.v.) for the fess point.
   Our good Abbess gives us regular instruction on the horrors of the abyss.
Abbot, see abate.
1. **Abel**: son of Adam, hence, a masculine personal name.
2. **ABLE**: capable.
   Is Abel able?
abettor, see abattoir.
1. **abject**: miserable; cringing; mean-spirited.
2. **OBJECT**: any material thing; one's aim or intention; the word in a sentence to which the verb is directed.
3. **OBJECT** (ob'ject): to protest; to disapprove; to offer opposition.
   I object to that abject object.
1. **ablation**: taking away; surgical excision; recession of pain; surface crumbling of rock.
2. **OBLATION**: offering, or giving to the deity; the offering of bread and wine in the Eucharist, hence, the whole Eucharist Service; sacrifice; almsgiving; an 'aid', or gift to the Sovereign; a pious gift.
   An ablation is needed to collect his oblation.
able, see Abel.
1. **abode**: place of residence.
2. **ADOBE** (a-doe-be): sun-baked brick.
   Say, Stranger, you seeking Two-gun Sam? Next turn o' the trail there's an adobe shack, that sure is his abode.
1. **abrade**: to grind; to shape against a grindstone; to rub a surface with hard grit.
2. **ABRAID**: to wrench a sword out; to make an effort; to shout.
3. **ABRASE**: alternative spelling of No. 1 above.
4. **ABRAY**: false.

5. UPBRAID: to censure; to rebuke; to adduce a subject as ground for censure.

It is quicker to abrade these shapes than to carve them, but if I do, the master will upbraid me.

abraid ⎫
abrase ⎬ see preceding group.
abray ⎭

abyss, see abbess.

1. Accadian: the language of ancient Accad, recorded in cuneiform characters.

2. ARCADIAN: pertaining to Arcadia, an imaginary country in which rural simplicity and bliss reign.

Is the Arcadian ideal found in Accadian literature?

1. accede: to receive, inherit, come into; to accent (q.v.); to support or adhere to.

2. EXCEED: to surpass; be greater than; be more than, go beyond; overrun limits.

He will accede to what remains of the estate, and exceed his father's extravagance.

1. accedence: agreement; approval; acceptance of an office.

2. ACCIDENCE: a term relating to inflexion of words; the rudiments of any subject.

3. ACCIDENTS: unexpected occurrences; undesired or disturbing events; mishaps; disasters; misfortunes.

Notwithstanding his accedence to my request that he exercise care when studying the accidence of Chemistry, he met with several accidents.

1. accent: stress upon a syllable or a word, hence upon any particular.

2. ACCENT: a cypher, or a mark denoting such stress.

3. ACCENT: the shape of speech in general, peculiar to an area.

4. ASCENT: the act of rising; to climb.

5. ASSENT: to give permission, to express agreement.

Having his father's assent, he attempted the ascent of the peak, where the accent is on endurance, not speed, and he announced his failure in a broad county accent.

1. accept: to take; to receive voluntarily; to agree with.

2. EXCEPT: to select in a negative way; to leave out; to overlook.

I accept the whole of his story except the part that makes of him a hero.

1. access: approach or entry; a means or way of approach or entry; an onset, particularly of illness.

2. AXES: pl of 'axe' (q.v.).

3. AXES: an obsolete spelling of No. 1 above, particularly when relating to an attack of illness.

4. AXESSE: an alternative spelling of No. 3 above.

5. AXEZ: a further alternative spelling of No. 3 above.

6. AXIS: an imaginary line around which a sphere revolves; an imaginary line about which the figures of solid geometry are evolved; a line bisecting a plain symmetrical figure; the major power, or influence, affecting international public affairs.

7. AXIS: a name given to an Indian deer, *Cervus axis*.

8. AXYS: another alternative spelling of No. 3 above.

9. EXCESS: surplus (q.v.); an amount, quantity or number above normal; too much; gluttony; drunkenness; loud vulgar behaviour; immorality; departure from social norms.

I make it your duty to prevent those men from gaining access to His Majesty: their sudden excess of loyal feeling is unconvincing, and I fear they are agents of the Ruritania-Urbolia axis: and even if I am wrong, it is certain that they have axes to grind.

accidence ⎫ see accedence.
accidents ⎭

1. accomplice: a partner, or a helper, in a criminal or a guilty enterprise.

2. ACCOMPLISH: to carry out a plan; to succeed in a task.

To accomplish a robbery in a Safe Deposit one must secure an accomplice on the staff.

accomplish, see preceding group.

1. accumbent: leaning against; reclining, particularly when at table.

2. INCUMBENT: exerting downward pres-

sure, hence, a duty to be performed, hence, that which is impending.

3. INCUMBENT: the clergyman appointed to the benefice; the holder of the Living, as distinct from a curate or a deacon.

At Easter, our Incumbent preached on why it is incumbent on the head of a Jewish house to be accumbent during the Passover feast.

1. accur: to go towards; to meet (q.v.).

2. occur: to happen; to present itself.

Does it not occur to you that the two evils will accur?

1. acetic: vinegar-like; an acid, C₂H₄O(OH), being the basic form of vinegar; an acid product of fermentation (q.v.).

2. AESTHETIC: having good taste; being appreciative of art and letters.

3. ASCETIC: to be austere; abstinent; self-denying.

A man who sprinkles brown acetic acid on fish and chips cannot claim to be aesthetic, though it might be allowed he is ascetic.

1. ache (ake): a dull, continuous pain.

2. ACHE (aitch): parsley, *Petroselinum*, an umbelliferous plant, used for decorating food.

3. ACHE (aitch): the eighth letter of the alphabet between G and I: H, h.

If that boy drops another ache I'll use a cane to such good account that he will ache all over.

1. acher: one who, or a limb or an organ that, aches.

2. ACHOR: dermatitis of the scalp; scald-head.

3. ACKER: a tidal-wave on an estuarine river.

4. ACRE: a unit of land measure equivalent to seventy yards square.

5. ACRE: a fortified city of antiquity, the last stronghold of the Knights Hospitallers of St John of Jerusalem, on the mainland of Palestine. (Fall of Acre, 1291 A.D.)

6. AKKA (sl): an Egyptian beggar's term for a piastre, hence, in the Army, a generic term for money.

7. AKRE: a name for the acorn.

When the acker burst the embankment every acre of woodland in the area was flooded; manning the pumps made each volunteer an acher that evening, and several pumps were put out of action through an akre or two choking the suction: Tom, an ex-soldier, remarked that the disaster would cost someone a stack of akka.

1. aching: suffering dull, persistent pain.

2. AKIN: related.

That woman's effect on me was akin to that of an aching tooth.

acker, see acher.

1. acme: the climax; the highest; the greatest achievement.

2. ACNE: an affection (q.v.) of the sebaceous glands manifested by an eruption of pustules on the face; blackheads.

That girl's face would be the acme of perfection could she but be rid of her acne.

acne, see preceding entry.

acre, see acher.

1. acts: pl (') of 'act', to proceed (q.v.); to do; a decision reached by a legislative body; one of the major divisions of a stage-play.

2. AXE: a tool, anciently a weapon, consisting of a bit (q.v. or blade socketed to the end of, and parallel with, a helve, haft or handle.

If he takes an axe and acts promptly all will be well.

1. actuate: to set in motion; to inspire; to cause a start to be made.

2. ACUATE: having a point, to bring to a point; to sharpen.

It requires but little to actuate his witty tongue which sometimes proves uncomfortably acuate.

acuate, see preceding group.

1. Ada: feminine personal name, possibly a diminutive of Adela.

2. ADAH: Hebrew masculine personal name.

3. EIDER: a duck, indigenous to the Arctic and sub-Arctic regions (*Somateria mollissima*), that lines (q.v.) its nest with down (q.v.).

4. IDA: a mountain in Phrygia.

5. IDA: a mountain in Crete.

6. IDA: a feminine personal name, diminutive of Idonia.

Ada wished to see Mount Ida, but Adah, to whom she was then engaged, did not approve, hence, she went to Norway with Ida to shoot eider-duck.

Adah, see preceding group.

1. **adapt:** to alter an object so that it may do the work of, or be used as, some other object; to make the best possible use of inferior tools, materials or machinery.

2. ADEPS: animal fat; lard.

3. ADEPT: to possess both knowledge and skill; to be exceedingly competent.

4. ADOPT: to take into use; to take as one's own; to assume, by process of law, responsibility for, and relationship to, a stranger in blood.

I will adopt his philosophy and adapt myself to the new conditions, for he was adept at introducing adeps into the grinding gears of circumstance.

1. **adds:** attaches one thing, or number, to another; increases quantity; reaches a sum or total.

2. ADZE: a carpenter's axe (q.v.) having the bit (q.v.) set at ninety degrees to the shaft.

Skill with the adze adds virtue to the man.

adeps ⎫
adept ⎬ see **adapt.**
adopt ⎭

1. **admirable:** a person, a thing, or a course of action that is exemplary, or pleasing, or inspiring.

2. ADMIRAL: a naval officer of the highest rank (q.v.); commander of a fleet (q.v.).

Nelson was an admirable Admiral.

Admiral, see preceding group.

adobe, see **abode.**

1. **advice:** information; suggestion how to act or behave; consultation; opinion; formal notice.

2. ADVISE: to inform; to suggest a course of behaviour; to give an opinion; to give formal notice.

I strongly advise you to ignore the advice John gave: he is himself fool enough to gruffly de-

mand delivery when he already has an advice-note on his desk.

advise, see preceding group.

adze, see **adds.**

1. **aerie:** a bird's nest built at a high altitude, hence, any dwelling high up in mountains.

2. AERY: alternative spelling of No. 1 above.

3. AIRY: well-ventilated; spacious (q.v.).

4. EERIE: ghostly; hair-raising, frightening in an abstract way; savouring of the occult.

5. EERY: alternative spelling of No. 4 above.

6. EYRIE: alternative spelling of No. 1 above.

7. EYRY: further alternative spelling of No. 1 above.

Visit the soothsayer in his aerie and the effect is most eerie, but in this airy hall his performance is not impressive.

aery, see preceding group.

aesthetic, see **acetic.**

1. **affect:** induced mood, or feeling; physical state; to induce some form of behaviour in another person; to make false claims of ability; to pretend.

2. AFFECT: to attack; seize; infect.

3. EFFECT: to be influenced; to cause.

4. EFFECT: the result of an effort, or labour; an article of property; the general appearance of a work of art.

The people who in these days affect to be artists affect one with anger, an effect that could not arise from even a poor, but true, artistic effect.

1. **affection:** a kindly feeling towards; love.

2. AFFECTION: illness; disease.

3. AFFLICTION: a calamity; disaster; sorrow; grief.

The affection of youth may become the affliction of age: the affection has a long incubation period.

1. **afflatus:** the breath of inspiration.

2. FLATUS: a blowing of wind, especially from the bowels.

The modern poet claimed that his work was a product of afflatus, but truth will out: the

printer left a space in place of
the first 'f' in the word.

affliction, see **affection.**

1. **aggravate:** to load heavily; to make
conditions or circumstances worse;
to annoy, irritate or incense.

2. AGGREGATE: collected into a mass; an
average; a mixture in close association.

You will aggravate the Professor of geology if you refer to
a granular basalt as an aggregate.

aggregate, see preceding group.

1. **agnize:** to believe in; to acknowledge
the existence of.

2. AGONIZE: to cause extreme suffering of
either a physical or a mental kind.

He will agonize himself in the
spirit in order to agnize the
elements of every new religion.

agonize, see preceding group.

1. **ah!:** an exclamation of grief, admiration, appeal, surprise, etc.

2. ARE: plural present indicative of 'be'
(q.v.).

3. ARE: a metric unit of land measure
equal to ten by ten metres.

4. R: the eighteenth letter of the alphabet, between Q and S: r.

5. R: an abbreviation of 'recipe',
hence, the initial symbol of a doctor's prescription (q.v.).

Ah! so you are buying a thousand are of France, are you?

1. **ail:** to suffer with poor health; to be
troubled; to be angry.

2. ALE: a beverage brewed from malt
and flavoured with bitters.

Sup ale and ail naught.

1. **ailment:** a sickness.

2. ALIMENT: food; that which sustains;
nourishment.

The cause of his ailment is his
aliment.

1. **air:** the earth's atmosphere.

2. AIR: manner; attitude.

3. AIR: tune; melody.

4. AIR: to dry, or to ventilate.

5. E'ER: contraction of 'ever'.

6. ERE: before.

7. EYRE: an archaic term for a circuit
Judge of Assize, or for such a
Court.

8. HEIR: one to whom title and property
automatically descends.

The rightful heir would have

come into his own ere this had
he not been breathing a foreign
air in a land where they do not
air rooms, and every bandit
wears the air of a prince: there
will be repercussions at the next
Court of Eyre, 'twas e'er thus:
but now let the village fiddler
strike up a lively air.

1. **airship:** a lighter than air flying
machine.

2. HEIRSHIP: the state or condition of
being heir (q.v.).

He can't raise a penny on his
heirship since his father ruined
himself by trying to perfect the
airship.

airy, see **aerie.**

1. **aisle:** the space on each side of the
nave (q.v.) in a church; the path
between the pews.

2. ILE: obsolete spelling of No. 1 above.

3. I'LL: contraction of 'I will'.

4. ILL: in bad health; evil; malevolent.

5. ISLE: a small island.

I'll lead you up the aisle and we'll
live on an isle where you'll never
be ill.

1. **ait:** a small island in a river.

2. ATE: pst tns of 'eat'.

3. EIGHT: a number between seven and
nine; 8; VIII; viii.

The rowing eight landed on the
ait and there ate their lunch.

akka ⎫ see **acher.**
akre ⎭

akin, see **aching.**

1. **Alan:** masculine personal name.

2. ALIEN: foreign in race or nationality;
unnatural, out of character.

3. ALIGN: to place, or to bring into line.

4. ALLEN: an English surname.

But Alan, you cannot align every
alien with those who are alien to
honesty: see *Allen's Guide to
Statistics.*

1. **alay:** a name for alabaster.

2. ALLAY: to alleviate; ease; subdue.

3. ALLEY: a narrow path.

4. ALLI: a colloquial abbreviation for
aluminium.

5. ALLOY: a solution of one metal in
another.

6. ALLY: to unite; to be on terms of
good relationship; to be party to
an agreement of friendship.

Allay your fears: we have a powerful commercial ally. Soon you will lay pavement of alay along the alley between your flower-beds, and you shall wear ornaments of gold without alloy: even your saucepans shall be of silver instead of common alli.

1. **alder:** a tree, *Alnus glutinosa*, related to the birch.
2. ALDER: senior; a chief or ruler.
3. ELDER: a shrub, *Sambucus nigra*, bearing berries (q.v.).
4. ELDER: comparative of age; one who is older than another; a member of the council, or committee that handles the affairs of a community.

A curative decoction made from mixed alder and elder, the elder sister said had been discovered by the alder.

ale, see **ail.**

1. **alec:** a herring; a sauce made from herrings.
2. ALEC: diminutive of Alexander, a masculine personal name.

Alec refused caviare, and asked for a wholesome grilled alec.

1. **alectryon:** a cock.
2. ELECTRON: a negative component of an atom.
3. ELECTRUM: a natural alloy (q.v.) of gold and silver; a commercial alloy of copper, zinc and nickel.

The sculptor's anger knew no bounds when his masterpiece, entitled *Alectryon*, cast in electrum, was described in the press as 'a thing called *Electron*, and made of it'.

1. **alegar:** fermented (malt) vinegar.
2. ALGA: a form of weed, common to both fresh and salt water, often used in the plural, algae (q.v.).
3. ALGOR: a condition of shivering preceding (q.v.) a fever.
4. ELGAR: surname of a great English musical composer.

The doctor said such a state of algor could be relieved only with essence of alga, and the patient, expecting death, made his last request; namely, that the record of Elgar should be played.

1. **alehoof:** a herb, *Nepeta glechoma*; ground-ivy.

2. ALOOF: the order to keep a ship's head to the wind; away to windward, hence, distant, withdrawn, superior to.

Drink a decoction of alehoof every morning and remain aloof from those tipplers.

1. **alepine:** a cloth of mixed wool and silk.
2. ALPINE: pertaining to the alps, hence to any mountain, or to a great height.

Windproof garments of alepine are best for alpine travel.

1. **Alf:** diminutive of the masculine personal name 'Alfred'.
2. ELF: one of the little people; a fairy of a special kind, male, bearded, clad in a green costume and a broad-brimmed high-crowned hat, who may be either friendly or antagonistic to human beings.

Alf saw an elf in the garden.

alga, see **alegar.**

1. **algae:** pl of 'alga' (q.v.).
2. ALGY: diminutive of the masculine personal name 'Algernon'.

Algy is the world's leading authority on algae.

algor, see **alegar.**

Algy, see **algae.**

alien, see **Alan.**

1. **alight:** to leave a vehicle; to descend from an altitude; to settle.
2. ALIGHT: on fire; emitting flames; in a luminous state.
3. ELATE: to excite; to put in a mood of exultation.
4. ELITE: the best; the superior; the leading members of a group.

It will elate them when they alight and find themselves among the elite, and all the fairy-lanterns alight.

align, see **Alan.**

aliment, see **ailment.**

1. **all:** everyone; the whole number or quantity; without surplus (q.v.).
2. AWL: a sharp-pointed tool used for piercing holes in material.
3. ORLE: in heraldry, a band, half the width of the bordure, following the contour of the shield, and at least its own width from the edge; small charges arranged in this position.

4. OWL: a nocturnal bird of prey; any bird of the sub-order *Striges*; the symbol of wisdom, and also of keen eyesight; a term of contempt applied to a stupid person.

We all know him for a wise old owl who, in spite of his successful book on *Do It Yourself Shoe-Repairs*, sticks to his awl and last.

allay, see alay.

Allen, see Alan.

1. allergy: a term introduced by Von Pirquet to describe a state (q.v.) of altered reaction to foreign protein, extended to include any state of exaggerated susceptibility to the effect of substances that normally are inert.
2. ALOGY: absurdity.
3. ELEGY: a poem, being a funeral oration; an inscription on a tombstone.
4. ELOGE: a funeral oration.
5. ELOGY: alternative spelling of No. 3 above.
6. EULOGY: enthusiastic praise.
7. -OLOGY: a suffix indicating a science.

He should become the subject of a study in abnormal psychology: consider the alogy of his allergy to 'Gray's Elegy', in relation to his eulogy of the productions of Walt Whitman.

alley ⎱ see alay.
alli ⎰

1. allowed: permitted; accepted as unarguable or irrefutable.
2. ALOUD: in a raised tone; noisily; audible at a distance.

It will be allowed by even the most lenient and least disciplined that the rule by which readers are not allowed to talk aloud in a library ought to be most rigorously enforced.

alloy: see alay.

1. allude: to make an indirect reference.
2. ELUDE: to escape from a person, a place, or an obligation in a clever way.

I did not allude to the occasion on which, to elude his opponents, he had to disguise himself as a Boy Scout.

1. allusion: an indirect, or an implied reference.
2. ELUSION: the act of making a nimble escape; of avoiding a meeting.
3. ILLUSION: deception; an appearance; belief in the objectivity of the subjective, or of the legendary.

I was sorry to hear your allusion to his elusion of work because it is your illusion.

ally, see alay.

1. almanner: inclusive of all kinds; a combined form of 'all', and 'manner'; of every sort (q.v.).
2. ALMONER: one who dispenses charity in a religious house, or, in a hospital, acts as Welfare Officer.

Almanner of folk come before the almoner.

almoner, see preceding group.

1. alms: sums of money distributed in charity.
2. ARMS: the upper limbs of the human body; any narrow branches or offshoots.
3. ARMS: heraldic devices emblazoned on a shield; the ensigns exclusive to a family, granted by Letters Patent.
4. ARMS: weapons of any kind.

Display a banner of your Arms when you distribute alms in the market-place, and have beside you men with lusty arms, and let them carry arms.

alogy, see allergy.

aloof, see alehoof.

aloud, see allowed.

alpine, see alepine.

1. altar: a platform, a table (q.v.) or a pillar (q.v.) before which the officiating priest stands in a place of worship.
2. ALTER: to change; to make different; to modify.

The iconoclasts of the Reformation set out to alter altar and service.

alter, see preceding group.

1. ample: sufficient.
2. AMPOULE: a small glass vessel, generally containing drugs.
3. AMPULE: alternative spelling of No. 2 above.
4. AMPULLA: a Roman flask; a pilgrim's bottle; vessel to contain oil for the ceremony of anointing.

Is the tenth of a cubic centi-
metre of fluid in the ampoule
ample to effect the cure?

ampule }
ampulla } see preceding group.

1. **an:** the article as used preceding
   (q.v.) a vowel.
2. ANA: an Indian coin of low value; a
   sixteenth of a rupee.
3. ANN: a feminine personal name.
4. ANNA: alternative spelling of Nos. 2
   and 3 above.
5. ANNE: alternative spelling of No. 3
   above.
6. ANNIE: alternative spelling of No. 3
   above.
   An anna Anna found was
   claimed by nine different coolies.

ana, see preceding group.

1. **anal:** pertaining to the anus.
2. ANNAL: a record of the events of one
   particular year.
3. ANNEAL: to treat by fire; to temper;
   to fuse in a kiln.
4. ANNUAL: yearly, recurring every
   twelve months.
5. ANNUL: to blot out; cancel; make
   void.
   The annal reveals how they
   learned to anneal glass, and ex-
   plains why they hold an annual
   feast in celebration, and annul
   certain debts.
1. **anchor:** an iron hook used to
   secure a ship to the ground.
2. ANKER: a wine measure of eight and a
   third gallons, hence, a cask of that
   capacity.
   We buoyed the anchor with an
   anker.
1. **anchorite:** a hermit.
2. ANKERITE: a mineral; iron-manganese
   ore (q.v.).
   The gentle anchorite was evicted
   from his cave when the avid
   prospectors found ankerite there-
   in.
1. **angel:** a spirit supposed to exist in
   human form, but of a quality
   superior to man.
2. ANGLE: the degree of inclination between a line and another when
   they are not parallel.
3. ANGLE: to catch fish by means of a
   barbed hook concealed in food.
4. ANGLE: a member of a race who

settled in England in the archaic
period, hence, an Englishman.
From whichever angle you view
his behaviour, it is manifest that
he will angle for compliments on
every occasion, and modesty is
more becoming to an Angle.

angle, see preceding group.
anker, see **anchor.**
ankerite, see **anchorite.**

Ann }
Anna } see **an.**

annal, see **anal.**
Anne, see **an.**

anneal }
annual } see **anal.**
annul }

1. **ant:** a herding insect of the order
   Hymenoptera.
2. AN'T: contracted form of 'are not',
   (colloquially used for 'is', 'have'
   and 'has not').
3. AUNT: sister of either parent; wife of
   one's uncle.
   An ant hurried past my aunt who
   snarled 'An't they jest pests!
1. **ante-:** a prefix indicating before,
   either in time or space.
2. ANTI-: a prefix indicating opposition
   (q.v.).
   Due to the benign syphonage of
   psycho-analysis she ante-dated
   the onset of her anti-humanity
   feelings by a decade.
anti, see preceding group.
1. **aphelia:** pl of 'aphelion', the point in
   an orbit farthest from the sun.
2. OPHELIA: the name of the leading
   female character in Shakespeare's
   tragedy *Hamlet.*
   All the talents of these amateur
   actresses put together would not
   make a satisfactory Ophelia:
   they are cold and dull as planets
   at their aphelia.
1. **apposite:** apt; witty; appropriate.
2. OPPOSITE: contrary in position, direction or opinion; of two objects
   facing each other across an intervening space; opposed.
   His remarks are always apposite,
   but his wife's are opposite.
1. **apposition:** of two things brought, or
   placed together, or side by side;
   one in contact with another; to be
   in juxtaposition.

2. OPPOSITION: contrariness; obstruction; competition; hostility.

Bringing his teeth firmly into apposition, he rose to lead the opposition.

1. **appraise:** to praise; to attach a value.
2. APPRISE: to inform.
3. APPRIZE: to offer for sale at a fixed price.

You appraise him so highly that I will apprise him of my wish for him to apprize my antiques.

apprise ⎫
apprize ⎭ see preceding group.

1. **arbor:** a spindle used to carry a grindstone, or other revolving fitting, or machine part.
2. ARBOUR: a shady nook in a garden.
3. HARBOUR: a place of refuge, chiefly for ships; to care for, to provide a refuge.

He sat in the arbour, wondering whether to harbour his degenerate kinsman, when he received the report that his factory was idle due to a broken arbor.

arbour, see preceding group.

1. **arc:** segment of the circumference of a circle; a luminous electrical discharge.
2. ARK: a box (q.v.), chest (q.v.), or coffer (q.v.).

The body of the scullion who pilfered the treasurer's ark swung in a slow arc from the gallows, and the film-producer's arc-lamp was visible in the trees.

Arcadian, see Accadian.

1. **arch:** an upward-curving span of building-construction.
2. ARCH-: a prefix denoting superiority; the chief; pre-eminent; leading.
3. ARCH: girlish; innocently artful.

The Archbishop passed under the arch and entered the cloisters.

are, see ah.

1. **area:** surface measure; superficial extent; the opening whereby light and air are admitted to a basement.
2. ARIA: a difficult song introduced into opera to enable the leading vocalists to display their glottal agility.
3. ARREAR: behind; late in making payments.

When Madame Excelentoni sings the aria it is hard to believe that she began her vocal career in the area of number nine Shrills Buildings, where they were perpetually in arrear with rent.

aria, see preceding group.

ark, see arc.

1. **armory:** pertaining to Coats of Arms; Armorial Bearings; Heraldry.
2. ARMOURY: a collection of weapons; a collection of suits of armour; a chamber where such collections are housed.

His interest in armory began when he observed the emblazonment on the weapons in the armoury of the Tower of London.

armoury, see preceding group.

arms, see alms.

1. **arrant:** notorious; absolute; downright.
2. ERRANT: one having an errand, or mission; itinerant; of a knight seeking opportunity to serve in the name of, or in the cause of, chivalry; of a judge on circuit.

The arrant folly of conferring Knighthood on those who would never become Knights-errant is intensified annually.

1. **arras:** tapestry, large tapestry sheets used to cover the walls of a chamber.
2. HARAS: a number of stallions and mares maintained for breeding purposes, hence, a stud (q.v.).
3. HARASS: to worry; to fatigue; to wear out by repeated attack.

I will harass him till I get the arras from his hall in exchange for a stallion from my haras.

arrear, see area.

1. **art:** creative ability in writing, painting, and other forms of representation; skill arising from practice; branches of learning that open the mind to more advanced knowledge; to follow the occupation of a fortune-teller or a magician; to exercise cunning, to be artful.
2. ART: a poetic form of 'are'.

Art thou yet proficient in thine art, boy?

1. **artesian:** a deep bore-hole sunk to tap (q.v.) a supply of water, mineral-oil, or natural gas.
2. ARTISAN: a worker by the hand; a skilled operative.
   The men engaged in sinking the artesian well seem to be of a more educated class than the average artisan.

ascent, see accent.

ascetic, see acetic.

1. **ash:** a tree yielding a hard, straight-grained timber; *Fraxinus excelsior.*
2. ASH: The non-inflammable residue left after a substance has been consumed by fire; an inorganic constituent of organic matter.
   Examination of the ash revealed that the incendiary machine had been contained in a case constructed of ash.

1. **asker:** one who asks; a beggar, a suppliant.
2. ASKER: a newt.
3. OSCAR: a masculine personal name.
   Let us put an asker in a jam-jar and take it to school; Miss Scarboys hates them: we can get a lot of questions about them out of the Encyclopaedia and confuse her—little innocent-looking Oscar can be the asker.

1. **aspic:** a form of jelly in which meat and other foods are set.
2. ASPIC: a name for lavender, or spike (q.v.), *Lavandula spica.*
3. ASPIC: a big gun.
   The enemy officers perfume themselves with aspic water, and at this hour sit at table over chicken-in-aspic, but we will sail in close to the land and provide them with the music of our aspic.

1. **assay:** to make an analysis of metal, or metal-bearing ore (q.v.), trial; experiment; an effort.
2. ESSAY: a short English composition on a subject; a monograph; a treatise (q.v.); an attempt to do something; to set oneself a task.
   I will essay to make an assay and write an essay on my findings.

assént, see accent.

1. **assistance:** help; aid; succour.

2. ASSISTANTS: those who help; those who serve.
   The shop runs at a loss because half the assistants are of no assistance.

assistants, see preceding group.

1. **atar:** essential oil, or wax (q.v.) of rose (q.v.) petals.
2. ATTAR: alternative spelling of No. 1 above.
3. OTTAR: alternative spelling of No. 1 above.
4. OTTER: a fish-eating mammal, having webbed feet and a flat tail, *Lutra vulgaris*; the fur of this creature.
5. OTTER: alternative spelling of No. 1 above.
6. OTTO: alternative spelling of No. 1 above; a masculine personal name.
   She sprayed atar of roses on her otter wrap.

ate, see ait.

attar, see preceding group.

1. **attendance:** the act of being present; on duty; ready to serve.
2. ATTENDANTS: those in waiting upon Royalty; those who are present in order to render service; those who follow or accompany.
   The Prince is not a fool: he keeps a careful record of the attendance of his attendants.

attendants, see preceding group.

1. **auger:** a tool designed for making deep holes in thick timber; a shipwright's drill (q.v.).
2. AUGUR: to prognosticate; to indicate or promise.
   To see that boy playing with the carpenter's auger does not augur well for the furniture and fittings.

1. **aught:** anything.
2. 0 (aught) (C): the tenth cypher of the Arabic system of numeration, having function, but no numerical value, hence, nothing, or naught, mispronounced as indicated.
3. ORT: a scrap of food left (q.v.) after a meal (q.v.).
4. OUGHT: an obligation or a duty.
   You know you ought to attend the funeral, but you can stay away for aught I care.

augur, see auger.

1. **auk:** any sea-bird of the family *Alcidae*; the little auk, the puffin,

the guillemot and the razor-bill largely inhabit Northern waters: the Great Auk, *Alea impennis*, became extinct in mid-nineteenth century.

2. AWK: contrary; in the wrong direction; upside down; back to front; awkward.

3. ORC: a kind of whale (q.v.); a cetacean of the genus *Orca*, family *Delphinidae*; the killer whale, *Orca gladiator*; any sea monster.

4. ORK: alternative spelling of No. 2 above.

You cannot hunt for either the great auk, or the whale orc, the one is extinct, the other almighty awk.

aunt, see ant.

1. aural: pertaining to impressions received via the ear; verbal, not written.

2. ORAL: by word of mouth; an exercise of the mouth.

The sergeant-major, by a feat of oral agility, condensed four words into one syllable, but the Colonel said aural instruction was not satisfactory.

1. aureole: a halo; the disc or circle of gold depicted surrounding the head of holy figures; the ring of light surrounding a total eclipse of the sun.

2. ORIOLE: a migratory bird of the genus *Oriolus*; any bird of the family *Oriolidae*.

The artist, entranced by the gay yellow and black plumage of the oriole, decided to substitute it for the dove in his masterpiece, and paint it with an aureole.

1. aviary: a large cage or other enclosure in which birds are housed.

2. IVORY: the hard, white, bone-like material (dentine) of which the tusks of elephants, walruses, and other creatures are composed.

3. OVERIE: in the name of the Church of St Mary Overie, Southwark, London, meaning 'over rie', that is, over the river, Southwark being on the south bank of the river Thames, opposite to the City.

4. OVARY: the female organ that produces eggs; the paramount part of

the female genital system; in plants (flowers), the lower section of the pistil (q.v.); the seed container.

The famous (publicity-minded) film star announced having erected an aviary of gold wire fitted with ivory perches in which she would breed piebald parrots by means of the ovary grafting system; and that she would celebrate the hatching of the first brood by making a donation of ten thousand dollars to the Church of St Mary Overie, London, England.

1. awe: fear; reverence.

2. OAR: a pole with a flattened end used to propel a boat.

3. OR: a comparative; an expression of alternative.

4. OR: the heraldic word for gold.

5. O'ER: contracted form of 'over'.

6. ORE: any mineral from which metal can be obtained.

While prospecting for ore they lost an oar and could get no help, because the natives held the river in awe; however, on the bed of the stream they found gold which they logged cryptically as Or, and then they had to decide whether to drift back, or proceed o'er land.

awl, see all.

1. axal: pertaining to, or in the nature of, an axis (q.v.).

2. AXIAL: alternative and more general spelling of No. 1 above.

3. AXIL: The upper surface of the angle at which the branch of a tree merges into the trunk; that location in the junction of a leaf-stem with the main stem of any plant (q.v.).

4. AXILE: belonging to an axis; an embryo orientated on the axis of the seed.

5. AXLE: the peg, rod or shaft passing through the centre of the hub, and upon which the wheel rotates.

He was making a journey into the jungle to study the comparative axil of certain plants when the axle broke, and prevented further progress, but he made good use of the waiting time by recording his observations on the axile of mature tropical seeds.

axe, see acts.

axes ⎱
axesse ⎰ see access.
axez

axial ⎱
axil ⎰ see axal.
axile

axis, see access.

axle, see axal.

axys, see access.

1. ayah: an Indian child's nurse.

2. IRE: anger.
   How dare you display ire to my ayah?

B

1. B: the second letter of the alphabet, between A and C; b.
2. BE: to exist.
3. BEE: a winged insect, *hymenopterous.*
4. BEE: a party, or a gathering, organized for joint intellectual amusement, or for light handicrafts.
5. BEE: a ring of metal, or of hardwood.
   If there is to be a confectionery-making bee, do not fail to invite the queen bee: she will bring honey.
1. baa: imitative of the bleat of a sheep.
2. BAH: an exclamation expressive of contempt, or of intense disgust, or disagreement.
3. BAR: a rigid rod of wood, or of metal, often used to act as a barrier; a rectangular block of material; a strip of inscribed metal crossing a medal ribbon, being an augmentation; in heraldry, one of a pair of transverse stripes crossing the field, each one-fifth of the shield's width; to exclude, to prohibit entry to a place.
4. BAR: a sand-bank obstructing the mouth of a harbour (q.v.).
5. BAR: the barrier at which the prisoner stands during a trial; the rail separating the seats of the Benchers of the Inns of Court from the body of the Hall, and to which qualified students are called, hence the title Barrister-at-Law.
7. BAR: a fish, *Sciaena aquila.*

8. BAR: a counter (q.v.) extending across a chamber in which alcoholic drinks are served; a barrier between the drinkers and the stock (q.v.) of liquor (q.v.), hence, a counter whereat drinks are served, and the chamber itself.
   Bah! that fellow angers me the way he behaves in a bar; going on all fours and shouting 'baa-baa, I'm a lamb!' No one would believe that he has the Military Medal and bar. I hear they are going to bar him if he does it again: they say he learned to drink when reading for the Bar— he was never called; now they should call him to receive a bar of soap.

1. bacon: the back and sides of a pig preserved by salting and smoking.
2. BEACON: a signal fire, hence, any conspicuous mark, as a painted pole (q.v.), a tower or a lighthouse; a hill on which a beacon-fire was formerly situated.
3. BECKON: to make a movement of the head, arm, or finger to invite a person to approach.
   Sent to the village to buy bacon, he went by way of the beacon where breeze-stirred grasses beckon.

bah, see baa.

1. bail: temporary release from arrest on security; the sum of money deposited as such a security; a person who guarantees one for such freedom.
2. BAIL: an arch, or semi-circle of bent-wood, or of iron, used to support the tilt (q.v.) of a van (q.v.) or an awning over a boat (q.v.).
3. BAIL: palisade, outer wall, advance fortifications around a fort or castle.
4. BAIL: one of the pieces of turned wood balanced on the top of the wicket (q.v.) in the game of cricket (q.v.).
5. BAIL: a ladle, or a bucket employed in removing water from a boat; to make use of such a ladle.
6. BALE: evil; malign influences; active malice; harm; death.
7. BALE: a large, round bundle or package.

8. BALE: misspelling of No. 5 above.
9. BAYLE: alternative spelling of No. 3 above.

Be careful: although you stood bail for him I observed his glance charged with bale when you asked him to bail the boat, and again when you told him to erect the bail over her so that he might sleep there: keep the bayle of your consciousness manned while he is near, and try to find out what he has hidden in that bale he carries.

1. **bain:** a warm bath; a hot spring; an apparatus for slow heating; to bask (q.v.) in warm water.
2. BANE: anything that causes distress, woe, misery; poison; anything destructive to life.

The paying guests were the bane of our existence till we put a big bain in the barn and called it the bathroom.

1. **bairn:** a child, particularly one's own child. (Chiefly Scottish.)
2. BARN: an extensive hollow building for the storage of bulk (q.v.) commodities, such as grain, on a farm, or waste-paper in industry.
3. BARNE: alternative spelling of No. 1 above.

Let the bairn play in the barn.

1. **bait:** to attack savagely; to give food to a horse when on a journey; to rest a while; to provoke.
2. BAIT: food placed on a hook, or in a trap, to lure fish or animals.
3. BATE: to force back; to reduce intensity.

He left his horse at the bait and livery stables, put bait on his hooks, and had to bate his breath while he fished.

1. **baize:** a strong woollen fabric, generally green in colour, used for aprons, covers, and for covering the underside of objects so as to soften their impact on a table (q.v.) or other surface.
2. BAYS: pl, or active inflexion of 'bay' (q.v.).

Finish the bottoms of the candlesticks with baize before you stand them in the bays of the cabinet.

1. **balance:** equilibrium; a weighing machine; the seventh sign of the Zodiac; the escapement mechanism of a watch (q.v.); harmony in the elements of a work of art; an account showing the difference between credit and debit.
2. BALANCE: remainder; residue; the portion of anything in excess (q.v.) of requirements; that which is left.

Use the best balance to weigh out that gold-powder, and put the balance back in the safe.

1. **bald:** lacking hair on the head to greater or less degree; bare of supracutaneous natural covering, as fur, or feathers; of a statement lacking in meaning.
2. BALLED: provided with, or decorated with, balls.
3. BAWLED: pst tns of 'bawl' q.v.).

'Call me " Curly "! ' bawled the bald man excitedly, and knocked his beer over on the balled-edged chenille table-cloth.

bale, see bail.

1. **balk:** a ridge; a piece of ground left solid between one breadth of furrow and another; a joist, or beam (q.v.) of timber; that part of a billiards table that is the shorter in relation to a permanent transverse line.
2. BALK: to neglect duty; to make a sudden stop; to obstruct.
3. BAULK: alternative spelling for the balk in billiards (No. 1, above).
4. BAWKE: an iron bucket in which coal is raised.
5. BOLK: to belch; to vomit.
6. BULK: volume; mass; the whole of a consignment of goods; the majority; the hold of a ship; a ship's entire cargo.

The last balk of timber was taken aboard, and the bulk of the crew was content, but a sea-lawyer among them, in order to balk the owners, began to bolk, and we delayed sailing due to his pretending to have contracted infection ashore.

1. **ball:** a sphere; a solid object having a continuous curving surface, any point on which is the same distance from the centre.

2. BALL: a social gathering at which the major (q.v.) entertainment is dancing to an orchestra's music.
3. BAWL: to shout in either excitement or temper (q.v.).
If you bawl like that you will not be invited to another ball, you'll find yourself left at home to play ball with the dog.
1. balm: aromatic resin from trees in genus *Balsamodendron*.
2. BALM: a healing, and pain-soothing ointment, hence, the next.
3. BALM: a soothing influence.
4. BARM: the yeasty froth of beer.
It was balm to his depressed spirit when a rich barm formed on his brew.
1. band: an endless strip of materials for the purpose of connecting, or of binding, objects together.
2. BAND: a company of people, usually having some common purpose, and particularly that of performing on musical instruments.
3. BANNED: outlawed; prohibited; of a book or a stage-play declared unsuitable for public entertainment.
An excited band of would-be buyers demonstrated in front of the shop, immediately the radio announced that the book secured with a paper band had been banned.
bane: see bain.
1. bank: a rising ridge of ground; a mass or cluster; the territory forming the edge of a stream or a lake.
2. BANK: an accumulation of money; a company that administers such an accumulation.
3. BANK: a long, narrow seat; a form (q.v.), or settle (q.v.).
4. BANK: to tilt an aeroplane sideways in making a turn.
Sitting upon a bank outside the bank-manager's office, he was thinking of the shady bank of a bickering stream.
banned, see band.
1. banner: a square flag (q.v.) worked with the armorial bearings, but neither the crest nor the supporters, of an armiger; extended to include gonfannons, and other flags.
2. BANNER: one who bans; a censor (q.v.).

The Lord Lyon King of Arms is a ruthless banner of a false banner.
bar, see baa.
1. barb: the beard, hence, to shave.
2. BARB: a rearward-pointing spike on a spear or a fish hook.
3. BARB: a breast and flank cloth for a horse.
4. BARB: a horse (or a pigeon) of the breed originally imported from Barbary (q.v.).
5. BARB: in heraldry, one of the five sections of the calix visible between, and beyond, the circumference of the petals.
The master's favourite barb threw him, and there was found in its barb a fish hook with a cruel barb which it was believed was put there by a foreign groom who had been told to have his dirty-looking barb shaved off.
1. Barbary: the Arab countries along the North Coast of Africa; the southern part of the Mediterranean Sea.
2. BARBERRY: the shrub *Berberis vulgaris*, having yellow flowers and red berries.
3. BARBERY: a barber's shop; the trade, or business, of a barber.
4. BERBERRY: alternative spelling of No. 2 above.
Captured by Barbary pirates, his art of barbery secured him a position in the Sheikh's household, where he attained to a Robe of Honour by making hair-dye from barberry bark.
barberry } see preceding group.
barbery }
1. bard: a poet who travels the countryside singing his own poems of chivalry, hence, any poet.
2. BARD: breast armour for a horse.
3. BARD: a slice of bacon when placed on the breast of a fowl while roasting.
4. BARRED: provided with bars; to be excluded from an event or a place.
There is a theory that 'the dark lady of the sonnets' was the hostess of a Bankside tavern from which the bard was barred.

3# BARE [15] BASTE

1. **bare:** unclothed; uncovered.
2. BEAR: a quadruped of heavy build that kills by crushing in its fore-limbs, *Ursus horribilis.*
3. BEAR: to sustain; support, endure.
4. BEAR: to produce offspring.

I can't bear to think of the poor pregnant bear with mange, behind the scenes in the circus; she sat shivering in her bare skin, locked in a cold cage where she will bear her cub.

1. **bark:** the protective outer skin of a tree.
2. BARK: the cry of a dog.
3. BARQUE: a three-masted ship with fore (q.v.) and main mast (q.v.) square-rigged, the mizzen fore-and-aft.

It is a far call from the pine-forest, the howl of the wolf, and the Indian's birch-bark canoe; to the stately barque moored at the wharf where the watchdogs bark.

barm, see **balm.**

barn ⎫
barne ⎭ see **bairn.**

1. **Baron:** a lord of Parliament.
2. BARREN: unfruitful.

The wife of Baron Barkard being barren, the title will go into abeyance.

barque, see **bark.**
barred, see **bard.**
barren, see **Baron.**

1. **barrow:** a hillock; a grave (q.v.) mound.
2. BARROW: a vehicle, smaller than a cart, and provided with, in addition to its wheel (q.v.) or wheels, legs to support it when stationary (q.v.).

In his avid search for celts he loaded the entire barrow on a barrow.

1. **base:** the foot; the bottom; the lowest extremity.
2. BASE: headquarters; the place from which a military unit is managed or controlled.
3. BAS-RELIEF: sculpture raised only slightly from its background.
4. BASS: a fresh-water fish (*Perca fluviatilis*), also a marine fish (*Labrax lupus*).
5. BASS: a vegetable fibre used in ropes, mats and the like.

7. BASS: low in the musical scale (q.v.).
6. BASS: a form of beer.
8. BASSE: alternative spelling of No. 4 above.
9. BASS-RELIEF: alternative spelling of No. 3 above.

They set out from base, the sergeant's bass voice audible above the din, and located the monolith carved in bas-relief to the base of which was secured a bass line sustaining in the river a net full of bass, and at the bottom, six bottles of Bass.

1. **based:** set upon a foundation, either material, or of ideas or opinions.
2. BAST: fibre obtained from the bark (q.v.) of the lime tree.
3. BAST: a pack-saddle.
4. BASTE: to secure in juxtaposition by means of loose (q.v.) stitches, parts of a garment; to tack (q.v.).
5. BASTE: to pour the dripping over meat while it is roasting.

The idea that a gardener may be recognized by a length of bast dangling from his pocket is not soundly based: does the thread he uses to baste garments typify the tailor? does the ladle used to baste beef brand the cook?

1. **bask:** to wallow, or soak (q.v.) in sunshine, to enjoy any sort of warmth.
2. BASKE: a variation of 'bash', to make ashamed; to dismay; to strike heavily.
3. BASQUE: the people inhabiting the Pyrenees who speak a non-Aryan language; this language.
4. BASQUE: a downward extension of a bodice forming a sort of diminutive skirt.

For his holidays he went to the Basque country to bask in the sun, but thinking that the Basque, walking with a lady, would not understand, he made a joke on her old-fashioned-looking basque, and received from her cavalier such a baske that he spent the rest of the time in hospital.

baske ⎫
Basque ⎭ see preceding group.

bass, see **base.**

bast ⎫
baste ⎭ see **based.**

1. **bat:** a nocturnal winged mammal of the order *Vespertilionidae*.
2. **BAT:** a club; an instrument for striking the ball (q.v.) used in a variety of games, hence, to use such instruments.
3. **BAT:** a pack-saddle.
4. **BAT:** to flutter.
He did not bat an eyelid when he struck with his bat at a bat he had mistaken for the ball.
bate, see bait.
1. **batell:** singular of 'batells', the provision of food, and the accounts in connection therewith, supplied to a member of a college in the University of Oxford.
2. **BATTEL:** alternative spelling of No. 1 above; nourishing grass; productive land.
3. **BATTLE:** a fight between opposing forces during a war; a single combat between champions; descriptive of any fight between either human beings or animals.
4. **BATTLE:** to fortify a building with crenellations; to embattle.
5. **BATTLE:** to beat clothes with a beetle (q.v.) during the process of washing.
There will be no verbal battle concerning batell: these Oxonians are gentlemen descended from ancestors who received licence to battle their houses, not from scullions and washerwomen who battle clothes to live.
battel: see preceding group.
1. **batten:** a strip of timber (q.v.) conforming to standard measurements, and employed for numerous purposes.
2. **BATTEN:** fatten; to improve in physical condition; to parasitically thrive to the detriment of another.
She will batten upon him till he dies: already she has had to strengthen, with a batten, the shelves of her storage cupboard.
1. **batter:** to strike severe repeated blows; to destroy by rough treatment.
2. **BATTER:** flour and water mixed for culinary use.
3. **BATTER:** the player in a game who is wielding the bat (q.v.).

4. **BATTER:** to slope, generally from the perpendicular.
Notwithstanding the batter of the wall, the batter sat in its shade eating cold batter pudding while the other members of the team threatened to batter him.
battle, see batell.
baulk, see balk.
1. **bawd:** keeper of a house of prostitution; a lewd, or immoral, woman.
2. **BOARD:** a plank of wood; any compound which, pressed into a hard sheet, can be used as a substitute for wood.
3. **BOARD:** a table at which meals are eaten.
4. **BOARD:** maintenance; the provision of meals.
5. **BOARD:** generally in the plural, the Stage, 'on the boards', of an actor.
6. **BOARD:** a ship's side, hence, to go onto a ship.
7. **BOARD:** a kind of committee; a body of persons having the duty of transacting some form of business, as Board of Trade, Board of Management, Board of Directors.
8. **BORED:** made tired by dull conversation, or from insufficient interest.
9. **BORED:** drilled with a hole.
The bawd, secured to a board bored so as to accommodate the straps, was towed to Tyburn and her flow of invective prevented the sightseers being bored.
bawke, see balk.
bawl, see ball.
bawled, see bald.
1. **bawn:** a fortified enclosure.
2. **BORN:** to be brought into being; to be ejected from the womb.
3. **BORNE:** endured.
4. **BOURN:** a stream.
5. **BOURNE:** a destination.
Man is born, and must alone defend the bawn of his life: much must be borne before he crosses the bourn of death and reaches the bourne from which there is no returning.
1. **bay:** the laurel bush, *Laurus nobilis*; leaves or berries of this.
2. **BAY:** an inward curve of coast-line.
3. **BAY:** a segment of a building, a division or recess for special use.

4. BAY: a reddish-brown colour, hence, an animal of that colour.
5. BAY: the long-drawn-out bark (q.v.) of a hound.
6. BEY: a Turkish title of honour for the governor of a province, or for either a naval or military officer.
  The Bey of Bahara, as he lay in the sick-bay of his palace, had placed upon his brow the wreath of bay in recognition of his promptitude, on hearing the hounds bay, of mounting his bay horse and galloping to the bay, where he held at bay, single-handed, the invaders who had there landed.

bayle, see **bail**.
bays, see **baize**.
be, see **B**.
1. **beach:** the sea-shore (q.v.).
2. BEECH: a tree of the genus *Fagus*.
  Beech trees do not grow on the beach.

beacon, see **bacon**.
1. **beadle:** a minor parish officer; a Town-crier; a crier at a court of law; one who makes announcements or proclamations.
2. BEDEL: an English university officer having duties chiefly processional in character.
3. BEDELL: alternative spelling of No. 2 above.
4. BEETLE: large wooden mallet as used by paviours.
5. BEETLE: an insect in the *coleoptorus* class.
6. BEETLE: to lower, frown, overhang.
  Our village Beadle will beetle his brow, and employ a fourteen-pound beetle to crush a black beetle.

1. **beam:** a squared tree-trunk; a wooden cylinder in a loom (q.v.); the main (q.v.) part of a plough-frame; the poised bar of a balance from the ends of which the pans are suspended; the greatest breadth of a ship or a boat.
2. BEAM: a ray of the sun; a ray, cylinder, or pencil of light; any wave motion or effect impelled or directed in a straight line; to emit a ray or rays; to smile.
3. BEAM: short for Whitebeam, a tree,

Pyrus aria, related to the apple, and having a white under-surface to its leaves (q.v.).
  The aircraft hostess continued to beam though she knew they were flying off-beam, and that she would be safer clinging to a beam adrift on a storm-tossed ocean: she thought, nostalgically, of the whitebeam at the bottom of her father's garden, but the beam of her smile, and the humorous beam of her eyes, never wavered.

1. **bean:** a flat, kidney-shaped seed borne in pods by the plants *Faba vulgaris* and *Plaseolus*; anything bean-like or bean-shape.
2. BEEN: pst ppl of 'be' (q.v.).
3. BEIN: pleasant, kindly, comfortable.
  I have been visiting my bein kinsman who has given me a golden bean for my bangle.

bear, see **bare**.
1. **beat:** to strike; to inflict corporal punishment.
2. BEAT: to defeat; to gain the ascendancy.
3. BEAT: musical sequences.
4. BEAT: the extent of a watchman's patrol.
5. BEAT: to sail to windward, hence, Am. sl. ' beat it ', go, irrespective of difficulty.
6. BEET: an edible root, *Chenopodiaceae*.
7. BETE: to mend, particularly to mend a fire, hence, add fuel.
  Don't beat about the bush. We have to beat our attackers. Do you hear that drum-beat stirring them? Bete the watch-fires, extend the beat of the look-out men and, since we have nothing else, cook that beastly beet-root for supper. Now beat it, and do as I say.

1. **beau:** beautiful; hence, a foppish, overdressed young man; also one paying court to a lady.
2. BOUGH: limb or branch of a tree.
3. BOW: an arch; hence anything bent or arched, particularly a rod held by a cord used for propelling arrows.
4. BOW: to bend the body in a form of greeting.

5. BOW: an ornamental knot having two pendent loops and ends.
6. BOW: the forward part of a ship.

Although the hawser at the bow of the enemy's ship might be severed by an arrow, and though I bow to your superior knowledge, I think that bough is too brittle to make into a bow, and I feel certain that a bow is the wrong knot to secure the cord, and that beau the wrong person to discharge the shaft.

1. beck: to nod as a signal of affirmation.
2. BECK: a rapid stream.

He answered by a beck when asked, 'Is this the beck?'

beckon, see bacon.
bedel } see beadle.
bedell }
bee, see B.
beech, see beach.
been, see bean.

1. beer: a fermented malt liquor.
2. BIER: a stretcher, particularly one on which a corpse is carried.

The folk-belief that a bier carried over a footpath establishes a right-of-way, has led to much carrying of beer.

beet, see beat.
beetle, see beadle.
bein, see bean.

1. bell: a hollow metal instrument, often bowl-shape, which, when struck, emits a musical note.
2. BELLE: a beautiful girl; the most beautiful of a party of girls.

She was declared the belle of the ball and the bell was struck in her honour.

belle, see preceding group.

1. bent: deflected from straight (q.v.); kinked; curved; of a drawn bow (q.v.).
2. BENT: natural inclination; capacity or ability.
3. BENT: coarse (q.v.) reed-like grass; a field of grass; pasture.

His natural bent seems to be to lounge day-long on the bent; maybe his mind is bent.

berberry, see Barbary.

1. bereave: to deprive of an abstract possession; to lose affection through death.

2. BRIEF: an official document.
3. BRIEF: short; reduced in either duration or extent; a curtailed form.
4. BRIEVE: a writ appointing a Tutor-at-Law to a ward in chancery.

His demise will bereave his son; give me, therefore, a brief version of the brieve we shall have to prepare.

1. berry: a stoneless soft fruit.
2. BURY: to inter.
3. BURY: a city, or a charter-town, often used as a suffix.

His ambition to bury a berry and raise a blackberry bush at Glastonbury was never achieved.

1. berth: sufficient sea-room for a ship to anchor, hence, sleeping room aboard ship.
2. BIRTH: nativity; production of offspring.

I gave up my berth for the ship's cat to give birth to kittens.

bete, see beat.

1. better: comparative of 'good'; beyond good; superior to; more desirable than; in excess of; more suitable; more advisable.
2. BETTER: one who has made, or who habitually makes, bets.
3. BETTOR: alternative spelling of No. 2 above.

Better be the bookie than the better.

Bey, see bay.

1. bi-: a prefix indicating duality.
2. BUY: to give money in exchange for goods or services.
3. BY: beside; near; not later than; in the course of; indicative of succession; indicative of cause or of effect.
4. BYE: secondary; incidental to; aside from.
5. 'BYE: an abbreviated form of 'good-bye'.
6. BYE-BYE: a familiar form of 'good-bye'; in child's language, bed or sleep.

Just by Barclay's Bank, at the end of the High Street, there is a bye-lane at the bottom of which is a blacksmith's where you can buy a child's stationary bicycle: he produces them as a bye-product of his main manufacture;

after exercise on that the difficult child will go bye-bye without trouble. Now hurry off and buy one—Bye-bye!

1. **bib:** a kerchief tied under a young child's chin during meals to protect the dress; an extension upward of an apron.
2. BIB: to imbibe; to drink; to get drunk.
3. BIB: a fish, *Gadus luscus*, also called whiting-pout (q.v.).
   You bib beer like a beast and need a bib.

bier, see beer.

1. **bight:** a curve, as the loop of a rope forming a knot (q.v.) or a shallow bay (q.v.) in a coast-line (q.v.).
2. BITE: to seize (q.v.) with the teeth; to masticate.
   While we were cruising in the Bight of Bungahoe we found, when fishing for sharks, that they would not bite; but we took several in a bowline-on-the-bight.
1. **bill:** a document, particularly the draft (q.v.) of a proposed Act of Parliament; an account of moneys.
2. BILL: a beak, specifically a bird's beak, but any beak-like projection.
3. BILL: a curved blade mounted on a pole used anciently, in time of peace, for cutting wood, and in war, as a weapon.
4. BILL: a diminutive of William, a masculine personal name.
   Standing on Portland Bill he took cake, which he had wrapped in an unpaid tailor's bill, and threw scraps into the air: a lightning-swift gull caught each piece in his bill, and the donor wondered how Bill Shakespeare would have described such aerial agility.
1. **billed:** to have sent, or to have received, a statement of account due for payment.
2. BILLED: having, or being provided with, a beak.
3. BUILD: to erect an edifice; to assemble materials to form a structure; to shape and join timber (q.v.), or metal (q.v.) in the form of a ship, a vehicle, or piece of machinery; to construct; to assemble ideas in the form (q.v.) of a fantasy or

theory; to anticipate, and form conclusions on a hint, or a hope.
They intend to build a public house and to call it *The Duck-billed Platypus*, but the contractor wants guarantees that they will pay when billed.

1. **bird:** a feathered, winged vertebrate animal.
2. BIRDE: breed (q.v.), family or nation.
3. BURD: archaic spelling of No. 1 above, retained in poetry with the meaning, a girl, a maiden.
4. BURRED: being covered in burs, the clinging seeds of burdock and other plants.
5. BURRED: of metal having a rough, or wire-edge finish to a cut; of a rivet when beaten, or swaged over a washer (q.v.) to secure it in place.
6. BURRED: a speech form in which the R is sounded heavily.
   'I made the bonnie burd a clockwork bird,' he burred, 'each feather fastened with a rivet burred tight, but she would not look at it even, for the cat had come in burred all over, and she wished to help remove them.'
1. **birr:** an energetic whirring sound; a strong wind.
2. BUR: The flower head of a burdock, *Arctium lappa*; any clinging seed-pod; to remove such seed-pods from wool, or from cat's fur (q.v.).
3. BURR: a washer placed over a rivet before it is hammered tight; to thus secure a rivet; a halo round the moon.
4. BURR: the sweetbread.
5. BURR: the external auditory meatus. [The cockney use of the term 'burr-hole' for the ear is justified.]
6. BURR: a rough, or wire-edge to a piece of metal.
7. BURR: a name for the rock from which millstones were made; a sharpening stone.
8. BURR: a strong sounding of the letter R, hence, dialectal speech.
9. BURR: the banyan tree, *Ficus indica*.
10. BURR: a rotary file, or milling cutter; a dentist's drill (q.v.).
    They say he is a local saint; he sits beneath a burr-tree uttering 'birr' in modulation, there is a

bur clinging to every square inch of him, he has a knife, the edge of which is one long burr, and the burr has worn off the rivets in the halves, you may shout in his burr and he does not hear, and should you drop a burr-stone on his pate he probably would not feel.

birth, see **berth.**

1. **bit:** a small piece.
2. BIT: that part of a tool in which the cutting quality is to be found.
3. BIT: the part of a key that engages the bolt (q.v.) of the lock.
4. BIT: the iron rod which, placed in a horse's mouth, enables the rider or the driver to guide the animal.
5. BIT: pst ppl of v to bite.
6. BITT: one of a pair of bollards attached to the deck of a ship used for securing lines.

He bit off more than he could chew when he undertook that bit of work because he had no suitable bit to fit the chuck, but you know what he is like when he gets the bit between his teeth.

bite, see **bight.**

bitt, see **bit.**

1. **Blaise:** an obsolete masculine personal name; St Blaise.
2. BLAZE: a white streak on the head of either cattle or dogs.
3. BLAZE: to create white marks on the trunks of trees by chipping the bark (q.v.), thus indicating a way through the woods, hence, to indicate a path.
4. BLAZE: a lively fire; a bright light.
5. BLAZE: misspelling of No. 1 above.

His ambition to blaze a new trail through the science of Pyrotechnics ended when his laboratory was consumed in one huge blaze.

1. **bleak:** a fresh-water fish, *Leuciscus alburnus.*
2. BLEAK: pallid, sickly; bare, inhospitable; barren; cold, exposed, windy.

This weather is too bleak to go fishing for bleak.

1. **blew:** pst tns of 'blow', a movement of wind.
2. BLUE: a colour; azure, cobalt, the colour of the sky, used to express a state of depression; applied to aristocratic blood; the colour of burning sulphur, hence symbolic of the Devil, of evil spirits of wizardry; applied to immoral or indecent cinematograph films, to books condemned as obscene, to foul language; conversely, symbolic of truth and reliability; the colour prefixing 'stocking', applied to an intellectual woman; symbolic colour of the Holy Mother's robes in art.

When a gust of wind blew the curtain down all that the blue-stocking could do was turn the air blue with her language. She blew the charwoman up over it, but that lady, claiming to be true-blue, refused to oblige any longer in a house where the people discuss blue films over meals.

1. **blow:** the motion of the wind; to emit breath in a thin stream; to sound (q.v.) a musical instrument by blowing into it.
2. BLOW: to lay (q.v.) eggs, particularly of a fly.
3. BLOW: to blossom.
4. BLOW: the impact of a fist, or a hammer; percussion.

You strike a blow at the fly but, perhaps, if it did not blow upon filth there would be no active manure to aid the rose to blow, and less pleasant smells would blow in at the window.

blue, see **blew.**

1. **boa:** a genus of large snake that kills by constriction, extended to include any large snake.
2. BOA: a form of ladies' neckwear in the shape of a snake, constructed (generally) of feathers extending outward from a central string, or braid (q.v.).
3. BOAR: a male pig (q.v.).
4. BOER: a South African farmer of Dutch origin.
5. BOOR: a Teutonic rustic, or peasant, hence, any brutal, insensitive and offensive person.
6. BORE: a hole (q.v.) of cylindrical form, hence, the internal diameter of a tube; to make such a hole.

7. BORE: pst tns of the v ' to bear' (q.v.).
8. BORE: a dull, talkative person; the state of enduring the attention of such a one.
9. BORE: a gigantic tidal wave occurring under special conditions on some estuarine rivers.

> The fellow is an utter boor and he will bore you to tears with the account of his witnessing the bore on the Severn: you bore him too well last time: your only escape will be to bore a hole in the floor and drop through, or else counter-attack like a boar at bay with your own yarn of what you did in the Boer War.

boar, see preceding group.
board, see **bawd.**
1. **boal:** a niche; an unglazed window aperture.
2. BOLE: the trunk of a tree.
3. BOLE: a form of clay often stained yellow, or red, by iron-oxide.
4. BOUL: anything bent into a curve, particularly a handle.
5. BOULE: an inlay of tortoiseshell in brass.
6. BOWL: a hollow hemisphere forming a vessel.
7. BOWL: a cheese-shaped disc used in the game of bowls.
8. BOWL: to roll along the ground, hence, to hurl the ball in the game of cricket.
9. BUHL: the name of the originator of No. 5 above, which is sometimes so spelt.

> The bowl you had turned from the bole of the oak, and fitted with a silver boul, looks better than the boule box did standing in the boal: I hear you will fill it with ale for them to drink after they bowl a man out at cricket: why not extend the idea to those elders who quietly bowl on the green?

1. **boarder:** one who has food, as well as accommodation for sleeping, at the house of another; a paying guest; a boy who lives in at school; a member of a boat's crew that swarms aboard, and takes, an enemy ship.

2. BORDA: under the Feudal System, one who gave service in exchange for the lord's permission to build and occupy a hut or cottage.
3. BORDER: an edge, margin or limit; a frontier; a line of plants along a flower bed.

> She has a favourite boarder who does the garden for her: he planted that herbaceous border: he is not a native, but comes from over the Border: it is said that were he to fall upon hard times she would let him stay in the capacity of a borda.

1. **boat:** a small, open vessel, propelled by rowing; extended to such vessels when provided with either sail or engine; further (q.v.) extended to fishing vessels, small steam- or oil-driven vessels, and even to major ocean liners; anything of the shape of a boat.
2. BOTE: an old word still employed in Law; the tenant's right to collect timber from the Lord of the Manor's woods to use in house repairs; other perquisites of a like nature.

> I know they had housebote, but in riparian areas had they a house-boat-bote?

1. **bode:** premonition; fore-knowledge; omen, to predict, portend.
2. BOWED: curved; bent like a bow (q.v.).

> It bode ill for the careless workman who had bowed the straight-edge.

1. **bodice:** the upper part of a woman's dress, often tight-fitting, sometimes stiffened with whalebone, or with steel laths.
2. BODIES: pl of body, the animal form; the trunk of a tree; a group, amount or quantity; a Committee, Board (q.v.), Organization or Society.
3. BODY'S: possessive of the body.

> They found five female bodies in the pond, each tight-laced in a leather bodice.

bodies ⎫
body's ⎭ see preceding group.

Boer, see **boa.**
1. **bogey:** a demon.
2. BOGIE: a frame supported on wheels acting as a specialized truck.

3. BOGY: alternative spelling of No. 1 above.

The bogie, falling down the stone stairs, made a din suggestive of a regiment of bogey-men on the war-path.

bogie ⎫
bogy ⎭ see preceding group.

1. **boil**: the state of liquid subjected to increasing heat when the temperature can be no further raised; to bring about such an increase; to convert liquid into gas by the application of heat.

2. BOIL: a pus-filled septic tumour, erupting particularly on the neck.

Boil water to bathe a boil.

1. **bolar**: pertaining to, or having the nature of, bole (q.v.) clay.

2. BOWLER: the player in the game of cricket (q.v.) who propels the ball at the wicket (q.v.).

3. BOWLER: a stiff felt (q.v.) hat with a domed crown.

4. BOWLER: one who often resorts to the bowl; a toper.

5. BOWLER: a workman who beats out the bowl of hand-made (usually silver) spoons.

I once witnessed a village cricket match, played on a very bolar pitch, in which the bowler refused to remove his bowler, and the umpire, being a bowler who had imbibed heavily for lunch, fell asleep.

1. **bold**: courageous; brave; daring; audacious.

2. BOLD: strong; outstanding; pronounced; noticeable.

3. BOLLED: of a plant that produces a boll, a ball-shaped seed-pod, as cotton; anything having, or being supplied with, a round knob.

4. BOWLED: in the game of cricket, to be out by the fall of the wicket; defeated by the bowler (q.v.).

The bold bowler bowled the batsman whose name was printed in bold type on the programme, and the boys bolled his jacket in the pavilion.

1. **bolder**: more bold (q.v.).

2. **BOULDER**: a water-worn stone; an erratic; a massive rock in isolation

having been carried and deposited by archaic glaciers (q.v.).

3. BOWLDER: alternative spelling of No. 2 above.

Now that his patent crane has lifted Blokalyth Boulder he is making bolder claims.

1. **bolt**: a sliding bar to secure a door; a cylindrical pin with a flange head on one end, and a screw-thread starting at the other and usually reaching about two thirds of the length.

2. BOLT: a roll of cloth containing thirty yards.

3. BOLT: to run away.

4. BOLT: to swallow food hastily.

5. BOLT: a broad arrow; a missile (q.v.).

6. BOULT: a sieve.

Boult the oats, and bolt the stable door (I've had it repaired with a bolt and nut): if you forget, the horse will bolt his oats and bolt, which news would strike his owner like a bolt from the blue.

1. **boom**: deep resonant cry of the bittern; a sound representing an explosion; the sound of big guns.

2. BOOM: a log (q.v.) or a spar secured at one end to the mast, and having the main sheet attached to the free end, and onto which the foot of the mainsail is lashed, in fore (q.v.) and aft rigged ships.

3. BOOM: heavy logs chained together and set as an obstruction in the mouth of a river, or the entrance of a harbour, as a war-time precaution against the enemy's fleet (q.v.).

4. BOOM: a sudden very marked improvement in business; an enhanced demand for a certain object or commodity; a speeding up of affairs.

Now the war is ended, and we hear no more the boom of the coastal defence battery, and the boom is removed from the river, business has begun to boom.

boor, see boa.

1. **boos**: cries of contempt or of derision.

2. BOOSE: a horse or cow stall.

3. BOOZE: alcoholic liquor; to drink to excess; to become intoxicated.

4. BOWSE: to lift with block and tackle.

We sail this tide: if you can't get

the cow into the boose, bowse her in and ignore the boos of the audience on the dockside, they are full of booze.

boose ⎱ see preceding group.
booze ⎰

borda ⎱ see boarder.
border ⎰

bore, see boa.

bored, see bawd.

born ⎱ see bawn.
borne ⎰

1. **Borough:** a town, or part of a town, governed by a Municipal Corporation.

2. BORROW: to accept either money or goods for temporary use on security, or against a promise to return.

3. BURROW: a tunnel underground excavated by rabbits for a dwelling place; any kind of tunnelling, the act of cutting a tunnel.

During the war the Borough Council would permit any adult to borrow tools to burrow out an air-raid shelter.

borrow, see preceding group.

1. **boss:** a protuberance; a projection; the ornamental underside of the keystone of a vault; any raised ornament.

2. BOSS: the employer; one to whom the employer's authority is delegated.

3. BOSS: to look; to stare.

4. BOSS: generally as a prefix to 'eye' or 'eyed'; to squint; to make inaccurate visual observation; to be askew, out of centre.

You must be boss-eyed the way you fixed that boss: you should have seen the boss boss at it!

bote, see boat.

bough, see beau.

boul, see boal.

boulder, see bolder.

boule, see boal.

boult, see bolt.

1. **bound:** to spring or leap.

2. BOUND: to be tied up; made secure; committed by oath or by promise.

3. BOUND: to be upon a course of progression.

4. BOUND: boundary.

If you saw him bound along the

street he was bound for the printers to get a book bound: you may be bound that he will make no such effort within the bound of his occupation.

bourn ⎱ see bawn.
bourne ⎰

bow, see beau.

bowed, see bode.

bowl, see boal.

bowlder, see bolder.

bowled, see bold.

bowler, see bolar.

bowse, see boos.

1. **box:** an evergreen shrub, *Buxus sempervirens*.

2. BOX: a container of wood, horn, metal or other material, used either for storage, or for protection during transport.

3. BOX: to strike with the palm of the hand; to engage in fisticuffs under restraining rules; the playful butting of young horned animals.

He has a boxwood box to hold the watch wherewith he times the boys who box.

1. **boy:** a young male human being, hence, a coloured house-servant, or porter, of any age.

2. BUOY: a float used to mark a channel, or to indicate a mooring berth (q.v.): sometimes provided with a light, or a bell.

The hotel's bell-boy ran a side line of sailing guests round the bell-buoy.

1. **brace:** a pair (q.v.); two similar articles.

2. BRACE: a strap, or a rope, a plank, or a beam, or an iron bar supporting, strengthening, or tightening something.

3. BRACE: the act of fixing or applying a brace (also metaphorically).

4. BRACE: a carpenter's crank for rotating a bit (q.v.), or drill (q.v.).

The saddler made a brace for the squire's coach, and the carpenter, in fixing it, broke his brace, and in reward of their labour they received but a brace of pheasants between them.

1. **brae:** the sloping bank of a river.

2. BRAY: the harsh cry of an animal, particularly the ass.

3. BRAY: to use a pestle and mortar; to crush; to pulverize.

4. BRAYE: forward position of a defensive earthwork.

The bray of an ass in the braye on the brae enabled us to positively bray the enemy.

1. **braes:** pl of 'brae' (q.v.).

2. BRAISE: to cook meat by stewing in a close pan.

3. BRAZE: to plate (q.v.) with brass; to join two pieces of metal with a solder containing brass.

You braise the steak while I braze the petrol-pipe and we'll lunch *alfresco* on the braes.

1. **braid:** a flat plait, or weave of fibres or wire, used for strengthening sewn seams, or for decoration on the edge of a garment; a sudden movement, a sharp turn; to draw a weapon; to burst into rapid speech; to scold.

2. BRAYED: pst tns of 'bray' (q.v.).

The Regimental pet ass brayed loudly as the sergeant-major, resplendent in his tunic decorated with gold braid, appeared on parade.

braise, see braes.

1. **brake:** a thicket of fern; an instrument for crushing, also used in the torture-chamber; a winder; a device for stopping a vehicle or a machine.

2. BREAK: to render into pieces by a blow (q.v.); a waggonette.

I saw the wheel break as it fouled a fern-brake and the break might have overturned had the brake failed.

1. **brat:** a contemptuous term of reference to a child.

2. BRAT: a cloak; outer garment; overall.

3. BRAT: turbot.

While the tinker's brat, pretending to shiver, begged for an old brat, they stole the brat from the larder.

bray ⎫
braye ⎭ see **brae.**

braze, see braes.

1. **breach:** to break (q.v.); failure to fulfil a contract; a hole (q.v.) through, or in; a forced opening.

2. BREECH: the buttocks; the butt (q.v.) end of the barrel of a gun.

It is a breach of discipline to open the breech without orders.

1. **breaches:** pl (') of 'breach' (q.v.).

2. BREECHES: masculine nether-garment descending to the knee where it terminates in a strap, but extended to include full-length trousers.

These breeches are full of breaches, I'll have to get a new pair.

1. **bread:** flour-paste baked with leaven.

2. BRED: pst ppl of 'breed' (see No. 6 below); pertaining to quality, to family, social type, line of descent.

3. BREDE: roast, boiled, toasted, cooked meat (q.v.).

4. BREDE: breadth.

5. BREDE: a form of 'braid'.

6. BREED: to develop, nourish, grow, give life; a particular physical or social type.

Men of his breed do not complain when in want of bread: from his kind, heroes are bred, and they breed true, generation after generation.

1. **breadth** (C): distance from side to side; the minor (q.v.) dimension of a rectangle; the minor axis of an oval; toleration; generosity of outlook.

2. BREATH: the air that is inhaled and exhaled in the act of respiration; vapour; odour.

3. BRETH: rage; fury; anger.

4. BRETHE: degenerate; self-ruined by excess.

He called his behaviour breadth-of-mind, but the villagers described him as brethe, and they said it was a judgement when, in a drunken breth, he caught his breath, choked, and so died.

break, see brake.

1. **breast:** glands in the female for the secretion of milk; the chest; the supposed seat of the affections; any broad, solid front; a section of wall between a window and floor.

2. BREST: a fortified seaport town of Western France.

3. BREST-LITOVSK: Russian town, an important railway, river and canal junction.

They pinned a medal on his breast when, after having booked a passage to Brest, he alighted at Brest-Litovsk.

breath, see breadth.

bred } see bread.
brede

breech, see breach.

breeches, see breaches.

breed, see bread.

1. breeze: a gadfly, *Oestruo*.
2. BREEZE: broken coal or coke, larger than dust; broken cinder used in making blocks for building.
3. BREEZE: a gentle, pleasing wind.
   The breeze blew the dust from the breeze blocks into my left eye and a breeze flew into the right.

Brest } see breast.
Brest-Litovsk

1. bret: a fish, *Rhombus vulgaris*; the spawn, or the fry (q.v.) of herring.
2. BRET: to bite; to crop; to break or bruise.
3. BRETT: shortened form of 'britzka', a horse-drawn four-wheeled carriage.
   From his brett, drawn up by the stream, he fished for bret and let his horses bret the wayside grass.

breth } see breadth.
brethe

1. brethel: a dissipated, degenerate person.
2. BROTHEL: a house of sexual prostitution; a 'red-lamp'.
3. BROTHFALL: a folk name for epilepsy.
   The brethel, entering the brothel, was seized with brothfall—a judgement on him.
1. Breton: a native, or a product, of Brittany.
2. BRITAIN: the island comprising England, Scotland and Wales; the Duchy of Bretaign, or Brittany.
3. BRITON: the ancient (pre-Roman) inhabitants of England; a native of Wales; any native of the island of Britain; all subjects of Her Britannic Majesty; an alternative form of No. 1 above.
   In seaport towns around the coast of Britain, many a lusty Briton feels it is his duty to offer to fight any Breton who says he is a Briton.

brett, see bret.

1. brewed: produced by the process of brewing; to mash and extract with hot water; to make.
2. BROOD: offspring, particularly of birds, hence, a family.
3. BROOD: to hatch eggs, hence, to concentrate the attention, particularly in a morbid manner.
   I never visit the O'Haggards now: the whole brood will brood over imagined wrongs, and they brewed a lot of real trouble for me.
1. brews: the various yields of a brew-house; to be occupied in brewing.
2. BRUISE: an injury to the flesh, caused by a blow (q.v.) that extravasates blood without breaking either the skin or bone; to pulverise; to grind, break into particles.
   His brews always turn out satisfactorily simply because he brews conscientiously: he does not neglect to bruise the raw material.
1. bridal: a wedding feast; pertaining to a bride.
2. BRIDLE: an arrangement of straps about the head of a horse to keep it under control.
   Immediately after the bridal he felt the tug of the bridle.

bridle, see preceding group.

brief } see bereave.
brieve

1. bright: vivid; shining; clear; agile-minded; suffused with light.
2. BRITE: description of the condition of grain when over-ripe.
   Very bright of John to have observed that the corn was brite.

Britain, see Breton.

brite, see bright.

Briton, see Breton.

1. broach: to open, particularly to start conversation on a particular subject.
2. BROACH: to turn unexpectedly bringing a ship's broadside into the wind.
3. BROACH: a tapering tool for boring; any rod tapering off at the ends.
4. BROOCH: an ornamental safety-pin, normally an article of jewellery.
   The ship may broach-to while the crew broach cargo, using a

broach to bore brandy kegs. In the bilge they may find the passenger's lost diamond brooch.

1. **broke:** to bargain; to deal; to follow the occupation of a broker.
2. BROKE: pertaining to breakage, fracture, damage or destruction by being forcibly rendered into two or more pieces; to be insolvent, ruined, penniless.

He broke on the Exchange for many years, but taking a holiday in a winter sports area he fell and broke his arm which was so ill-attended, and took so long to knit, that he came home broke.

brooch, see **broach.**
brood, see **brewed.**
1. **brook:** a stream.
2. BROOK: to digest, hence, to tolerate.

Damp I do not mind, but I cannot brook the brook flowing on my kitchen floor.

1. **broom:** a shrub bearing yellow flowers and prickly spines, *Genista*, as well as *Sarothamnus*, and *Cytisus scoparius*; any similar plant.
2. BROOM: a tool having knots of hair or of bristle extending downward from a wooden rectangle, with a long cylindrical handle extending upward, used for sweeping.
3. BRUM: contraction of 'Brummagen', a form of Birmingham, applied to the place, the people, and goods made in that city.
4. BRUME: fog; haze; mist.

When you work all the week in a broom factory in Brum you appreciate a walk through the broom come Sunday, even on a day of drifting brume.

brothel ⎫ see **brethel.**
brothfell ⎭
1. **brough** (bruff): a halo round the moon, or around any luminous body.
2. BROUGH: a round tower.

There is a brough about the moon—an ill-omen—yet we attack the brough at midnight.

1. **brows:** pl of 'eyebrow'; the forehead.
2. BROWSE: twigs and young shoots of shrubs used as fodder for cattle; to feed on such leaves and twigs; extended to include graze (q.v.);

further extended to the act of light rapid reading in one book after another.

Look at his lofty brows and have no doubt but that he will browse in a bookshop for hours.

browse, see preceding group.
bruise, see **brews.**
1. **bruit:** noise, clamour; rumour; to spread a rumour.
2. BRUTE: any animal considered lower than mankind; a person who is crude, rough, insensitive, cruel.
3. BRUTE: a form of the masculine given name, Brutus, the legendary first King of Britain; a Briton; a Welshman; a term used to describe a hero.

They bruit about that he is a veritable Brute, but the fact is simply that he behaves like a brute.

Brum ⎫ see **broom.**
brume ⎭

brute, see **bruit.**
1. **buck:** male deer, goat, hare or rabbit.
2. BUCK: male Red Indian or Negro.
3. BUCK: a dashing ostentatious young man.
4. BUCK: to leap in the air and arch the back, particularly of a horse.
5. BUCK: a wash-tub.
6. BUCK (Am. sl): a dollar.

'That young buck laid me a buck he'd ride your buck-jumper. Now all his clothes are in the buck and the station buck-Nigger is washing them, while a buck-Indian medicine-man named Snorting Buck plasters his bruises,' said the disrespectful Limey tenderfoot.

1 **buckle:** a belt fastener, a frame of metal provided with a transverse tongue, or rod, that engages in a hole punched in the free end of a strap or belt.
2. BUCKLE: to bend.

If you pull that strap too tight you will buckle the buckle.

1. **budge:** move; make room for another.
2. BUDGE: lamb's skin with wool outward used for making garments.
3. BUDGE: abbreviated form of budgerigar, Australian grass parakeet.

That fellow in the budge jacket

won't budge an inch to let that
poor woman carrying a caged
budge sit down.

1. **buff**: stout leather, tanned yellow and
impregnated with oil; such leather
made into jackets and worn in
preference to plate-armour when
gunpowder was first introduced.
2. BUFF: yellowish-brown colour, from
that of the leather.
3. BUFF: a soldier of the Buffs, the third
Regiment of the Line, afterwards,
East Kent Regiment.
4. BUFF: one's bare (q.v.) skin.
5. BUFF: to burst into laughter; to emit a
sound as does a bladder when
struck.
6. BUFF: to polish, or burnish; the revolving pad employed for this
purpose.
There he stood in a buff overall
holding against the spinning buff
a pouch sewn up from buff-
leather, which, he said, would
hold his costume when he went
swimming in the buff.
1. **buffer**: an apparatus for neutralizing
a sudden impact, fitted to each end
of railway vehicles, and at the
head of a railway bay (q.v.).
2. BUFFER: a brass-finisher; one who
works with a buff (q.v.).
3. BUFFER: a person, generally prefixed
with 'old'.
4. BUFFER: a stammerer.
An old buffer stood on the platform looking at the hydraulic
buffer, and insisting that it would
work better if sent for polishing
to the buffer.
1. **buffet**: to strike with the fist; to shake
up, treat roughly.
2. BUFFET: a sideboard laden with
viands; a refreshment bar, particularly when in a railway station or
other place to and from which
passenger transport is organized.
3. BUFFET: a foot-stool.
They buffet you about on their
rackety old vehicles, then have
the impertinence to charge fancy
prices at the buffet.
1. **bugle**: a bull.
2. BUGLE: short for bugle-horn, a
musical instrument made from a
shed horn; extended to include the

copper short trumpet used by
infantry regiments.
3. BUGLE: a tubular bead of slightly
greater diameter in the middle than
at the ends, used as trimming on
ladies' gowns; when black, particularly when cut from jet (q.v.), a
form of mourning (q.v.) jewellery.
As the bugle sounded 'Last Post'
over his grave, a tear from his
widow's eye fell on the jet bugle
at her neck.
Buhl, see **boal**.
build, see **billed**.
bulk, see **balk**.
1. **bunk**: a shelf-like fixture used as a
sleeping berth (q.v.) at sea, or elsewhere.
2. BUNK: short for 'Buncombe', or 'Bunkum'; to make a deceptive speech;
to talk nonsense.
3. BUNK (sl): to run away.
4. BUNK (sl): to lift, or assist in climbing.
The boys had been told that the
retired seaman kept a bear in his
bunk, which they accepted as
bunk, but to find out for certain
Harry gave Jack a bunk up but
they made so much noise that
they decided to do a bunk.
buoy, see **boy**.
bur, see **birr**.
burd, see **bird**.
1. **burden**: load; responsibility; carrying capacity, particularly of a ship.
2. BURDEN: chorus, refrain (q.v.), a repeated phrase (q.v.), or verse, in a
poem or a song, generally marking
the end of a stanza or a verse.
3. BURDON: a hybrid between a horse and
a she-ass.
4. BURTHEN: alternative spelling of Nos.
1 and 2 above.
You burden me with the task of
entertaining the troops—I know
but one song; however, they will
enjoy shouting the burthen.
burdon, see preceding group.
1. **burn**: a stream.
2. BURN: a mark, blister, or other effect
of excessive heat: to be consumed
by fire; to be ignited, in a state of
combustion; to smart or tingle as
if burnt; to be damaged or consumed by acid.

Burn all documents and deposit the ashes in the burn.

burr, see **birr.**

burred, see **bird.**

burrow, see **Borough.**

burthen, see **burden.**

bury, see **berry.**

1. **bust:** a sculptured or painted representation of the sitter's head and shoulders.

2. BUST: the bosom, hence the measurement round the bosom.

3. BUST: vulgar or facetious pronunciation of 'burst'; slang for a spell of drunken roistering.
   After sitting for his bust he decided that he must go on a bust or bust.

1. **bustle:** activity with unnecessary noise and excitement.

2. BUSTLE: the wire dress extender that followed the crinoline, now not worn.
   Think of the bustle of the Victorian bedroom when madam got into her bustle and stays (q.v.).

1. **but:** except; on the contrary; if not; unless, nevertheless.

2. BUTT: halibut, and other flat fish.

3. BUTT: a wine barrel.

4. BUTT: the base, rump, or thicker end.

5. BUTT: a mound; often an artificial mound set up behind targets, on a rifle (q.v.) range, hence, of a person who is the victim of a joke.

6. BUTT: to charge (q.v.) with the head.

7. BUTT: thick leather.

8. BUTTE (bewt): a sudden peak or hill in otherwise flat landscape.
   The American Wild West Infantry Regiment had a rifle-range a mile north of Big Butte. Tethered near the first butt they kept their regimental goat who was sure to butt, but they invariably gave him a kick on his butt, and as their service-boots were soled in good butt-leather, it was considered a fair exchange. The Company with which I served won the Cup that year, and the Captain stood us a feast of boiled butt, and provided a butt of white wine.

butt ⎫ see preceding group.
butte ⎭

1. **butter:** a goat, or other horned animal, with the reputation of butting.

2. BUTTER: the fat content of milk.
   Which of you boys let that old butter go gambolling into the creamery when the girls were making butter?

buy, see **bi-.**

1. **buyer:** one who exchanges money for goods; who makes a purchase; one employed for the purpose of keeping stocks replenished and up to date at the lowest price obtainable.

2. BYRE: a building in which cattle are housed.
   Farmer Graspal has found an American buyer for the old byre.

by
bye ⎬ see **bi-.**
bye-bye

byre, see **buyer.**

C

1. **C:** the third letter of the alphabet, between B and D; c.

2. SEA: the ocean; the earth's envelope (q.v.) of salt water.

3. SEE: to possess the faculty of sight; to cognize optically; to comprehend.

4. SEE: territory under the authority of a Bishop.
   I see the See is now extended to the sea.

1. **Cs:** pl of 'C' (q.v.).

2. SEAS: pl of 'sea' (q.v.).

3. SEES: pl of episcopal See (q.v.); the act of seeing.

4. SEISE: to put one in possession of a freehold estate.

5. SEIZE: to clutch eagerly; to catch hold with hands, teeth or claws; to take an opportunity when presented; to take legal possession of property; to understand instantly; the stoppage of an engine due to expansion of parts, or the introduction of foreign matter.
   I will seize the opportunity to seise him of his cottage on the understanding that he sees to my car so that it will not again seize up.

1. **cabaan:** a white shoulder-cloth, being an item of Arab attire.
2. CABAN: alternative spelling of No. 1 above.
3. CABIN: a small private apartment in a ship; a small room; a crude hut or other humble dwelling-place; a temporary shelter.
   The Arab Sheikh, occupying the first-class luxury cabin, called Allah to witness that the dog of an infidel steward had used his best cabaan for a table-cloth!
1. **cabal:** a secret alliance of persons who aim to secure private ends out of public affairs; a caucus.
2. CABALL: a horse.
3. CABLE: a thick, strong hempen rope, particularly that carrying a ship's anchor, hence, a steel (q.v.) rope, or a chain, employed for that purpose.
4. CABLE: a marine measurement of one hundred fathoms, standardized in charts at 607·56 feet (q.v.).
5. CABLE: a number of insulated conductor wires twisted together as rope and encased in a leaden pipe, employed to carry the current (q.v.) in the transmission of telegraphy and telephony between continents, hence, an overseas telegram.
6. CABLE: an ornamental moulding having the appearance of rope.
   I attempted to cable the King of Antiquania to inform him of our discovery of the cabal in our government, but they had already acquired sufficient power to get the submarine cable cut. In days of old a stout caball was all one needed in such an emergency.

caban ⎫
cabin ⎭ see **cabaan.**

1. **cache:** an underground store, or hiding place, particularly for provisions.
2. CASH: coin, treasury notes, money.
3. CATCH: to capture; to overtake; to come upon unexpectedly; to grasp an object in motion; to contract illness by contact with a sufferer; to hear what is said; to attract attention; to snare, capture or detect, to cheat.

4. CATCH: a device for holding something, as a hook on a doorpost, or a bolt (q.v.) on a window.
5. CATCH: a roundsong.
   The rescue party, happening to catch sight of the lost explorer's cache, were so elated that they sang the old school catch for four voices.
1. **caddie:** an odd-jobs man, hence, the boy, or man, employed by golfers to carry clubs (q.v.).
2. CADDY: a box, usually lined with lead (q.v.) foil (q.v.), for the purpose of holding tea (q.v.).
3. CADDY: alternative spelling of No. 1 above.
   The Golf Club tea-party was a failure due to the caddie having put his tee in the caddy.

caddy, see preceding group.

1. **Caen:** historic university town of North-Western France.
2. CAIN: son of Adam; a symbol of murder, or misspent life.
3. CANE: a rod of bamboo or rattan.
   The conscientious schoolmaster who did not spare the cane sometimes spared the boy the curse of Cain.

Cain, see preceding group.

1. **calendar:** a sheet (q.v.) or a series of sheets inscribed with the number of the year, the name of the month, the days of the week and their numerical sequence; the system whereby the year is subdivided, as the Arabic, the Hebrew, the Julian, the Gregorian calendar; an index to archives.
2. CALENDER: a series of rollers varying in the pressure they exert, used in finishing paper, or cloth; to submit a material to such treatment.
3. CALENDER: an Islamic monk; a Mohammedan Order of mendicant dervishes.
4. COLANDER: a hemispherical vessel perforated, and set upon a ring-shaped foot, used for draining and straining in cooking processes.
5. CULLENDER: alternative spelling of No. 4 above.
   According to my calendar (which seems to have been printed on paper that had not been through

the calender), the Calender Missionary arrives from Turkey next week, so we'd better buy a new colander for him to wash his vegetables or he will think he is violating their strict food tabus.

calender, see preceding group.

1. **calf:** the young of certain animals, as the cow, the deer, the whale, the elephant.
2. **CALF:** the muscular rear portion of the leg between ankle and knee.

He ran to see the new calf and strained his calf.

1. **caliver:** a matchlock musket; a soldier so armed.
2. **CAVALIER:** a gentleman; a Royalist; a horseman; a gay soldier.

Roundhead caliver daunts not the Cavalier.

1. **call:** to shout.
2. **CALL:** to visit.
3. **CALL:** to habitually fulfil one's task in an inspired manner.
4. **CALL:** to bestow a name upon a person or thing.
5. **CAUL:** the amniotic sac, particularly when enveloping a child at birth.
6. **CAWL:** a basket.

Call at the Inn and call for Waterproof (that's what they call the 'boots' there, because he was born in a caul); he will hand you the cawl.

1. **calorie:** a unit of measurement of heat; a great, or major calorie, the amount of heat required to raise one kilogramme of water one degree centigrade; a lesser, or minor calorie, the amount of heat required to raise one gramme of water one degree centigrade.
2. **CALORY:** alternative spelling of No. 1 above.
3. **COLLERY:** name of one of the non-Aryan peoples of India.
4. **COLLIERY:** a coal-mine; a place where coal is handled; a coal-yard.
5. **COLORY:** descriptive of produce having a good colour, indicative of high quality.
6. **COLOURY:** alternative spelling of No. 5 above.

You can't sell the Collery coffee that isn't coloury, you'd as soon

get them to work in a colliery, digging out the solid calorie.

calory } see preceding group.
colliery }

1. **Calvary:** the mount of the Crucifixion.
2. **CAVALLY:** in the seventeenth century a name applied by navigators to horse-mackerel.
3. **CAVALRY:** mounted troops; Lancers; Dragoons; horsemanship in general.

The old soldier, who had served with the Cavalry in Palestine, was never tired of telling of his visit to Calvary.

1. **calve:** of a cow giving birth to a calf (q.v.); of an iceberg from which a considerable mass of ice breaks away.
2. **CARVE:** to create statuary from stone, wood or other medium; to produce a scene, or a pattern in relief; to cut; to slice meat.

The cow was about to calve and the farmer's boy busied himself with a knife on the beam of the barn, keeping alive the old custom to carve a notch on such an occasion.

1. **can:** to possess ability; to have received sanction.
2. **CAN:** a cylindrical vessel made of metal and used as a container, chiefly of preserved food or liquids.
3. **KEN:** to know; to realize.
4. **KIN:** blood relations.

I ken well he is of my kin so I can offer him a can of beer.

1. **candid:** frank; forthright; truthful; without concealment.
2. **CANDIED:** an edible substance, generally peel (q.v.) of fruit, preserved with, and covered with, sugar.

The candid cook condemned the candied peel.

candied, see preceding group.

Cain. } see **Caen.**
cane }

1. **cannon:** a big gun.
2. **CANNON:** the ring, or ear, by which a church-bell is suspended.
3. **CANON:** laws, rules and ordinances (q.v.) laid down by the Church, hence, an accepted standard of behaviour.

4. CANON: a clergyman of advanced rank; a member of an ecclesiastical Chapter.
5. CANYON: a deep rift with clifflike sides and a water-course at the bottom.

The Canon, relating religion to the Christian as the cannon to the bell, thundered like a cannon from the pulpit on the canon of morality, and his voice echoed far down the canyon.

canon, see preceding group.
1. **cant:** hypocrisy; to ape piety; to whine.
2. CANT: tilt (q.v.) or deflect; incline; slope.
3. CANT: a graphic pun; a pictorial phonetic representation of an armiger's name in his heraldic device.
4. CANT: to sing, chant or intone.
5. CANT: to sell by auction.
6. CANT: to divide.
7. CANT: secret language as used in the underworld; trade jargon.
8. CAN'T: contraction of 'cannot'.

He can't deceive me with his pious cant for the cant of the thieves' kitchen would sit better on him.

1. **cantar:** a measure of capacity in countries bordering the Mediterranean Sea.
2. CANTER: one who uses the slang of the underworld; one who talks hypocritically.
3. CANTER: a moderate gallop.
4. CANTOR: one who sings liturgical music.

The cantor mounted his horse, proceeded at a canter, but he was stopped by a vagabond who would have robbed him had he not, as a hobby, studied slang, and so became a vigorous canter.

canter } see preceding group.
cantor }
1. **canvas:** strong cloth of flax or hemp used for making sails, tents, and articles subject to hard wear.
2. CANVASS: to solicit orders for goods, votes in an election, or patronage to secure a place.

She volunteered to canvass but the candidate, noting her dirty canvas bag, did not accept.

canvass, see preceding group.
canyon, see cannon.
1. **cape:** a land mass extending seaward.
2. CAPE: a sleeveless outergarment that hangs from the shoulders.

The cape is a garment worn everywhere between Inverness and the Cape of Good Hope.

1. **caper:** a shrub, *Capparis spinsoa*, indigenous to Southern Europe, the flower-buds of which are used for pickling.
2. CAPER: to leap in a playful manner; to execute frolicsome dance steps.

They caper with joy when caper sauce is on the menu.

1. **capital:** the head, or chief; at the head of; the flat stone on the top of a pillar (q.v.); the foundation of money on which affairs depend.
2. CAPITOL: a hill-top fort; the Roman Temple of Jupiter Optimus Maximus; the building housing the Congress of the U.S.A., or the building housing a State senate.
3. CAPITOUL: the municipal magistrates of Toulouse.

It sure was a capital idea to put Sam K. Gagattah in the Capitol, now he's invested capital in this burg, and if he wants us to call him Capitoul that don't give me no grief.

capitol } see preceding group.
Capitoul }
1. **carat:** a standard of fineness, or purity of gold, 24 carat being absolute purity; a standard of weight used for precious stones equal to 3·2 grains; a bean of the carob-tree, *Ceratonia siliqua*.
2. CARROT: a plant, *Daucus carota*, having a red, conical edible root.
3. CHARACT: a monogram; a mark; a sigil; a written sign supposed to possess occult powers.

The craftsman made a shank of 24-carat gold to hold the huge stone weighing many a carat and carved in the shape of a carat-bean conjoined to a carrot which he had been informed represented in the round, a magician's charact of enormous potency.

1. **card:** pasteboard used for many purposes and in numerous processes; to comb wool or other fibre in preparation of spinning.
2. CAR'D: travelled by motor-car.
   A messenger brought his visiting card on which was written 'help', so we car'd immediately to his house.
1. **career:** progress along a course (q.v.), hence, advancement in an occupation.
2. CHOREA: convulsive involuntary muscular contractions; St. Vitus's Dance; choreomania.
3. KOREA: a peninsula to the south-east of Manchuria, subject to political upheavals.
   He hopes for a career in Korea.
1. **carol:** a joyous song, specifically a Christmas hymn (q.v.).
2. CHORAL: sung by a choir (q.v.).
3. CHORALE: a hymn set to a devotional tune.
4. CORAL: the continuous shell built and inhabited by colonies of minute marine organisms (polyps); beads, and other pieces of jewellery made from this.
5. CORRAL: a fenced-in pasture, set aside for the use of horses.
6. KRAAL: a Zulu village.
   The children from the kraal, marshalled by the Mission-worker, stood in a group in the corral where they were each given a necklace of cheap coral beads, and a travelling pastor led them in singing a carol.
1. **carp:** the fresh-water fish *Cyprinus carpio*; goldfish.
2. CARP: to find fault; to be captious; to be censorious.
   I keep carp and you can carp.
1. **carosse:** a form of carriage.
2. CAROUSE: a drinking bout.
   After a carouse he fell out of his carosse.
carouse, see preceding group.
carrot, see carat.
1. **cart:** a strongly built vehicle designed for conveyance of goods; to undertake the removal of goods by the aid of such a vehicle.
2. CARTE: a chart; a bill-of-fare; a visiting card; a playing card.

3. QUART (carte): a position assumed in swordplay; a sequence of four cards in certain card-games.
4. QUART (kwart): a measure of capacity equal to two pints.
   He descended from the driving seat of the cart, entered the inn, ordered a quart of ale and, being hungry, asked to see the carte, but the landlord drew back in a swordsmanlike quart, at the idea of a common cart driver using the dining-room.
carte, see preceding group.
1. **carton:** a box, generally of corrugated cardboard, made to fit a specific number of a certain object, hence, a box designed for transportation of goods.
2. CARTOON: a design on paper for tapestry, mosaic (q.v.) or stained glass; a comic drawing having a political slant; an animated drawing, projected by cinematograph.
   The cartoon that decided the issue in the election was first drawn with a charred stick on the lid of a carton.
carve, see calve.
1. **case:** an occurrence; the matter for decision by a Court of Law; a state of illness.
2. CASE: a box, container, or covering for an object, or a number of objects.
   In case you forget, tomorrow the case of the stolen spectacle case will be heard.
1. **cashier:** one who handles inward and outward payments in a bank; one who receives cash payments in a shop or other establishment.
2. CASHIER: to dismiss, particularly an officer from a Service.
   He refused to handle the Mess (q.v.) accounts on the grounds that he was not a skilled cashier, and would get into a muddle that might result in their having to cashier him.
1. **cask:** a barrel; a vessel of staves, hoops and heads cut and assembled by the cooper.
2. CASQUE: a helmet; the head piece of a suit of armour.
   The stage property casque having

been lost, was substituted by a small cask with the bung-hole enlarged.

casque, see preceding group.

1. **cast:** to throw; a mass thrown off; to throw a thing, or a person, down.
2. **CAST:** to form by pouring a liquid that will ultimately solidify, into a mould (q.v.); the object thus formed.
3. **CAST:** the part that is to be played by an actor; the company of actors in a play; to choose actors to suit the parts in a play.
4. **CAST:** to keep accounts; to add a column of figures.
5. **CASTE:** a social group or sect that keeps itself apart, or aloof, from the bulk of the population; a social status.

The high-caste Indian, cast in the international mould of the tycoon, cast caution to the winds and produced European drama with an all-Indian cast, after which he had to employ extra clerks to cast his accounts.

caste, see preceding group.

1. **caster:** that part of a typesetting machine where the molten metal is introduced into the moulds (q.v.).
2. **CASTOR:** a substance obtained from the beaver, and used in perfumery.
3. **CASTOR:** a small jar (q.v.) the lid of which, perforated, screws securely on, and which inverted and shaken dispenses a powdered foodstuff, as pepper or sugar.
4. **CASTOR:** a small swivelled wheel, one of which secured to each leg of a heavy piece of household furniture enables it to be moved easily.
5. **CASTOR:** name of a vegetable oil obtained from the seeds of the 'castor-oil plant', *Ricinus communis,* used as a purgative.
6. **CASTOR:** the name of the twin brother of Pollux, sons of Tyndareus and Leda; the first star in the constellation Gemini.

While Tom was shaking castor-sugar on his stewed apple, Mother remarked that he must put the castor on grandfather's arm-chair, which he facetiously

did, and it was spilled all over the old man who was already in a bad temper, he having accidentally taken double his routine dose of castor oil.

castor, see preceding group.

1. **cat:** a domestic, furred quadruped, of high intelligence, having an affectionate nature, and a strong individuality, *Felis domesticus*; any member of the genus *Felis*.
2. **CATT:** a broad, flat-bottomed boat; a coal barge.

Sir Richard Whittington's fortune was derived of his catt, not his cat.

catch, see **cache.**

1. **cate:** an article of food, but particularly choice, dainty food. Usually pl.
2. **KATE:** a diminutive of the feminine personal name Katherine, Catherine or Cathleen.

catt, see **cat.**

1. **caudal:** the tail (q.v.) or something in the nature of a tail, or something near to, or related to, a tail.
2. **CAUDLE:** a hot drink consisting of thin gruel laced with wine and spice; to mix or make a caudle.

The veterinary surgeon sipped caudle and surveyed the horse suffering from a caudal contusion.

caudle, see preceding group.

1. **caught:** pst tns & ppl of 'catch' (q.v.).
2. **COURT:** the place of residence of the Sovereign; an assembly held by the Sovereign; the persons attending the Sovereign, and their proceedings.
3. **COURT:** an assembly of judges, or magistrates or others appointed who hear and determine causes at law; the building, or the chamber, in which such hearings and judgements take place.
4. **COURT:** a square surrounded by buildings; a quadrangle; a space enclosed for the purpose of sport or games such as tennis; a narrow way between buildings.
5. **COURT:** to pay attention in order to gain an end.

He was caught while obtaining credit by pretending to be

attached to the Court, and when he came up in court the magistrate caught a resentful murmur from the public gallery which he ordered to be cleared, as he did not care to court disaster.

1. **cauk:** a form of lime.
2. CAULK: to seal the seams of a ship; to make watertight; to make draught-proof.
3. CORK: the bark (q.v.) of the oak-tree, *Quercus suber*; anything made of this, particularly stoppers for bottles.

Caulk with powdered cork mixed with watered cauk.

caul, see **call.**
caulk, see **cauk.**
Cavalier, see **caliver.**
cavally } see **Calvary.**
cavalry }

1. **cause:** a thing, or a number of things, persons, emotions or circumstances that bring about an action, or that influence behaviour; a principle, or an objective to be striven after; action at law.
2. CAWS: pl of 'caw' (q.v.).
3. CORES: pl of 'core' (q.v.).

The caws of the rooks cause the house to remain uninhabited; the late owner supported the cause of 'Freedom for fur, fin and feather', and he raised no complaint when the birds left nothing but the cores of his apples.

1. **caw:** the rasping cry of the crow.
2. COPS: a shackle; a bolt (q.v.); a fastener.
3. COPSE: a thicket cultivated to produce small wood.
4. CORE: the central, non-edible part of an apple or a pear, containing husk and seed; the heart, or the essence, of any matter.
5. CORPS: a body of soldiers or others under discipline.
6. CORPSE: the dead body of a human being.
7. CORPUS: a body of writings on a particular subject.

There is a corpus of literature on military funeral etiquette and the disposal of a soldier's corpse: the core of the matter is that a man may be buried without ceremony in a copse, his obsequies being accompanied only by the caw of the rooks; or a whole army corps with bands and banners may form the funeral procession.

1. **cawed:** pst tns of 'caw' (q.v.).
2. CHORD: a number of harmonious musical notes.
3. CORD: any line of small circumference but especially that which is woven, or plaited rather than laid or twisted; a cord-like ridge woven in cloth; any structure in the animal body that resembles a cord; a standard of measure applied to timber, or to stone being a mass, eight feet by four by four high.

He struck a chord, and even the local rooks cawed musically when he offered me mahogany at half-a-crown a cord on the understanding that I should tie it up in small bundles using my own cord.

caws, see **cause.**

1. **Cecily:** a feminine personal name.
2. SICILY: an island in the Mediterranean off the coast of Italy.

Since Cecily returned from the tour she talks only of Sicily.

1. **cedar:** a tree, *Abies cedrus*, known as Cedar of Lebanon from its famous early mention in literature; wood of this tree.
2. CIDER: an intoxicating drink, being fermented apple juice (q.v.).
3. SEDER: the name of the Hebrew Religious Rite (q.v.) performed in the home, in celebration of Passover.

The cedarwood box in which was kept the book of the Service for Passover was on the table, but the Seder could not be celebrated because, by accident, a bottle of cider had been included with the wine.

1. **cede:** to surrender something to somebody; to voluntarily give an opponent victory, or partial victory.
2. SEED: the male, fertilizing germ in animals; the fertilized ovules in plants; the tangible beginning of a new organism; anything from

which something may grow and develop; religious and moral instruction.

I cede you a point when you state that the much-vaunted 'Youth Movement' sows the seed of juvenile delinquency.

1. **ceil:** to cover the walls of a room (q.v.) with panelling or with plaster; so to treat the underside of a roof, or a floor; to construct a ceiling (q.v.).

2. CIEL: alternative spelling of No. 1 above.

3. SEAL: a sea-mammal, *Phoca vitulina*.

4. SEAL: a disc of wax (q.v.), impressed with a device, and attached to documents either for security, or for authentication; to attach such a device; to enclose anything very securely.

5. SEEL: to blind, particularly to blind a bird.

His seal, a seal naiant, is in the plaster because he paid for them to ceil the roof.

1. **ceiling:** the area of (usually) plaster spanning from wall to wall at the top of a room; a canopy or cover; an agreed maximum height, as that at which an aircraft flies; the figure beyond which prices may not rise.

2. SEALING: the act of affixing a seal (q.v.).

He was sealing his own brother's death warrant when the ceiling fell and killed him.

1. **celanese:** the name of a sheer (q.v.) fabric woven from synthetic fibre.

2. CEYLONESE: a person, or a product, from Ceylon.

The Ceylonese ladies were clad in celanese saris.

1. **celery:** a plant, *Apium graveolens*, the stalks of which enjoy the reputation of being edible.

2. SALARY: weekly, or monthly, payments for work other than manual labour.

Notwithstanding his high salary he lives on celery and dry biscuits.

1. **cell:** the simplest form of organic matter; the elemental form of life; a compartment; a cubicle inhabited by one person only; an arrangement

of chemicals to generate electricity; a small organization dependent on, and representing, a larger one.

2. SELL: to dispose of goods for money; to betray; to be deceived.

Sell me a cell in a monastery.

1. **cellar:** a store room, particularly when below ground level.

2. SELLER: one who sells; one who exchanges goods for money.

In a dark, damp cellar the seller of mushrooms raised his produce.

1. **Celt** (Kelt): an ethnic group including the populations of Cornwall, Wales, Scotland and Ireland.

2. CELT (selt): a prehistoric stone implement.

3. KELT: an alternative spelling of No. 1 above.

4. SILT: waterlaid geological stratum.

Geological evidence shows that the celt was in the silt before the Celt was in the country.

1. **cemetery:** a burial ground.

2. SYMMETRY: balance; equal distance in lines of contour from a centre line; regular proportions.

The memorial monument recently erected in the cemetery is all out of symmetry.

1. **cense:** to estimate; to perfume with the vapour of burning incense.

2. CENTS: plural of 'cent' (q.v.).

3. SENSE: intelligence; ability to exercise judgement; meaning; the faculties of physical perception.

I cense it better to be without cents than without sense.

1. **censer:** a small ornamental portable stove in which incense is burned.

2. CENSOR: an official having the duty of eliminating from public entertainment any indecent passage or one likely to induce lascivious thoughts in members of the audience; one who deletes from any written matter passages that are, for the time being, held to be detrimental.

3. CENSURE: condemnatory criticism; admonition.

The poor girl is continually subject to paternal censure, for her father, who carries the censer in church on Sunday, is chairman of the local Watch Committee, and self-appointed censor.

censor, see preceding group.

1. **censual:** pertaining to a cenus.
2. SENSUAL: physical; lewd; immoral; gross (q.v.); greedy; unconcerned with intellectual or with spiritual matters; materialistic; irreligious.

A report based on censual information calculates that 90 per cent of the population is sensual.

1. **cent:** a hundred; a coin (q.v.) of small value (in U.S.A. one hundredth part of a dollar); a generic term for money.
2. SENT: pst ppl of the v 'to send'.
3. SCENT: a liquid that exudes an artificial odour; the odour of flowers; the track of an animal that can be followed by a dog having a keen sense of smell; the sense of smell itself.

The film-actress sent for an expensive bottle of scent though she had not a cent to pay for it, and the shop detective was immediately on the scent.

1. **Centaur:** a mythical creature having the body and legs of a horse and, in place of the neck, the trunk, head and arms of a man.
2. CENTRE: a point equidistant from the periphery of a figure or object; the middle; a focal point; a point, or place, of concentration.

Granny Wiggs made herself the centre of attraction at the Welfare Centre by complaining that a Centaur had entered her bedroom.

1. **centaury:** a plant of the species *Chlora perfoliata* and *Erythraea centaureum.*
2. CENTURY: a hundred; specifically a period of 100 years.
3. SENTRY: an armed guard stationed at a particular point.

The sentry, who felt as though he'd been on duty for at least a century, stamped savagely upon the centaury growing along his beat.

centre, see **Centaur.**

cents, see **cense.**

century, see **centaury.**

1. **cere:** to enwrap a body in cloth with wax (q.v.) and spices; to mummify.
2. SEAR: to scorch or carbonize by heat, to burn; to dry up; to lose vitality; to wither (q.v.).
3. SEER: one who sees; one having spiritual inspiration, or clairvoyance, second sight, precognition; one gifted with a wide and conscious field of extra-sensory perception, particularly in the area of subjective vision; a soothsayer; a scryer or crystal-gazer; a wizard; a magician; one having great wisdom.
4. SEER: an Indian expression of weight varying locally, averagely, 2 lb; an Indian standard of capacity equal to a litre; 1·76 pints.
5. SERE: alternative spelling of No. 1 above.

The seer, sear in the flesh, is vital in spirit.

1. **cereal:** wheat, oats, and the like; any grass, specialized and modified, suitable for human consumption; any material sold in gaudily printed packets and recommended (by the maker) as a breakfast food.
2. SERIAL: following in regular procession; a literary work, particularly a novel, published in periodical instalments.

Every morning I eat my cereal and read my serial.

1. **cession:** abdication; the vacating of an office or a benefice; the ceding of rights, or of property; voluntarily surrendering goods in payment of debt.
2. SESSION: the period of time during which a court sits, a committee meets, or an academical body is engaged in teaching.
3. SESSION: short for Session of the Peace, a court for the trial of criminal causes held periodically.

After the fraudulent bankruptcy, the cession of his personal property, and more than one session with his solicitors and learned counsel, did not save him from appearing for trial at Session.

Ceylonese, see **celanese.**

1. **chagrin:** annoyance; anger; mortification due to a failure.

2. SHAGREEN: a form of leather; shark-skin; any imitation of this; a leather with an abrasive surface; thin, green leather.

To my chagrin I failed to secure the shagreen spectacle-case.

1. chair: a seat for one person; a light car or carriage for the conveyance of one person; symbolic of authority, as the Chair of Philology, i.e., a Professorship; short for chairman, one who presides over a formal meeting; one of the iron sockets that secure a railway line (q.v.) to the sleeper (q.v.).

2. CHAR: a recurring irksome humble task; housework.

3. CHAR: a fish, *Salmo salvelinus*, inhabiting mountain lakes.

4. CHAR: to scorch; to carbonize by the application of heat.

5. CHARE: alternative spelling of No. 2 above.

6. CHARE: a narrow lane; an alley (q.v.).

7. CHARE: to turn away; to be chary, careful, cautious.

8. CHORE: alternative spelling of No. 2 above.

You will take the chair at the meeting to decide who shall execute the disputed chore, but chare from the suggestion of our providing a new armchair for the charwoman; the old one will do though she did let the leg char off by the fire while she sat at ease preparing the char for the frying pan, 'but', she explained, 'I ain't no chef.'

1. chaise: a light carriage.

2. CHASE: to pursue, hunt, run after; a tract (q.v.) of land preserved for hunting over; a landowner's right of breeding and keeping cattle for hunting.

3. CHASE: a groove, trench or slot (q.v.); a gun barrel; a steel (q.v.) frame in which printing type is set.

4. CHASE: to produce on sheet metal a raised pattern by hammering.

5. CHASSE: a receptacle for the relics of a saint.

6. CHASSE: liquor taken to inhibit the after-flavour of coffee.

7. CHASSÉ: a gliding dance step.

8. CHASSEZ: to dismiss.

9. CHASSIS: the base-frame of a motor vehicle.

The silversmith had to chase his assistant in order to get him to chase the urgently required chasse; he found him in a saloon, taking a chasse of brandy, and executing a chassé, but knew that he could not hand out the chassez; on the contrary, he enticed him back to the bench by offering a day off in which to dig the chase for the drain-pipe in his garden, and another in which to clean the chassis of his car.

1. chance: an occurrence without previous organization; an accident; a risk; an opportunity; a probability.

2. CHANTS: pl of 'chant', a simple melody used for intoning psalms, prayers and other religious utterances.

It was by chance that he was offered the chance of rendering the solo chants but the choirmaster was satisfied that there was a fair chance of his making a success of it, and it was worth taking a chance.

1. chantie: a rhythmic song, or chorus, intoned in unison by a team (particularly of sailors), at work, in order to secure coordination of effort.

2. SHANTY: alternative spelling of No. 1 above.

3. SHANTY: a flimsy, roughly constructed hut; a lean-to.

Paddy was the best chantie-man on the ship and, during watch below, he'd bring tears to the eyes of our bucko mate by singing about a shattered Irish shanty.

chants, see chance.

1. chap: a split or crack descending into the subcutaneous tissue, generally caused by frost.

2. CHAP: the jaw, particularly of an animal, hence, the jaw of a vice (q.v.).

3. CHAP: to vend or barter.

4. CHAP: a person.

5. CHAP: a leather leg covering, tanned with the hair on, as worn by cowboys.

When the chapman came to the village I bought a new chap for my vice: I was sorry for the poor chap: on each of his hands was a terrible chap.

char, see **chair**.

charact, see **carat**.

chare, see **chair**.

1. **charge**: the sum of money demanded for either goods or services; any pecuniary liability; trust or responsibility; a person under the care of another; an order or an instruction; an accusation.
2. CHARGE: the quantity of material appropriate to a receptacle, as the amount of tobacco required to fill a pipe.
3. CHARGE: in heraldry, any single shape, or object, depicted upon the field.
4. CHARGE: to attack with vigour; the bugle- or trumpet-call ordering the attack.
5. CHARGÉ: the Diplomatic Officer who takes command at an embassy in the absence of the Ambassador.

His lordship will charge in here tomorrow morning and complain that we charge too much for painting the augmentative charge on his Coat of Arms; you will be in charge, so remember to take it quietly; it is a little habit that he developed while Chargé d'affaires at the Italian Embassy: don't charge him with using insulting language.

1. **charger**: a large dish, generally circular in shape, and often having a ridge on the underside forming a foot.
2. CHARGER: a military officer's horse; a war-horse.
3. CHARGER: a person who demands abnormally high rates of payment for either goods or services.

He has in the window a beautiful Chinese charger on which is depicted, in that vivid blue the Oriental potters used, a warrior in raw-hide armour mounted upon his charger: I yearn to acquire it but I dare not so much as ask the price, knowing what a charger he is.

chase, see **chaise**.

1. **chased**: pst ppl of the v 'to chase' (q.v.); pursued, hunted.
2. CHASED: decorated with a design in relief.
3. CHASTE: restrained in manner; moral in behaviour; sexually pure.

That girl (wearing the chased silver bangle) is chased by every young man she meets, and her mother (knowing the girl to be chaste) raises no objection.

chasse
chassez }see **chaise**.
chassis

chaste, see **chased**.

1. **cheap**: inexpensive; a bargain; weak unseemly behaviour or remarks.
2. CHEEP: the shrill, but weak, cry of a young bird, of a mouse or a bat.

He made himself cheap by haggling with a huckster to get the canary cheap, and it can but cheep.

1. **check**: to obstruct, restrain, control or supervise.
2. CHECK: to investigate, particularly for the accuracy of work.
3. CHECK: a pattern of squares repeating alternately in two colours.
4. CHECK: a term used in the game of chess.
5. CHEQUE: an authorization for a banker to pay money out of a customer's account.

The way to check the leakage is to check every cheque made payable to a weaver of check tweed.

1. **cheek**: the side of the face.
2. CHEEK: impertinence.

Cheek me, my boy, and I'll leave my finger marks on each cheek.

cheep, see **cheap**.

1. **cheery**: cheerful; in abounding good spirits; a pleasing place, sight or situation; gladdening news.
2. CHERRY: a small, sweet, red stone-fruit of the tree *Prunus cerasus*.

The cheery atmosphere of the gathering was enhanced by cherry-brandy.

cheque, see **check**.

cherry, see **cheery**.

1. **chesil**: gravel, or grain.
2. CHESSEL: a cheese cask.
3. CHISEL: an edged tool, long rectangular in shape, bevelled and

sharpened at one end and mounted in a handle at the other, used by carpenters and other woodworkers; a bar of steel, hardened and tapered at one end, used by masons and other workers in stone.

4. CHISSAL: a kind of pear (q.v.).
5. CHISSEL: bran, or wholemeal.

She invented a fruit pie made with chesil, chissal and chissel; then she sulked when her husband said he needed his chisel to cut it.

chessel, see preceding group.

1. **chest:** a coffer; a strong box; a box in which a seaman carries his personal belongings; a container of standard dimensions for the transport of tea (q.v.), hence, a measure of tonnage by bulk (q.v.); a semipoetic name for a coffin.
2. CHEST: the upper ventral area of the body; the lung cavity.

A gnarled seaman with his chest on his shoulder, and on his chest tattooed a clipper-ship under sail, swung into the inn and gave, with the full power of his deep chest, a shout for rum.

1. **chews:** third person present tns of the v 'to chew'; the act of crushing food between the teeth; to masticate.
2. CHOSE: pst tns of No. 3 following.
3. CHOOSE: to demonstrate preference; to select one or more from a greater number.

When asked to choose, he chose coconut toffee and there he sits and chews it.

1. **Chile:** a country on the Pacific coast of the South American continent.
2. CHILE (chio-l): Am. form of 'child'; an endearment, shaped by the Southern accent (q.v.).
3. CHILLI: the pods of red pepper, *Capsicum.*
4. CHILLY: cold.
5. CHILLY: alternative spelling of No. 3 above.

Know somepin', honey chile? the weather's turned chilly so he's taking pleny chilli soup, and he plans to be back home in lil ole Chile before the European winter really sets in.

chilli ⎱ see preceding group.
chilly ⎰

chisel ⎫
chissal ⎬ see **chesil.**
chissel ⎭

1. **choir:** an organized group of vocalists; the space, or stalls, reserved for the vocalists in a church.
2. COIR: coconut fibre woven into either rope, or matting.
3. COYER: a comparative of 'coy', more coy, or shy.
4. QUIRE: twenty-four sheets of writing paper; printing sheets folded to form a signature of a book; a complete literary work, a monograph, making an octavo book of sixteen pages.

The choir-master, a scholar and a gentleman, used a whole quire of note-paper in writing letters to save the monumental brasses from a covering of coir matting: he wrote, subsequently, a quire on the antiques, which sold for a shilling to the profit of the Church.

1. **choler:** irascibility; bad temper.
2. COLLAR: the part of a garment that surrounds the neck; the chain of an Order of Chivalry; a strap about the neck of an animal; a ring through which a rod, forming part of a machine, passes; an eye-splice in a rope.
3. COLLAR (sl): to seize.

A speck on his shirt-collar roused his choler.

choose, see **chews.**

1. **chop:** to cut by a blow with an axe, or other heavy edged tool, hence, a piece of meat severed from the bulk by a cleaver (q.v.); pertaining to the sea when waves of low amplitude and short pitch (q.v.) are running with high frequency.
2. CHOP: the jaw; the mouth; the sides of the face; the cheek; to snap with the jaws; the entrance of a valley, or of a channel.
3. CHOP: in eastern trade a seal, trademark or brand, hence, a comparative of quality.
4. CHOP: to change; to conduct transactions by barter.
5. SHOP: a room or a chamber open to

the street, where retail trading takes place; a room devoted to the execution of, usually, manual work.

6. SHOP: business, or occupation.

7. SHOP (sl): The Royal Military Academy.

8. SHOP (sl): to betray.

How the weather does chop and change: this morning we arranged to go for a sail, but now there is a nasty chop running— if I go aboard I'll be sick—the chop I had for lunch which was bought at a strange shop was decidedly second chop. I will admit that the dog to whom I gave more than half did not share my opinion judging by the way he licked his chop. No. Let us stay ashore and laze, and talk shop. I know we promised not to, but no one will shop us.

choral ⎫
chorale ⎭ see **carol.**

chord, see **cawed.**

chore, see **chair.**

chose, see **chews.**

1. **chough** (chuff): a small black bird having red legs and beak, indigenous to Cornwall.

2. CHUFF: fat; chubby; a boorish rustic.

That chuff chuff claims to know the breeding ground of the chough.

1. **Chris:** diminutive of Christopher, a masculine personal name.

2. KRIS: a Malay native short sword.

Chris brought home a kris.

1. **chuck:** a chicken; a term of endearment; the sound uttered by a hen calling chickens.

2. CHUCK: a gentle tap (q.v.) under the chin.

3. CHUCK: a gripping mechanism by means of which material is held in a lathe or by which the bit (q.v.) is held in a brace (q.v.) or by which any material or any tool is held while being rotated.

4. CHUCK: to throw, specifically, to throw gently.

When the female fitter called for a chuck the apprentice said he'd chuck one over, but the foreman, addressing her as 'chuck', offered her a chuck under the chin.

chuff, see **chough.**

1. **chute:** a steeply sloping duct to carry a heavy fall of water, and also objects afloat on the water; a similar duct down which coal (q.v.), sand, gravel, minerals or grain may be handled.

2. SHOOT: to discharge missiles; to kill by discharging an arrow or a bullet; an armed party of men who kill a rabbit or a bird; a young branch growing out of a plant-stem or a tree-trunk; a sharp forward advance; a sudden pain; a sudden slope, that forms a rapid in a water course; an alternative spelling of No. 1 above.

3. SHUTE: alternative spelling of No. 1 above.

Shoot off to the chute, and don't let them shoot the coal down, or the master, who is out on a shoot, will shoot me when he returns.

cider, see **cedar.**

1. **cinq:** five; a combination of five in the game of dice; in bell-ringing, the name for changes on eleven bells.

2. CINQUE PORTS: ancient English seaports, originally five in number, namely, Hastings, Sandwich, Dover, Romney, Hythe, to which was added Rye and Winchelsea.

3. SANK: pst tns of 'sink'; subsided; disappeared beneath the surface of water, snow, bog or any yielding medium; to have gone down; to have passed from a higher to a lower position, state or condition; to have declined in health; to have excavated, or to have carved a pattern in relief; to have invested money.

Full many a fair ship sank in foul weather within sight of a Cinque port.

Cinque, see preceding group.

1. **cion:** the uvula; the nasal septum.

2. SCION: a twig or branch, a graft, a son (q.v.); an heir (q.v.); a descendant; a cadet.

He is without doubt a scion of that noble house: note the bent cion that has marked the race for generations.

1. **cipher:** the Arabic figure '0', of no value; one who is a nonentity; a secret alphabet; continuous emission of sound from an organ pipe through a defective valve.
2. **CYPHER:** alternative spelling of No. 1 above.
3. **SYPHER:** a carpenter's long chamfer joint.

   The village carpenter made a sypher in the sixteen-foot organ pipe in an endeavour to hush its cipher.

1. **circa:** at about that time.
2. **CIRCAR:** a province of Hindustan under the Moguls.
3. **SIRKAR:** the court of an Indian prince; a native house-steward; a native clerk, accountant or agent.

   Zahir-ud-din Mohammed Babur the Lion entered India circa 1525 and inaugurated the circar system: my sirkar will give you a written note of the facts.

circar, see preceding group.

1. **cist:** a sepulchral chamber either cut in rock or built up of stone slabs.
2. **CYST:** a hollow, ball-shaped cavity in the body of an animal, hence, the bladder; a morbid growth in an animal being a cavity containing pus.
3. **SIST:** to stop proceedings in progress before a Court of Law by a Judicial decree.

   The body in the newly excavated cist was so well preserved that it was possible to observe that death had been caused by a cyst in the throat.

1. **cite:** to quote a precedent as an example.
2. **SIGHT:** the faculty of cognizance in the visual field; that which is visually cognized; an impressive scene (q.v.) or object; an example of building, of town-planning or of costume that is ugly, out-of-place or ill-suited.
3. **SITE:** a plot of land set aside for a specific use.

   My sight is poor: does the notice announce that the site is sold? If so, we may expect a perfect sight of a modern building: I cite the example of London, where

tradition is sacrificed to Mammon.

1. **cited:** pst tns of 'cite' (q.v.).
2. **SIGHTED:** having the faculty of visual cognizance; having visual power of a certain kind.
3. **SITED:** having place or position; allocated to a site (q.v.).

   He was cited as an eye-witness, but cross-examination revealed that he was too short-sighted to have observed the incident on account of the position in which the building is sited.

1. **claimant:** one who asserts a claim, or a right to a possession or an office.
2. **CLAMANT:** clamorous; insistent; loud; noisy.

   The claimant is so clamant that we'd better give way.

clamant, see preceding group.

1. **clause:** a self-contained section of a compound sentence; a single paragraph from a document.
2. **CLAWS:** the horny terminal of the toes of birds, and of some quadrupeds.

   There is a clause in the cat's service agreement whereby he shall not sharpen his claws on furniture.

claws, see preceding group.

1. **cleave:** to split into two; to cut, generally by heavy blows.
2. **CLEAVE:** to adhere firmly; to follow, or be attached to a person, or party, or idea, steadfastly.
3. **CLEEVE:** a form of cliff, sometimes appearing in English place-names.
4. **CLEVE:** alternative spelling of No. 3 above.

   The whole population of Clevewell-on-Sea talks of how I cleave to you though you try to cleave my friendship.

1. **cleaver:** a meat (q.v.) axe; a butcher's tool used for splitting a carcass in two.
2. **CLEVER:** having superior intellect, or manual skill; possessing ability; nimble; dexterous.

   The butcher's boy is clever with a cleaver.

1. **cleek:** a large strong hook.
2. **CLICK:** a sharp, non-musical sound

as of metal lightly striking against metal.

3. CLIQUE: a small, exclusive circle or coterie; a group of people having unconventional ideas.

The cleek snapped with a click to the discomfiture of the clique of theorists.

cleeve, see cleave.

1. clef: a cypher inscribed on the left-hand side of a line of music to indicate pitch (q.v.).

2. CLEFT: pst tns & ppl of 'cleave', to cut in two, split; bifurcated; a ravine or deep valley; a deep cut.

3. CLEFT: the pin on which the beam (q.v.) of a balance is poised.

The composer in a frenzy cleft his manuscript in two with an axe, and it was wrongly re-assembled by the editor, who put the treble clef against the bass part, hence, it was hailed as a work of genius.

1. clem: to starve.

2. CLEM: diminutive of Clement, a masculine personal name.

If Clem were our master we'd all clem.

cleve, see cleave.

clever, see cleaver.

click, see cleek.

1. climb: to ascend laboriously; to mount upward by means of an instrument; to reach an altitude by use both of hands and feet.

2. CLIME: a literary or a poetic form of the word 'climate', i.e. a belt between any two parallels of latitude in relation to its prevailing weather conditions; the weather conditions prevailing in any area; a place or a country.

The natives of that clime climb trees like monkeys.

clime, see preceding group.

clique, see cleek.

1. cloche: a bell (q.v.).

2. CLOCHE: a bell-shaped glass cover, or shade, hence, a small enclosure constructed from sheets of glass inclined at an angle against each other, and supported by wire, used for protecting young plants.

3. CLOCHE: a felt (q.v.) hood, or hat.

It was raining, and Mother sent John upstairs to get her cloche, but he brought her the shade from the group of wax-fruit in Grannie's bedroom.

1. clock: a bell (q.v.), hence, a time-piece that chimes the hours, hence, any timepiece larger than a watch (q.v.).

2. CLOCK: an ornamental pattern woven into the side of a sock, or of a stocking.

3. CLOCK: to sit upon, and hatch eggs.

4. CLOCK: a popular name for any beetle.

Farmer Giles was unable to inform the Ministry of Agriculture how long each of his hens would clock, because the village clock had stopped due to a black-clock having crawled into the works.

1. close: shut; secret; hot, damp weather; reserved in manner, un-communicative; ungenerous; in juxtaposition; near together; with a minimum of intervening space.

2. CLOZE (cloze): to shut; to bring a matter to an end; a quadrangle; a passage or alley (q.v.) way; to reach agreement; to conclude a trans-action.

3. CLOTHES (C): garments; dress.

The day was close, and we had been seated close together in the bus and our clothes stuck to our skins: we opened a window but the driver insisted that we close it again, therefore the cool Cathedral close seemed like the threshold of Heaven.

clothes, see preceding group.

1. clove: a spice, being the flower bud of the plant *Carophyllus aromaticus*.

2. CLOVE: a species of Pink, *Dianthus caryophyllus*.

3. CLOVE: a segment of a fruit or of a root, such as garlic.

4. CLOVE: a weight of between seven and eight pounds, formerly used for both wool and cheese.

5. CLOVE: a cleft, or gap, in rocky, mountainous places.

6. CLOVE: pst tns of 'cleave', to cut in two.

7. CLOVE: a hitch for securing a line (q.v.) to a spar (q.v.).

The children, looking for clove-pinks, got lost in Deadman's Clove: the search party, after making fast with a clove-hitch, lowered them with a block and tackle, and a hot clove drink soon revived them, but the men aloft, who had clove the spar on which the pulley was fixed, found it too weak to support them, and there they remained, sustained on a clove of garlic, till a second rescue party was organized.

cloze, see close.

1. club: a mace; a stick bulging conspicuously at one end, used as a weapon.

2. CLUB: a gathering of people cooperating for a set purpose either social or intellectual; a group of persons contributing funds so that each member in turn may benefit by the total; sums of money contributed for the purchase of goods or services that shall benefit the entire group.

I suggest that we club together and buy a club to act as a hint to all club-members that one does not talk in the library.

1. clutch: to hatch young birds.

2. CLUTCH: a device whereby the working part of a machine may be engaged with, and disengaged from, the moving part.

3. CLUTCH: a bird's claw, hence, to grasp greedily.

The farmer with a clutch of chicks for sale would not let the basket out of his clutch, but, jumping into his car, he let in the clutch with a jerk.

1. coach: a four-wheeled vehicle for carrying passengers.

2. COACH: to give concentrated or specialized instruction; to prepare a student for examination or a sportsman for an event.

He won the coach-driving contest having had old John for a coach.

1. coal: carbon; wood out of which the oils have been driven by destructive distillation; a hard black mineral used for burning, and from which numerous by-products are obtained.

2. COLE: popular name of plants in the genus *Brassica*, a family of vegetables of which the cabbage and the turnip are the most familiar, and among which certain edible sea-weeds are popularly included.

3. KHOL: a misspelling of No. 4 below.

4. KOHL: a pigment used in the East to darken the eyelids, hence, any form of make-up for the eyes.

5. KOHL: short for Kohlrabi, the turnip-cabbage.

She will black her eyes with Kohl but will not black her hands with coal so I have let the fire go out and I will not cook the cole.

1. coaled: provided with coal (q.v.).

2. COLD: at a low temperature.

While the ship was waiting to be coaled, the boilers grew cold.

1. coarse: of rough texture; of large particles; vulgar; indelicate.

2. CORSE: a dead body.

3. CORSE: vending or bartering, particularly horses.

4. COURSE: forward movement along a path; the path itself; passage; normal procedure; customary, or expected, behaviour or result.

Of course, they corse upon the race-course to the accompaniment of language coarse enough to raise a corse.

1. coarser: a comparative, more coarse (q.v.).

2. CORSAIR: a Barbary privateer, having letters of marque (q.v.) from the Turkish Government, but condemned as pirates by the Christians whom they attacked.

3. COURSER: a dog used in coursing; a person engaged in that sport; a race-horse.

4. COURSER: a block of stone used to form a course in building.

5. COURSER: a fast-running bird of the genus *Cursorius*.

The corsair, captured and brought home for trial, being a professional courser when not at sea, and having the good fortune to go before a magistrate whose tastes were coarser than they should have been, was dismissed with a caution, and given charge of the gentleman's dogs.

1. **coat:** an outer garment; normal masculine attire for the upper part of the body; the external covering, as the hair or fur of animals.
2. COTE: a shed; a covered compartment; a nesting-box.
   Put on an old coat and give the dove-cote a coat of paint.
1. **cobble:** a rounded stone formerly used for paving.
2. COBBLE: to mend, particularly shoes; to mend crudely.
3. COBBLE: a flat-bottomed boat; a ferry boat.
   The cobble struck a cobble and we could but cobble her.
1. **cock:** a male bird, particularly of the domestic fowl (q.v.) *Gallus domesticus.*
2. COCK: a device for controlling flow.
3. COCK: a cone-shaped pile of hay, straw, or other farm-produce.
4. COCK: a smart upward turning, particularly of a hat-brim.
5. COCK: to place the trigger-mechanism of a fire-arm in a position ready for discharge.
6. COCK: a vulgar term for the penis (q.v.).
   With the water-butt cock dripping, and the barnyard cock crowing on top of the hay cock, the sportsman didn't know whether to cock his hat or cock his gun.
1. **cockle:** a mollusc much used for food, *Cardium edule.*
2. COCKLE: a fault in alignment; a blister, or bulge on a flat surface.
3. COCKLE: a plant, *Lychnis or Agrostemma githago,* which grows among corn (q.v.).
   The farmer on a day trip folded a cockle in his guide to London when he found a cockle-stall selling fish instead of flowers.
1. **cod:** a bag, husk or pod; the sac (q.v.) enclosing peas and beans; a husk.
2. COD: a seafish, *Gadus morrhua.*
3. COD: to misinform, to make a fool of.
   We named our little cabincruiser 'Peascod', and when a local longshoreman asked why,

we decided to cod him, and said it was because we intended using her to fish for cod.

1. **coddling:** pampering; spoiling; making a fuss of; to nurse as if an invalid.
2. CODLIN: a variety of cooking apple.
3. CODLING: a young cod (q.v.); in Am. applied to the allied fish *Phycis.*
4. CODLING: timber sawn into staves.
   It's no use your coddling that boy—if he will not eat wholesome boiled codling followed by stewed codlin and custard, let him stay hungry!

codlin ⎫
codling ⎭ see preceding group.

1. **coffer:** a strong-box; a storage place for money and gems; a sunken ornamental pane (q.v.); a hollow space in a wall filled with cement; a water-tight pallisade of piles, driven in a river bed, forming a dry cavity in the water to enable a bridge-pier (q.v.) to be erected; a caisson.
2. COUGHER: one who habitually coughs.
   He, being a cougher, attracted the attention of the guard, and so failed to rob the coffer.
1. **coffin:** a box, constructed from the best timber, and by the best craftsmanship, to contain a corpse, and be buried.
2. COUGHING: the act of expelling air violently and noisily from the lungs.
   From the sound of his coughing he seems right for his coffin.
1. **coign:** a projecting corner.
2. COIN: a disc of metal stamped with the insignia of a State (q.v.) employed as currency within the State.
3. COYN: a name for the quince.
4. COYNYE: the billeting of the armed followers of an Irish overlord upon civilian tenants.
5. QUOIN: a wedge, particularly that used by printers to secure type in the forme.
   The mad Irish compositor, from a coign of vantage in the caseroom, brooding upon how his ancestors had rebelled against 'coynye and livery', tossed a

coin to decide, and tossed a quoin into the gears of the new typesetting machine.

coin, see preceding group.

coir, see **choir.**

colander, see **calendar.**

1. **colation:** to strain or filter.
2. COLLATION: bringing together; placing sheets of a book, or folios of a manuscript, in numerical order; comparison of documents; a light meal, originally taken in Benedictine monasteries after the reading of Collationes.

   The Abbot took a cold collation between superintending the colation of the wine in the cellar and the collation of the records in the library.

cold, see **coaled.**

cole, see **coal.**

collar, see **choler.**

collation, see **colation.**

collery }
colliery } see **calorie.**

1. **colonel:** the officer in command of a regiment; the rank superior to a lieutenant-colonel, and inferior to a general.
2. CRENEL: an embattlement.
3. KERNEL: a fruit seed; the soft interior of a nut; the central theme of any matter or situation.

   The Colonel, protected behind a crenel, surveyed the attacking force below, and revealed to his officers the kernel of his plan of defence.

colory }
coloury } see **calorie.**

1. **colt:** a young male horse.
2. COLT: a type of multi-charge pistol invented by Samuel Colt (1814–1862); a revolver.
3. CULT: worship; a form of ritual; adhesion, or devotion, to an idea, or to a person.

   It ent a fair election if they make a cult of the multi-racial society idea. Guess I'll ride my chestnut colt into town and attend the next meeting with my Colt loaded in every chamber.

1. **coma:** an ultra-sleep state; total unconsciousness.
2. COMA: the arrangement of the

branches forming the head of a tree; fine hair on certain seeds.

3. COMMA: a punctuation mark, being a point with a curved descender, that separates the smallest section of a sentence; the same mark used supra-lineally, to enclose a quotation, or to indicate possessive case.

   That new typist girl must be in a state of coma: she puts a comma after every fifth word.

comma, see preceding group.

1. **comb:** a utensil consisting of a strip of suitable material having, projecting from the edge (or edges), a series of teeth, used for drawing through hair or other fibre; to use such a utensil.
2. COOM: dust, particularly sawdust, and coal-dust.
3. COOMB: a small, deep valley.
4. COOMB: a capacity of four bushels; a brewing vat.
5. COOMBE: alternative spelling of No. 3 above.

   We comb the bleak hillsides for firewood, and regard a coomb of coom as a luxury.

1. **compatible:** able to be admitted together; having accord; agreeing.
2. COMPETIBLE: befitting; suitable; applicable.

   Although sheep are compatible with goats, there is no profit in the latter since wool is not competible to them.

competible, see preceding group.

1. **complement:** completion; fullness; an addition to make whole.
2. COMPLIMENT: praise, a gift expressive of admiration.
3. COMPLIMENT (compli`ment): to pay a compliment.

   When you meet the professor compliment him on his discovery of the complement of the period's poetry: he likes a compliment.

compliment, see preceding group.

1. **compound:** combined, mixed, or blended into a composite whole; to settle matters by agreed payments; a chemical substance, being a combination of two or more other substances, from each of which it differs.

2. COMPOUND: an enclosure within which houses, offices, factories and other European buildings stand in Oriental and other countries.

There was a sudden infestation of insects in the compound, and the Medical Officer made up a compound that inhibited them.

1. concent: harmony; blending of voices; accord.

2. CONSENT: permission; agreement; acquiescence.

Having gained consent their voices rose in concent.

1. concurs: agrees; coincides.

2. CONKERS: a game played with horse-chestnuts, hence, a name for the nuts.

3. CONQUERS: gains ascendancy, or victory; subdues; overcomes.

If Jack concurs, when next we play conkers the one who conquers shall take all the nuts.

1. confidant: one who is trusted with knowledge of another's private affairs.

2. CONFIDENT: self-reliant; assured; without fear of failure or error.

I am confident of finding a confidant.

confident, see preceding group.

1. conjur (kunjer): to employ sleight of hand; to perform tricks having the appearance of magic.

2. CONJURE (con'jure): to plead with; implore; to bind by oath.

Useless to conjure, the boy will neglect his mathematics and watch the clown conjur.

conkers ⎱ see concurs.
conquers ⎰

consent, see concent.

1. Consol: singular of 'Consols', the short name of a government security, 'Consolidated Annuities', started in 1751.

2. CONSOLE: a corbel; a bracket; an ornamental projection.

3. CONSOLE: that part of an organ containing the keyboards and stops, whereat the organist sits.

4. CONSOLE: to comfort; to sympathize with; to alleviate grief.

5. CONSUL: the official representative of a Sovereign. State, resident in a foreign town, generally a seaport, to protect the commercial, trading and other rights enjoyed by its subjects there.

When Madam Pantancri lost her Consol certificates which, she insisted, had been stolen from the console-table in the hall, she complained to her national Consul, but try as he would he could not console her. On her way home she entered a church to pray for the return of her securities, and felt herself growing calmer as the organist seated himself at the console.

console ⎱ see preceding group.
Consul ⎰

1. content (con'tent): satisfied; not willing to change conditions; not desirous of acquiring additional property or greater riches.

2. CONTENT (con'tent): that which is contained; capacity; the purport of a document; the theme of a book.

Be content with the content of your bank account.

1. continent: a major, continuous landmass which may contain numerous nations, as Europe, or several races, as Africa.

2. CONTINENT: self-disciplined; restrained; controlled and moderate in bodily functions.

We insular islanders cannot believe that on the Continent men are continent.

1. coo: the irritating bubbling sound made by pigeons.

2. COOP: to enclose; confine; particularly of fowls.

3. CO-OP: abbreviation for Cooperative Stores.

4. COUP: a brilliant manoeuvre; usurpation of political power; sudden successful action.

5. COUPÉ: a carriage of small dimensions; a vehicle built to carry two passengers.

They could not coop him in the office after he heard the pigeons coo and made a recording of it, for the Director of the Co-op regarded this as a coup, gave him an outdoor job and a cash bounty with which he bought a racing coupé and killed himself.

coom
coomb } see comb.
coombe

coop, see coo.

1. cope: an item of ecclesiastical vestment.
2. COPE: to haggle; to bargain.
3. COPE: to encounter; match with; struggle against; strive with; tackle; manage.
4. COPE: to provide a waterproof, and rain-diverting inclined top-course to a brick-wall.

The Bishop removed his cope and, glancing at the documents to be dealt with, enquired of his secretary, 'Can you cope?'

1. copper: a metallic element, Cu; the basis of all alloys of yellow metal, as brass and bronze; a vessel made from copper; money made from bronze; wire of high electrical conductivity.
2. COPPER (sl): one who cops, or catches, hence, a police-constable.

He drove away a lorry loaded with copper ingots, but at the first traffic block, in climbed a copper.

cops } see caw.
copse

coral, see carol.
cord, see cawed.
core, see caw.
cores, see caws.

1. co-respondent: a man charged with adultery appearing in a divorce court.
2. CORRESPONDENT: one who writes letters; one who is employed by a newspaper to supply news on a particular subject, or from a particular place.

The co-respondent, who insisted that he was not guilty, might have obtained the benefit of the doubt had he been a more cautious correspondent.

cork, see cauk.

1. corn: the seed of cereal plants.
2. CORN: a horn-like hardening and thickening of the skin due to pressure.

Everyone helped gather the corn harvest except John, who pleaded a painful corn.

1. corporal: pertaining to the body; bodily needs.
2. CORPORAL: a military non-commissioned rank; the first promotion above the rank of private.
3. CORPORAL: the cloth upon which consecrated wafers rest at the service of Mass (q.v.).
4. CORPOREAL: pertaining to the body, not to the spirit; animal; mortal; tangible; material.

Our Regimental Sergeant-Major asserts that when he was an acting, unpaid Lance-Corporal corporal punishment was still employed in the army.

corps
corpse } see caw.
corpus

corral, see carol.

1. correspondence: a collection of letters; likeness; agreement; similarity.
2. CORRESPONDENTS: those who write letters to each other.

Over a ton of correspondence passes annually between those two correspondents.

correspondent, see co-respondent.
correspondents, see correspondence.
corsair, see coarser.
corse, see coarse.

1. cosier: comparative of 'cosy', 'cosey' or 'cozy'; more cosy, snug or comfortable than some previous, or other, state of cosiness.
2. COZIER: a cobbler; a repairer of boots and shoes; alternative spelling of No. 1 above.

Having found a better cozier my slippers are now much cosier.

cote, see coat.

1. cosine: a term used in trigonometry.
2. COUSIN: the son or daughter of the brother or sister of one's father (q.v.) or mother; extended to include other collateral relations; a term of address employed by sovereigns one to another, and by sovereigns to the higher ranking peers.
3. COZEN: to deceive; to cheat; to mislead.
4. CUISINE: standard achieved in cooking and catering; the kitchen.

It will require a super-con-man

to cozen my cousin, Diana, particularly in the matter of cuisine.

1. **cotton**: fibre from the plant *Gossypium*; thread or fabric made from this fibre.

2. COTTON: to be attracted to another person; to be friendly with, hence, to approve of an idea or a proposition.

I found that though I could cotton on to Jack, his scheme for importing cotton was one I could not cotton to.

1. **couch**: an article of furniture on which to lie down; a settee; a bed.

2. COUCH: to lay paper-pulp on felt (q.v.) for pressing.

3. COUCH: to embody in words; to express in writing.

4. COUCH: a form of grass, *Triticum repens*.

Before seeking my couch, I must couch, in a few words, my note on couch grass.

1. **couché**: in heraldry, of a shield canted over to the dexter.

2. COUCHEE: an evening reception on a lavish scale.

3. CUSHY (sl): easy, comfortable, not strenuous.

The fatigue-party told off for duty at the couchee given by the Viceroy were on a cushy number; all they had to do was each hold a painted wooden shield à couché.

couchee, see preceding group.

1. **coucher**: one who is employed in the hand-made paper trade to lay pulp on felt (q.v.).

2. COUCHER: a book, permanently resting on a desk, or a table, in a public office, in which estate transactions are recorded.

Consulting the coucher book he observed that his appointment as coucher in the Manorial paper mill was not recorded.

cougher, see **coffer**.

coughing, see **coffin**.

1. **council**: a body of persons gathered together for discussion; a committee.

2. COUNSEL: advice.

3. COUNSEL: a Barrister-at-Law.

Do not pay to consult Counsel: he will merely counsel you to keep clear of the Borough Council.

counsel, see preceding group.

1. **count**: to add to another in reaching a total.

2. COUNT: to be a matter, or a person, of importance.

3. COUNT: a continental title of nobility. The average Englishman holds the opinion that a foreign Count does not count, and he does not count the cost abroad of such folly.

1. **counter**: a person who counts; a machine that counts, an abacus.

2. COUNTER: a disc, stamped like a coin (q.v.), used for counting; any piece of ivory, bone, pearl and the like used for counting points gained in a game.

3. COUNTER: the long narrow barrier in a shop over which business is transacted and on which money paid is counted.

4. COUNTER: the stiff piece of the upper of a boot or shoe covering the heel (q.v.).

5. COUNTER: in opposition; contrary; opposite; a check.

6. COUNTER: the cut-away stern (q.v.) of a ship.

The counter, behind the bank counter, found a counter in a bag of silver coins: this runs counter to the best banking theory, and in his hurry to report to the Manager, his foot slipped from his shoe and he trod down the counter.

coup ⎫
coupé ⎭ see **coo**.

1. **courier**: a servant who goes ahead to prepare the way for his master when on a journey; a running footman; a messenger; a light horseman acting as scout.

2. CURRIER: a leather-dresser; one who dyes and polishes leather after it has been tanned.

The courier must call on the currier to get the leather for the saddler.

course, see **coarse**.

courser, see **coarser**.

court, see caught.
cousin, see cosine.
coyer, see choir.
coyn
coynye } see coign.

1. coz: an abbreviated form of 'cousin' (q.v.), employed in addressing both relations and familiar friends.
2. COZE: a heart-to-heart talk; a friendly chat.
   Come coz, let us coze.
coze, see preceding group.
cozen, see cousin.
cozier, see cosier.
1. crab: a crustaceous marine spider, Brachyura.
2. CRAB: the wild apple, any small, sour apple.
3. CRAB: a South American nut tree, Carapa guianensis.
4. CRAB: to oppose; to irritate; to anger.
5. CRAB: of hawks when they fight.
6. CRAB: a portable crane (q.v.).
   Old Jasper would crab an angel; his diet is crab-claw salad made with crab-apples, crab-nuts and dressed in crab-nut oil.
1. crane: a long-legged bird of the family Gruidae.
2. CRANE: a device used for hoisting heavy and bulky material, as building construction units, or cargo into or out of a ship's hold (q.v.).
   All work stopped when a crane perched on the crane.
1. crank: of anything bent at right (q.v.) angles; a machine part, so bent to convert a reciprocal to a rotary motion; a triangular plate, or fret, pivoted, and fixed to the wall at its 90° angle, the other two angles being fixed to a wire to carry the impulse on a pull-bell round a corner, or from vertical to horizontal.
2. CRANK: a twisting path; a twist in speech, a smart utterance; full of high spirits.
3. CRANK: a ship that carries too little ballast for her cloud of canvas.
4. CRANK: a minor sickness, hence, one who malingers. ·
5. CRANK: an eccentric person; one with fixed, often erroneous, ideas.
   He was a perfect crank: in the days of the dear departed steam

railway engine he invariably went to the front and asked the driver to examine the crank.
1. creak: a vibrant grinding noise as emitted by a dry hinge, or a basket under strain (q.v.).
2. CREEK: a narrow, streamlike tidal water.
3. CRICK: a sharp pain in the muscles of the neck.
   We sailed into a creek to investigate a creak that had developed in the aft hold which the skipper said gave him a crick in the neck.
1. credible: believable.
2. CREDITABLE: an action that earns praise; one who may safely be given credit.
   It is hardly credible that he has executed so creditable a work as this.
creditable, see preceding group.
creek, see creak.
crenel, see colonel.
1. crevasse: a crack, or an opening, usually of great depth, in a glacier.
2. CREVICE: a crack, split or opening; a rift or break; a narrow opening or fold.
3. CREVISE: a crayfish; a freshwater lobster; Astacus fluviatilis.
   While he rambled on concerning his adventure in a crevasse, I searched the crevice between the arm and the seat of the chair where I knew he kept the key of the cupboard containing the tinned crevise.
crevice
crevise } see preceding group.

1. crew: a ship's company; a group constituting a team that functions under a leader; a party of men trained to serve with a machine or an appliance; any group of persons motivated by a common aim.
2. CREW: pst tns of 'crow' (q.v.), the cry of a cock (q.v.).
   'And as the cock crew those who stood before
   The Tavern shouted, "Open thou the door".'
   (Rubaiyat of Omar Khayyam)
   Evidently a boozy crew!

1. **crewed:** being manned by a crew (q.v.).
2. CRUDE: in a natural, unrefined state; unmannerly; uncouth; rough; without cultivation; bawdy.

> That yacht is crewed by a crude crowd.

1. **crewel:** a form of thread used in making tapestry and embroidery.
2. CRUEL: callous; merciless; severe; to inflict pain; to cause distress.

> The tapestry turned out by the local ladies' guild was a cruel waste of crewel yarn.

1. **crews:** pl (') of 'crew' (q.v.).
2. CROUSE: vivacious; lively.
3. CRUISE: to sail, or to make a voyage usually, but not necessarily, for pleasure; sailing about in an area, or over a route, for non-commercial reasons.
4. CRUSE: a small vessel, pot, or jar (q.v.) to contain liquid.

> Even the crews were crouse, and enjoyed the cruise, taking their daily cruse of lime-juice without complaint.

crick, see creak.

1. **cricket:** the English national summer game played between two teams each of eleven players being fielders, bowlers and batsmen.
2. CRICKET: an insect that produces a note by rubbing the wings with the hindmost legs, *Acheta domestica.*
3. CRICKET: a footstool.

> Grandpa sat at the open window, his feet upon the cricket on the floor, his eye on the cricket on the green, and his thoughts on the cricket on the hearth.

1. **crop:** a harvest, particularly of food-plants.
2. CROP: part of the digestive system of a bird.
3. CROP: the handle of a horse-whip.
4. CROP: to cut short.

> The abundance of the potato crop will crop prices and Farmer Giles will not get a silver-mounted riding crop this season.

crouse, see crews.

1. **crow:** a bird of the genus *Corvus*; a rook.
2. CROW: the cry of a cock.
3. CROW: the mesentery of an animal.

4. CROW: a crow-bar, a rod of steel having a bifurcated wedge-shaped end turned at an angle from the shaft, used for levering or wrenching.

> So you can't find the crow-bar, can't you? Well, that's nothing to crow about. When the boss hears he'll make crow-bait of you.

crude, see crewed.

cruel, see crewel.

cruise ⎫
cruse ⎭ see crews.

1. **cue:** a word, or a gesture indicating to an actor that his part is about to begin.
2. CUE: a tapering wooden shaft, or rod, used to impel the ball in the game of billiards.
3. KEW: a suburb of London, famous for its Botanical Gardens.
4. Q: the seventeenth letter of the alphabet, between P and R; q.
5. QUEUE: a file of people generally waiting for something.

> You, being a new member of this club, must mind yours ps and qs—take your cue from me or you will queue for a billiard cue longer than for a ticket for Kew Gardens on a fine day.

1. **cuff:** the termination of the sleeve by a band (q.v.) at the wrist; the starched end of a shirt-sleeve; a detachable piece to terminate a sleeve.
2. CUFF: a blow with the hand.

> I gave the boy a cuff on the ear for deliberately soiling my cuff with ink.

1. **cuirass:** body armour consisting of breast-plate and back-plate.
2. CURIOUS: inquisitive; having unusual characteristics.

> He was curious about a curious cuirass.

cullender, see calender.

cult, see colt.

1. **curaçao:** an orange-flavoured liqueur (q.v.); the name of one of the Caribbean islands.
2. CURASSOW: a South American bird similar to the turkey, *Crax alector.*

> After drinking half a bottle of curaçao he called a canary a crested curassow.

1. **curb:** a chain passing under the horse's jaw, and attached to the bit, used for the purpose of imposing restraint, hence, anything of a restraining nature; to impose restraint; to curtail freedom.
2. KERB: the granite edge of the pavement, or footpath, forming a step down into the road or carriageway; a protective edging or dwarf wall; the fender about the domestic hearth.
   Curb that child or he'll fall down the kerb.
1. **cure:** treatment to remove illness; to restore health; a drug, or a process having this effect; to rectify.
2. CURE: the spiritual pastor of a parish; a clergyman.
3. CURÉ: a French parish priest.
4. CURE (sl): a humorist.
   Oppressed with the cure of souls he suffered a breakdown and visited a spa for a cure; there he made friends with a French curé who, in his wisdom, took the sufferer to a Music Hall where a comedian, a perfect cure, completed his cure.

curious, see **cuirass.**

1. **currant:** a form of imported dried fruit akin to the raisin; a homegrown berry, *Ribes nigrum* and *Ribes rubrum.*
2. CURRENT: in progress; in the news; contemporaneous; in circulation; electromotive force in operation.
   There is a current rumour that Professor Dr Phisone was bribed by the Levantine Export Trade to declare that the currant has slimming value.

current, see preceding group.

currier, see **courier.**

1. **curry:** a piquant Indian dish served with rice.
2. CURRY: to dress and finish leather after tanning.
3. CURRY: to seek favour by sycophantish behaviour.
4. CURRY: part of the process of grooming a horse by combing the coat.
5. CURRY: meat from a hunted animal thrown to the hounds; to inflict a beating.
   To curry favour he cooks curry for the master twice a week, and he has offered to curry the leather for the new saddle: he complains that we do not curry the horses correctly, and that we do waste venison to curry the hounds, hence, we have arranged for a local lad to curry his hide for him.

cushy, see **couché.**

1. **custardy:** of a foodstuff such as stewed fruit, or a fruit tart (q.v.) generously supplied with custard.
2. CUSTODE: one who has custody.
3. CUSTODY: safe-keeping; in the care of a responsible person; under arrest.
   While he was in custody his wife wrote informing his custode, the jailer, that her husband liked his stewed prunes very custardy.

custode ⎱ see preceding group.
custody ⎰

1. **cygnet:** a young swan.
2. SIGNET: a small seal (q.v.).
   His signet is a cygnet Or.
1. **cymbal:** one of a pair of metal discs which, when struck together, emit a musical note.
2. SYMBOL: a sigil, a sign, a cypher, a shape or an object that represents an idea, or a myth, or a supernatural being; any occurrence that is associated with the mystical or the esoteric; something acceptable as representative.
   The clash of the cymbal was the symbol of the High Priest's power.
1. **cynical:** having, or using cynicism; a sneering disbelief in the sincerity of good works; to belittle.
2. SINICAL: relating to a sine, one of the trigonometrical functions.
   The captain was rather cynical concerning the accuracy of my sinical calculation.

cypher, see **cipher.**

1. **cypre:** the shrub *Lawsonia alba* or *inermis*, sometimes confused with No. 3 below.
2. CY PRES: as near as possible. A term applied to the activities of the Board (q.v.) or Committee of an old-established Charity, the purpose of which can no longer be

carried out to the letter, and is therefore implemented as near as possible within the framework of the constitution.

3. CYPRESS: a coniferous tree, *Cupressus sempervirens*, having dark foliage, sprigs of which were formerly carried in funeral processions, hence, a symbol of death.

4. CYPRESS: the name of a textile-like cloth of gold, a satin, or lawn (q.v.).

5. CYPRIS: a small freshwater bivalve.

6. CYPRUS: alternative spelling of No. 4 above.

7. CYPRUS: an island at the eastern end of the Mediterranean Sea.

8. SUPPRESS: to prohibit, or put down either by force or authority; to ban; to prevent publication or circulation of printed matter; to subdue desires; to keep secret; to refrain from revealing what ought to be revealed.

The Chairman had no right to suppress the fact that the Charity was functioning *cy pres* in so far as girls about to be married are now given seven yards of nylon instead of cypress, but he himself has been sent to winter in Cyprus for it is likely that we will soon be carrying cypress before him.

cy pres ⎫
cypress ⎪
cypris ⎬ see preceding group.
cyprus ⎭

cyst, see cist.

D

1. **dace:** a general term for freshwater fish including *Lucisus vulgaris*, *Rhinichthys* and *Minnilus cornutus*.

2. DAIS: a raised platform; a plinth, or a stage (q.v.).

3. DAYS: pl (') of 'day' (q.v.).

4. DAZE: to stupefy; benumb; confuse; dazzle; bewilder.

That dame's day's work is just sitting: she thinks she can pose on a dais and daze the boys all the days of her life.

1. **Dairi:** the Palace of the Mikado.

2. DAIRY: a place where milk, cream, butter and cheese are prepared for use; a shop that sells dairy produce.

3. DIARY: a record of events written each day; a journal or log (q.v.); an account book showing a daily record of transactions; a book printed with headings dated for each day in a year.

It was from a traveller's diary that we first heard of the ceremonies performed in the dairy attached to the Dairi.

dairy, see preceding group.

dais, see dace.

1. **daisies:** pl of 'daisy', a small flat wild flower having a ring of white petals extending as a disc out of a yellow centre, *Bellis peronnis*; other flowers of this form, as *Chrysanthemum leucanthemum*.

2. DAISY'S: possessive case of 'daisy'.

3. DAZES: the effect (q.v.) of that which induces daze (q.v.).

The daisy's bed is overcrowded: so great a mass of daisies dazes me.

daisy's, see preceding group.

1. **dam:** a bank of earth, or of other material, constructed to form a barrier against, for example, water.

2. DAM: a female parent, applicable chiefly to quadrupeds.

3. DAM: each separate piece in a set of draughts (q.v.); the game itself.

4. DAMN: to condemn, used profanely against both things and people, used singly as an expletive.

We lost the dam and all her lambs because George sat engraving the Lord's Prayer with a needle on the back of a dam, and Hodge argued with Robin that 'a tinker's damn' is swearing, and that it does not refer to the clay plug used to dam the hole to be soldered.

damn, see preceding group.

1. **Dane:** a native of Denmark, but in antiquity, description of any Norseman; a breed of large, short-haired dog.

2. DEIGN: to condescend; to bestow, or to accept, in a haughty manner.

The captured Dane would not deign to accept food from one of lesser rank than himself.

1. **darn:** to mend fabric by weaving a patch with needle and yarn (q.v.), the patch so woven.
2. DARN: short for 'damnation', a euphemism for 'damn', employed chiefly in U.S.A.
3. DERM: the skin of an animal.
4. DERN: a door, or a gate, post.
5. DURN: alternative spelling of No. 2 above.

I walked into the darned dern, and as well as knocking the derm off my nose I made a hole in my jacket and now I've got to darn the durn thing.

1. **date:** fruit of the date-palm, *Phoenix dactylifera.*
2. DATE: the numeration of days in a month and of months in a year.
3. DATE: the writing of the day in its numerical sequence on a document; to fix in time.
4. DATE (Am.): an appointment usually with a member of the opposite sex.

I forget the date, but only recently—not much more than a week ago—a girl who ate a date in a television 'commercial' had several hundred 'phone calls from men trying to date her.

1. **daw:** a bird, *Corvus monedula*; a jackdaw.
2. DOOR: a barrier of wood or other material, poised in a manner to be easily moved, guarding an entrance or an exit, or giving access to a cupboard.
3. DOR: the night-flying dung beetle, *Geotrupes stercorarius*; a hornet; a bumble bee.
4. DOR: to mock, scoff at.
5. DORR: to tone down a colour.
6. DORRE: alternative spelling of No. 4 above.

Behind that door is the picture he painted of a daw picking a gem out of a mass of brilliant colour, but he became obsessed with the idea that the dor beetle's hum was a dorre at him, and he started to dorr it down and so spoilt it.

1. **day:** the natural alternation of light

and dark during one rotation of the earth on its axis (q.v.); a span of twenty-four hours; the passage of time; the hours of light distinct from the hours of darkness; in Christendom, the span of time from midnight to midnight; in Islam, from sunset to sunset.

2. DEY: a person, formerly a woman, later of either sex, having responsibility for the conduct of a dairy (q.v.).
3. DEY: maternal uncle in the Turkish language, hence, a friendly and respectful term of address for an elderly person, hence, the title of the officer commanding the Janissaries of Algiers, who became ruler.

Greeting, and Allah be with you O Dey: is this a propitious day for a poor household dey to report the death of the milk-giver to his master?

days ⎱ see **dace.**
daze ⎰

dazes, see **daisies.**

1. **deal:** a log of wood (q.v.), nine by three inches, and not less than six feet long; a general name for timber cut from trees of the genus *Pinus.*
2. DEAL: quantity; amount; a portion or an allowance; a considerable quantity.
3. DEAL: a business transaction; an agreement between commercial or political parties for their own benefit; to distribute playing cards; to take action in a matter.

It seems there is a great deal of deal in the consignment of mixed timber, and the deal was for not more than ten per cent: you had better deal with it.

1. **Dean:** a person holding authority in either the Church, or a university.
2. DENE: a deep, narrow, wooded valley having a stream running through it.

The Dean of St Dedellun, suffering from strain, was advised to take a camping holiday in a local dene.

1. **dear:** an expression of affection, esteem or good-will.

2. DEAR!: an exclamation of surprise, regret or anxiety.
3. DEAR: expensive; costly.
4. DEER: a quadruped distinguished by its graceful form and impressive antlers.

Oh dear! now we've won the pools dear Lionel says he is setting up as an English Squire, but he refuses to consider stocking his park with deer because they're too dear.

1. decad: the number of ten, anciently thought to be a perfect number.
2. DECADE: a period of ten years; a ten-day week.
3. DECAYED: deteriorated; fallen into a ruinous condition; withered away; ravaged by disease; rotted; destroyed by decrepitation.

The abandoned yacht in the saltings decayed a decade then sank.

decade ⎫
decayed ⎭ see preceding group.

1. decease: to die.
2. DISEASE: a morbid condition; sickness; infection; illness; infestation with parasites, spores or bacteria.

He has contracted a disease that ensures his decease.

1. deck: a platform extending from side to side of a ship, being a covering for the space below, as well as a floor; the roof of an omnibus, particularly when converted to a compartment to accommodate passengers; a pier, jetty or landing stage.
2. DECK: a pack of playing cards.
3. DECK: to adorn with clothing.
4. DECK (sl): the ground, the floor.

If you deck yourself out in your Sunday best, do not travel on the top of a tramcar, nor carry a deck of cards in your pocket, and, if it's muddy, don't slip and sprawl on the deck.

1. decline: a slope downward; to decrease; to fail in health; decay; to sink or sit.
2. DECLINE: to refuse.

The poor old professor is in a decline, can barely leave his bed, and so must decline your invitation to address your Society.

1. decree: judgement given without the verdict of a jury in certain Courts of Law; an order or a rule promulgated on authority, and having the force of law.
2. DEGREE: a step, stair or round of a ladder; each of the layers in a step-like plinth; a step in descent, hence, measurement of consanguinity between collateral relations; a step up or down a scale (q.v.) or measurement; the angle between two lines from the centre to the circumference of a circle enclosing one three-hundred-and-sixtieth part of the circumference; a stage in the social scale, a rank of nobility; a stage of proficiency in scholarship confirmed by a university, and indicated by post-nominal initials.

The Chancellor of the University issued a decree demanding a higher standard of achievement to attain a B.A. degree.

degree, see preceding group.
deign, see **Dane.**
dene, see **Dean.**

1. dental: pertaining to the teeth; of a word pronounced by contact of the tongue with the front teeth.
2. DENTEL: a design in wood, stone, plaster (q.v.) or other material consisting of rectangular relief like a row of teeth.
3. DENTELLE: a lace-like design tooled in leather and used in fine bookbinding.
4. DENTIL: alternative spelling of No. 2 above.
5. DENTILE: further alternative spelling of No. 2 above.

Dental decay attacking the incisors, the lecturer found difficulty in pronouncing dentals, and dreaded speaking on the arts of the Middle Ages with their use of the dentils in architecture and the dentelle in bookbinding.

dentel ⎫
dentelle ⎪
dentil ⎬ see preceding group.
dentile ⎭

1. dependant: one who looks to another for support.
2. DEPENDENT: hanging; relying upon something or someone for support.

He is not the only dependant to be entirely dependent upon me.

dependent, see preceding group.

1. **depose:** to dismiss from a position of authority; to remove from office.

2. DEPOSE: to give evidence on oath.

3. DÉPÔTS: pl of 'dépôt', a regiment's headquarters where their stores and equipment are centred, recruits trained, and old soldiers left to vegetate pending their discharge; a railway station or a marshalling yard; a warehouse.

The congestion in railway dépôts throughout the country will not be relieved until they depose the dictator of the goods traffic section. I'd gladly go and depose against him were he on trial for criminal incompetence.

dépôts, see preceding group.

1. **depraved:** to have lax morals; to display an appetite for normally repulsive food; to behave habitually in a bestial manner.

2. DEPRIVED: kept out; prevented from obtaining; not supplied with; dismissed from an office.

At the first sign of his becoming depraved, he was deprived of his Living.

1. **deprecate:** to plead against; to seek deliverance from; to express strong disapproval.

2. DEPRECIATE: to belittle; to sneer at; to undervalue; to reduce the purchasing power of currency.

3. DEPREDATE: to plunder; to prey upon; waste; destroy.

You may deprecate the way they depredate the land as they advance, but you cannot depreciate their prowess as fighting men.

depreciate ⎫
depredate ⎭ see preceding group.

deprived, see **depraved.**

derm ⎫
dern ⎭ see **darn.**

1. **descent:** progress downward; movement from a higher to a lower position or status; a slope; a means of getting down to a different level; the progress of a family from one

generation to another; the fact of being the offspring of one's father (q.v.); the transmission of estate from father to son.

2. DISSENT: disagreement; difference of opinion; to leave an established Church; to become a Nonconformist.

There can be no dissent on the matter of his descent.

1. **desert:** that fate merited or deserved, generally plural.

2. DESERT: a waterless expanse of territory; an uninhabited place.

3. DESERT: to abandon a person, place or thing; to absent oneself from duty without the intention of returning.

4. DESSERT: fruit served as the last course of a meal.

Once again the Colonel entertained the Officers' Mess over dessert with his story of how a soldier, attempting to desert, got his desert[s] by being wrecked on a desert island.

dessert, see preceding group.

1. **deter:** to restrain, or to inhibit an activity; to be aware of danger; to be put off by some consideration.

2. DETOUR: deviation from a direct route (q.v.); to journey round instead of through some point on a highway, such as a road-junction.

3. DETUR: Latin for 'let there be given', hence, a prize, consisting of a book, bestowed upon students displaying merit at Harvard University, U.S.A.

You have not merited a detur but do not let that deter you, try again.

detour ⎫
detur ⎭ see preceding group.

1. **deuce:** two in dice, or in card-games; duality (or two) in sports.

2. DEUCE: the devil; mischief; bad luck; an exclamation indicating surprise or incredulity; a negative exclamation.

3. JUICE: the liquid that can be expressed from fruits and vegetables; the natural moisture that can be obtained from vegetable or animal matter.

4. JUICE (sl): electricity; petrol; mineral oil used in vehicles or in heating apparatus.

He's been in this state the deuce of a time: first, he would not pay the electricity account and they cut off the juice so he bought an oil-stove, but he will not put any juice into it: now he sits all day sipping neat lime-juice, and he flies into the deuce of a rage if one refers to it as anything but whisky.

1. device: a utensil, or an object brought into being out of imagination; a notion, or a plan; a stratagem; an armorial achievement devised and granted.
2. DEVISE: to leave real estate by will (q.v.); to think out; to invent; to design armorial bearings.

It would help a Herald to devise original arms if there was a device for revealing all previous grants made to armigers of the same name.

1. devices: pl of 'device' (q.v.).
2. DEVISES: the act of devising.
3. DEVIZES: a market-town in Wiltshire.

The Recorder of Devizes devises devices to make locks pick-proof.

devise, see device.

1. deviser: one who invents, or who makes an original design; a designer of armorial bearings; a testator of realty.
2. DIVISOR: the number by which another number is to be divided.

He is the deviser of the attachment to the adding machine that finds the answer to the application of a divisor to a total.

devises } see devices.
Devizes }

1. dew: moisture of condensation that is precipitated in the small hours.
2. DUE: that which is owing in either a material or abstract sense.
3. JEW: one who, assuming descent from the ancient Israelites or Hebrews, professes the religion of the Old Testament.

Due to the dew, the Jew was late for the Synagogue.

dey, see day.
1. di-: a prefix denoting duality, used chiefly in technical words.
2. DI: diminutive of the feminine personal name, Diana.
3. DIE: to reach the end of life.
4. DIE: an engraved seal (q.v.) or printing-plate.
5. DIE: a dice, hence, fate, chance, luck.
6. DYE: a chemical substance that imparts a permanent colour to fibres, fabric, wood or the like.

The die is cast, poor little Di must die, for she has sucked the dicyanide dye out of the woollen cot-cover.

1. diarist: one who records daily events; one who has become famous by the publication of a diary (q.v.).
2. DIREST: the superlative of dire (q.v.).

The prevailing distress of the period, as revealed by the contemporary diarist, was the direst in social history.

diary, see Dairi.
die, see di-.
1. diet: food taken each day in the normal course of life; food of a special variety prescribed; to be restricted in both quantity and quality of food.
2. DIET: an appointed day or time, particularly for an appearance in court; a conference, or a committee held on a certain day; a name for the governmental assemblies of certain Teutonic and Eastern European states.

The facetious schoolmaster said the boy who wrote the worst essay on The Diet of Worms (q.v.) should be put on a diet of worms.

1. dire: distressing; disastrous; calamitous.
2. DYER: one who dyes cloth.
3. DYER: one who dies.

The dyer is in a dire condition with blood-poisoning and looks like being a dyer.

direst, see diarist.
1. discreate: destroy; obliterate; annihilate.
2. DISCREET: judicious; circumspect; cautious; restrained in speech.

3. DISCRETE: detached; separate; discontinuous.

In future, statesmen will be discreet, for the possession of the discrete atom might discreate the universe.

discreet⎰ see preceding group.
discrete⎱

1. discus: a disc, used in ancient Greek sports, for throwing.
2. DISCUSS: to talk over; to reach a conclusion as a result of debates; to investigate by argument.

It took the Committee several hours to discuss the question of whether or not we should have an item 'throwing the discus' in our village sports.

discuss, see preceding group.

1. discussed: pst tns of 'discuss' (q.v.).
2. DISGUST: strong dislike or distaste; repugnance; nausea.

To my disgust, they discussed the matter in my absence.

disease, see decease.
disgust, see discussed.

1. dispence: do without; bestow, or give; to give judgement; to grant permission for an act normally contrary to law.
2. DISPENSE: alternative, and more usual, spelling of No. 1 above; to make medicine; to compound from a prescription (q.v.).

The proprietors of the chemist's shop told him they could dispence with his services, but forgot to send, in his place, a qualified man to dispense the medicines.

dispense, see preceding group.
dissent, see descent.

1. divers: different; not of the same kind, or at the same time, or in the same place; assorted; not connected one with another.
2. DIVERS: those who commence to swim by descending, head foremost, from an altitude into the water; those who, clad in a waterproof suit into which air is introduced, undertake subaquatic work; any water-birds who plunge beneath the surface, *Colymbidae*.
3. DIVERSE: varied; opposed; differing.

On divers occasions divers were at work, for diverse reasons, in the harbour.

diverse, see preceding group.

1. divine: pertaining to the deity; sacred.
2. DIVINE: a theologian, a priest having superior learning.
3. DIVINE: to discover, or to know, by extra-sensory perception.

During divine service last Sunday we had a travelling Divine preaching, who declared it laudable to divine water but wicked to divine mineral deposits.

divisor, see deviser.

1. dock: a place constructed to accommodate ships during lading and discharge; dry-dock, a similar place for repairing ships, hence, any repair-shop, including a hospital.
2. DOCK: the fleshy part of a horse's tail on which the hair grows, hence, the act of removing such hair, hence, to cut, or curtail generally.
3. DOCK: a plant distinguished by its large coarse leaves, *Rumex*.
4. DOCK: the cubicle wherein stands the accused in a Criminal Court.

He was stung by nettles growing in the dry-dock, used dock-leaf as an antidote and, later, went into dock with a septic arm. While he's there they will dock his wages, so when he is cured he will qualify for the role of prisoner in the dock.

1. doctoring: fulfilling the functions of a Doctor of Medicine; prescribing remedies; performing castration on animals.
2. DOCTRINE: the teaching of a religion or a science; that which is accepted as true; dogma; theory.

The doctrine of prohibiting any but qualified men from practising as veterinary surgeons will prevent ignorant, brutal cat's meat men from doctoring kittens.

doctrine, see preceding group.

1. doe: a female animal particularly a deer (q.v.), hare or rabbit.
2. DOH: a sound symbol used in the tonic sol-fa system of notation.
3. DOUGH: flour and water paste prepared for cooking.

4. DOUGH: suet pudding, either with or without fruit—colloquially and jocularly pronounced *duff*.
5. DOUGH (sl): money.
6. DUFF: of poor quality.
   He blamed my buck rabbit, but I told him his doe was duff, and no wonder seeing he feeds her on dough, but he said he'd paid plenty of dough for her.
1. does (dohs): pl of 'doe' (q.v.), the female red deer (q.v.).
2. DOES (duz): the third person singular present indicative of 'do'.
3. DOZE: a semi-sleep state; a dull, drowsy condition.
   He does doze, and the does stray.
doh, see doe.
1. dollar: the standard unit of coinage in U.S.A.; $; general name given to various foreign coins; five shillings; 5/–; 5s.
2. DOLOR: misery; grief; physical pain.
3. DOLOUR: alternative spelling of No. 2 above.
   He gave vent to some dolour when he lost a dollar.

dolor ⎫
dolour ⎭ see preceding group.

1. Dom: a title of rank (q.v.) bestowed by royal authority, current in both Portugal and Brazil.
2. DOM: a title bestowed within the Roman Catholic Church on certain dignitaries.
3. DOM: a cathedral church.
4. -DOM: a suffix indicative of state or condition.
5. DON: originally a Spanish title of rank (q.v.), now a form of address equivalent to 'Mr.'; a Spaniard.
6. DON: a tutor at a university.
7. DON: to assume an article of attire; to dress.
8. DON: a gift.
   Dom Benedict, walking in solemn procession in the great dom of Santa Katrina, reflected that although the Prince had created him a Secular Dom, his kingdom must remain the cure of souls, and he must resist the don of an Office of State: never should he don the gaudy uniform of State Authority in which every Don in the country glorified: far better return to Cambridge, and there fill the modest role of a don.
don, see preceding group.
1. done: finished; settled.
2. DUN: to aggressively and persistently apply for payment.
3. DUN: a dull rusty grey colour.
4. DUN: a primitive archaic Irish hill-fortress.
   The archaeologist set out upon an expedition to discover a dun, but a debt-collector, wearing a dun coat, began to dun for payment of money still due from the previous expedition, so it was never done.

door ⎫
dor ⎪
dorr ⎬ see daw.
dorre ⎭

1. dossed: slept, particularly at a common lodging-house.
2. DOST: a poetic form of 'do', 'do you', 'dost thou'.
3. DUST: finely pulverized solids; such solids blown by the wind, or carried by the air; to remove from an object a layer of such settled particles; any form of domestic refuse put out for collection and disposal by the Municipal Authority.
   His clothes were so deeply impregnated with dust that it seemed he had dossed in a doorway: I simply put them in the bin with the other dust.
dost, see preceding group.
1. dot: a point; a mark made with the point of a pen or a pencil by pressure only, without movement; the diacritic of lowercase i or j; a full stop, or period.
2. DOT: a little child, or young animal.
3. DOT: to scatter; to place at irregular intervals.
4. DOT: a dowry, or marriage portion; before the Married Woman's Property Act, a dowry of which the interest, but not the capital, was under the husband's jurisdiction.
5. DOT: a diminutive of the feminine personal name Dorothy.

6. DOT: the head of a boil (q.v.).
The old Baron will dot unwanted chapels and schools all over the landscape, his youngest child by his fifth wife is but a dot for whom he declares he has made a sufficient provision to secure her dot, on which document he has but to dot the i's and cross the t's, but his eldest daughter by his first wife— Lady Dot, as she is called— says her father ought to be under restraint, he being dotty.

1. doubt: a state of uncertainty; disbelief.

2. DOUT: do out, hence, to extinguish fire, hence, a chemical, or other, fire-extinguisher.
I doubt his ability to dout a candle.

dough, see doe.

dout, see doubt.

1. down: undulating pasturage, generally considerably above sea-level

2. DOWN: soft feather, or young hair, on animal or plant.

3. DOWN: descent; to travel from London; to be down upon, i.e. object to; to fall; to be in ill health, or in mental depression; to pay prompt cash.
He went down to Sussex and as he walked over the down he stroked the down on his chin reflecting that having made a down payment he had asserted his manliness, demonstrated his dignity and then, treading upon a rabbit hole, he fell down.

doze, see does.

1. drachm: a standard of weight; Troy —sixty grains, one eighth of an ounce; Avoirdupois—twenty-seven and a third grains, one sixteenth of an ounce.

2. DRAM: a standard measure of volume equal to one eighth of a fluid ounce, hence, a draft of medicine, or a drink of spirits.

3. DRAM: short for Drammen, timber exported therefrom.
The skipper, having been ashore where he had found some pyrites, which, naturally, he thought to be gold, sat in his cabin with the medicine chest open: he had weighed his find, which was over a drachm, hence, in good spirits, he promised every member of the crew a dram when we reached the port of Drammen where we were to load with Dram.

1. draft: a group, or a party, taken for a special purpose out of a larger group; a cheque (q.v.), or an order, calling a sum of money out of a banking account; a chisel mark around the edge of a stone to indicate the level of the finished surface; the angle of a millstone furrow in relation to the radius of the stone; the first writing, subject to revision, of any English composition; a rough sketch, or drawing from which the finished copy will be made.

2. DRAUGHT: an irritating and dangerous flow of air through open, or ill-fitting, doors and windows, mistakenly described as fresh air; the act of pulling something along; descriptive of animals used for such pulling; the act of pulling a net through the sea to catch fish; a measure, 20 lb. of eels; to drink; the liquid imbibed in drinking; the depth to which a ship sinks into the water; a game played by moving discs about a chequered board. (The last, generally in the pl.)
The men on draft for the front were given a free draught of ale, and a draft map of the terrain.

dram, see drachm.

draught, see draft.

1. drill: military or other physical exercise; a routine method laid down to be followed in achieving specific ends.

2. DRILL: a tool for boring holes.

3. DRILL: a small slow stream; to influence gradually.

4. DRILL: a groove, or miniature furrow in which seeds are planted.

5. DRILL: a refined sort of canvas (q.v.), or coarse cotton cloth.
Having finished the drill on his allotment he drew water from the adjacent drill reflecting the while that he'd have to instruct

the new workman in the firm's drill for drawing a drill from the stores.

1. **drone:** the male honey-bee, hence, applied to any lazy dependent person.
2. DRONE: a long-drawn-out deep humming sound.
3. DRONE: the bass (q.v.) pipe of a Highland bagpipe.

The irate mother condemned him as a drone who would do no work, but whose voice would drone for hours on end from the attic as though he read aloud, but how proud she was of her Sandy when he won the trophy for chanting Highland lays, and took the prize for playing on the pipes, his use of the drone being specially mentioned.

1. **droop:** to hang down; to become limp or inert; to languish; to be dejected, dispirited, devitalized; to fail.
2. DRUPE: a general term for pulpy fruits that enclose a stone, as the peach, plum (q.v.), cherry (q.v.).

The prize drupe will droop in this drought.

drupe, see preceding group.

1. **dual:** double; relating to duplication; pertaining to two (q.v.).
2. DUEL: a fight with lethal weapons between two people, or two parties.
3. JEWEL: a gem, or a precious metal artistically worked, worn (q.v.) as an ornament.

The quarrel arose out of a remark concerning a lady's jewel, and the duel was a dual tragedy for both the contestants died of their wounds.

1. **duck:** a freshwater bird of the genus *Anas*, and particularly the hen (male, *drake*).
2. DUCK: a form of refined canvas used for certain types of clothing.
3. DUCK: a rapid downward jerk of the head and body, usually in evasion or defence.
4. DUCK: to dive, plunge in water.

The wild duck swooped low: it made John duck and split his duck trousers, tumble overboard and take a duck.

1. **ducked:** dipped beneath the surface of water.
2. DUCT: a tube, pipe, channel or other conduit to convey a flow of water or other liquid; leading; confining to a course (q.v.); directing to, or towards, an end, or an achievement; the flow of the strokes in handwriting.

He ducked the soiled parchment into the adjacent water duct, then commenced to study the duct of the calligraphy.

duct, see preceding group.

due, see dew.

duel, see dual.

1. **dug:** pst tns and ppl of 'dig', to penetrate the soil with a spade or other suitable instrument; to stab; to penetrate beneath a surface; to obtain information from an unwilling informer.
2. DUG: the udder, or the nipple, of the female mammal.
3. DUG: a type of red-worm used as bait (q.v.) by fishermen.

Having dug for an hour without unearthing a single dug he went to the slaughter-house and bought a cow's dug.

1. **Dumbie:** a nickname often bestowed upon a dumb person.
2. DUMMY: an unreal representative; a specimen for show purposes; a sham or a counterfeit.

Dumbie Brown made a fortune by inventing an improved, hygienic unswallowable dummy-teat.

dummy, see preceding group.

dun, see **done.**

durn, see **darn.**

dust, see **dossed.**

dye, see **di-**

dyer, see **dire.**

1. **dune:** a natural sea-wall consisting of a ridge, or hillock, of sand built up along the coast by onshore winds.
2. JUNE: the sixth month of the year between May (q.v.) and July; the month of the summer solstice in the Northern Hemisphere; a modern, and not very popular, feminine personal name.

John, walking along a sand-dune

during his holiday last June, met a girl named June and they will be married next June.

E

1. **ear:** the auditory apparatus; the external cartilage of the organ; to have ability to distinguish musical sound; to pay attention to an utterance.
2. EAR: the cluster of grain (q.v.) at the head of corn (q.v.) or other cereal (q.v.) plant.
3. EAR: the plough, or the act of ploughing.

   Give ear to the philosophical injunction: 'ear thy field and bless each ear of wheat that filled thy land'.

1. **earing:** cords used for securing a square-sail to the yard-arm.
2. EARRING: an ornament worn on the ear.
3. ERRING: in error; wrong in judgement or opinion; to pursue a course of inadvisable action.

   The erring seaman redeemed his character by being first aloft to secure the broken earing, his earring glittering like a signal in the sunshine.

1. **earn:** to produce labour in exchange for money; to deserve.
2. ERNE: an eagle.
3. URN: a vessel to contain the ashes of a cremated corpse, or the relics of a saint; a water-boiler provided with a draw-off tap.

   On the fair-ground they earn good money by supplying tea from an urn, yet it would ruin the digestion of an erne.

earring, see earing.
1. **eaten:** masticated and swallowed; to have taken food.
2. ETON: a town on the north bank of the River Thames in Buckinghamshire, opposite to Windsor, Famous for the School, founded by by King Henry VI.

   At Eton, when they have eaten they take exercise on the Thames.

1. **eaves:** the projecting part of a roof.

2. EVES: pl (') of 'eve', the evening, particularly the evening preceding a festival.
3. EVE'S: possessive of 'Eve', a feminine personal name.

   Christmas eves come and go, and every year Grandfather hangs Eve's present under the eaves for her.

1. **éclair:** a tubular, or cigar-shaped, hollow crust of pastry, filled with cream and often coated with chocolate.
2. ÉCLAT (ekla): renown; success; applause; brilliancy.
3. ECLÂT: miswriting of No. 2 above.

   She made the grandest éclat when she made the grandest éclair.

éclat, see preceding group.
1. **eel:** snake-like, small-finned fish of the family *Anguillidae*.
2. EL: applied in U.S.A. to the elevated railway.
3. ELL: a measure of length equal to 42 inches.
4. ELL: applied in U.S.A. to an L-shaped room or building.
5. ILL: diseased; in a morbid condition; not in good health; bad; evil; unlucky; incompetent; unskilful.
6. ILL.: an abbreviation of 'Illinois'.
7. I'LL: contracted form of 'I will'.
8. L: The twelfth letter of the alphabet between K and M; l. (Printed in red on a white ground, and displayed both back and front of a motor vehicle, it warns drivers of a learner.)

   I'll tell you what happened to that L-driver. He ate an eel an ell long and was taken ill.

e'er, see air.
eerie }
eery } see aerie.
effect, see affect.
1. **egg:** a parabolic mass, held within a shell, or container of calcium carbonate, enclosing the elements of a reproduction of the parents, laid by, and kept warm by, the female bird, or other animal.
2. EGG: to provoke; to encourage a person to take a specific step, or perform some act.

   They egg him on in vain to throw an egg at the speaker.

eh!, see A.
eider, see Ada.
eight, see ait.
elate, see alight.
elder, see alder.
electron ⎫ see alectryon.
electrum ⎭
elf, see Alf.
Elgar, see alegar.
1. elicit: to draw out; to evoke; stimulate response.
2. ILLICIT: illegal; not sanctioned or tolerated, irregular.
   Rumour of an illicit still will elicit an immediate response from the Revenue officers.
1. eligible: fit; suitable; ready; likely to be chosen to fill a place or office.
2. LEGIBLE: of handwriting that is well-formed, clear and readable.
   I am not eligible for the job; they specify legible handwriting.
elite, see alight.
ell, see eel.
elegy ⎫
eloge ⎬ see allergy
elogy ⎭
elude, see alude.
elusion, see allusion.
1. em: a unit of measurement used in setting printing type.
2. EM-: a prefix, often interchangeable with 'im-'.
3. 'EM: dative and accusative third person plural; a short form of 'them'.
4. M: the thirteenth letter of the alphabet, between L and N; m; the Roman cypher for a thousand; 1,000; used in modern newspapers for a million; 1,000,000.
   An em is called an em because it is the space into which an M will fit, and don't you make no mistake about it when you sit for the Print Employment Exam, or you'll have 'em fail you for certain: I'll lay a M to one on it!
1. ember: the glowing cinder and red-hot ash of an expiring fire.
2. EMBER: the name of the three fast-days in each of the four seasons.
3. EMBER: a sea-bird of the variety *Columbus immer*.
4. EMMER: alternative spelling of No. 3 above.

5. IMBER: further alternative spelling of No. 3 above.
6. IMMER: further alternative spelling of No. 3 above.
   The lone traveller sat by the ember of his fire when an ember-goose settled beside him, reminding him that it was the first ember day after Whit Sunday.
1. emigrant: one who abandons his native land and settles permanently in another; one who leaves his country without intending to return.
2. IMMIGRANT: one who enters a country other than his own, with the intention of settling there.
   A country loses nothing with an emigrant; and seldom gains anything with an immigrant.
1. eminent: exalted; high; distinguished; outstanding.
2. IMMINENT: impending; threatening; to be expected soon.
   The imminent smear campaign was anticipated by the eminent statesman.
1. encurtain: to enclose with curtains; to defend a strongpoint by surrounding with a wall; to conceal.
2. INCURSION: a foray; a raid; an attack; invasion, or infiltration; the performance of a blameworthy act.
   His incursion of blame was so manifest that the effort to encurtain him failed utterly.
1. ensure: to make certain.
2. INSURE: to provide for the receipt of compensation in case of loss, damage or other disaster.
   Insure your life and ensure your wife receiving an income if left a widow.
1. enter: to go in; to offer oneself as a candidate for examination; to record.
2. INTER (in'ter): to bury (q.v.).
3. INTER (int'er): between.
   With your intermediate ideas, you can enter the hall and enter yourself as a political candidate, but if, on leaving, you receive a black eye, you can inter all hope of being elected.
1. envelop (envel'op): to surround; to cover; to act as a container.

2. ENVELOPE (en'velope): a prefabricated wrapper for a letter; the calyx of a plant.

Envelop yourself in an ulster and journey through the blizzard for tonight the mysterious envelope will be opened.

envelope, see preceding group.

1. envoi: a concluding essay to a prose work, or stanza to a poem.

2. ENVOY: alternative spelling of No. 1 above.

3. ENVOY: a messenger; specifically a Diplomatic Officer ranking less than an Ambassador, representing a State.

4. ENVY: ill-will, or hatred induced by the success, or the good fortune of another; a strong desire to have oneself succeeded, or becomes possessed of, or experienced, the good fortune of another.

I envy you the distinction of being the author of an envoi so brilliant as that concluding your recent book on the life of our Turkish Envoy in Tudor times.

ere, see air.

erne, see earn.

errant, see arrant.

erring, see earring.

essay, see assay.

1. escallop: a shell-fish of the genus *Pecten*, the shell of which is used as an art motif; in heraldry, the conventionalized representation of this shell, being the insignae of St James the Great, Patron of Pilgrims, signalizes a traveller.

2. SCALLOP: an edge decoration formed by cutting semi-circles outward from the cloth; to invect.

3. SCOLLOP: alternative spelling of No. 2 above.

The fishmonger who applied for a grant of armorial bearings said he would like to have an escallop: and he was granted a fess invected which, the herald informed him, had one scallop beside another right along both edges.

Eton, see eaten.

1. even: flat; balanced; equal; without variation.

2. EVEN: although; a form of emphasis.

3. EVEN: evening (q.v.).

Even though they complain, an even division must be made, and the money distributed before eventide.

1. evening: the early part of the night; the hours immediately following sunset.

2. EVENING: the act of making even (q.v.).

By this evening they will be evening the portions.

eves, see eaves.

1. ewe: a female sheep.

2. U: the twenty-first letter of the alphabet, between T and V; u; prefix to the name of articles of that shape.

3. YEW: a tree, *Taxus laccata*, having sombre foliage, often grown in a churchyard, it being symbolic of mourning (q.v.); the correct timber (q.v.) from which to construct the archer's bow (q.v.).

4. YOU: yourself; the person or group of persons to whom speech is directed.

You, Tom, and all of you, please see that my ewe lambs do not graze under the churchyard yew: you can swing a hammock from it, and suck iced lemonade through a U-tube.

1. ewer: a large jug; a vessel having a wide neck, a broad lip, and ear-shape handles, employed for holding water.

2. URE: usage; utility; function.

3. YAW: a jolt sustained by a ship through bad steering.

4. YAW: one of the sores appearing in connection with yaws (q.v.).

5. YORE: of old; in days gone by.

6. YOUR: possessed by, belonging to or pertaining to you (q.v.).

7. YOU'RE: contracted form of 'you are'.

Your oriental ewer, which hath been in ure in days of yore, was smashed when the yacht gave a horrid yaw, and as it was yourself at the helm you're unable to make a fuss.

1. ewes: pl (') of 'ewe' (q.v.).

2. U's: pl of 'U' (q.v.).

3. USE (yews): to employ; to put an object, or a substance, or a faculty to the task for which it was made, or supplied, or provided; to consume; to avail oneself of; to become accustomed.
4. USE (youce): the act of employing for a purpose; a habit, or a custom; the ability to employ for a purpose; to be desirable; to be suitable for employment.
5. YEWS: pl (') of 'yew' (q.v.).
I asked you, boy, to prevent my ewes from grazing under the yews—a simple enough task, if you use your common sense—I fear you are of no use at all!

exceed, see accede.
except, see accept.
excess, see access.
1. excise: to cut a part out; to cut a piece off; a tax payable on certain home-manufactured products.
2. EXERCISE: repetition in order to secure greater proficiency of either body or mind; to employ or use (q.v.); to perform one's normal occupation; religious observance.
3. EXORCISE: to dispel or drive out, by the sign of the cross, the repetition of the Holy Name, and a special dispensation, a demon or other evil spirit or malefic force or entity.
4. EXORCIZE: alternative, and preferable spelling of No. 3 above.
They exercise miraculous surgical skill when they excise a cerebral tumour, but this operation does not exorcize the demon in possession of their patient's soul.

exercise ⎫
exorcise ⎬ see preceding group.
exorcize ⎭
eye, see aye.
1. eyelet: a round hole in fabric reinforced by buttonhole stitching, or by a metal washer (q.v.).
2. ISLET: a very small island.
The islet on that lake is in proportion as an eyelet hole in a marquee tent.
eyre, see air.
eyrie ⎫
eyry ⎬ see aerie.

F

1. face: that part of the body between chin and forehead; the countenance; impudence; aspect; appearance; a surface, or front; the written, or printed side of a sheet (q.v.) of paper or parchment; the side or surface for presentation; the dial of a clock or other measuring instrument with a revolving pointer; one third of a sign of the Zodiac extending over ten degrees; the offsetting surface of a print-type; to confront; to accept the challenge of circumstance; to look in a given direction; to attach to a garment ornamental coverings of specified parts with a material differing in either texture or colour; to veneer.
2. FAYS: pl (') of 'fay' (q.v.), a fairy.
3. PHASE: an aspect of the moon determined by her illumination; any one aspect of a thing subject to change; a state; an operation, complete in itself but merely a unit in a whole scheme; one movement in a recurring sequence; vibration; one of the oscillations of an alternating electric current.
Let us face the fact that during that phase of our hero's career, notwithstanding the bold face he assumed, he was in fact face to face with a disaster from which he was rescued by the acceptance of his invention of the faceplate, a device that could be manufactured only by the application of the three-phase electric welding arc, by means of which they now fuse the face of a weather-proof brick, and he certainly did not acquire his knowledge of science from the fays.

1. factor: an agent, or representative who trades on his own account, but whose income is derived from commission, not by profit; a land-agent, or estate steward.
2. FACTOR: one of two or more numbers that multiplied together result in a given number.
3. FACTOR: any circumstance, or condition, that contributes to a result.

A factor leading to the exposure of His Lordship's dishonest Factor, was the latter's disregard of the auditor's ability to use a factor in checking accounts.

1. **fag:** an uncongenial task; an effort that induces undue fatigue; to toil.
2. **FAG:** a system of degrading slave-labour, encouraged in Public Schools, whereby a little boy is forced to become the servant of a big boy who sometimes has powers of inflicting corporal (q.v.) punishment; one of the victims of this iniquity.
3. **FAG** (sl): a cigarette.

When Beather Major asked Fienon of the Sixth Form why he did not flog his fag for smoking a fag the former replied that it was too much fag.

1. **fail:** to fall short; to not succeed.
2. **FOUL:** unclean; filthy; bad; repulsive; behaviour that is not acceptable.
3. **FOWL:** a bird, particularly the domestic breed of the genus *Gallus*.

The farmer sold us a foul fowl; fail to complain and he'll do it again.

1. **fain:** pleased; well-disposed towards; to wish for.
2. **FAIN:** an expression of the wish to discontinue, particularly to retire from a game.
3. **FANE:** a flag-like weather vane.
4. **FANE:** a pagan temple.
5. **FEIGN:** pretend.

I fain would have climbed and secured the fane on the pinnacle of the fane; but Jack, who will unblushingly feign sickness when beaten, cried, 'Fain I!' and so stopped the contest.

1. **faint:** to become unconscious; to swoon; weak; indistinct.
2. **FEINT:** a sham attack to mislead the enemy; a deceptive action.

Did he faint, or did he feint?

1. **fair:** a conflux of vendors and purchasers taking place at a specified periodic time, and in a prescribed place; an itinerant collection of apparatus for amusement, set up for restricted periods.
2. **FAIR:** pleasing to the eye.

3. **FAIR:** of light (q.v.) coloured hair and complexion.
4. **FAIR:** just (q.v.); without either prejudice or favouritism.
5. **FARE:** to journey; to proceed; money paid for a place on a vehicle.
6. **FARE:** food; diet.
7. **PHARE:** a lighthouse; a channel illuminated for navigation; a name for the Strait (q.v.) of Messina.

After the annual horse-fair, the gypsies set up their fair, and the coloured lights created a fair spectacle: a fair gypsy presided over a 'Dream of Beauty' booth: her mother, who was dark, ran the tea-bar and provided good fare for sixpence. I paid my fare and went for a ride on the roundabout, but the big dipper stood idle: the Portreeve had prohibited it in case it interfered with the beams of the phare.

1. **fallow:** ground ploughed but not planted.
2. **FALLOW:** prefix of 'deer' (q.v.), a small breed of *Dama vulgaris*.
3. **FALLOW:** yellow; to wither; to turn pale.

A herd of hungry fallow-deer invaded a fallow field, and found nothing between its fallow hedges.

1. **fan:** an instrument used for creating a current (q.v.) of air; to create such a current.
2. **FAN:** a fanatic; hence, an enthusiast, an admirer of, or a supporter of, a public figure.

The photo of the film-star peeping coyly from behind a fan is selling by the dozen to every fan.

1. **fanatic:** an enthusiast (see **fan**).
2. **PHONETIC:** the representation by visible symbols of vocal sounds.

He was a phonetic alphabet fanatic.

fane, see **fain.**
fare, see **fair.**

1. **farrow:** a young pig, hence, to produce a litter.
2. **FARROW:** a cow that has ceased to produce young; of a cow between her pregnancies.

3. FURROW: a narrow, shallow, long groove cut upon the surface of the land by the plough; any similar groove; the wrinkles in the face caused by advancing years; to make or cut furrows.
The farrow destroyed the seedlings in every furrow.
1. **farther:** at a greater distance; forward in time; to a greater extent; to assist; to facilitate; in addition to.
2. FATHER: a male parent; a male ancestor; a founder, or an originator; the senior male member of a group; the title of a Catholic priest; First Person of the Trinity.
3. FURTHER: alternative spelling of No. 1 above.
I have knitted father a bedsock: I'd have made him a pair if the wool had gone farther.
1. **fast:** a period of abstinence from food.
2. FAST: fixed; immovable.
3. FAST: at a high speed.
4. FAST: wanton; dissipated; immoral.
A fast young man driving a fast car arrogantly attempted to pass through a closed gate, but it was fast, and now he will fast in hospital.
1. **fat:** corpulent; obese.
2. FAT: the oily, or greasy layers of flesh.
3. FAT: rich; profitable.
4. FAT: slow-witted; dull; inert.
5. FAT: a measure of capacity; a vat; a dry-goods cask.
He is a fat-head: because he is fat he thinks he must not eat fat but, being both wealthy and greedy, he gorges himself on the fat of the land.
1. **fate:** inevitable events; destiny; the preordained course of life.
2. FÊTE: an entertainment on a lavish scale; a Saint's day.
Mary, who had refused to attend the fête, allowed herself to be persuaded, and there met John who ultimately became her husband; they attributed their meeting to fate.
father, see **farther.**
1. **fawn:** a young deer.

2. FAWN: a light brown colour.
3. FAWN: to express a servile fondness.
The keeper has invited me to see the fawn but I shall not accept: he will be wearing his fawn coat, and he will fawn upon me.
1. **fay:** a fairy.
2. FAY: to clean and polish metal; the skewings removed in the process.
3. FAY: to fit, join, fix.
4. FAY': a sloven, or an abbreviated, or a euphemistic shape of the word 'faith', particularly when in the form of an oath.
5. FAY: fated; doomed; having second sight.
6. FAY: a feminine personal name.
7. FEIGH: alternative spelling of No. 2 above.
8. FEY: alternative spelling of No. 5 above.
By my 'fay', that one is fey: a year ago she said my son in Canada would feigh, and here's a letter telling how he set up a shop to fay and finish antique articles of metal.
fays, see **face.**
1. **fear:** cowardice; panic; timorousness; dread; anxiety; solicitude; reverence.
2. FEARE: companion; husband; wife; an equal; to be sound, in good health.
3. FERE: alternative, and more usual, spelling of No. 2 above.
4. VEER: to change direction; to change course; to be variable; to pay out cable.
Jack is a good feare, and full of fun till Maggie, his feare, comes nigh; then you see fear written on his face and he'll veer right round and say not a word.
feare, see preceding group.
1. **feat:** notable achievement.
2. FEET: the parts of the anatomy that, when a person or an animal is standing, are in contact with the ground; that part of portable objects on which they stand; the underside of objects in contact with the ground; pl of 'foot' (q.v.).
3. FEET: units of measurement equal to twelve inches, or one third of a yard.

The doting parents regarded it as a remarkable feat when their offspring could stand on his feet and repeat, 'Three feet one yard'.

1. **feed:** to ingest food; to provide food for another or for an animal; to appease hunger; to supply wants; to nourish; to insert raw material into a machine.
2. FEED: to derive an income from payments made for professional services; bound in feudal ervice, a Feedman; to be seized of estate in feudal fee.
   When your lawyers have been feed, and your case comes up for judgement, you will only feed public curiosity.

feet, see **feat.**
feigh, see **fay.**
feign, see **fain.**
feint, see **faint.**

1. **fell:** a pelt (q.v.); animal's skin with hair, fur or wool on.
2. FELL: lower slopes of a mountain; hilly moor (q.v.) land.
3. FELL: to strike, or cut down (q.v.).
4. FELL: pst tns of 'fall'.
   He went over the fell to collect a fell and to fell some fir-trees but he fell and broke his neck.

1. **felloe:** a sector, usually one eighth, of the circumferential rim of a wooden wheel.
2. FELLOW: a companion; one who shares something with another; a contemporary; any other person, generally, but not necessarily, male; member of an inner circle, or higher group, in a society.
   That fellow with the beard is the Fellow of the Flapchatian Society who showed that a felloe does not carry the load that rests upon it. I know him for a fool, we were fellow students at Oxford.

fellow, see preceding group.

1. **felt:** pst ppl of the v to feel.
2. FELT: a fabric made by compressing, instead of weaving, fibres; descriptive of any article made of this.
   In the dark I extended my hand and felt felt.

1. **fence:** a partition; a defence against

trespass; a guard against the active part of a machine.
2. FENCE: to engage in swordsmanship.
3. FENCE (sl): a receiver of stolen property.
4. FENTS: tailor's cuttings.
   Now that the fence has been arrested, the yard where they sort fents is available for me to teach you to fence: there will be no audience, the fence is very high.

fents, see preceding group.
fere, see **fear.**

1. **fermentation:** the chemical and physical reactions brought about by the growth of yeast in various substances, namely, the generation of heat, distillation of alcohol, and exudation of carbon dioxide; the working-up of emotions, often for political ends.
2. FOMENTATION: a cloth, dipped in hot water, and applied to the skin for its therapeutical effect; the application of such treatment to a boil (q.v.) or other septic (q.v.) focus, to draw pus; a stimulus; encouragement.
   Fermentation was the cause of fire by spontaneous ignition breaking out in the wastepaper warehouse: one of the firemen cut his hand on rusty wire and was ordered to apply a hot fomentation.

1. **ferule:** a stick or cane, once used by schoolmasters to enforce discipline.
2. FERRULE: a cap in the form of a truncated cone placed at the bottom of a walking stick: a ring of metal placed on a handle or other object to prevent splitting.
   The schoolmaster sadly fitted a ferrule to his ferule, and on long, lonely walks meditated on the good old days.

ferrule, see preceding group.
fête, see **fate.**

1. **feu:** a feudal fee; a tract of land held in exchange for fee of either grain or cash; a feu-farm.
2. FEW: not many; not much.
   Few farms are feu-farms.

few, see preceding group.

fey, see fay.

1. **field**: an open expanse of land; the site (q.v.) of an activity such as a battle, or a sport; the players in a game or sport; in heraldry, the surface of the shield, the background; a sphere of interest or activity.
2. **FILLED**: supplied with as much as can be contained; of an office or function that is not vacant; to fulfil; of a porous surface treated with a homogeneous medium.

   The position is now filled, but there is a wide field of allied situations vacant.

1. **file**: a number of men standing, or marching, one behind another; to place articles, or documents, one behind another, hence, a collection of documents arranged in order.
2. **FILE**: a steel bar (q.v.) cut in ridges and hardened, used for the purpose of cutting and smoothing metal.
3. **PHIAL**: a small glass bottle for holding drugs.
4. **VIAL**: alternative spelling of No. 3 above.
5. **VILE**: base; depraved; disgusting; filthy; intensive of 'bad'.
6. **VIOL**: a violin-like musical instrument.

   In the archives was found a secret file on the life of the great musician: it had been secured with steel bands which, having rusted, we were compelled to cut with a file, and from the contents we learned that the fame of his recitals on the viol ought to be attributed to the Apothecary who supplied the contents of the phial he always carried about with him; without resorting to its aid his performance, it seems, was vile.

filled, see field.

1. **filter**: a porous bed, or membrane, through which a liquid, but not minute solids held in suspension, may pass.
2. **PHILTRE**: a love-potion; any drink that is supposed to have a magical effect.

   Filter the philtre before taking.

1. **fin**: the tough, external organs by means of which fish propel and steer themselves through the water.
2. **FINN**: a nordic people speaking the Ural-Altaic language.

   The Finn who owned the fishing rights in the fiord was said by his neighbours to have grown a dorsal fin.

1. **fine**: a sum of money paid for a fellowship in a society, or for some other privilege.
2. **FINE**: a payment made in lieu of serving a term of imprisonment.
3. **FINE**: thin; delicate; superior, good.
4. **FINE**: an Irish sept, family or group having close consanguinity.

   There is a fine line of distinction between buying a bogus degree, and paying a fine for one.

Finn, see fin.

1. **fiord**: an inlet of the sea (q.v.) deep and narrow in comparison with its length, typical of the Scandinavian coast.
2. **FORD**: a shallow place in a river with a hard bottom, where a crossing can be made.
3. **FORD**: a type of motor vehicle named after its maker, Henry Ford.

   We reached the ford and our old Ford, probably mistaking it for a fiord, stopped dead.

1. **fir**: an inclusive name for trees of the genus *Pinus*.
2. **FUR**: short soft hair of very narrow gauge growing profusely on the skin of some animals.
3. **FUR**: a deposit of calcium carbonate which forms in kettles, boilers and pipes wherein hard water is boiled.

   My aunt Elsie, having heard that a ball of fir placed in the kettle would inhibit fur, proceeded to make a ball of fur from her old fur coat.

1. **firs**: pl (') of 'fir' (q.v.), trees of the genus *Pinus*.
2. **FURS**: pl (') of 'fur' (q.v.), having particular reference to garments of fur.
3. **FURZE**: a shrub, bearing yellow flowers, which grows on heathland, and other open, uncultivated spaces.

   He named his newly-built house

'The Firs' although the nearest trees were sycamores: one jealous of his prosperity said sarcastically that the name served the purpose of calling attention to his wife's numerous and expensive furs; another of them said it must refer to the furze proliferating on the land he called his park.

1. **fisher:** a name for the pekan, or Pennant's marten, *Mustela pennanti*; any animal (including man) that catches fish.
2. FISSURE: a cut, or cleft, either natural or artificial; an obsolete heraldic term for a diminutive of the bend-sinister.

   The fisher, who lived a mile inland, had discovered a short cut to his boat on the beach, through a fissure in the cliff.

fissure, see preceding group.

1. **fit:** a paroxysm; a seizure; an epileptic attack.
2. FIT: to conform in dimensions.
3. FIT: in good health.
4. FIT: suitable; proper.
5. FIT: prepared; ready.
6. FIT: a mood or a whim.
7. FIT: to supply.

   When father is feeling fit, and the fit takes him, he will tell mother to make the children fit, and he will take them to town and fit them with new clothes, making sure that they fit, while he himself will remain in rags scarcely fit for a tramp, and one dares not remark on it in case he is seized with a fit.

1. **fitting:** the action of the v 'to fit' (q.v.).
2. FITTING: a part; an accessory; an adjunct to some object; the assembling of parts of an engine; the making of parts to fit other parts.
3. FITTING: suitable; correct; appropriate.

   It is not fitting for a woman to be fitting so heavy a fitting.

1. **fizz:** a hissing sound, hence, a slang name for champagne.
2. PHIZ: abbreviation of 'physiognomy', the face.

   When I said I'd stand a bottle of fizz you should have seen his phiz!

1. **flag:** a flowering plant; the iris, *Iris pseudacorus*.
2. FLAG: a rectangular stone used for paving.
3. FLAG: a square, or an oblong or a triangular cloth, of either silk or bunting, emblazoned with either national or personal armorial devices, hoisted to fly at a mast-head.
4. FLAG: to droop; to lose (q.v.) vigour; to evince fatigue.

   The sole of the mast was set on a flag-stone in the midst of a mound whereon the flag flourished, and at the top his household flag was seen to flag in the breathless heat of noon.

1. **flair:** keen perception, hence, special ability.
2. FLAIR: a strong, offensive odour.
3. FLAIR: a flat fish, the ray (q.v.) or skate (q.v.).
4. FLARE: a sudden burst of flame.
5. FLARE: a flag or other object riding in the wind.
6. FLARE: a bulge outward and upward.

   She has a flair for dressmaking, note how well she set the flare in this skirt. Her husband goes out at night to fish for flare, and once, when he lost his oars, had to light a flare. Never cross the bay in his boat—pooh!—the flare! I did once and when my hair blew out in the wind he said it was a flare like a red flag.

flare, see preceding group.

1. **flatter:** to pay compliments (q.v.); to represent in too (q.v.) favourable terms.
2. FLATTER: of a surface more free from depressions and elevations than is some other surface.
3. FLATTER: a blacksmith's broad-faced hammer.

   I don't wish to flatter you, but yours is flatter though you used a small hammer and he employed a flatter.

flatus, see afflatus.

1. **flaw:** a fault; a defect.
2. FLOOR: the boards, or other material,

constituting the bottom of the cube forming a room, the platform from wall to wall on which the contents of a room stand.

The mosaic floor had a curious flaw in its design.

1. **flay:** to remove the skin.
2. FLY: any winged insect.
3. FLY: to be volant; on the wing.
4. FLY: a light, fast-moving carriage.
5. FLY: a tent-flap, an entrance cover; a button-hole cover.
6. FLY: the free end of a flag (q.v.) when hoisted.
7. FLY: the vault over the stage in a theatre.
8. FLY: to depart speedily; to escape.
9. FLY (sl): cunning; sharp.

That fly fellow you employ has hoisted your banner with the fly to the mast: fly home and flay him, I'll lend you my fly, and I hope that is the only fly in the ointment: make sure he hasn't pitched the tent and torn off the fly, or let all your prize birds fly away.

1. **flea:** a parasite insect, *Pullex irritans*, that progresses by leaping.
2. FLEE: to depart hastily in order to evade danger; to escape.

' "Let us flee!" said the fly:
"Let us fly!" said the flea.'

flee, see preceding group.

1. **fleece:** the wool covering of sheep; the quantity of wool yielded by a sheep when shorn.
2. FLEECE: to rob; to extract money and goods in a particularly brutal and callous way.

The farmer who received a good price per fleece for his yield of wool, fearing to enter a tavern for food lest someone should fleece him, fainted from hunger and became a victim of the pickpockets.

1. **fleet:** a number of ships under the command of an admiral (q.v.).
2. FLEET: swiftness of living things either physical or mental.
3. FLEET: a (now) underground river, tributary of the Thames, giving its name to a district and now, to a main street.

The King of Sidon sent a fleet-footed messenger to Tyre with orders for the Admiral of the Fleet.

1. **flew:** pst tns of the v 'to fly' (q.v.).
2. 'FLU: abbreviation of 'influenza' which itself is a euphemism for a slight cold.
3. FLUE: a conduit through which products of combustion pass from the stove to the chimney.
4. FLUE: fluff.
5. 'FLUE: alternative spelling of No. 2 above.

'A flea and a fly flew into a flue' revolved in my aching head as I lay sick with 'flu, watching a little curl of flue pirouetting on the polished floor.

1. **Flo:** a familiar diminutive of the feminine personal name Florence.
2. FLOE: an extensive sheet of floating ice.
3. FLOW: to run smoothly and unobstructedly; the progressive movement of water or other liquid, of air or other gas, of electricity, of information.

The large thick floe drifting southward disturbed the flow of shipping, and an incessant flow of information reached the Admiralty.

1. **flock:** a group or large conclave of people, animals or birds acting without organization but with one accord.
2. FLOCK: a mass of fibres of wool, cotton, or other similar material used for padding beds and chairs.

A huge flock of housewives held up traffic in the High Street when they surged to the sale of flock mattresses.

1. **flocks:** pl of 'flock' (q.v.).
2. PHLOX: plants of the order *Polemoniaceae*, indigenous to North America; a name, phlox-worm, given to the larvae (q.v.) of the moth *Heliothis phlogophagus*, which feeds on the phlox plant.

The American tycoon whose hobby was the cultivation of phlox, endowed a chair of Natural History at a universiy, and opened an Experimental Laboratory to find flocks of birds that could be imported to feed on the phlox-worm.

floe, see **Flo.**

floor, see **flaw.**

1. **flounder:** a small flat fish, *Pleuronectes flesus.*

2. FLOUNDER: to walk with a stumbling awkward gait (q.v.); to struggle through deep mud.

He will flounder about on the beach for hours and catch not so much as a single flounder.

1. **flour:** a fine soft powder, particularly that of wheat.

2. FLOWER: the brilliant coloured complex excrescence at the terminal of a twig or stem, being the reproductive organ in plants; to come into flower.

He said my roses would not flower unless I dusted the leaves with flour-of-sulphur, and he was astonished when I handed him a flower.

flow, see **Flo.**

flower, see **flour.**

flue, see **flew.**

1. **fluke:** a flat fish, *Pleuronectes flesus.*

2. FLUKE: the broad-arrow shaped terminal of the arm of an anchor.

3. FLUKE: success by luck rather than skill.

4. FLUKE: the tail of a whale (q.v.).

5. FLUKE: a parasite worm infesting the livers of sheep.

It was by a fluke that the vet discovered fluke infecting our sheep: a neighbour told us that if we got some fluke from the fishmonger it would effect a cure, but grandma said modern people knew nothing: it was only a piece of the fluke of a dead whale brought to the surface on the fluke of a pirate's anchor at midnight during a storm that had healing power.

1. **flute:** a mellow, high-pitch musical instrument in the woodwind group; anything long, narrow and tubular resembling a flute.

2. FLUTE: to provide a garment with pleats; to render the edge of a fabric engrailed or wavy.

She is the only woman flute-soloist: I designed and made her impressive platform costume: it took me many hours to flute the skirt.

fly, see **flay.**

1. **foaled:** of a mare, to have given birth to a foal.

2. FOLD: to bring opposite edges into apposition by bending; the line created in some material thus bent.

3. FOLD: an enclosure to protect animals, particularly sheep.

Fold back the doors of the barn, and lead in my mare for she has foaled in the sheep-fold.

1. **foil:** a leaf, hence, metal beaten to a thin sheet.

2. FOIL: thin burnished sheet metal affixed to the underside of imitations of precious stone, hence anything that is applied to increase apparent value.

3. FOIL: to defeat, to outwit.

4. FOIL: a small, blunt sword, the point covered by a disc, used in fencing.

We must foil his design to uncover the point of the foil. This contest may scrape the foil off and reveal his artificiality.

fold, see **foaled.**

fomentation, see **fermentation.**

1. **foot:** the organ below the ankle on which one stands, hence, that part of any object on which it stands.

2. FOOT: a measure of rhythm in poetry.

3. FOOT: a lineal measurement of twelve inches; the third part of a yard.

He stood on one foot about a foot from the foot of the wall and marked each foot of his recitation with a drum-beat which he achieved with his free foot.

1. **for:** in exchange.

2. FOR: to be in favour of; to support.

3. FOR: to have purpose; to attain.

4. FOR: to bestow; to serve; to please.

5. FOR: because of; in order that.

6. FORE: in front of.

7. FOUR: the number between three and five; 4; IV; iiij.

'Fore and aft!' shouted the captain for drill purposes, and four bluejackets were put in irons for an hour for being slow: heavy punishment for light offence, and some of the crew were for drawing up a Round Robin for, they argued, that was the least one could do for distressed shipmates.

1. **foramen:** an opening in a bone as, for example, the foramen magnum through which the spinal column connects with the brain.
2. FOREMEN: pl of 'foreman', a workman, who, having some minor superiority, is put in charge of, and permitted to organize, the activities of other workmen; a charge (q.v.) hand, a *primus inter pares.*

We thought him the best, and the men thought him the worst, of all our foremen: incidentally, the men were correct—he died raving and foaming at the mouth, and it was discovered that his foramen magnum was malformed.

1. **forbar:** to exclude; prohibit; discriminate against; bar (q.v.).
2. FORBEAR: an ancestor.
3. FORBEAR: refrain; withhold action; show mercy; to abstain from enforcing, particularly the payment of debt; to do without.
4. FOREBAR: alternative spelling of No. 1 above.
5. FOREBEAR: alternative spelling of both Nos. 2 and 3 above.

Forbear to forebar him out of respect for the memory of his noble forebear.

1. **forcene:** engaged in using force; violence; frenzy; blind fury; in heraldry, descriptive of a horse (stallion) standing on its hind hoofs, rearing, its forelegs raised and flexed.
2. FORESEEN: seen in advance; anticipated; awareness of the future effect of a present cause.

It might have been foreseen that the horse forcene in his arms would be mis-named as salient, and mis-drawn as rampant.

ford, see **fiord.**
fore, see **for.**
1. **forego:** to precede; to go in front.
2. FORGO: to pass; to relinquish; to abandon; to do without.

A cavalry band will forego the State Coach, and I will forgo my dinner in order to see it pass.

foremen, see **foramen.**
1. **forge:** a blacksmith's, or a founder's hearth; the workshop in which such a hearth is erected; to work metal by heating and beating; to make, or manufacture.
2. FORGE: (generally followed by 'ahead') of a ship when it makes way, or progress, without receiving impulse, drifting forward by momentum, or carried on a current.
3. FORGE: to fabricate, duplicate, imitate, and offer as genuine; to copy a signature; to produce spurious coinage; to adulterate.

Skilful in his iniquity, he was able to forge a conveyance, and forge ahead selling to an American visitor the village blacksmith's forge.

forgo, see **forego.**
1. **form:** shape; condition; to make.
2. FORM: a group of scholars sufficiently qualified in a set of studies to enter upon another set.
3. FORM: a board (q.v.) supported on legs forming a multiple seat.
4. FORM: a standardized set of questions printed with (usually inadequate) space for answers; a standardized letter sent by civil servants in order to avoid responsibility.
5. FORME: a steel frame for holding type on a printing machine.

Up to the third form they sit on a form as stated in the form parents are required to fill, which is printed in the same forme as the school's rules: the headmaster, when in form, administers a form of punishment that will form character.

1. **formally:** conventionally; according to accepted rules; correctly; to fulfil a rule or custom.
2. FORMERLY: at a time previous; in the past; before.

They were formerly formally given notice to quit.

forme, see **form.**
formerly, see **formally.**
1. **fort:** earthworks, or a building

housing guns and a garrison for defence.
2. FORTE: special aptitude, ability.
3. FORTY: the multiple of four tens; 40; XL; xl; XXXX; used figuratively to express size, or quantity.
4. FOUGHT: pst ppl of the v 'to fight'.
He made forty mistakes—holding a fort was not his forte though he fought hard to do so.
forte, see preceding group.
1. **forth:** forward; outward.
2. FOURTH: the ordinal of cardinal four; 4th; IVth; iiijth.
The boy who goes forth into the world, and has no trade, will remain fourth-rate all his life.
forty ⎫ see **fort.**
fought ⎭
foul, see **fail.**
1. **found:** pst ppl of the v 'to find'; to have recovered that which was lost, or mislaid; to have discovered.
2. FOUND: to cast (q.v.) metal; to be a founder (q.v.); to work in a foundry.
3. FOUND: to establish; to create; to be the originator; to build.
I am going to found a society to collect money for charity from folk like grandfather, whose spectacles, when lost, are found on their noses: I shall need cast-iron collecting boxes: I wonder who will found them?
1. **founder:** one who starts something, as a school or a charity; an originator.
2. FOUNDER: one who casts metal.
3. FOUNDER: certain diseases of both hoof and chest in horses.
4. FOUNDER: to collapse; fall; to sink in a bog; of a ship, to sink, to turn turtle.
He made his fortune as a founder, and became the founder of a charity for seamen, becasue, in his youth, he had seen a ship founder.
four, see **for.**
fourth, see **forth.**
fowl, see **fail.**
1. **fraise:** the mesentery of a calf.
2. FRAISE: a ruff (q.v.); a pallisade.
3. FRAISE: to ream, or enlarge a drill-

hole; the tool used in this operation; to cut teeth in a wheel forming a cog, in watchmaking.
4. FRAISE: in heraldry, a cinquefoil representing a strawberry flower (q.v.).
5. FRAISE: a bacon omelette.
6. FRAYS: of cloth that unravels easily; to fray (q.v.).
7. FROISE: alternative spelling of No. 5 above.
8. PHRASE: a group of words expressive of an idea, and part of a sentence; a pithy expression; a style of diction; a short passage of music being part of a longer passage.
This 'ere overall frays that easy that I shed half my sleeve each time I fraise a hole: to coin a phrase, as they say, it ain't no blooming good.
1. **fray:** a fight; a contest.
2. FRAY: to unravel fabric generally by wear (q.v.).
3. FRY: fish newly hatched, hence, a term descriptive of all small fish; offspring; a family; the roe (q.v.) of a female fish; a disparaging description of a group of either people or objects.
4. FRY: to cook in a shallow, open pan, or skillet, in fat over direct heat; to be affected by excessively hot weather; to torture, or to tortured, by exposure to fire.
5. FRY: a name applied to such items of offal as are normally cooked by frying.
I sent him out for a pound of pig's fry and he came back with young herrings: he thought I'd said 'big fry': I suppose I'll have to fry them, but I'd like to fry him. When he does such things my nerves fray to pieces. One day I'll hit him and that will start a real fray.
frays, see **fraise.**
1. **frees:** that which releases, removes obstructions, gives liberty.
2. FREEZE: excessive reduction in temperature; to solidify by coldness; to immobilize.
3. FRIEZE: a form of cloth.
4. FRIEZE: a strip or band of decoration.

Painting the frieze in the hall frees the servants from outdoor tasks where, dressed in their frieze livery only, they are likely to freeze.

freeze⎫ see preceding group.
frieze⎭

1. **fret**: ornamental pierced work in either wood or metal.
2. FRET: a pattern made by a number of parallel lines interlaced with a like number set at right-angles.
3. FRET: to grieve or pine (q.v.), to complain querulously.

Don't fret over the destruction of the ornate panel of fret on the front of grandmother's piano: we shall replace it with a repeat design of the Harrington fret—and there is nothing fishy about that.

1. **frog**: an amphibious, tailless quadruped, *Rana*, or *Ranidae*.
2. FROG: the centre of a horse's hoof.
3. FROG: the detachable socket hanging from the belt, for the purpose of carrying a sword.
4. FROG: a fabric-faced button which engages with a cord-loop, to fasten a cloak.
5. FROG (sl): a Frenchman.

That Frog cavalry officer has sold me a horse with a diseased frog, and when I catch up with him I'll cut every frog off his cloak with his own sword and then cut the frog so that he can't go so grandly armed again in a hurry.

froise, see fraise.
fur, see fir.
furs, see firs.
further, see farther.
furze, see firs.

G

1. **gabble**: inarticulate, incoherent speech; foolish speech.
2. GABEL: taxation, particularly tax levied on salt.
3. GABELLE: alternative spelling of No. 2 above.
4. GABLE: the triangular termination of

the end walls of a building having a sloping roof.
5. GABLE: alternative spelling of No. 2 above.

The farmer did not cease to gabble about the 'gabelle falling heavy', but we townsmen assumed that he meant that the gable of the barn was in an unsound condition, so we departed hurriedly.

gabel ⎫
gabelle ⎬ see preceding group.
gable ⎭

1. **gage**: an object deposited in the form of a pledge; a gauntlet thrown down as a pledge to fight, hence, a challenge.
2. GAUGE: to measure the diameter; diameter used as a standard of comparative thickness as in the case of wire; an instrument for measuring diameter; a rough estimate.

He threw down his gage challenging his workmate to gauge the number of eight-gauge nails in the sack.

1. **gait**: characteristic manner of walking.
2. GATE: a door, or a doorway, giving admittance to an enclosure other than a building; the sum of money received as entrance fees to an enclosure wherein a sporting event takes place.

As the visiting team marched, with a swaggering gait, round the field the entrance gate was closed and the managers beamed with satisfaction over the record gate now being counted by the cashiers.

1. **gall**: bile; the secretion of the liver; intense bitterness; hence, bitterness of character; resentment.
2. GALL: a chafe, or a sore occasioned by friction; a blister.
3. GALL: a bare, unfertile patch in cultivated ground, or in woodland.
4. GALL: tannic acid; an excrescence of the oak-tree in protection against insects of the genus *Cynips*.
5. GAUL: the *Gallia Transalpina* of the Romans, modern France and Belgium; inhabitants of this area, hence, a Frenchman.

6. GHOLE: alternative spelling of No. 7 below.

7. GHOUL: an evil spirit, particularly one haunting burial-places and consuming corpses.

'You gall me when you call me "Gaul",' cried Alphonse Dupont, who thought we were accusing him of necrophilia and of being necrophagous by calling him a ghoul.

1. gamb: the leg.

2. JAM: a conserve of fruit and sugar.

3. JAM: to crowd together; to overcrowd; to obstruct by overcrowding.

4. JAMB: alternative spelling of No. 1 above.

5. JAMB: a door post.

I saw him jam the last of his bread and jam into his mouth, lean against the door-jamb as he swallowed it, and declare that a jamb in both British heraldry and American slang is spelt with initial 'g'.

1. gamble: to risk money on unknown results.

2. GAMBOL: to leap and frisk playfully.

If you keep a pet lamb do not gamble that it will gambol before your guests.

gambol, see preceding group.

1. gaol: a prison; a house of correction; a penitentiary.

2. GOAL: an objective; a destination; a winning post; the net suspended between two posts towards, and into, which the ball is violently propelled in the game of football; a similar base (q.v.) or 'home', in other games.

3. JAIL: alternative (and more popular) spelling of No. 1 above.

He makes his goal gaol.

1. garb: fashion of dress, particularly official costume.

2. GARB: in heraldry, a wheat-sheaf, or a sheaf of other grain.

When he wears his official garb you will see a garb on the buttons.

1. garth: an area of land, enclosed, and adjacent to a house or other building; a private garden; a grass-grown quadrangle.

2. GIRTH: a strap passing round the body of a horse to secure the saddle, or other load; measurement of the circumference of any object that has a rotundity.

I wandered absent-mindedly onto the greensward of the garth within the cloisters and cognized the presence of an armed man, of enormous girth, who ordered me off.

gate, see gait.

1. gateau: a cake, generally rich in quality, and ornate in appearance.

2. GHETTO: a section of, or district in, a town that is inhabited by a specific group of people, generally Jews.

A ghetto gateau is the best.

1. gaud: a larger bead threaded between the decades of aves in a rosary.

2. GAUD: a trick; a pastime; a florid thing, or a piece of finery; to make merry.

3. GORED: tossed, or wounded by a bull, or other horned animal.

Father Dominic delcared we should not gaud about within the precincts of the Cathedral, and for penance made us say a long prayer at each gaud when telling our beads; he said he had once seen a boy gored by a bull out of Divine wrath at less.

gauge, see gage.

Gaul, see gall.

1. gaur: an Indian wild ox, *Bos gaurus*.

2. GORE: alternative spelling of No. 1 above.

3. GORE: blood, particularly when in a semi-coagulated condition.

4. GORE: to pierce or wound (q.v.), particularly with horns.

5. GORE: a triangular piece of land.

6. GORE: a triangular panel of cloth, generally a section of a skirt.

7. GORE: in heraldry, a now obsolete sub-ordinary.

8. GOUR: alternative spelling of No. 1 above.

Bear in mind that you are in the country, not safely in Kensington Gore: the farmer's bull, loose on that gore, may gore you if you go out in that green skirt with the red gore, and if he does, your white blouse will be as red with your own gore.

1. **gauze:** a woven network having a minute mesh; such a fabric employed as a surgical dressing; woven of wire and employed as a strainer or filter (q.v.).
2. GORES: the act of a horned beast in wounding.
3. GORES: pl of 'gore' (q.v.), a panel of cloth.
4. GORSL: a name for furze (q.v.) or whin (q.v.).

No matter how many gores you have in your skirt, nor how fast you can run: the bull can run faster, particularly over gorse, and if he gores you it will not be rectified simply by the application of a little surgical gauze.

1. **gazer:** one who looks fixedly; an interested spectator.
2. GEYSER: a natural hot spring, hence, an apparatus for giving a supply of hot water.
3. GEYSER (sl): a person.

The geyser up from the country was the champion gazer at the geyser on show in the maker's window.

1. **gest:** a romance, or a poetic narration of notable exploits.
2. GEST: bearing, carriage.
3. GEST: the stages of a Royal progress.
4. JESSED: of a hawk, provided with jesses, or a strap about the claw.
5. JEST: a joke; merriment; a form of entertainment.

For a jest he clad himself in the costume of a troubadour, and strolled into her garden singing a gest, but the hawk on his wrist was stuffed and she called out— 'Why not jessed, varlet?'

geyser, see gazer.

ghetto, see gateau.

ghole ⎫ see gall.
ghoul ⎭

1. **ghyll:** a spelling of No. 7 hereunder, first employed by the poet Wordsworth, and so authenticated.
2. GILL: the organ of respiration in water-breathing organisms; *branchiae.*

3. GILL (jill): a quarter of a pint.
4. GILL (Jill): a feminine personal name, hence, any girl; a diminutive of Gillian, itself a shape of Guiliana.
5. GILL: a method of catching fish; to gut fish before cooking.
6. GILL: a flax-comb.
7. GILL: a rocky cleft, having a watercourse through it; a brook.

Jill went down the ghyll to help Jack draw the gill-net, but the work was hard and the wind biting, so they called at the inn for a gill of cordial spirit.

1. **gibb:** to pass a sail (q.v.) and boom (q.v.) from one side of a ship to the other when sailing.
2. GIBE: to scoff or sneer, to jeer at.
3. GIBE: a form of the word 'gibbet'.
4. GIBE: to handle roughly in a game; to play rough.
5. GYBE: alternative, and more usual, form of No. 1 above.
6. JIB: further alternative spelling of No. 1 above.
7. JIB: a triangular sail.
8. JIB: the beam (q.v.) or arm (q.v.) that extends outward from the platform of a crane (q.v.).
9. JIB: to stop; back away; show strong disinclination to proceed, or to perform a task; of a horse that stubbornly refuses to act, hence, of a human being.
10. JIB: the nose, the mouth; the face.
11. JIBE: alternative spelling of No. 2 above.
12. JIBE: to be in harmony with.

He does jib at a simple task, but do not gibe at him: he has had two serious head-injuries: once when the jib of a crane fell on him, and again when the helmsman failed to cry 'gybe ho!' on going about.

gibe, see preceding group.

1. **gild:** to plate (q.v.) with gold; to apply gold leaf, or gold paint, to a surface.
2. GILLED: having gills, as a fish.
3. GUILD: a confraternity, usually of craftsmen, who set standards, and meet (q.v.) for the purposes of studying, improving and protecting their craft.

The Christian Guild of Scriveners now gild the initial capital letter of their certificate, but the symbolic fish in the border remain blue gilled.

gill, see **ghyll.**

gilled, see **gild.**

1. **gilt:** gold plating upon silver; any metal given a surface of gold.
2. GUILT: responsibility of having committed a crime, or of giving offence.

He admitted his guilt in selling brass-plated iron as silver gilt.

1. **gin:** a particularly brutal type of trap.
2. GIN: an intoxicating spirit flavoured with juniper.
3. 'GIN: (coll) [hard 'g'] against.
4. JINN: gigantic spiritual forces, able to take human or animal form, very active in Islamic folk-lore.

A farmer who sets a gin trap should be seized by a jinn made savage with gin. There should be a law 'gin 'em.

1. **gird:** encircle; prepare; afix a belt.
2. GIRD: strike; revile.

Gird yourself well, the foreman, filled with wrath, seeks one to gird for last week's low output.

girth, see **garth.**

1. **glacier:** a river of ice formed from the incessant snow on high mountains.
2. GLAZER: one who applies glaze to pottery.
3. GLAZIER: one who renews glass in broken windows.

During the Christmas holidays, Jack destroyed the refrigerator while demonstrating how a glacier is formed, Tom set the outhouse on fire experimenting in being a glazer, and Fred, innocently playing cricket in the garden, provided work on every floor for the glazier.

1. **glair:** the white of an egg; anything made with white of egg; anything slimy.
2. GLARE: strong light; an unrelieved white surface, as a snowfield, or a sheet of ice; to give a fierce, threatening look.

The chef's glare when the scullion spilled a basinful of beaten glair would have melted the alpine glare.

glare, see preceding group.

glazer }
glazier } see **glacier.**

1. **gleam:** to shine; to emit light (q.v.); a subdued light.
2. GLEAN: to gather in small quantities; to gather the corn (q.v.) left standing after the reaping is done.
3. GLEAN: the placenta of a cow.
4. GLEAN: a warm burst of sunshine.
5. GLEEN: alternative spelling of No. 4 above.
6. GLENE: the eye-ball; the socket in which the eye-ball moves; a glenoid cavity, the concave socket in the end of a bone into which the ball-shaped projection of the adjoining bone fits.

He did manage to glean some knowledge of anatomy at the local reference library, and it came to him as a gleam of light that a cow's glean was not the glene of the human knee joint and this revelation warmed him like a gleen.

glean }
gleen } see preceding group.
glene }

1. **glose:** to give a definition of a word; to explain; comment, annotate; to gloss (q.v.).
2. GLOWS: that which emits light and heat; is incandescent; is warm, healthy, brilliant.
3. GLOZE: alternative spelling of No. 1 above.

The learned monk's face glows with joy as he carefully pens his Latin glose above the line of the Saxon manuscript.

1. **gloss:** an alternative spelling of 'glose' (q.v.); an explanatory note; a brief dictionary; a glossary.
2. GLOSS: shine; superficial polish; a semblance, or deceptive appearance.

Scrape from that foreigner his gloss, and his every action would need a gloss.

glows }
gloze } see **glose.**

1. **gnat:** any fly of the genus *Culex*, particularly *Culex pipens* and *Culex mosquito*.
2. NAT: diminutive of Nathaniel, a masculine personal name.
   Nat died of a septic gnat-bite.
1. **gnaw:** to grind with the teeth; to destroy or damage by biting.
2. NOAH: the righteous man who, by means of the Ark (q.v.), was saved, with his family and animals, from the Deluge; a masculine personal name.
3. NOR: a comparative, indicating negative choice between two.
4. NOR: than.
5. NOR': abbreviated form of 'North'.
6. NORE: a sandbank in Thames estuary marked by a light, three miles off the Kentish coast, and 47¼ miles below London Bridge.
   Nor Noah nor I gnaw nuts.
1. **gnu:** a horned quadruped indigenous to South Africa, *Catoblepas gnu*.
2. KNEW: pst tns of 'know'; to have had knowledge; to have been informed; to have been aware of.
3. NEW: fresh: not yet used; seen or heard for the first time; recent; having but recently become wealthy.
   I knew the gnu was new to him.
1. **goffer:** to give to a starched frill a wavy finish; to crimp.
2. GOLFER: one who plays golf :q.v.).
   The Scottish widow told her son he'd do better to stay home and help her goffer than go carrying sticks for a golfer.
1. **golf:** a game in which a small resilient ball is driven forward by a blow from a club (q.v.).
2. GULF: a deep concavity in the coastline.
3. GULPH: alternative spelling of No. 2 above.
   They have applied for permission to lay down a golf-links on the beach of the gulf.
golfer, see goffer.
gore, see gaur.
gored, see gaud.
gores, see gauze.
gour, see gaur.
1. **Graf:** a Teutonic title equivalent to Count.

2. GRAFF: a trench, or moat (q.v.), provided for fortification.
3. GRIEF: sorrow; suffering; a wrong or an injury; distress; weeping.
4. GRIFF: to spread a false report; to deceive; to cheat; sl for news.
5. GRIFF: a claw.
6. GRIFF: the offspring of a Negro and a mulatto.
7. GRIFF: a jig (q.v.) employed in weaving.
8. GRIFFE: alternative spelling of No. 6 above.
   Yes, I will give you the griff: a griffe, working at the hotel, stole from a Graf staying there a diamond-studded tie-pin in the form of a bird's griff: he was tracked down, and from behind a graff shot twelve of his would-be captors: he certainly spread some grief.
graff: see preceding group.
1. **graft:** tissue, either animal or vegetable, taken from one organism and attached, in its living form, to another.
2. GRAFT: dishonest dealing, particularly in politics.
3. GRAFT (sl): work, particularly hard work.
   There is a lot of graft going on behind the scenes in the gland-graft racket, and the doctors get only the hard graft.
1. **grain:** wheat, or similar food crops; any small round hard piece of matter; the smallest part; a standard of weight equal to 1/7000 of a pound (q.v.).
2. GRAIN: the texture in some manufactured materials; a kind of stratification in some natural materials, making cutting in the direction of the grain easy and smooth, but cutting across it hard and rough, hence, feelings of pleasure and approval, or of displeasure.
   It goes against the grain that governments give concessions to big buyers of grain.
1. **grate:** to reduce to small particles by scraping; to emit a harsh sound; to annoy (or be annoyed) by crude, irritating behaviour.
2. GRATE: a cage of iron bars, particu-

larly such a cage used to contain a fire.

3. GREAT: large, important, exalted.

He sat by the grate reflecting that a man might be considered great who had invented only a new way to grate cheese.

1. **grater:** a tool consisting of a surface pierced with numerous holes and the intervening metal turned at an angle to form a cutting edge, used for shredding or reducing to powder various forms of food.

2. GREATER: a comparative of great, exceeding what is great.

In these days the tin-opener is of greater importance than the grater.

1. Gratz (grays): capital of the Duchy of Styria, Austria.

2. GRAYS: short form of Grays-Thurrock, a town on the north bank of the River Thames in Essex.

3. GRAZ: alternative spelling of No. 1 above.

4. GRAZE: a surface wound consisting in damage to an area of the skin; an abrasion; any light wound; to inflict such a wound.

5. GRAZE: to feed upon grass.

6. GREYS: pl of 'grey', a colour between black and white, not in the spectrum, of which there are many shades; heraldic name for a badger; grey clothing.

Greys graze, and graze themselves on the barbed wire where the hunter from Grays tore the seat out of his best suit of greys. This mishap angered him, hence, he challenged a foreign gentleman to fight after calling him a liar because he said he came from Graz.

1. **grave:** a place of burial or interment.

2. GRAVE: serious; dangerous; demanding very close attention; sombre; not a subject, or an occasion, for mirth.

3. GRAVE: cut, carve or sculpt; to engrave.

4. GRAVE: a civic rank or dignity formerly employed in Yorkshire.

5. GRAVE: a continental title of nobility, a Landgrave.

He looked grave as he stood beside the grave of the late Landgrave, and on his return he gave orders to grave a headstone.

Grays ⎫
Graz ⎬ see **Gratz.**
graze ⎭

1. **grease:** fat or oil of either animal or vegetable origin.

2. GRECE: a number of steps or stairs.

3. GREECE: an ancient geographical area, consisting of a group of islands as well as part of the mainland at the eastern end of the Mediterranean Sea.

4. GRIECE: alternative spelling, used in heraldry, of No. 2 above.

In ancient Greece they spread grease on the grece supporting statuary of unpopular characters.

great, see **grate.**
greater, see **grater.**

1. **greave:** brushwood.

2. GREAVE: armour for the shin.

3. GRIEVE: a farm foreman.

4. GRIEVE: to cause distress; to persecute; to cause pain; to hurt.

5. GRIEVE: to suffer deep distress.

The farmer has employed a new grieve who will, by claiming greave as his perquisite, grieve him.

grece ⎫
Greece ⎬ see **grease.**

1. **greet:** to meet; to welcome; to hail with expressions of friendliness and goodwill; any action, or thing, signalizing a meeting. or a commencement.

2. GREET: to weep; to lament; to express grief.

3. GRETE: an obsolete spelling of No. 2 above, and also of 'great' (q.v.).

Have I not cause to greet? Proud of having been selected to greet our distinguished guests I descended the steps of the Town Hall and what should greet me but a fusillade of bad eggs and brickbats.

greys, see **Gratz.**
griece, see **grease.**

grief ⎫
griff ⎬ see **Graf.**
griffe ⎭

grieve, see **greave.**

1. **griffin**: one of the fictitious beasts of heraldry, having the forequarters of an eagle, the head complete with ears, and the hindquarters of a lion.
2. GRIFFIN: a European newly arrived in India, hence a novice in any society.
3. GRIFFON: alternative spelling of No. 1 above.
4. GRYPHON: further alternative spelling of No. 1 above.
   Every griffin in Bombay stays at the sign of the 'green gryphon'.

griffon: see preceding group.

1. **grill**: a gridiron; food cooked on a gridiron; a room, chamber or restaurant specializing in such dishes.
2. GRILLE: a portcullis; the visor of a close-helmet; any arrangement of bars of metal interlaced, or otherwise joined together at right angles.
   There is a grille between the grill-room and the bar.

grille, see preceding group.

1. **grilles**: pl of 'grille' (q.v.).
2. GRILLS: pl of 'grill' (q.v.); the act of grilling.
3. GRILSE: a young salmon.
   Have you ever attended the ceremony of the closing of the grilles while the chef grills grilse at Notdun Restaurant?

grills
grilse } see preceding group.

1. **grisly**: horrible; causative of fear; uncanny; ghastly.
2. GRISTLY: having the tough nature of cartilage.
3. GRIZZLY: grey-haired.
   Though old and grizzly, gristly meat is his favourite.

gristly
grizzly } see preceding group.

1. **groan**: to express, by a moaning sound, either pain or grief.
2. GROWAN: a form of soft granite found in association with tin in Cornwall.
3. GROWN: pst ppl of 'grow'; to have increased in size (q.v.); to have developed from a germ, or from seed; to have advanced by degrees from one state to another.
   He emitted a groan as his pick-axe struck growan, for he had grown old prospecting for tin.

1. **grocer**: a wholesaler; a dealer in spices; a supplier of provisions.
2. GROSSER: a comparative, more than gross (q.v.).
   That grocer is gross, and grows grosser.

1. **groin**: the fold in the flesh where the abdomen joins the thigh.
2. GROIN: the stone (or timber) ridge formed by the junction of two vaults.
3. GROYNE: a fence of either timber or stone built on a beach (q.v.) to prevent sand (etc.) being carried out on the falling tide.
   The boy, climbing on the groyne, fell and drove a spike into his groin: as stated on the brass commemoration plate near the third groin in the crypt of the local church.

1. **grope**: to search for something in the dark by using the hands; to investigate.
2. GROUP: an assemblage of things or people; a number of persons connected by their support of, or their adhesion to, an idea, or a party; a means of classification.
3. GROUPE: alternative spelling of No. 2 above.
   The Nudist Camp Reform group grope blindly for facts.

1. **gross**: a quantity, twelve dozen; one hundred and forty-four; 12 x 12; 144.
2. GROSS: coarse; rough; fat; massive; florid; lacking refinement.
   He's greedy and gross, when I have a dozen oysters, he orders a gross.

grosser, see **grocer**.

1. **ground**: the surface of the earth or to powder by crushing; to have been distinct from water; the space, enclosure, or arena whereon contests are held or games played; a surface or base on which something may stand, or be erected; matter suitable for discussion or for study; an undercoat of paint; the prevailing background colour of a picture; a field or area on which a design appears; particles of solid

precipitated out of liquid; sediment.

2. GROUND: pst ppl of 'grind', to reduce to powder by crushing; to have been shaped or sharpened by pressure against a revolving stone; to treat, or form by the application of abrasives.

He took the knife to be ground, and had no ground for complaint; however, on the way home he dropped it onto stony ground, and accidentally treading on it, ground it against a nodule of flint that turned the edge and in a towering rage he tossed it over the wall of the football ground where it broke the ground-glass window of the booking-office.

group ⎫ see grope.
groupe ⎭

1. grouse: birds of the genera *Tetrao*, and *Lagopus*, also applied to birds of the genera *Syrrhaptes* and *Pteroclea*.
2. GROUSE (sl): to complain; to grumble; to criticize adversely.

Give the troops grouse and still they grouse.

growan ⎫ see groan.
grown ⎭

groyne, see groin.

1. grub: the larva (q.v.) of a beetle or of a fly; a serious student at a university.
2. GRUB: to rummage; to dig superficially; to remove roots from the ground; to be engaged on a mean (q.v.) task; to be a literary hack (q.v.).
3. GRUB (sl): food.

The natives collected a certain large-sized grub and made stew, but the white men despised such grub and preferred to grub about for edible roots.

gryphon, see griffin.

1. guessed: pst tns of 'guess', to conjecture; to make a judgement without evidence; a supposition; to reach a conclusion without grounds; to estimate roughly.
2. GUEST: one who stays at the house of, or who eats or drinks at the invitation of, another; a person one

entertains and for whose comfort and wellbeing one holds oneself responsible; a person staying at an hotel, or in a boarding house.

When I saw the blaze of lights I guessed you had a guest.

guest, see preceding group.

1. guide: one who directs others on a journey; indicates a path or a way; instructs in moral standards; a book of elementary instruction; an object that directs the movement of another object, as in parts of machinery, tools, and the like; a post, a notice, a mark or some other indicator of a route (q.v.); one who belongs to the feminine equivalent of the Boy Scouts' Association.
2. GUYED: made a fool of; held up to ridicule; made to look absurd.

Further on you'll see a guidepost telling where to turn off for the school: they don't guide the boys there so well as they used; last summer they acted a play and in it guyed our local volunteer Fire Brigade.

guild, see gild.

guilt, see gilt.

1. guise: manner, custom or style; one's behaviour, conduct, general habit; costume; appearance; to assume fancy dress; or an unaccustomed mode of attire.
2. GUYS: pl (') of 'guy' (q.v.).

They hired dress-clothes for the occasion and in that guise looked perfect guys.

gulf, see golf.

1. gull: any long-winged web-footed sea bird; birds of the family *Laridae*, sub-family *Larinae*, genus *Larus*.
2. GULL: a simpleton; a credulous person; to take advantage of such a one.
3. GULL: a channel, or a rut (q.v.) created by running water.

It's fun to gull him; I told him a gull had, for its own convenience, cut the gull across the meadow.

gulph, see golf.

1. gum: the flesh covering the jawbones through which the teeth erupt.

2. GUM: a vegetable excretion in the nature of a resin, but soluble in water; colloquially extended to include indiarubber, and other substances not gum.

To cure a sore gum chew gum.

1. guy: old clothes stuffed, and surmounted with a paper mask, supposed to be an effigy of Guy Fawkes, carried about the streets by importunate children, who let off fireworks on the night of 5 November.

2. GUY: a rope used to hold fast any object that might be carried away by the wind as an awning at sea, or a tent on land.

The boys wantonly cut a guy-rope from a tent to tie their guy to a chair.

guyed, see guide.

guys, see guise.

H

H, see ache.

1. habit: dress; costume, particularly the semi-uniform style adopted by members of a calling.

2. HABIT: custom; instinct; usual mode of behaviour.

The pickpocket's dress-habit was a clergyman's habit.

1. hack: a tool of the mattock variety, suitable for rough cutting; the result of unskilful use of a more refined cutting tool; a gash; a broad deep cut; a saw (q.v.) for severing metal.

2. HACK: a serviceable, but not elegant, horse.

3. HACK: one who makes a meagre living by writing.

Any literary hack can hack out a Western novel by glorifying the cowboy's hack.

4. HACK (Am sl): a taxi-cab.

1. haggis: a kind of sausage used in Scotland.

2. HAGGISH: having the appearance, nature and manner of a vindictive old woman.

Sandy's wife is so haggish he never gets haggis.

haggish, see preceding group.

1. haie: an artificial hedge woven from cut branches.

2. HAY: grass cut and dried for winter fodder.

3. HEIGH: an exclamation to attract attention.

4. HEY: alternative spelling of No. 3 above.

Hey! John! Dang they goats! Put a haie round yon hay-stack.

1. hail: nodules of ice, being frozen rain-drops, that fall from the clouds.

2. HAIL: whole, hence, healthy.

3. HAIL!: a greeting, to shout to someone at a distance.

4. HALE: alternative spelling of No. 2 above.

The sailor on the raft, still hale and healthy, decided to hail the distant ship in spite of the hailstorm.

1. hair: a soft flexible fibre that rises from the epidermis of mammals, and from some plants.

2. HARE: a small quadruped of the genus Lepus, famous for its speed.

When Harold lost his hair his wife made him a wig from the pelt of a hare.

hale, see hair.

1. hall: an extensive chamber used for receptions and such gatherings; a building used as a headquarters by a Guild or a Livery Company.

2. HAUL: to pull; to convey by some vehicle; to sail close to the wind; to make excessive profit; to obtain a great number.

The Admiral at the ball was heard to say that the duchess should close haul somewhat when entering the hall.

1. hallo: to shout; to call dogs in hunting.

2. HALLOW: to make holy (q.v.); to regard as holy.

3. HALLOW: a form of No. 1 above; a term of greeting.

4. HALO: a nebulous circle surrounding a luminous body; a disc as of light, placed about the head of a saint in sacred art.

5. HOLLOW: concave; empty; cavernous; echoing.

6. HULLO: alternative spelling of No. 1 above.

> There was a halo round the moon which seemed to hallow the place, and from the hollow hills there came a faint hallo.

hallow, see preceding group.

1. halm: stalks of peas, beans, hops and other plant-stems used in thatching.
2. HARM: damage; injury; mischief; distress.
3. HAULM: alternative spelling of No. 1 above.
4. HELM: further alternative spelling of No. 1 above.
5. HELM: the large 'pot' helmet employed when plate armour emerged.
6. HELM: the steering apparatus of a ship.

> During the ship's fancy-dress ball the rating in helm and harness had to take his trick, so clad, at the helm, which did no harm, but later, the man wrapped about in halm, who represented rustic craft, was soaked, and his dress was ruined.

halo, see hallo.

1. halt: a temporary stopping place; to stop, or be stopped in one's progress.
2. HALT: lame, limping.

> The sergeant brought the squad to a halt and said they ought to be transferred to the halt lame and blind battalion.

1. hamper: a large, generally rectangular basket with a lid.
2. HAMPER: to impede, obstruct, overburden.
3. HANAPER: a small round basket; a department of Chancery taking fees for sealing documents.

> Before 1914 a commercial traveller had to hamper his mobility by a big hamper of samples.

hanaper, see preceding group.

1. hands: the terminals of the arms (q.v.); the palm (q.v.) and five fingers; the organ of prehension.
2. HANDS: the pointers of a clock.
3. HANDS: persons in employment.
4. HANS: German masculine personal name.

> Hans, the refugee, will not be given work by me: I like to keep my hands clean, and I am most particular about the hands I employ.

1. hangar: a large shed, specifically for housing grounded aircraft.
2. HANGER: a wood, growing on a steep hill.
3. HANGER: a person engaged upon suspending something, as paper for wall-covering; anything used for suspending something else; anything that hangs, or delays.
4. HANGER: a short, curved sword.

> They built a hangar on the hillside, and employed a paperhanger to disguise it as a hanger, but the General condemned it as too flimsy, declaring that one of his old-time cavalrymen could cut it up for firewood with his hanger.

hanger, see preceding group.

Hans, see hands.

haras } see arras.
harass }

harbour, see arbor.

hare, see hair.

harm, see halm.

1. hart: a male deer more than five years of age; a stag.
2. HEART: the cardiac; the muscular organ that circulates the blood; the innermost part, the core, of anything; the vital part of a thing or of an idea; courage or spirit; will to refrain from a cruel or objectionable act.

> He hadn't the heart to shoot the hart through the heart.

haul, see hall.

haulm, see halm.

1. hause: a depression between two heights; a pass, or upland valley (q.v.) between two hills.
2. HAWS: pl of 'haw' (q.v.).
3. HAWSE: the part of a ship's bows through which a pipe is set to accommodate the anchor-chain; that part of the cables or chains between the outer end of the hawse-pipe and the water when a ship rides on two anchors.
4. WHORES: plural of 'whore' (q.v.).

> We hurried our prisoner over

the hause fearing that to get under way this tide we'd need to cut our cables at the hawse, while our leader, slashing savagely with a stick at the hedgerow haws that lined our route, held forth incessantly on the evils of sailormen dallying with whores ashore.

1. **haw:** the berry of the hawthorn.
2. HOAR: white, hence, old.
3. WHORE: an immoral woman; to frequent houses of prostitution.

She bore the village reputation of having been a whore, but now she was hoar and above suspicion so she was consulted on sundry matters which she answered from her stock of adages such as, 'full haw harvest tells of fresh hoar-frost'.

1. **hawk:** a bird of prey (*Falconidae*) trained and used in the bloodthirsty sport of falconry.
2. HAWK: to clear the throat.
3. HAWK: to offer goods for sale in a humble way; to carry goods for sale from door (q.v.) to door.

The penniless falconer said he'd hawk his hawk, whereupon his companion was moved to hawk and spit upon the ground.

haws } see **hause.**
hawse }
hay, see **haie.**

1. **heal:** to repair, to become whole; the growing together of a wound; recovery from sickness.
2. HEEL: the rear portion of the foot; the rear, elevated portion of a boot or shoe; the last crust of a loaf of bread; the last section of a round cheese.
3. HEEL: to lay a ship over; to incline to port (q.v.) or starboard when sailing.
4. HEEL (Am. sl): a low, or bad charactered person.
5. HELL: the nether regions; the supposed fiery pit wherein sinners will dwell for eternity; the abode of Satan and all evil spirits; applied to a miserable life, or to an unpleasant place.
6. HELL: to burnish precious metals.
7. HE'LL: contracted form of 'he will'.

The heel will always heel the ship over when at the helm, and he'll cringe round the afterguard for a heel of bread and cheese; he's that packed with poison that if he got a blister on his heel it would never heal. He makes life hell for the rest of the crew, but I doubt if even Old Nick would give him a berth in hell.

1. **hear:** to receive auditory impressions; to listen; to conduct a trial or an enquiry.
2. HERE: in this place; an exclamation of summons, hence, to secure attention.

Here! Hear this!

1. **heard:** pst tns and ppl of the v 'to hear'; to have received an impression in the auditory field.
2. HERD: a group of domestic, or wild animals, particularly horned cattle.

I heard that the farmer lost a valuable herd of short-horns.

heart, see **hart.**
heel, see **heal.**
heigh, see **haie.**

1. **height:** elevation; altitude; measurement from the foot upward; of exalted rank or estate; in heraldry, one row of feathers in a pyramid, or panache of feathers.
2. HIGHT: to order, command; to call by name; to confirm, by vow, a statement.

Hight the good soldier who will demonstrate by obedience the height of his training.

heir, see **air.**
heirship, see **airship.**

1. **heliacal:** in the sun; the rising or the setting of a star close to the sun.
2. HELICAL: spiral, hence applied to screws, gears, and other machine parts.

The Ancient Egyptians discovered the heliacal rising of Sirius without the benefit of micro-helical-geared telescopes.

helical, see preceding group.
he'll, see **heal.**
helm, see **halm.**

1. **hem!:** an ejaculation to give warn-

ing, attract attention or express doubt.
2. HEM: the edge of a garment, turned over and sewn down.
3. HEM: confine; obstruct; crowd upon; hem in.
   Hem! You want me to believe they hem you in with restrictive regulations, but that you are too idle to put a stitch in the hem of your coat is manifested by its hanging down.
herd, see **heard.**
here, see **hear.**
1. **hew:** to hack, or chop.
2. HUE: loud and insistent outcry.
3. HUE: colour.
4. HUGH: masculine personal name.
   I asked Hugh to hew a few sticks: his face changed hue and he raised a horrible hue.
hey!, see **haie.**
1. **hi!:** an exclamation, being a shape of 'hey' (q.v.).
2. HIE: to go; to make a journey; to hurry.
3. HIGH: extensive upward; to be above; in a position of authority; at the top (q.v.); to be greatly esteemed.
   Hi! Hie you to the High Priest and buy me a blessing.
1. **hide:** a skin suitable for tanning; a skin tanned; one's own skin; any-one's skin.
2. HIDE: to conceal.
3. HIED: to have gone without delay.
   Angus hied into the heather to hide when he heard the Excise men were after his hide.
hie, see **hi.**
hied, see **hide.**
high, see **hie.**
1. **higher:** an elevation greater than another elevation; a person of more exalted rank or status; comparative of 'high' (q.v.).
2. HIRE: to have the use of an object, or of a person's services, or of a place, for the duration of a period for which payment is made.
   The roof here is higher, hire this hall.
hight, see **height.**
1. **him:** masculine pronoun of the third person singular; of persons or animals of the male sex.

2. HYMN: a poem, generally set to music, of praise to the Deity; vocal interpolations in the Church service.
   All day long you hear him hum that hymn.
1. **hind:** a female red deer (q.v.).
2. HIND: a fish of the family *Serrinadae*, genus *Epinephalus*.
3. HIND: a servant; a farm-labourer for whom a cottage is provided; a farm bailiff or steward.
4. HIND: in the rear; posterior.
5. HIND: an archaic name for India.
   The hind-quarters of a hind and a basket of hind were the annual rental that the hind rendered to the landlord.
1. **hip:** the outward lateral curvature of the human body below the waist (q.v.).
2. HIP: the fruit of the rose.
3. HIP: the word of warning given to secure unity in cheering.
   The president of the beauty culture club, calling for three cheers for the doctor who had discovered that hip-syrup increases hip-measurement, led with a feeble 'Hip-hip...'
hire, see **higher.**
1. **his:** possessive of 'him' (q.v.).
2. HISS: the sibilant sound made by geese, snakes and, when angered, cats; the sound of escaping gas, or steam, under pressure; to imitate this sound as an expression of disapproval.
   His snakes hiss.
hiss, see preceding group.
1. **hissed:** pst tns of 'hiss' (q.v.).
2. HIST!: an exclamation either calling attention, or warning to silence.
   'Hist!' he hissed angrily.
hist, see preceding group.
1. **ho!:** a seaman's cry to secure unity of effort in hauling.
2. HO!: an exclamation used to call a halt either to a draught (q.v.) animal, or to a person.
3. HOE: a ridge of land bordering the sea.
4. HOE: a tool used for piling the earth around the roots of growing plants, or for eradicating weeds; for working the top soil.
   Heave ho! my hearties and this

noon we'll make our landfall on Plymouth Hoe, and every man-jack among you shall hoe his wife's potato patch this eve.

hoar, see haw.

1. **hoard:** to save in a greedy, miserly manner; money or treasure hidden or buried; an accumulation of loot (q.v.).

2. HORDE: a large, army-like mass of semi-disciplined barbarians.

3. WHORED: pst tns & ppl of the v 'to whore' (q.v.)

A horde of Huns overran the civilized settlement: they whored, and murdered and burned; they desecrated the holy places and added much plunder to their hoard.

1. **hoarse:** gruff of voice.

2. HORSE: a quadruped of large stature (q.v.), *Equus caballus*, employed for riding, and as a draught (q.v.) animal.

3. HORSE: an article of furniture for hanging clothes upon; an apparatus for gymnastic exercise.

He came on horse-back, was drenched and shivering and very hoarse, but warmed himself on the vaulting-horse while his garments dried upon the clothes-horse.

1. **hock:** a name for malvaceous plants.

2. HOCK: the joint between the knee and the fetlock in a quadruped's hind leg.

3. HOCK: a form of sparkling white wine.

The veterinary surgeon applied hollyhock balm to the injured hock, and drank the rider's health in a glass of hock.

hoe, see ho!

1. **hoes:** plural of 'hoe' (q.v.).

2. HOSE: stockings.

3. HOSE: a flexible pipe, or tube used for conveying water or other liquids.

These townsmen cultivate their gardens with the hose; perhaps they fear to soil their hose if they employ their hoes.

1. **hold:** to grasp, seize or grip; to possess; to contain; the cargo room of a ship; to stop.

2. HOLED: provided with a hole (q.v.), perforated.

After he had addressed the crew they were content to hold on, although the ship was holed and there was ten feet of water in the hold.

1. **hole:** an aperture, break or way through any substance or object; a pit or a cavity; a chamber scraped in the earth by an animal to provide shelter; a cell or dungeon; a mean, dirty, or otherwise undesirable dwelling; a disparaging term, descriptive of any place that the speaker dislikes.

2. HOLL: an alternative spelling, being a dialectal form of No. 1 above.

3. HULL: a cavity; a hollow container or envelope; shell, pod or husk; rind of fruit; the covering of a chrysalis; the body of a ship; a ship's hold.

4. WHOLE: in one piece, unbroken, intact; all of the parts, pieces or elements contained in, and formative of, a set (q.v.) or group (q.v.); in good health; undamaged; uninjured; unabridged.

Upon him was cast the whole blame for the insanitary hole the Remand Home was revealed, at the enquiry, to be: the report stated, *inter alia*, that the building was as overcrowded and as verminous as had been the hull of a convict transport in the eighteenth and early nineteenth centuries.

holed, see hold.

1. **holey:** pierced with numerous holes.

2. HOLLY: an evergreen shrub, *Ilex aquifolium*, having engrailed spined leaves and bright red berries.

3. HOLLY: an archaic, but also a dialect form of No. 5 below.

4. HOLY: dedicated to religious use; having a sacred, or a divine (q.v.) character.

5. WHOLLY: in its entirety; thoroughly; exclusively.

Brother Dominic noticed, while decorating the church with holly, that the priest's vestments, though wholly holy, were holey.

holl, see hole.

1. **Holland:** the kingdom of the Netherlands; the country of the Dutch nation.
2. HOLLAND: a thin, tightly woven linen fabric used for roller window-blinds, for mounting maps, charts and the like, and for covering the boards between which a book has' been bound.
3. HOLLAND[S]: a name for gin.

He is an admirable craftsman, and a curious eccentric: he has a bottle of holland[s] for his breakfast, binds books in holland that appears like vellum, and every year he goes to Holland for a holiday.

hollow, see hallo.
holly, see holey.

1. **holm:** a name for holly (q.v.).
2. HOLME: flat, low-lying land on the bank of a stream; an island in a river.
3. HOME: the residence of a family; one's native place.

My home, on a windy holme, is sheltered by a thick holm hedge.

holme, see preceding group.
holy, see holey.
home, see holm.

1. **homo:** Latin for 'man'.
2. HOMO-: Greek for 'the same as'.

One doubts the sapience of *Homo sapiens* considering he makes no effort to become homocentric in social and political affairs.

1. **hoop:** a ring of metal, wood, or any other material.
2. HOOP: a bullfinch.
3. WHOOP: a cry or vocal sound expressing excitement; the hoot of an owl; the sound made at the end of a fit of coughing in whooping-cough.

The village idiot plays with a hoop all day, and now and then you hear him give a whoop of glee at having seen a hoop in the hedge: after dark he spends the time imitating the whoop of an owl.

1. **hoove:** a cap or other head-dress; a caul (q.v.).

2. HOOVE: a bovine disorder causing dilation of the stomach.
3. HOUVE: alternative spelling of No. 1 above.
4. HOVE: an alternative name for 'ale-hoof' (q.v.).
5. HOVE: temperateness.
6. HOVE: to linger.
7. HOVE: to hover; to remain suspended as a bird in air, or a vessel in water.
8. HOVE: to heave.
9. HOVE: the name of an unidentified round building of antiquity, formerly near Carron, Stirling-shire; generally in combination with Arthur's, or with Julian's, possibly derived from 'stove', or from 'oven'.
10. HOVE: a seaside resort adjacent to Brighton, on the coast of Sussex.

As I was walking along the front at Hove, Jack hove into view.

1. **hop:** the cones of a female vine, *Humulus lupulus*, used to impart flavour to beer.
2. HOP: to proceed by short leaps forward; to leap while standing on one foot.
3. HOP (sl): go.

While the children play at hop-scotch, I'll hop along and get some hop branches to decorate the room.

1. **hopping:** leaping upon one foot; leaping in either pleasure or anger.
2. HOPPING: gathering the hop harvest.

The kids in the alley were hopping with delight at the prospect of going hopping, but the social worker was hopping mad at having our young Jack in the party.

horde, see hoard.

1. **horn:** a hard excrescence on the head of certain animals; anything made from this substance; objects of this shape; hoof material.
2. HORN: a musical instrument developed from a simple horn cut short at the point.

Having performed upon the French-horn for fifty years his lips were as hard as horn.

horse, see hoarse.
hose, see hoes.

1. **host:** a large number of people; an army.
2. HOST: one who entertains another.
   France was an unwilling host to Hitler's host.
1. **hour:** the twenty-fourth part of a day measured from noon to noon; sixty minutes.
2. OUR: possessive of 'us'.
   The length of our lives grows less each hour.
1. **house:** a dwelling place.
2. HOUSE (how′ze): to provide with a dwelling place.
3. HOW'S: contraction of 'how is'.
   How's your house going to house all your guests?
how's, see preceding group.
hue ⎫
Hugh ⎭ see **hew.**
hull, see **hole.**
hullo, see **hallo.**
1. **humerus:** the bone of the arm between shoulder and elbow.
2. HUMOROUS: amusing, jocular; of a nature to induce laughter.
   He will not think a broken humerus humorous.
1. **humour:** moisture; any fluid exuded by an animal or a plant; the liquid content of the eye.
2. HUMOUR: a mood; a whim; an attitude of mind not subject to reason.
3. HUMOUR: the amusing quality of a thing, or a situation.
   We praised the hermit's cave just to humour him but we could see the humour of his living within those humour-dripping walls.
humorous, see **humerus.**
hymn, see **him.**

I

I, see **aye.**
1. **Ian:** a masculine personal name, the Scottish form of John.
2. ION: either of the elements that form a salt, or other chemical compound, when submitted to electrolysis.
3. -ION: part of the compound suffix '-ation', formative of nouns of action.

4. IRON: an abundant base metal, Fe, which, in many forms of alloy, is universally employed; a tool of iron; a tool, not necessarily of iron, but used for smoothing, hence, a copper-bit (q.v.) or soldering iron.
   Ian submitted the mysterious salt to ionization and found iron, copper, lead and zinc, hence he jocularly described it as quintoxide of old soldering iron.
Ida, see **Ada.**
1. **idle:** unoccupied; not in use; lazy.
2. IDOL: an image worshipped in primitive religions; a person who receives too much attention.
3. IDYLL: a poem descriptive of rural life.
   He published an idyll, became a public idol, and was idle ever after.
idol ⎫
idyll ⎭ see **idle.**
ile ⎫
I'll ⎭ see **aisle.**
ill, see **eel.**
illicit, see **elicit.**
illusion, see **allusion.**
immigrant, see **emigrant.**
imber ⎫
immer ⎭ see **ember.**
imminent, see **eminent.**
1. **impost:** tax; customs duty; an imposition.
2. IMPOST (sl): the weight a horse carries in a handicap.
3. IMPOST: the top slab of stone of a pillar (q.v.) on which the arch rests; the top cross, or bridging stone of a trilithon.
   The iniquitous impost on imported stone prevented the restoration of the collapsed impost of the trilithon in the stone circle.
1. **impostor:** a cheat; one who assumes a false identity in order to profit.
2. IMPOSTURE: the act of cheating by assuming a false identity; unjust and oppressive demands.
   It is an imposture to be forced to accept that impostor.
imposture, see preceding group.
1. **impressed:** a mark, cypher or pattern on a medium such as leather,

or sheet-metal, made by the application of pressure; to have exerted pressure or force; to have given or to have received a deep, indelible effect upon the mind or the emotions; to have been strongly (and favourably) affected by something.
2. IMPRESSED: taken by force to serve in the Navy; of goods or money, taken by force in the service of the State.
3. IMPRESSED: the pay of a military or naval officer when a portion has been excised by the State on the supposition of debt incurred upon government property in his charge (q.v.) being unaccounted for.
4. IMPREST: a sum of money advanced by an employer to an employee to be expended by the latter on behalf of the former.
I was not impressed by his boast of the enormous imprest his firm allows him.
imprest, see preceding group.
1. in: an inclusion, in a place, a group, a space or a period of time; to be contained; of a kind; to be at home.
2. INN: a house providing lodgment for travellers; a hostel for students; a Society of Lawyers; the buildings and estate belonging to the four Societies of Lawyers.
We slept in an inn.
1. incense (in'cense): aromatic gums burned to disperse a sweet odour during a religious ceremony.
2. INCENSE (in'cense): to anger exceedingly.
You will incense the colonel if you suggest the use of incense during the festival.
1. incidence: coming in contact; falling upon; angle of approach.
2. INCIDENTS: pl of 'incident'; a happening, or occurrence; a circumstance.
The gravity of the incidents can be judged only in relation to their incidence on current affairs.
incidents, see preceding group.
1. incite: to set in motion; to stimulate (q.v.); to influence; to inspire or encourage; to urge. .

2. INSIGHT: deep, and particularly shrewd understanding; mental vision; extra-sensory perception; complete mastery of a subject, or of a situation.
It needs but little insight to conclude that the parents incite the children to steal.
incumbent, see accumbent.
incursion, see encurtain.
1. indent: to knock a depression into a surface; make a pit, or dent.
2. INDENT: to commence a new paragraph a few spaces to the right of the margin.
3. INDENT: to enter into a two-part agreement, of the kind originally indented, that is, cut into two by a wavy severance; to be bound apprentice by indenture.
4. INDENT: to place an order for goods.
We must indent for some sheets of vellum so that we can formally indent the new apprentice: indent a new paragraph under the stationery sub-heading—the document is in the box with an indented lid.
1. indict: to bring a charge, or an accusation of felony against a person.
2. INDICT: a misspelling of No. 3 below.
3. INDITE: to set down in writing; to compose, particularly a poem.
To indict a man verbally is not enough, if you bear true testimony take up your pen and indite your evidence.
indite, see preceding group.
1. inflect: to bend, particularly inward; to vary the end of a word to accommodate its relationship to the other words in a sentence; to flatten, or to sharpen a musical note. [Inflected forms sometimes create homonyms: see throughout the glossary.]
2. INFLICT: to force something, as, for example, punishment, upon a person.
He will inflict his vocal efforts upon you, and you will observe how he will inflect every note.
inflict, see preceding group.
1. ingenious: clever; having simplicity

combined with effectiveness; being of an inventive turn of mind; being possessed of a ready wit.

2. INGENUOUS: guileless; unguarded in speech; simple; direct in thought and action; unprepared for iniquity in others.

He is very ingenuous, but has an ingenious way of escaping from rascals.

ingenuous, see preceding group.

inn, see in.

insight, see incite.

insure, see ensure.

1. intense: excessive; to a high degree; ardent; highly-strung; over-enthusiastic; strenuous in activities.

2. INTENTS: pl, purpose; premeditation; the will to act.

He is too intense: for all intents and purposes he is a liability, not an asset.

intents, see preceding group.

inter, see enter.

1. invalid: weak; sick; in bad health; a patient (q.v.).

2. INVALID (in'valid): not appropriate; not suitable; not legal.

The invalid in his chair remained all night at the railway station, his ticket being invalid.

ion, see Ian.

ire, see ayah.

iron, see Ian.

isle, see aisle.

islet, see eyelet.

1. its: possessive of 'it'.

2. IT'S: contracted form of 'it is'.

It's its end.

ivory, see aviary.

J

1. J: the tenth letter of the alphabet, between I and K; j.

2. JAY: a species of bird, *Garrulus glandarius*; a talkative person; a simple, or a foolish person.

Not to mention names—you know who I mean—J. He's a perfect jay.

1. jacket: a short coat, hence applied to numerous different kinds of covering; the skin of roast pota-

toes, the wrapper of a book, a hot-water jacket.

2. JAGGED: a ragged, notched or indented edge.

The book's title appeared in jagged letters on the jacket.

jagged, see preceding group.

jam ⎫ see gamb.
jamb ⎭

1. jar: a discord; a harsh sound; a blow, or physical shock.

2. JAR: a container of earthenware, glass, or other substance, cylindrical in form, and generally handleless.

A jar of jam dropped will jar on any grocer's nerves.

jay, see J.

jessed ⎫ see gest.
jest ⎭

1. jet: a form of lignite commonly found in the district of Whitby, at one time a popular form of mourning (q.v.) jewellery.

2. JET: black, very dark, as the colour of the mineral.

3. JET: a stream of liquid, or of gas, forcibly propelled through a narrow aperture.

4. JET: an aircraft driven by a jet-engine.

When the jet crashed on the jet-warehouse, the skilful firemen directed their jet onto the heart of the fire and instantly the night became black as jet.

Jew, see dew.

jewel, see dual.

1. Jewry: Jews collectively; a place where Jews live.

2. JURY: a committee of citizens brought into being for the purpose of hearing the evidence and returning the verdict in a criminal trial; a committee formed to give a verdict on any matter.

3. JURY: makeshift.

When the ship, under jury-rig, reached port, a jury was assembled and, pending a Court of Admiralty, evidence was taken in a house in the Old Jewry.

jib ⎫ see gibb.
jibe ⎭

1. jig: a folk-dance favoured by the Irish peasantry; a form of music

suitable to accompany such a dance; any boisterous form of group-dance.

2. JIG: a mechanical device, less than a machine and more than a tool, employed in manufacturing processes; a kind of separator used in mining.

Jack designed a jig to hold four parts and nine screws all at once, and when it was approved by the chief engineer, the whole staff knocked off and had a jig in the canteen.

1. jinks: quick turns in order to escape from pursuit; boisterousness; lively frolics.

2. JINX: a minor demon, or imp, that attaches itself to an individual and causes all his endeavours to fail.

He has a jinx having high jinks with his affairs.

jinn, see gin.
jinx, see jinks.

1. joust: a combat with the lance between two equestrian knights; a tournament.

2. JUST: alternative spelling of No. 1 above.

3. JUST: fair; without bias; equitable; moral; lawful; fitting.

4. JUST: exactly; accurately; precisely; merely; barely.

He arrived just in time to joust in the last item of the tournament, and just missed the victory by a point: he said the score was accurate and the umpire just.

juice, see deuce.
June, see dune.
jury, see Jewry.
just, see joust.

K

Kate, see cate.

1. keel: the central ridge from fore (q.v.) to aft in a ship, hence, applied to the whole ship.

2. KEEL: to cool by pouring from one vessel to another.

3. KILL: to destroy life; to destroy, utterly, any object, or a project; the birds or animals slaughtered in a day's sport.

I was engaged in the galley, and just about to keel some soup when our keel came in contact with the ground and I remarked that I would kill the helmsman.

1. keen: sharp; eager; fierce; competitive; piercing.

2. KEEN: to wail (q.v.) in mourning (q.v.) for the dead.

I went over to Ireland simply because I was keen to hear the old women keen.

ken, see can.
kerb, see curb.
kernel, see colonel.
Kew, see cue.

1. key: an instrument of metal cut so as to pass the wards of a lock and thus move the bolt (q.v.) back and forth (q.v.), hence, anything either material or abstract that helps in the opening, understanding, or unfolding of something else.

2. KEY: a range of musical notes having relationship to the lowest note in a scale.

3. KEY: an external lever that operates an internal mechanism; the fingerplates on a musical instrument that control the notes.

4. KEY: the final truncated wedge-shape stone that holds the span of an arch rigid.

5. KEY: a rough surface on which a layer of cement, or of plaster (q.v.) will hold (q.v.).

6. KEY: a winged seed such as that of the ash (q.v.).

7. KEY: a rectilinear pattern, employed by the ancient Greeks.

8. KEY: the elected section of the Government of the Isle of Man.

9. QUAY: a stout (q.v.) stone platform alongside of which a ship may be brought for loading and unloading.

The Mate gazed with unseeing eyes at the Greek key pattern he had painted for a frieze round his cabin as he played a dismal dirge, all out of key, on his piccolo, and every now and then pressed the wrong key: the key to the solution of the mystery of his behaviour was that he felt the key-stone had fallen from the arch of his career, he having lost the key to the skipper's rum cupboard which it was his duty to open as soon as the vessel tied up at the quay.

khol, see **coal**.

1. **kid:** young of the goat.
2. KID: a bundle of sticks.
3. KID: a child; a young person.
4. KID: a verbal hoax.

Don't try to kid me that that kid carried that kid up here from the farm.

kill, see **keel.**
kin, see **can.**

1. **kind:** a class or a group; a variety of animal; an assortment of objects having some points of similarity.
2. KIND: gentle; good-natured; affectionate; unselfish; thoughtful for the welfare of others; charitable; generous.

He is the kind of man who is kind to man as well as to animals.

1. **kite:** a bird of prey, *Falconidæ milvinae.*
2. KITE: a toy consisting of a triangular frame having a semi-circular base over which paper is stretched. This, secured by a line, or string, rides on the wind and rises to a considerable height.
3. KITE: the belly.
4. KITE (sl): in aeronautical circles, an aeroplane; in the realm of commerce, a Bill of Accommodation; in the underworld, a false cheque (q.v.).

When the boy asked his father to buy him a kite, the latter replied cryptically that he had just presented the landlord with a kite that would give him a pain in the kite.

1. **knag:** the stump of a sawn-off branch of a tree; any short rigid projection; a coat-hook, or peg; a pointed rock; anything jagged (q.v.).
2. NAG: a small breed of horse suitable for general riding.
3. NAG: to worry, irritate, find fault with, or scold incessantly.

She has a tongue like a knag and she could nag the hind leg off a nag.

1. **knap:** an abrupt snap of the jaws; to bite; break by a sharp blow, particularly stones; to strike.
2. KNAP: the brow of a hill.
3. NAP: projecting thread forming a fur-like surface on cloth.
4. NAP: a game of cards.
5. NAP: a short, light sleep without preparation.

He wore the nap from the seat of his trousers by a combination of taking a nap and playing at nap, but when I said so he gave me a knap that made me see stars.

1. **knave:** a rogue, but frequently applied in a friendly jocular sense.
2. NAVE: the hub, or central element of a wooden wheel (q.v.).
3. NAVE: the lofty arched central chamber of a church.

The sexton pushed a barrow down the nave: the wheel was broken, and the cunning knave made the nave serve as a roller.

1. **knead:** to mash and mix into a smooth stiff paste; to thus form dough (q.v.) from flour (q.v.) and water.
2. KNEED: having knees; of a beast descriptive of joints equivalent to human knees; of an object bent like a knee; to strike with the knee.
3. NEED: a lack (q.v.); a want; a necessity; a requirement.

The bakery engine will not knead for need of a kneed plunger.

kneed, see preceding group.

1. **knell:** slow ringing of bells to announce death, or at a funeral.
2. NELL: feminine given name, diminutive of Eleanor.

They tolled a knell for poor old Nell.

knew, see **gnu.**

1. **knight:** a person honoured by the accolade and given the title of 'Sir' by the Sovereign; a rank in an Order of Chivalry.
2. NIGHT: the hours of darkness between sunset and sunrise.

Mr John Bull goes to bed for

the last time this night for to-morrow he becomes a knight.
1. **knit:** to weave a fabric by interlocking loops of yarn; to unite.
2. NIT: the egg of a louse.
    She has to knit for a living, but who will buy from her? I distinctly saw a nit in her hair.
1. **knock:** to strike against; to come into contact with; to drum upon a door to attract attention; to beat, or hammer; to make a strong impression; a morbid rattling or drumming sound from an engine.
2. KNOCK: a hill, or a sand bank.
3. NOCK: the horn terminals of a bow (q.v.) to which the string is attached; the notch of an arrow.
4. NOCK: the forward corner aloft of a boomsail, or of a square-tack staysail.
    Beating into London river, dangerously close to the Kentish knock, a sail carried away at the nock, came down with a run, and gave the Old Man a nasty knock on the head.
1. **knot:** a bend, or hitch by which two cords, or two ends of one cord, may be joined.
2. KNOT: a hard, cross-grained cylinder in a plank of wood formed where a branch had joined the trunk (q.v.) in the growing tree.
3. NOT: an expression of negation.
    Pass the line through the knot hole in the plank and make a figure-of-eight knot, it will not slip.
1. **know:** to have knowledge; to be acquainted with; to be sure; to understand.
2. NO: negative; not (q.v.); none (q.v.); refusal; expressive of rejection or of opposition.
3. No.: the accepted abbreviation of 'number'.
    No, I know no-one at No. nine.
1. **knows:** possesses acquaintanceship with a person or a fact; has knowledge.
2. NOES: that section of an assembly that votes against the matter put.
3. NOSE: the facial organ through which the breath is inhaled, and in which is seated the sense of smell.

When he is on his feet his expression of countenance implies that his aristocratic nose knows noes.
kohl, see coal.
Korea, see career.
kraal, see carol.
kris, see Chris.

L

L, see eel.
1. **lac:** a hard, red incrustation formed on trees in India and other Asiatic countries, as a defence against the insect *Coccus lacca*.
2. LAC: Hindustani for a hundred thousand, used figuratively for any unspecified large sum of money.
3. LACK: to be short of; in need of.
4. LAKH: alternative spelling of No. 2 above.
    He does not lack a lac of rupees since he cornered the lac market.
lack, see lac.
1. **lacks:** needs; requires; suffering from a deficiency.
2. LAX: loose; careless; negligent.
    Discipline is lax and the Regiment lacks pride.
1. **lacquer:** a form of hard varnish made from lac (q.v.).
2. LICKER: one who licks, generally used in combination with 'up'.
3. LIQUEUR: a potent type of wine.
4. LIQUOR: any prepared liquid, but particularly alcoholic drinks.
    You, being a licker-up of local scandal, will be glad to learn that to celebrate Father's seventieth birthday we all got tight on liqueur except Aunt Priscilla who is anti-all-liquor, but she knocked some over and ruined the lacquer table.
1. **lade:** to fill a ship's hold with cargo.
2. LADE: a channel or a water-course; a mill-race.
3. LADE: to bail (q.v.); to lift water with a ladle.
4. LAID: pst ppl of the v 'to lay' (q.v.).
    The officer whose duty was to lade the ship in a seamanlike manner laid sheets between the bags of corn and the bags of

cement, and said though we steamed up a lade, and had to lade vigorously, no damage would be done.

laid, see preceding group.

1. **lain,** pst ppl of the v 'to lie'.
2. LANE: a passage or way.
   The basket of crockery left by the picnic-party has lain in the lane over a year.
1. **lair:** a resting place; the place in which wild animals sleep.
2. LAYER: a stratum; a spread of material superimposed upon some other material; one who lays.
   The archaeologist cut through a layer of sand, and unearthed the lair of a sabre-toothed tiger.
1. **lake:** an expanse of water surrounded by land.
2. LAKE: an artist's pigment based on an oxide.
3. LAKE: to take a holiday (chiefly North of England usage).
   Last time he was on lake he painted a picture of a lake at sunset using only crimson lake.
lakh, see lac.
1. **lam:** to beat soundly.
2. LAM: part of a loom (q.v.).
3. LAM (Am.): pertaining to running, particularly running away.
4. LAMB: the young of the sheep; a term of endearment.
   Atta boy! Can that lamb take it on the lam! I guess he must have figured the ram was going to lam him.
1. **lama:** a Buddhist priest of Tibet.
2. LLAMA: an animal similar to the camel, *Auchenia llama*.
   The lama rode a llama.
lamb, see lam.
lane, see lain.
1. **lantern:** a ventilated box (q.v.) or case (q.v.) of a translucent, or a transparent material, constructed to enclose a light (q.v.).
2. LANTHORN: alternative spelling of No. 1 above.
3. LENTEN: pertaining to, or appropriate to Lent (q.v.).
4. LENTERN: alternative spelling of No. 3 above.
   He carried a lantern in the Lentern procession.

lanthorn, see preceding group.
1. **lap:** a hollow, hence, the ventral surface of the thighs, particularly when sitting.
2. LAP: to drink by raising liquid with the tongue, particularly of cats and dogs, but colloquially of human beings.
3. LAP: the sound made by waves or ripples against the hull of a ship, or against some other solid.
4. LAP: to project; to overhang.
5. LAP: a distance, or a section, as in a race.
6. LAPP: a member of the Mongoloid race inhabiting Lapland, Northern Scandinavia.
   I heard the water lap alongside as we rode at anchor in the lap of the land, and the ship's cat sat on my lap to lap milk, kindly contributed by the ship's cook, a Lapp, and she let her tail lap over my knees.
Lapp, see preceding group.
1. **Lapps:** pl (') of 'Lapp' (q.v.).
2. LAPS: pl of 'lap' (q.v.).
3. LAPSE: a slip (q.v.); an error; a failure to perform; a falling off; decline; decay; termination.
   Due to a lapse of memory on the part of the Navigation Officer, the ship grounded on a lea shore and went to pieces, the floating part of the cargo falling into the laps of the longshore Lapps.
laps }
lapse } see preceding group.
1. **lark:** a bird that soars singing high in the air; a skylark; *Alanda arvensis*.
2. LARK (sl): to create a humorous situation; to join in general hilarity; to witness an amusing occurrence.
   Just for lark, go and tell Father there is a lark in his seed-bed.
1. **Larry:** a diminutive of the masculine personal name Lawrence.
2. LAURIE: another diminutive of Lawrence.
3. LORRY: a flat, four-wheeled vehicle; a truck.
4. LORY: a bird of the parrot family, common in Australia and parts of Asia, *Loriinae*.

5. LURY: alternative form of No. 3 above.

Laurie carries a caged lory in his lorry.

1. larva: the maggot stage in an insect's metamorphosis; the form assumed between egg and pupa.

2. LATHER: the mass of bubbles created by agitating a solution of soap or of detergent powder.

3. LAVA: the form assumed, when cool, of the liquid rock that issues from a volcanic exudation.

4. LAVER: a name given to edible marine algae (q.v.).

5. LAVER: a vessel used to hold (q.v.) water for (particularly ceremonial) ablution; the basin of a fountain.

The lava, like lather overflowing from a giant laver, submerged and preserved the form of everything in its path: even larva of an insect on a leaf.

1. last: the final one; the end.

2. LAST: to continue, to endure.

3. LAST: in the fullness of time.

4. LAST: a block of either wood or iron used in making or in mending footwear.

At last the cobbler, feeling his patience would last no longer, reminded his nagging wife that she had received the last warning, and threw his last at her.

1. lath: a thin, narrow, rectangular length of wood.

2. LATHE: a machine for rotating a piece of raw material for the purpose of shaping it by the application of cutters; a machine for turning.

3. LATHE: one of the five areas into which the County of Kent is divided for administrative purposes; a barn.

4. LAVE: to wash; to ladle water, to pour out.

5. LAVE: to droop (q.v.); hang down.

Carter! Give that lave-eared horse a whack with this lath, I have promised to deliver this lathe to the wood-turner in the next Lathe, and I want to be in time to lave our tonsils at the inn.

lathe, see preceding group.

lather, see larva.

1. Latin: the language of the Ancient Romans; the population of Southern Europe, distinct from Greek.

2. LATTEN: an old term for brass.

Monumental tablets of latten inscribed in Latin.

latten, see preceding group.

1. latter: the second of two; the hind part.

2. LETTER: an alphabetical symbol.

3. LETTER: a written document; a communication.

4. LETTER: one who lets; one who hires out goods or accommodation at rental.

5. LITTER: a bed suspended in a frame for transport.

6. LITTER: the multiple young brought forth at a birth by some animals.

7. LITTER: straw and like substances used to bed horses.

8. LITTER: scraps of paper, empty bottles, tins and other rubbish thrown down by a wanton, careless, selfish public.

He began life raking litter and could not read a single letter, but he attended night school, and prospered till he became the letter of a big house: towards the latter end of his life he wrote a letter to all who had known him as litter-boy, informing them that his wealth would go to founding a scholarship and to supporting the anti-litter campaign: he was a keen supporter of the latter.

1. laud: to praise.

2. LORD: the Lord God; a rank of the peerage; a baron (q.v.) of parliament; one to whom respect and obedience is due.

'The Lord laud exceedingly,' said the Lord Archbishop.

1. laura: an assemblage of separate cells each tenanted by a recluse, under the guidance of a Superior, found in Egypt, and in the desert near the River Jordan.

2. LAURA: a feminine personal name.

The Ladies' Archaeological expedition was put into a state of panic when they lost Laura in the desert, but they found her, safe and sound, the honoured guest of a laura.

Laurie, see **Larry.**

lava, see **larva.**

lave, see **lath.**

1. **law:** the rules of conduct, the prohibitions, the customs and general behaviour that govern civilized life; statutes enacted and enforced for the general peace and welfare; the forces of justice; that which occurs in nature under given circumstances.

2. LAW: a conical hill; a tumulus or a cairn.

3. LOR'!: an exclamation expressive of astonishment, or of disbelief.

4. LORE: teaching; learning; the tradition surrounding, or in connection with, some particular subject.

5. LORE: a strap, or a rein (q.v.).

6. LORE: the space between a bird's eyes and the upper mandible; between the eyes and the nostrils of a reptile.

The farmer said he'd have the law on the students of folk-lore if they touched the sepulchral law on his land, concluding his tirade with, 'Lor! What these town folk do be adoing.'

1. **lawn:** fine linen.

2. LAWN: an area of garden ground under grass kept mown (q.v.).

3. LORN: desolate; forsaken; doomed; in a condition of despair.

A lorn lady in lawn on a lawn.

lax, see **lacks.**

1. **lay:** a poem or song.

2. LAY: to speculate money on a bet.

3. LAY: the direction of the twist of the strands of cordage.

4. LAY: not sanctified; acting in, but not belonging to, a profession.

5. LAY: pst tns and ppl of 'laid' (q.v.).

6. LAY: to overthrow; to place an object on its side, or in a state of greatest equilibrium.

7. LAY: to reveal; to put a case (q.v.).

8. LAY: to set (q.v.); to arrange in good order.

9. LAY: an alloy (q.v.) similar to pewter.

10. LAY: to sprinkle water before sweeping a floor to prevent dust from rising.

11. LAY: to dispel a ghost, or other spirit.

12. LAY: the action of a bird in depositing an egg.

13. LAY: to spread a cloth, and arrange cutlery etc. on a table in preparation of a meal.

14. LAY (sl): one's occupation.

To hear him lay the matter before the committee will sound like a performance of *The Lay of the Last Mimic.* I'll lay long odds he is a lay-preacher on Sunday, but last Saturday he lay on his lawn and entertained some low-looking characters: I wonder what his lay is? They don't lay a cloth for meals, but simply muck-in like pigs. I look forward to the day when someone will lay him low, and I'd be pleased to pay for a line with a left-hand lay to hang him.

layer, see **lair.**

1. **lays:** pl of 'lay' (q.v.).

2. LAZE: to be deliberately idle; laziness.

I shall enjoy my holiday: I shall simply laze about and re-read Macaulay's *Lays of Ancient Rome.*

laze, see preceding group.

1. **lea:** a meadow; arable land under grass.

2. LEA: a measure of yarn; worsted, 80 yards; silk or cotton, 120 yards.

3. LEE: sheltered; away from the wind.

4. LEE: sediment from wine (q.v.).

5. LEW: alternative spelling of No. 3 above.

6. LEW: diminutive of the masculine personal name, Louis.

7. LOU: diminutive of the feminine personal name, Louise.

Lew spent his holiday lounging with Lou on a lea in the lee of a hill.

1. **leach:** to extract soluble elements from an insoluble mass by percolating the solvent as in a filter.

2. LEECH: an aquatic slug or worm, *Hirundinea,* used in medicine for drawing blood.

3. LEECH: a semi-slang term for a doctor of medicine.

4. LEECH: the edge of a sail furthest from the mast.

If you amateur sailors would watch the leech and steer by it, instead of asking if the sail was tanned in leach, and sitting with your feet in the water, and catching a leech, we'd make our moorings the quicker.

1. lead (led): a heavy, soft, grey metal, of low melting point and high malleability, *Plumbum*.

2. LEAD (leed): to guide by example; to go ahead; to direct; to be foremost.

3. LED: pst ppl of No. 2 above.

When he received orders to lead the cavalry charge his heart sank like lead, but he led with distinction.

1. leaf: the green blades that extend from the stem of a plant, or the branches of a tree, that appear before the flower and stay after the flower has fructified.

2. LEAF: one pane (q.v.) of a folded sheet (q.v.) of paper, making two pages in a printed book.

3. LEAF: gold, or other metal, when beaten to its ultimate thinness.

4. LEAF: a section of an expanding table.

5. LEAF: the moving part of a bascule-bridge.

6. LIEF: to be eager; willing; to make a choice.

We may as well take a leaf out his book, he'd as lief eat the leaf as the fruit.

1. league: a number of persons, organizations, States, or other groups banded together to add strength in gaining an end.

2. LEAGUE: a variable measure of distance, generally considered equal to three miles.

Seven-league boots do not help to form a League of Nations.

1. leak: the passing, by seepage, of a fluid, either liquid or gas, generally through faulty fittings or containers; the unofficial and undesirable publication of information.

2. LEEK: a plant, *Allium porrum*, allied to the onion, adopted as the national plant-badge of Wales (q.v.).

Due to a leak, a leek plated with gold for the Welsh reunion was stolen.

1. lean: thin, meagre, poor; the muscular tissue of meat (q.v.).

2. LEAN: to incline out of the perpendicular; to rest against an object; to depend upon.

3. LIEN: right to retain property pending payment of debt.

You'll have a lean time if you lean on Lena: you have a lien on her house, take possession, and let her eat the fat with the lean.

1. leant: pst tns and ppl of 'lean' (q.v.); to incline.

2. LENT: the period from Ash Wednesday to Easter Saturday.

3. LENT: pst ppl of the v 'to lend', to give a person use of, or access to, for a period. .

He leant over and whispered, 'It was the first Sunday in Lent last year that I lent you £5 for a week —what about it?'

1. lease: a contract of conveyance of property from landlord to tenant for a stipulated period subject to the payment of rent (q.v.).

2. LEASH: a thong or strap by which a dog is led (q.v.).

3. LEASH: a term used in weaving.

4. LEES: the dregs of wine (q.v.).

5. LEESE: to lose; spoil, destroy.

That a hound on a leash is led round the bounds every Quarter Day is one of the terms of the lease; failure to comply would cause the family to leese their lands.

1. leased: of property let upon lease (q.v.).

2. LEAST: superlative of little; the smallest; fewest; of most minor (q.v.) importance.

That the property was leased was least of his troubles.

1. leaser: one who holds property on lease (q.v.).

2. LESSER: the second comparative of less; between less and least.

3. LESSOR: one who grants tenancy on lease.

Is the leaser lesser than the lessor?

leash, see lease.
least, see leased.
1. **leave:** permission to take some action; permission to be absent from one's post.
2. **LEAVE:** to direct, by Will (q.v.), the disposal of property to successors; to permit things, on conditions, to remain as they are; that part of a meal, or of an article of food that remains uneaten.
3. **LEAVE:** to depart, or to deviate from a place or a course of action.
   If my uncle should leave me his fortune I'd not simply ask leave of absence to attend the funeral, I'd leave the job for good.
1. **leaver:** one who leaves.
2. **LEVER:** a rod (q.v.) or a bar (q.v.) poised upon a fulcrum, and used for lifting heavy objects; an upright shaft or handle to move gears, or points, or other parts of machinery.
3. **LIEFER:** comparative of 'lief' (q.v.).
   I'd liefer use the news of his being a leaver as a lever, than try some other way.
1. **leaves:** pl of 'leaf' (q.v.).
2. **LEAVES:** the act of departure; the act of bequeathing; the act of abandoning.
   Our gardener leaves leaves to make mold.
led, see lead.
lee, see lea.
leech, see leach.
leek, see leak.
lees ⎱ see lease.
leese ⎰
1. **left:** the side of the body that is to the west when one faces north.
2. **LEFT:** pst ppl of the v 'to leave'.
   He said he left a pair of shoes behind, but both were for the left foot.
legible, see eligible.
lent, see leant.
lenten ⎱ see lantern.
lentern ⎰
1. **lessen:** to make less; to reduce; to subtract from; to become smaller; to diminish; to lower or degrade.
2. **LESSON:** that which is, or is to be, learnt; an exposition for another's enlightenment; a lecture; one sec-

tion of a course of study; an example; a portion of scripture read during service.
3. **LISTEN:** to cognize by auditory intake; to pay attention to words spoken; hark; hear (q.v.).
   Listen! it may lessen his self-esteem if he is not asked to read the Lesson in church next Sunday, but passing him over may be a lesson to him.
lesser, see leaser.
lesson, see lessen.
lessor, see leaser.
1. **let:** to give, or receive, permission; to be granted freedom; to permit to pass; to shed; to grant a tenancy at rent (q.v.).
2. **LET:** to obstruct; to hinder.
3. **LETT:** an ethnic group inhabiting North Eastern Europe.
   He let water in the street, and it was discovered that he was a Lett in improper possession of a British passport: they would not let him remain here and go about without let or hindrance, but he was permitted to let his house before deportation.
Lett, see preceding group.
letter, see latter.
1. **Lettice:** a feminine personal name.
2. **LETTISH:** pertaining to the Letts (q.v.).
3. **LETTUCE:** any plant of the genus *Lactuna*, but particularly *Lactuna sativa*, garden lettuce, used in salad.
   Lettice laid lettuce on the table when we entertained the Lettish Consul.
Lettish ⎱ see preceding group.
lettuce ⎰
1. **levee:** a reception for men only held by the Sovereign.
2. **LEVEE:** an embankment along a river; a landing-place for river craft.
3. **LEVY:** to impose taxes, or a fine (q.v.); to enforce attendance at a place, or for a purpose; to raise an army, or a body of armed men.
4. **LEVY:** a surname of Hebraic origin.
   Councillor Levy moves that we levy a toll upon all folk who go strolling on the levee.

lever, see leaver.
levy, see levee.
Lew, see lea.
1. **liar**: an habitual speaker of falsehood.
2. LYRE: a stringed musical instrument of ancient Greek origin, taken as the symbol of lyric poetry.
  When he says he plays the lyre he plays the liar.
1. **lichen** (li'ken): a minute plant that grows in clusters on rock, roofs, walls, and sometimes on tree trunks.
2. LIKEN: to draw a parallel between two things, or two circumstances.
  You can liken lichen to mould.
licker, see lacquer.
1. **lie**: an untrue statement.
2. LIE: to be extended in rest.
3. LYE: alkali used in soap-making.
  It's no lie: he can lie in lye.
lief, see leaf.
liefer, see leaver.
lien, see lean.
1. **lieu**: instead; in place of.
2. LO!: an exclamation equivalent to 'look'.
3. LOO: a card game popular in the eighteenth century.
4. LOO: a mask worn in the seventeenth century by ladies to protect the complexion.
5. LOUP: a wolf, *Lupus cervarius*.
6. LOW: not reaching a normal height; nearer to the ground; simple; humble; subdued.
7. LOW: the sound made by a cow.
8. LOWE: a leaping flame.
  Lo! the kine low on the lea and those low-livers, playing at loo in lieu of working, would leave them to the fangs of the loup and fear not a lowe of avenging flame from on high.
1. **light**: the vibration to which the eye responds; the radiation from a luminous or an incandescent body.
2. LIGHT: having little weight; a substance that is attracted less by gravity than is some other substance of equal bulk (q.v.); of little consequence; requiring a minimum of attention.
  It feels light, but with no light I cannot identify it.

1. **lighten**: to suffuse with light; to brighten; to reduce the intensity of a colour.
2. LIGHTEN: to reduce weight; to unload a ship; to relieve from pressure; to restore peace of mind.
  Lighten the darkness of the hold, lighten the ship, and so lighten my mind.
1. **lighter**: having, or reflecting, more luminosity than some other object; receiving more of the sun's rays, or those of an artificial luminant.
2. LIGHTER: having less weight; being not so heavy as something else.
3. LIGHTER: a square-built, flat-bottomed vessel (miscalled a barge) into which a ship's cargo may be discharged, and transported up a tidal river.
4. LIGHTER: a device whereby a spark is thrown onto a wick soaked in an inflammable liquid, used for igniting some other object.
  I dropped my lighter last night into this lighter when loading: now she's lighter I may find it, when the sun is up and it's lighter.
1. **lightening**: reducing in weight; discharging cargo from a ship; alleviating; removing a burden.
2. LIGHTENING: illuminating; brightening.
3. LIGHTNING: the visible high-tension electrical discharge from clouds to earth.
  Lightning was lightening the scene as we worked at lightening the ship.
lightening, see preceding group.
1. **lights**: a number of points of illumination; a number of ports (q.v.) through which light may be admitted.
2. LIGHTS: the lungs of sheep, bullocks, and other animals sold as food for cats and dogs.
  There were but two small lights burning in the shop, so I did not see these lights were not fit for a mangy dog.
1. **ligne**: Old French measure, still employed to give the diameter of buttons.
2. LINE: cordage.

3. LINE: a particular course of action.
4. LINE: a scratch, or mark made upon a surface by drawing a scribing instrument from one point to another.
5. LINE: a brand, or type of merchandise.
6. LINE: to face the inside of a garment, or the back of some article of fabric, with a different kind of fabric.
7. LINE: to fill, hence, copulation in some animals.
8. LINE: a note or letter.

Drop me a line concerning the line you have to offer: I will draw a line under the items of interest to me; I require a great deal of cable-laid line and hundreds of thirty-ligne bone buttons: we will take a strong line against those who oppose you, so come, let us line our stomachs.

liken, see lichen.
1. limb: part of the animal body other than the head and trunk (q.v.); the branch of a tree; a projecting section being part of a whole (q.v.).
2. LIMN: to execute illumination of manuscript; to paint in watercolours.

The Abbot, observing the monk's deformed limb, wondered that he could limn so beautifully.

1. lime: calcium oxide, CaO; caustic calcium; quicklime; an ingredient of cement.
2. LIME: any sticky substance; birdlime.
3. LIME: a globular juicy fruit, allied to the orange and the lemon; *Citrus medica*.
4. LIME: a tree, *Tila europea*, the linden tree.

He sat under a lime-tree to drink his lime-juice and found the ground had been covered with bird-lime, but how thankful he was that it was not quick-lime.

limn, see limb.
1. limp: to walk with uneven steps.
2. LIMP: soft; lacking stiffening; flexible.

My efforts to limp home on my damaged foot made me go limp.

line, see ligne.
1. lineament: facial appearance, outline; any distinctive feature.
2. LINIMENT: an embrocation; an ointment.

She tried to improve her lineament by the nocturnal application of liniment.

1. ling: a sea fish, *Holva molva*, usually salted and dried.
2. LING: a variety of heather, *Calluna vulgaris*.
3. LING: a bird, the meadow-pipit, *Anthus pratensis*.
4. -LING: a suffix having power of diminishing or disparaging; of reducing; as codling (q.v.), lordling, etc.

A cold ling pie eaten among the smeet-smelling ling, and accompanied by the song of the ling, is better than the banquet laid on for a princeling.

liniment, see lineament.
1. link: a ring, a number of which interlaced form a chain; a unit of measurement employed by surveyors; to join, connect, or associate.
2. LINK: a flat expanse of sea-beach: on such the game of golf (q.v.) was first played.
3. LINK: a torch.

Some boys, each bearing a lighted link, searched at low tide on the link for eggs of the sea-serpent, thus forming a link between modern times and the Middle Ages.

1. links: pl of 'link' (q.v.).
2. LYNX: an animal of the cat family, *Felis lynx*.

Wandering over the links looking for his lost ball, it occurred to him that there are no links between a lynx and a hawk save proverbially sharp sight.

liqueur } see lacquer.
liquor }
1. list: a border; the selvage (q.v.) of cloth.
2. LIST: boundary; the barriers enclosing a space in which a contest, specifically a tournament, will be held.

3. LIST: desire; pleasure.
4. LIST: a catalogue, particularly of names.
5. LIST: an incline to one side, particularly of a ship.
6. LIST': a poetic form of 'listen'.

As you list, Sir Gwain, but methinks our list is not suitable for the tournament since the grandstand took a list backward: your steward has made a list of the dilapidations.

listen, see **lessen.**

1. **literal:** pertaining to the letters of the alphabet; exact, to-the-letter, transcription or translation; without secondary meaning.
2. LITTORAL: the coastal area pertaining to the sea-shore (q.v.); living, or growing or taking place on or near the shore.

There was a literal gold-mine along the West African littoral.

1. **literally:** in the same words; according to the words; verily, truthfully.
2. LITERARY: relating to the alphabet; relating to books; written composition; having knowledge of literature; being engaged in the profession of authorship.

As a literary man I literally writhe when I read some of the stuff that gets printed.

literary, see preceding group.
litter, see **latter.**
littoral, see **literal.**

1. **live** (lye-ve): having life; having great energy; containing explosive; being connected to an electrical generator.
2. LIVE (liv): to be alive; to spend one's time in a specific way; to pass one's life in a certain place; to produce works that preserve one's memory after death.

My name will live in the annals of folly for I live piously on the lip of a live volcano.

1. **liver:** the organ that secretes bile and purifies the blood.
2. LIVER: one who lives, particularly in a specific way.

He'll not be a long liver for he's been a loose liver and has ruined his liver.

1. **livery:** food and clothes provided for servants, hence, a type of uniform; food for horses.
2. LIVERY: as, or like the liver; to be suffering from a disfunction of the liver.

The gay livery suited him ill because of his livery complexion and character.

llama, see **lama.**
lo!, see **lieu.**

1. **load:** burden; pressure; resistance; a standard of weight or measure normally carried, or traded as a unit.
2. LODE: a watercourse; a channel; a track; a streak or layer of metal ore (q.v.) in a line (q.v.).
3. LOWED: pst tns of 'low' (q.v.).

The oxen lowed as their load was increased by the yield of the lode.

1. **loaf:** a mass of bread (q.v.) of specific size and shape.
2. LOAF: to waste time.

I know you want to loaf before the fire, but if you don't go out and buy a loaf there'll be no bread for tea.

1. **loafer:** an idle person; one who wastes time; a ne'er-do-well.
2. LOOFAH: the fibre of the plant *Luffa aegyptiaca*, used as a toilet sponge.
3. LOUVER: a chimney-like erection on a roof, having in its sides lateral slats sloping outward and downward, through which smoke can make exit, but rain can not enter.
4. LUCIFER: the fallen archangel; Satan; the Devil; Mephistopheles; the chief guest at a witches' sabbat; the enemy of Adonis; the Grand Master of the cultus of the left-hand; the chief of the demons; the spirit of evil.
5. LUCIFER: an early type of friction match (q.v.); the morning star.

He is no son of mine. He is a loafer who does nothing save lounge in the hall striking lucifer after lucifer. He has burnt the loofah I bought when last in town. I would that Lucifer entered by the louver and carried him off.

1. **loan:** goods or money belonging to

another that are subject to being returned; words taken out of a foreign language into current English usage.

2. LONE: isolated; reserved in manner; without friends or companions; unequalled.

He is a lone, unsociable wight, with thousands of pounds in War Loan.

1. loath: unwilling.

2. LOATHE: to dislike intensely; to hate.

3. LOTH: alternative spelling of No. 1 above.

The average Englishman is loath to loathe his enemies.

loathe, see preceding group.

1. loch: a Scottish lake.

2. LOCK: a tuft, or tress of hair.

3. LOCK: a device by means of which a door, or a lid, or a valve, can be secured.

4. LOCK: that part of a fire-arm that is actuated to effect the discharge.

5. LOCK: a length of a waterway between sluice gates, used for raising and lowering vessels between levels.

6. LUCK: chance; good or evil fortune; events affecting a person's welfare.

7. LUCK: an object of superstition, generally supposed to have been obtained from a fairy, on the safe-keeping of which object the welfare and destiny of a family depend.

'If that glass ever break or fall, Farewell the luck of Eden Hall.'
She unfastened the lock of the coffer and gave the youth a lock of hair for luck, it being from the head of the first Laird of the Loch, and she warned him to keep the lock of his pistol clean, and watch his boat in the lock worked by the Sasunnach.

lock, see preceding group.

lode, see load.

1. lodger: one who hires accommodation in a house tenanted by another person.

2. LOGGIA: a covered balcony.

When the lodger complained that the outer wall of his room had fallen down, the landlady said she would have to increase the rent for the luxury of a loggia.

1. log: a felled tree-trunk, or a branch; any piece of raw timber.

2. LOG: an apparatus for measuring a ship's rate of progress.

3. LOG: a book in which a ship's progress is recorded, as well as incidents and observations made during a voyage, hence, a diary (q.v.), a journal, a record of daily events.

Captain Spanker, in his retirement, kept a log from force of habit, and made his daily entries at a desk he had built from a log cut in his own garden.

loggia, see lodger.

lone, see loan.

1. long: extending in either space or time; of great distance from end to end, or from start to finish.

2. LONG: yearning; strong desire.

I long for a long cool drink.

loo, see lieu.

loofah, see loafer.

1. loom: a machine used to weave fabrics.

2. LOOM: a vessel, bucket, tub or vat.

3. LOOM: a name for a species of guillemot, *Alca brunennichi*.

4. LOOM: the inboard section of the shaft of an oar (q.v.).

5. LOOM: to come into view indistinctly.

Dimly through the fog we saw the land loom ahead, and as we rested on our oars a loom perched on the loom of the forward rower, and we then felt reassured of our safety.

1. loot: goods seized by an invading army; plunder.

2. LUTE: a stringed musical instrument; a washer (q.v.), often of clay, to make an airtight joint.

Among the loot was a lute inlaid with gold, and a lute of yellow clay which they thought was gold.

lord, see laud.

lor' ⎱ see law.
lore ⎰

lorn, see lawn.

lorry ⎱ see Larry.
lory ⎰

1. loose: not tight; not fixed; relaxed; easily movable.

2. LOSE: to cease to have; to be deprived; to be defeated; opposite to 'gain', hence, decrease; to become immersed in a subject.
If his head were loose he'd lose it.

lose, see preceding group.

1. lot: a decision reached by picking counters from a receptacle, hence, fate or destiny.

2. LOT: a group of animals, or of persons.

3. LOT: an item, either single or multiple, put to auction.

4. LOT: many; abundance; a large quantity.

5. LOT: a piece of land.
The cattle will go as one lot but for next to nothing, they are a poor lot; the farm lot will not fetch a lot, and I'd not consider it a hard lot to stay away from the Sale.

loth, see loath.
Lou, see lea.
loup, see lieu.
louver, see loafer.
low
lowe } see lieu.
lowed, see load.

1. Lucan: pertaining to St Luke.

2. LUCARNE: a skylight, or a dormer window.

3. LUCERN: the lynx (q.v.); the fur of the lynx.

4. LUCERN: a fodder crop resembling clover, *Medicago sativa*.

5. LUCERNE: alternative spelling of No. 4 above.

6. LUCERNE: the name of severally a Swiss lake, canton and city.

7. LUCIAN: a Greek writer of dialogues, sometimes referred to as Lucian of Samosata.

8. LUKAN: alternative spelling of No.1 above.
The Congress of Live Religions held at Lucerne had filled the town: I was in an attic, and as I looked out of the lucarne I could distinguish a field of lucern on the hillside and was thankful for my lucern sight. Turning from the window I took my copy of Lucian out of my bag, but paused—had I not better study the Lukan theme of tomorrow's meeting?

lucarne
lucern
lucerne } see preceding group.
Lucian

Lucifer, see loafer.
luck, see loch.
Lukan, see Lucan.

1. lumbar: pertaining to the loin; situated in the loin.

2. LUMBER: unwanted articles for which there is no use; anything that is not worth the space it occupies.

3. LUMBER: to move in a heavy, graceless manner.

4. LUMBER: a pawnbroker's shop, hence to pawn goods, to put away privately, hence to be imprisoned.

5. LUMBER: a Canadian term for timber (q.v.).
You'll see him lumber about among that load of lumber he calls antique furniture, bent double with a pain in the lumbar region, and muttering that if he thought he'd get a good price he'd lumber the lot.

lumber, see preceding group.

1. lurch: to move in short, sharp purposeless and directionless spurts.

2. LURCH: to cheat; to act cunningly; to take advantage of a competitor, hence, disadvantage; to be left in adverse circumstances.

3. LURCH: a term used in certain games of cards.
Keep your eye on him, he will borrow your money, get drunk, lurch about all over the town and ultimately leave you in the lurch.

lurry, see Larry.
lute, see loot.
lye, see lie.
lynx, see links.
lyre, see liar.

M

M: see em.

1. Mabel: a feminine personal name.

2. MAPLE: a tree, *Acer campestre*; timber from this tree; a syrup prepared from this tree.

3. MAYPOLE: a pole erected, painted and

decorated on the 1st of May, round which dancing takes place.

Mabel blamed her sick-headache on the combined effect of the Maypole and the maple syrup.

1. **mace:** a club (q.v.) originally a weapon, now a symbol of authority.
2. MACE: a spice consisting of the outer part of the nutmeg.
3. MACE: a Malayan coin, and a standard of weight.

A mace worth of mace in a mace weight of rice makes mace swingers fierce.

1. **madder:** the climbing plant, *Rubia tinctorum*; dye (q.v.) made from this.
2. MADDER: comparative of 'mad'; more mad; less sane than formerly, or than some other lunatic.

As she went madder she described more and more colours as brown madder.

1. **made:** manufactured; assembled; produced from raw material.
2. MADE: forced, compelled, influenced.
3. MAID: shortened form of 'maiden'; a young girl; a virgin; a spinster; a female servant.

The old maid made heavy knitted vests and made her maid wear them.

maid, see preceding group.
1. **mail:** a consignment of letters.
2. MAIL: chain, particularly chain armour.
3. MALE: the sex in which is vested the function of fertilizing.

He received by mail a sample of the mail he would wear in the play, and he declared it too flimsy for a belligerent male of the twelfth century.

1. **main:** the chief; the largest; the most important; superior; having great strength.
2. MAIN: the sea.
3. MAIN: exceedingly.
4. MANE: the abundant, long protective hair that grows about an animal's neck.

The main attraction at the circus is a lion whose mane is tied with bows of pink and blue baby-ribbon, and I consider it main disgraceful.

1. **mainour:** stolen goods, when found in the thief's possession, taken in the act.
2. MANNA: a form of food dropped out of Heaven to feed the wandering Israelites, hence, spiritual nourishment; Holy Communion; the exudation of *Tamarix gallica*; exudation of the Manna Ash tree, *Fravinus ornus*; a name for Hungarian or Italian millet, *Setaria panicum*; a name for frankincense.
3. MANNER: customary method of procedure; conduct or style (q.v.); rules of behaviour; politeness; morality.
4. MANNER: alternative spelling of No. 1 above.
5. MANOR: under the Feudal System a large tract of land of which a Baron was seized, and over which he had jurisdiction; now, a house of major proportions with some surrounding land.
6. MANOR (sl): a police area; a constable's beat (q.v.).

I was strolling quietly along my manor when my attention was attracted to the prisoner by his peculiar manner of walking, so I was able to take him with the mainour, being silver candlesticks stolen from the manor house: he fell into my hands like manna from heaven, in a manner of speaking, Your Worship.

1. **mahal:** in India, a tract of land; an estate; a territorial division; a section of a town; a palace or a house; an apartment.
2. MAHL: generally followed by the word 'stick'. A rigid stick, about two (q.v.) feet (q.v.) in length, fitted with a soft ferrule, or pad (q.v.) at one end, used by a sign-writer to rest his hand.
3. MALL: a sheltered path, used as a promenade.
4. MAUL: a large, heavy hammer used by both paviours and shipwrights.
5. MAUL: to beat very severely; the rending and crushing inflicted by a wild animal.
6. MAUL: alternative spelling of No. 2 above.

7. MAWLE: alternative spelling of No. 1 above.

The infuriated sign-writer used his maul stick to maul the children who smudged his work. He chased them down the Mall and had he not caught them would recklessly have followed them into the native mahal.

mahl, see preceding group.

1. maize: an American food plant, *Zea mays*; Indian corn.

2. MAYS: pl of 'May' (q.v.).

3. MAY'S: possessive of 'May' (q.v.), the feminine personal name.

4. MAZE: a confusion of paths within a confined space.

These many Mays past May's brother had the offer to carry the ceremonial dish of maize through the holy maze.

1. Major: a military rank, superior to a captain or, non-commissioned, superior to a sergeant.

2. MAJOR: of more importance or of greater (q.v.) size (q.v.); a larger number; a term used in music.

The major part of the Club membership did not like the Major.

1. malady: sickness; ill-health, a morbid condition.

2. MELODY: a pleasing musical sequence; a tune; euphonious and rhythmic arrangement of words in a sentence.

The malady of modern poetry and music is lack of melody.

male, see mail.

Mall, see mahal.

1. Mammy: a child's word for 'mother'.

2. MUMMY: alternative spelling of No. 1 above.

3. MUMMY: an embalmed body; a name for various medicines.

When we went to the Museum and saw a mummy Mummy fainted.

1. manakin: a small, brightly coloured bird of the Passerine family, *Pipridae*, indigenous to Central America.

2. MANIKIN: an artist's lay-figure; a model of the human body used in medical schools; a dwarf or pigmy; a figure used in the practice of witchcraft.

3. MANNEQUIN: a girl employed by expensive dressmakers to wear and demonstrate the becomingness of newly designed styles.

The mannequin suggested coming in with a manakin in a cage, placing it centre stage, then reaching up and taking a manikin from a cupboard.

1. manciple: a servant of an academy who buys the provisions for Fellows, students, and other residents.

2. MANIPLE: a handful, hence, a small subdivision of the Roman legion; an item of the Eucharistic vestments, being a strip of material wrapped round the left wrist, the ends, each about a foot long, hanging.

At the University of Munchonburg the manciple, clad in a white sleeved gown, with a maniple at each wrist, attends at High Table.

1. Mandarin: a Counsellor, or an official in Imperial China.

2. MANDARIN: the language spoken by the educated Chinese people.

3. MANDARIN: a doll, dressed in Chinese costume, and having the head poised so as to continue to nod when the doll is given a gentle push.

4. MANDARIN: a small perfumed orange, loose (q.v.) in its skin; the name of the yellowish-red colour that matches this orange skin.

5. MANDARINE: alternative spelling of No. 4 above.

6. MANDOLIN: a musical instrument having six wire strings and a deep, well-rounded sound-box, or body.

7. MANDOLINE: alternative spelling of No. 6 above.

A Mandarin who had travelled far and wide sat at ease eating a mandarine while a boy sitting at his feet entertained him with the music of the mandolin.

1. mandil: a turban.

2. MANDREL: a spindle, or an arbor (q.v.) to carry a grindstone, or a circular saw; the shaft, terminating in the chuck (q.v.) of a lathe (q.v.).

3. MANDRIL: alternative spelling of No. 2 above.

4. MANDRILL: a large, fierce West African baboon, *Cynocephalus mormon.*

An Indian conjurer wearing a mandil, and leading by the hand a huge mandrill, juggled with a mandrel, a file, a chisel and a key-hole saw.

mandoline, see **Mandarin.**

mandrel ⎫
mandril ⎬ see **mandil**
mandrill ⎭

mane, see **main.**

manikin, see **manakin.**

maniple, see **manciple.**

manna, see **mainour.**

mannequin, see **manakin.**

manner ⎫ see **mainour.**
manor ⎭

1. **manse:** a mansion; an ecclesiastical dwelling; applied chiefly to the house of a parish minister in Scotland.
2. MEN'S: the property, or attributes, of men; masculine plural possessive.
3. MENSE: neatness; tidiness; decorous; discreet.

The first-class men's outfitters in the High Street are always mense in their window-display, but they supply the manse.

1. **mantel:** a shelf fixed over a fireplace.
2. MANTLE: a cloak; a covering; applied variously to coverings in zoology, biology and engineering.

Maria cut up Grandfather's discarded mantle and made drapery for the mantel.

mantle, see preceding group.

maple, see **Mabel.**

1. **march:** the action of walking in rank (q.v.) and file (q.v.) and in step of a party of disciplined men; the forward progress of an army; the average distance an army can advance in a day; any hard long walk; figuratively, any forward movement.
2. MARCH: the frontier between two countries, the boundary between two estates.
3. MARCH: the third month of the Christian year, between February and April.

Next March there will be a cere-monial march along the tracks where Wales and England march together.

1. **mare:** a female horse.
2. MAYA: a people, and a cultural system, flourishing in Central America during the archaic period.
3. MAYA: a Hindu philosophical term expressing illusion.
4. MAYOR: the first citizen; the head, or leader, of a municipal corporation.
5. MIRE: swamp or bog, hence, mud.
6. MYER: a name, generally a surname, but sometimes a masculine personal name.

Professor Myer, the expert on Maya remains, fails to observe when he is splashed with mire, and when the Mayor, who breeds racehorses, spoke of selling a mare, the Professor replied that the entire universe was but Hindu maya.

1. **mark:** a discoloration or a stain; a cypher; an impression.
2. MARK: a Continental coin.
3. MARQUE: reprisal; to seize goods as a pledge; to take.

During the French war he received Letters of Marque and made his mark on the history of Privateering: when a foreign ship-master offered a sackful of money, he replied grandly that he did not regard the mark as money, and he dropped it overboard.

1. **maroon:** to place a person in an isolated position from which there is no escape as, for example, on an island.
2. MAROON: a package of gunpowder or other explosive which, when fired, gives warning to the general populace of some impending event.
3. MAROON: a colour between red and brown; a wine colour.
4. MAROON: a large sweet chestnut.

The maroon distilled from the wild maroon a liquid that he drank till his nose turned maroon and every few minutes he thought he heard a maroon.

marque, see **mark.**

1. **marriage:** a contract of union be-

tween two persons of opposite sex; the splicing of two ropes; the welding of two pieces of metal.

2. MIRAGE: an optical illusion of water in the desert; an image in a mirror; a pleasing fantasy.

The marriage mirage is 'happy ever after'.

1. **marry:** to join together; to enter a state of legal wedlock; to splice ropes with a long-splice; to weld (q.v.).

2. MARRY!: an exclamation expressive of surprise or indignation; a term of confirmation or agreement; a form of mild oath.

3. MERRY: cheerful, bright, amusing, entertaining, lively.

4. MERRY: a dark-coloured cherry.

Marry! that merry fellow is about to marry!

1. **marshal:** a high officer of the Court; a high officer of state; a military commander; an officer of the City of London who arranges and controls banquets; an officer of a Court of Law; to gather together and arrange in order; in heraldry, to display more than one Coat of Arms in proper order on an escutcheon.

2. MARTIAL: pertaining to the Army; military in character; warlike.

The Marshal ordered a general parade accompanied by appropriate martial music, and he advised the government to marshal our national resources.

1. **marten:** a fur-bearing quadruped, *Mustela.*

2. MARTIAN: pertaining to the planet Mars, or to the month of March; pertaining to war.

3. MARTIN: a bird similar to the swallow, *Chelidon urbica.*

4. MARTIN: the name of St Martin, Bishop of Tours (4th cent.), hence, a masculine given name.

Martin, dear little fellow! dressed himself up in his mother's new marten cloak to play at being a Martian, in which role he climbed a barbed wire fence, and fell into a ditch while trying to reach a nest built by a martin.

martial, see **marshal.**

Martian } see **marten.**
Martin }

1. **mask:** a strip of black silk, velvet or other cloth having holes for vision, and strings to tie behind the head, worn (q.v.) for a disguise; a hollow cast (q.v.) of the human face; a human face moulded in clay; anything that conceals or covers something else.

2. MASQUE: a form of stage-play; a masked ball.

He attended the masque wearing a mask of cloth of gold.

masque, see preceding group.

1. **Mass:** the Eucharistic Service celebrated by the Roman Catholic Church.

2. MASS: a large quantity; a large number; a wide expanse of colour; a co-operative gathering of bands of musicians.

A huge mass of people attend Mass.

1. **Massa:** a negro pronunciation of 'master'.

2. MASSÉ: a stroke in the game of billiards.

3. MASSER: a priest who conducts the Mass (q.v.) service.

Massa! You make massé first: then come: Masser, him wait.

massé, see preceding group.

1. **massed:** gathered together for a particular purpose, or on a special occasion.

2. MAST: a spar, pole, or post set upright to carry a ship's sails, or to elevate a flag.

3. MAST: a pig-food made from acorns, beech-nuts and horse-chestnuts.

The massed bands round the flag-mast played popular airs while the Squire's prize pigs made minor music with their snouts in a trough of mast.

Masser, see **Massa**

1. **match:** to be equal; to be suited one to another; to contend, generally in sport and games, against another; a person regarded as a suitable partner in marriage.

2. MATCH: a wick; a taper, a splint of wood treated with a substance to secure steady burning.

He proved a match for the entire tribe of armed savages by simply striking a match.

1. **mate:** friend; companion; assistant, hence, in the Merchant Navy, the first officer after the master mariner.
2. MATE: a move in the game of chess (q.v.); to render helpless,.
3. MATE: to pair (q.v.) animals or birds for breeding; to marry.
4. MATÉ: South American tea (q.v.) leaves (q.v.) of the shrub *Ilex paraguayensis*; a drink brewed from the leaves.

When I was in Paraguay my mate took to maté, and took to mate a native woman and I could not checkmate the affair.

maul, see **mahal.**

1. **maw:** the last of a ruminant beast's four stomachs, hence, figuratively, to be deeply involved; to be in some other person's power.
2. MORE: an addition; to be greater in number or extent; further; longer; again.
3. MOOR: a tract of heath land; uncultivated and unenclosed upland areas.
4. MOOR: to make a ship fast; to tie up to a buoy (q.v.) or a post (q.v.); to anchor (q.v.).
5. MOOR: one of the Berber Arabs who invaded, and occupied, the Iberian Peninsula, hence, any Arab.

I have ridden across the moor to warn you not to trust that Moor any more: his advice has caused you to moor your cutter in a dangerous channel: he seems to have got you in his maw.

mawle, see **mahal.**

1. **May:** the fifth month of the Christian year, between April and June.
2. MAY: a name for the hawthorn tree and particularly its blossom, *Crataegus oxyacantha.*
3. MAY: a term of permission or sanction.
4. MAY: a term expressive of doubt in connection with an event, or a person's ability or willingness.
5. MAY: a feminine personal name

If May-blossom appears early, May may be a hot month: if it

is I may go camping; father says I may, but my sister May says I may catch cold.

Maya } see **mare.**
Mayor }

Mays } see **maize.**
maze }

1. **mead:** meadow; pasture.
2. MEAD: an intoxicating beverage, produced from fermented honey.
3. MEED: a merited portion of praise.

The Industrial Revoultion put the mill on the mead, mead on the luxury list, and made agitators candidates for a generous meed.

1. **meak:** an agricultural implement, used for cutting bracken, or pulling peas.
2. MEEK: submissive; tame; gentle; not prone to complaining.

Jack's meek, give him the meak, I'm taking the tractor.

1. **meal:** a conventionally set and timed repast; nourishing food.
2. MEAL: any edible grain (q.v.) reduced to powder.

One can make a meal of oatmeal.

1. **mean:** to have specific reference; to indicate sense; to intend; to aim at.
2. MEAN: midway; equidistant from each of two points; average.
3. MEAN: ungenerous; of poor type or quality; contemptible.
4. MEAN: (Am.) a violent, unstable, or otherwise dangerous character.
5. MIEN: bearing, manner.

When I say my uncle is mean. I mean he lives in a mean street and is too mean to have milk delivered: I mean to provide for him in his dotage, but in the meantime he is a menace: however, his mien is that of a gentleman.

1. **mear:** rare alternative spelling of No. 3 below.
2. MERE: a swamp or marsh; a mountain pool; an arm of the sea (q.v.).
3. MERE: a landmark or boundary.
4. MERE: inconsiderable; not more in either quantity or quality than is stated.

He claims a mere mere as a mear and calls it a lake.

1. **meat:** food in general; the edible pulp of fruit; the edible part of shellfish; the flesh of animals.
2. MEET: to come face to face with; enter the presence of; to congregate.
3. MEET: fitting; proper.
4. METE: to measure, generally of rewards and punishments.

It is not meet that Parliament may meet for the members to take meat together, then mete out a heavier burden of taxation.

1. **medal:** a disc of metal, moulded and inscribed, suspended from a ribbon, and bestowed in distinction.
2. MEDDLE: to interfere; to act the busybody.

Were it but brave to meddle, that woman would qualify for the gold medal.

meddle, see preceding group.

1. **meddler:** one who meddles (q.v.); one who interferes; a busybody.
2. MEDLAR: the fruit of the medlar tree, *Mespilus germanica*, edible only when decayed.

She, being an inveterate meddler, mistaking the medlar for a russet apple, said it might be eaten, though it was not yet decayed.

medlar, see preceding group.

meed, see mead.

meek, see meak.

meet, see meat.

melody, see malady.

1. **melt:** to liquefy as temperature rises; to soften; to dissolve; to be softened by compassion.
2. MELT: the spleen, used largely for animal food.
3. MILT: alternative spelling of No. 2 above.

The way the cat tucks into stewed melt suggests that it must melt in his mouth.

1. **memorize:** to commit to memory.
2. MESMERIZE: to put a person in a hypnotic trance.

Mesmerize the man and make him memorize the code.

men's, see manse.

1. **mensal:** pertaining to the table (q.v.); used at table; land set aside by the Irish Roman Catholic Church for the maintenance of the table.
2. MENSAL: monthly.

I hate to hear the squire, at his mensal dinners, bid his guests draw up the mensal chairs.

mense, see manse.

mere, see mear.

merry, see marry.

mesmerize, see memorize.

1. **mess:** a company of persons who take meals together.
2. MESS: untidiness; litter; confusion; disorder.

He has got the mess accounts into a mess.

1. **message:** a communication, either oral or written, from one person to another.
2. MESSUAGE (mes we): a house, its appurtenances, and land surrounding.

If you decide to buy the messuage, send a message before twelve o'clock.

messuage, see preceding group.

1. **metal:** any member of a group of elements having certain common characteristics, such as high specific gravity, fusibility, high electrical conductivity, affinity for oxygen (with exceptions) and the ability to dissolve in acid (with exceptions) forming salts.
2. METTLE: temperament; vigour; courage; high spirits.

Here's a chance to show your mettle, carry that sackful of scrap-metal upstairs.

mete, see meat.

1. **meteor:** a nodule of matter free in space, attracted earthward, and made visible by contact with the atmosphere; a shooting star.
2. METER: an instrument for measuring and recording the passage of a fluid (gas, water or electricity) through it.
3. METIER: occupation; speciality.
4. METRE: rhythm in poetry.
5. METRE: the unit of linear measurement used in the decimal system; one ten-millionth part of a quarter of a meridian circle; 39·37 inches.

My metier is to read poetry aloud, and emphasize the metre,

yet I live by putting a metre of adhesive tape in a packet labelled 'Repair your own gas-meter', and these household novelties blaze through the trade like a meteor.

meter ⎫
metier ⎬ see preceding group.
metre ⎭

mettle, see metal.

1. **meuse:** a gap in a hedge used by hares (q.v.) and other small animals, particularly as a means of escape when hunted, hence, a loop-hole, or a means of escape.

2. MEWS: originally a house for hawks; later, stables disposed round a yard (q.v.) or on each side of a paved track; now, such stables converted into dwelling houses.

3. MUSE: one of the nine Greek goddesses who inspire learning, art and poetry.

4. MUSE: to be absorbed in thought; to ponder; to concentrate the mind.

He bought a mews-flat for £10,000, saying it was his meuse from the City; there he could sit and muse, and even seek the Muse.

1. **mew:** representative of the normal cry of a cat.

2. MEW: to moult, or cast (q.v.) horns.

3. MEW: a bird-cage.

4. MEW: a sea-bird, seamew or gull (q.v.).

The cat would mew, and rub her head affectionately against the seamew with a broken wing.

1. **mewl:** to weep as an infant; to whine (q.v.).

2. MULE: the offspring of a male ass and a female horse, extended to include offspring of a stallion and a female ass, and further (q.v.) extended to include any hybrid.

That child, as obstinate as a mule, will mewl all day.

mews, see meuse.

mien, see mean.

1. **might:** strength; power; ability to impose one's will.

2. MIGHT: pst tns of 'may' (q.v.).

3. MITE: a small maggot, particularly the cheese-mite, *Tyroglyphus domesticus*.

4. MITE: a coin of very low (q.v.) value; a weight equal to one twentieth of a grain troy; any small thing.

Now he demonstrates his might, but he might yet remember the days when he was about as important as a cheese-mite, and often cadged a mite from me.

milt, see melt.

1. **mina:** a unit of weight used in ancient Greece (q.v.).

2. MINA: any bird of the starling family found in south-east Asia, *Eulabes religiosa*, and *Acridotheres tristis*.

3. MINER: one who works in a mine (q.v.).

4. MINOR: a person who is under 21 years of age; an object, or a circumstance, of little importance; the smaller of two objects, or the younger of two people.

Is it a matter of minor importance if a minor, whose parents plan to make him a doctor, declares his intention of being a miner?

1. **mince:** to cut into small pieces, particularly meat (q.v.); to speak with affected elegance of pronunciation; to walk in an affected manner.

2. MINTS: plural of 'mint' (q.v.) generally applied to confectionery, and patent medicine flavoured with mint.

If mince gives you indigestion, suck Dr. Belcher's Mints.

1. **mind:** the faculty of thinking, reasoning and remembering.

2. MIND: to exercise caution; to beware of.

3. MIND!: an admonitory, or a cautionary ejaculation.

4. MIND: to take care of an object; to remain conscious of; to keep in active thought.

5. MIND: object (q.v.); to offer opposition; to enquire whether another person does, or will, object.

6. MINED: of any substance brought up from a mine (q.v.); of land that has been reduced in agrarian value by mining operations in the vicinity; an area of either sea or land, or a building that is either menaced or protected by an infernal machine charged with explosives.

I do not mind accepting the mission though the place is mined: I'll mind how I go, and do you mind if I ask you to mind my watch? Mind! do not scratch it, the gold, which was mined in Wales, is very soft. If I return it will be a victory of mind over matter.

1. **mine:** a series of shafts and tunnels in the earth out of which metals, and other products, are excavated.

2. MINE: an explosive infernal machine concealed beneath the surface of either land or sea, or placed in buildings.

3. MINE: belonging to me.
   Lay off! That mine is mine, and I have concealed a mine in every entrance.

mined, see **mind.**

miner, see **mina.**

1. **minister:** to serve, or attend upon; to render aid to one, or to those, in need; to supply; to suggest or prompt.

2. MINISTER: an officer of State, being a member of the Cabinet, and the supreme head of a department; a clergyman, and particularly a nonconformist, or a non-Christian, having the power of conducting Services; one having authority in religious affairs.

3. MINSTER: a church attached to a monastery; now, a Collegiate, or Cathedral church; any large church.
   As a boy he sang in the choir at the Minster, and though it was noticed how he was apt to minister to the needy, none who then knew him would have believed that forty years on he would be Her Majesty's Minister of National Assistance.

1. **ministral:** pertaining to the function, office or duty of a Minister (q.v.).

2. MINSTREL: in the Middle Ages a poet and musician who composed, and chanted to his own musical accompaniment, lyric, romantic and heroic poetry; any poet, vocalist or musician; a member of a team of entertainers who, with blackened faces, sing, play the banjo and crack pseudo-American Negro jokes.
   He fills, with dignity and efficiency, the ministral office; yet his pre-Parliamentary occupation was that of a Corner-man in a Nigger-minstrel troupe.

minor, see **mina.**

Minster, see **minister.**

minstrel, see **ministral.**

1. **mint:** coin; a place where metal is converted into coinage; the machinery for manufacturing coinage; to make coin; a very large sum of money.

2. MINT: of an antique book in perfect condition.

3. MINT: an aromatic plant of the genus *Mentha.*
   He said the book was mint and he charged me the mint; nevertheless, a piece of mint was pressed between the pages.

mints, see **mince.**

1. **minuet:** a dance, and music of a character appropriate to accompany such a dance.

2. MINUTE (min'et): the sixtieth part of an hour; a record of the decision reached by a committee.

3. MINUTE (my'nute): very small.
   Minute the decision that the minuet, being minute, may be extended by a minute and a half.

minute, see preceding group.

mirage, see **marriage.**

mire, see **mare.**

1. **Miss:** a contracted form of Mistress, now specialized as the title of an unmarried woman.

2. MISS: to fail to reach, or strike, or catch; to be conscious of a lack or a loss.
   Miss Hounder will miss the last bus, and then she will miss her car.

1. **Missal:** a book of prayer used in the service of the Mass (q.v.).

2. MISSEL: the mistletoe, a parasite plant growing on apple- and on oak-trees, *Viscum album*; the name of a thrush, *Turdus viscivorus*, that feeds on mistletoe berries.

3. MISSILE: that which is thrown either by hand or power.

She gazed at her Missal, illuminated by a miniature of a missel-thrush feeding on a sprig of missel, and she grieved to think of the innocent creatures killed by a missile from the catapult of a wanton boy.

1. missed: noted absence of a thing or a person; failure to catch, or strike, or reach; failure to follow a route (q.v.).

2. MIST: vapour in a state of suspension in the atmosphere, hence, all weather (q.v.) conditions varying between fog and very light rain (q.v.).

In the mist he missed the way.

missel } see **Missal.**
missile }

mite, see might.

1. mitre: the head-dress of a Bishop.

2. MITRE: a carpenter's joint in which the faces in apposition bisect the angle made by the parts.

The Bishop refused to pay the carpenter for the mitre-case because he did not mitre the joints.

1. moan: a weak (q.v.) groan (q.v.); an expression of anguish; to complain.

2. MOWN: pst ppl of 'mow' (q.v.).

The harvest is mown and the farmers moan.

1. moat: a deep and wide water-filled trench surrounding a fortified position.

2. MOTE: a minute (q.v.) piece of matter; a particle of dust.

A mote fell into the seneschal's eye, and he fell into the moat.

1. mode: a tune, or air (q.v.); a measure of music.

2. MODE: the style or fashion for the time being.

3. MOWED: pst tns of 'mow' (q.v.).

He whistled a syncopated mode in the mode of the period as he mowed the lawn.

1. modest: not boastful; not ostentatious; not expensive or extravagant; within reasonable limits.

2. MODISTE: a dressmaker, particularly a fashionable, expensive dressmaker.

'But mam'selle is too modest!' cried the modiste, hopefully.

modiste, see preceding group.

1. moil: toil; drudgery; unpleasant labour.

2. MOIL: to wade (q.v.) through mud.

3. MOILE: a mule (q.v.).

4. MOYL: alternative spelling of No. 3 above.

The farm-labourer must toil and moil like a moile, then moil homeward.

moile, see preceding group.

1. mola: a pathogenetic mass formed in the womb in some cases of pseudo-pregnancy.

2. MOLAR: a large back tooth that has a grinding action.

The section of mola under microscopic examination revealed a proto-molar.

molar, see preceding group.

1. mold: fertile surface soil.

2. MOULD: a hollow receptacle shaped for the purpose of forming a casting; to make, or shape, or fashion.

3. MOULD: microscopic fungus that grows on appropriate media under suitable conditions, in the form of clusters.

4. MOULD: alternative spelling of No. 1 above.

A circular mould is used to mould cakes of mold on which experimental mould is grown.

1. mole: a raised pigmented area on the human skin.

2. MOLE: a burrowing small mammal, *Talpa curopaea.*

3. MOLE: a massive stone groyne (q.v.) extending into the sea and forming an artificial harbour (q.v.).

Strolling on the mole to display his new mole-skin jacket he unconsciously displayed more effectively through his open-neck shirt a disfiguring mole on his chest.

1. moment: a short, unspecified division of time.

2. MOMENT: a factor used in expressing comparative leverage, hence, a term used to indicate the weightiness, or the importance, of a matter.

Just a moment! You can't go yet—this is a matter of moment.

moor, see **maw.**

1. **Moorish:** pertaining to the Arab invaders of Spain.
2. MOREISH (sl): pleasant; attractive; of a nature to cause one to desire further quantities, particularly of food and drink.

Moorish wine is moreish.

1. **moose:** an animal of the genus *Cervinus*; the North American elk.
2. MOUSE: small rodent of the genus *Mus*; the domestic mouse, *Mus musculus*; the field mouse, *Mus sylvaticus*.
3. MOUSSE: a sweet made of cream.

Whether a mouse or a moose walks on a mousse it is of no further use.

1. **moot:** a committee, or other assembly, forming a court to hear and determine in local disputes; subject to doubt, or discussion.
2. MUTE: silent; without power of vocal expression; a professional attendant at funerals; to soften the sound of a musical instrument.
3. MUTE: the droppings of birds, particularly of hawks.

When the British Museum pigeons mute their target, visitors do not remain mute, and how to handle the situation is a moot point.

1. **moral:** right; correct behaviour; virtue; restraint in sexual relationship.
2. MORALE: cheerfulness in adversity; confidence; discipline; reliability.

British troops are famous for their excellent morale and they are excellently moral.

morale, see preceding group.

more, see **maw.**

moreish, see **Moorish.**

1. **morn:** dawn; sunrise; the morning.
2. MORNÉ: in heraldry, of a lion deprived of its armament.
3. MORNE: a tilting spear with a rebated point.
4. MOURN: to feel, and to express grief at someone's death.

She will mourn the death of her champion who, tilting this morn, died accidentally from the thrust

of a lance not morne. The wielder thereof suffered an armorial abatement in the form of his arms debruised by a lion rampant morne tenné.

morne, see preceding group.

1. **morning:** the early part of the day; the time between dawn and midday.
2. MOURNING: sorrowing; lamenting; black clothes symbolic of grief; flags flying at half-mast, and any other symbol of death.

Saturday morning 30 January 1965, saw the whole world mourning for Sir Winston Churchill K.G., 'the voice and inspiration of the Nation that saved the world'.

1. **Mosaic:** relating to Moses; the Corpus (q.v.) of Law laid down by, or attributed to, him.
2. MOSAIC: the art of creating pictures or patterns by cementing fragments of coloured material, particularly stone, in appropriate positions; the decorations thus created.

Along the corridor of the monastery the Mosaic Law was inlaid in mosaic.

1. **mot** (moh): a word, particularly a precise witty word to suit the occasion.
2. MOW: to cut down a harvest of hay, corn, or other produce; the harvest thus gathered in; to slaughter many in battle.
3. MOW: a grimace often made in derision.

Observe the mow these rustics make as our friend from the City, voluntarily helping with the mow, gives tongue to an occasional mot.

mote, see **moat.**

mould, see **mold.**

mourn, see **morn.**

mourning, see **morning.**

mouse ⎱ see **moose.**
mousse ⎰

mow, see **mot.**

mowed, see **mode.**

mown, see **moan.**

moyl, see **moil.**

1. **muff:** a term of contempt applied to

a German; a dull, stupid person; a person who is not good at games.

2. MUFF: a short, hollow cylinder, often provided with an internal screw thread, for joining pipes; a short, hollow cylinder of fur to protect the hands in cold weather; any covering used as a special protection from frost.

That muff of a driver did not put the muff on the radiator, and we are now marooned.

1. **Mufti:** a priest of Islam; Grand Mufti, head of the Turkish State Church.
2. MUFTI: civilian clothes worn (q.v.) by a soldier or a sailor instead of service uniform, hence non-professional garb.

The local Mufti in mufti went on a spree.

mule, see mewl.

1. **mull:** flour (q.v.); dust or ashes; anything pulverized.
2. MULL: in Scotland a headland.
3. MULL: a form of madder (q.v.).
4. MULL: to spoil; to fail in a task.
5. MULL: to make ale (q.v.) or wine (q.v.) hot and to add spices.

I asked you to mull the mull-madder, and, plain as the Mull of Kintire, you mull the job and expect me to give you permission to mull the ale.

1. **mullet:** a name applied to a fish of the genus *Mullus,* and to related fish.
2. MULLET: in heraldry a solid pentogram being a conventionalized representation of a spur rowel; the mark of cadency for a third son.
3. MULLET: a pair of tweezers.

On the birth of his third son the Lord of the Manor gave a feast of mullet to the villagers and displayed a shield of his arms differenced by a mullet.

mummy, see Mammy.

1. **muscle:** the tough ligatures between joints that enable animals to move; strength.
2. MUSSEL: an edible bivalve mollusc; those indigenous to salt water, of the family *Mytilacea;* those in fresh water, of the family *Unionacea.*

3. MUZZLE: that part of an animal's face that comprises the nose and mouth; the extreme end of a gun from which the bullet emerges; a nozzle; a strap or straps used to keep an animal's mouth shut.

You cannot muscle-in on the mussel trade: the local press wears a muzzle on matters affecting the longshoremen.

muse, see meuse.
mussel, see muscle.

1. **must:** compulsion; duty; that which cannot be avoided.
2. MUST: fruit juice in process of fermentation.
3. MUST: the cause of mustiness; mouldy; earthy-smelling.
4. MUSTH: a state of bad temper, dangerous violence, that sometimes breaks out in an elephant.

When the elephant was in a state of musth the keeper felt he must face the animal, and asked for a quart of must.

1. **mustard:** a condiment produced from the seed of the mustard plant, *Sinapis.*
2. MUSTERED: assembled.

When the servants were mustered the butler enquired who had spilled the mustard.

mustered, see preceding group.
musth, see must.
mute, see moot.
muzzle, see muscle.
Myer, see mare.

N

nag, see knag.

1. **nail:** the hard, horn-like protective formation on the extremities of the dorsal surfaces of fingers and toes; the hooves in ungulates, the claws in carnivora and in birds.
2. NAIL: a spike of metal, generally iron, made in numerous different sizes, the shapes varying for specific purposes, used for driving into wood, leather, or other material to hold, or to fix.

My thumb-nail will come off: I hit it while driving a nail in the fence.

nap, see knap.

nat, see gnat.

1. **Naval:** pertaining to the Royal Navy.

2. NAVEL: a circular fold, or convolution in the surface of the abdomen, being the scar of the umbilical cord, hence, the centre of a thing.

Naval rations may include navel oranges.

nave, see knave.

navel, see Naval.

1. **nay:** no; negative; an expression of dissent, objection or disapproval.

2. NEIGH: the vocal expression of a horse.

If you hear the horse neigh don't back it. That is nay straight from the horse's mouth.

1. **near:** close; in juxtaposition; related; miserly.

2. NE'ER: a contraction of 'never'.

It ne'er will do for them to wed, they are too near in blood.

1. **neat:** horned cattle; an ox, a bullock, cow or heifer.

2. NEAT: clean; tidy; refined; precise; clever; witty.

3. NEAT: undiluted.

It was a very neat trick to make him drink neat-foot oil in mistake for neat whisky.

need, see knead.

ne'er, see near.

neigh, see nay.

Nell, see knell.

1. **net:** a fabric, or skeleton fabric, created by continuous mesh woven either in yarn (q.v.) or in wire.

2. NETT: not subject to reduction; the maintained standard selling price.

You cannot get cheap net, it's nett.

new, see gnu.

night, see knight.

nit, see knit.

nock, see knock.

noes, see knows.

1. **none:** no one; not any.

2. NONE: the third quarter of the day.

3. NONES: a service conducted each day at the ninth hour.

4. NOON: twelve o'clock mid-day and twelve o'clock midnight, i.e. the noon of night.

5. NUN: a woman who has taken the veil; has vowed poverty, chastity and obedience and who lives the religious life in a convent.

The good nun said nones at noon and at none, and none joined with her.

nones ⎫
noon ⎬ see preceding group.

nor ⎫
Nore ⎬ see gnaw.

nose, see knows.

not, see knot.

1. **note:** a letter, or a communication in writing.

2. NOTE: a brief abstract; a guide to memory.

3. NOTE: auxiliary information, connected with, but not part of, the matter in a book.

4. NOTE: a musical sound.

5. NOTE: to take notice; pay attention.

I want you to note that I am sending a note to the author of this book to point out that his footnote on the note of the lark is at variance with Professor Plonk's idea, a note of which I took when attending his lecture.

O

1. **O:** fifteenth letter of the alphabet, between N and P; o; the fourth (q.v.) vowel; the tenth cipher of the Arabic system of number; zero; often pronounced 'aught' (q.v.).

2. O!: an exclamation used to express divers (q.v.) emotions, a form of supplication; an expression of pain.

3. O': an abbreviated form of both 'of' and 'on', as in 'o'clock'.

4. OH!: as No. 2 above.

5. OWE: to have the obligation of paying either money or service; indebtedness.

Oh! I owe you a penny.

oar, see awe.

1. **oast:** a kiln, particularly one used for drying hops.

2. OUST: to eject, or deprive.

Should they oust me from my cottage I plan to take up residence in the disused oast, and so set them a problem.

object, see abject.

oblation, see ablation.

occur, see accur.

1. **ode:** a dignified rhymed poem usually in the form of an address.

2. OWED: that which is to be paid, either money or service; the subject of a debt.

> The poet who owed to the grocer £5, wrote, 'Ode to the Grocer'.

o'er, see awe.

1. **often** (awfen): many times; frequently; again and again; of common occurrence.

2. ORPHAN: one who is deprived of a parent, or parents, by death; a child left without father (q.v.) or mother, or both.

> The orphan often laughs.

-ology, see allergy.

1. **one:** a unit; a group taken as a unit; a person, oneself.

2. WON: to have achieved an object; to have succeeded; to have gained first place when in competition; to have conquered.

> He won one prize.

Ophelia, see aphelia.

opposite, see apposite.

opposition, see apposition.

or, see awe.

oral, see aural.

orc, see awk.

1. **Order:** an exclusive group; a decoration of honour.

2. ORDER: sequence; neatness; correctness.

3. ORDER: a command; a request for goods to be supplied.

4. ORDURE: anything foul (q.v.) or offensive; obscene language.

> He received the Order of the British Empire which was out of order, for his contemporaries knew he was of that order of people who mutter ordure under the breath upon receipt of an order.

1. **ordinance:** arrangement in rows (q.v.); the placing of things or matters in order (q.v.); commands, or orders; ceremonial usage.

2. ORDNANCE: artillery; big guns; any machine for propelling missiles (q.v.).

3. ORDONNANCE: system in art; the arrangement of details for a picture, or a building, or a literary work.

> The ordonnance for the Military Field Day was studied carefully, and the Colonel sent a secret ordinance to the Officer Commanding our ordnance.

ordnance } see preceding group.
ordonnance }

ore, see awe.

1. **organ:** any part of an animal, or of a vegetable body that is endowed with a special function.

2. ORGAN: a musical instrument of major proportions and importance, actuated by wind passing in pipes of varying lengths.

3. ORGAN: a newspaper, or other periodical, representing a party.

> His organ of digestion was upset for a week through reading the organ of the Radicalists on Saturday, and missing the Organ Voluntary on Sunday.

oriole, see aureole.

ork, see awk.

orle, see all.

orphan, see often.

ort, see aught.

Oscar, see asker.

ottar }
otter } see atar.
otto }

ought, see aught.

1. **ounce:** a standard of weight (q.v.); one sixteenth part of a pound (q.v.) avoirdupois; one twelfth of a pound Troy; expressive of a small quantity of anything.

2. OUNCE: a great cat; the cheetah, puma or cougar; the snow-leopard; the mountain panther; *Felis uncia.*

> If you had an ounce of brains, you'd keep well away from the ounce, and hunt rabbits in safety.

owed, see ode.

owl, see all.

P

1. **P:** the sixteenth letter of the alphabet, between O and Q; p.

2. PEA: the edible seed of the climbing plant, *Pistum sativum*.

3. PEE: phonetic spelling of the letter 'p', No. 1 above, being a euphemistic abbreviation of 'piss', which word is considered to be vulgar.

When the medical student's mother asked him what the yellow powder in the test-tube marked 'P' was, he replied cryptically, 'Dried P'.

1. paced: measured by counting footsteps; the act of taking slow and deliberate footsteps; pst tns of 'pace', to step; controlled in speed.

2. PASTE: a mixture of flour and water, with fat (q.v.); dough (q.v.); a mixture of flour and water, or of other materials used for joining paper etc.; imitation jewellery.

He paced meditatively up and down, concerned with the fact that the Duchess's diamonds, on which he'd lent the money, were but paste.

1. packed: goods secured in a wrapper, or a box, for protection, particularly during transport; filled; crowded.

2. PACT: an agreement, particularly one between nations, or factions, relating to peace between them.

While the two gang leaders sat making a pact, the street was packed with armed thugs.

1. packet: a small parcel.

2. PACKET: a ship plying regularly between two ports, specifically for the purpose of carrying the mail (q.v.).

3. POCKET: a bag provided as part of one's clothing; a bag-like natural cavity in rock, particularly when containing a deposit of mineral.

We must not be suspected of having found the pocket of diamonds: we can send a small packet home each week on the packet, and so gradually fill our pocket.

1. packs: the action of making a packet or parcel.

2. PAX: peace; a representation of the crucifixion kissed by the priest and the congregation at Mass (q.v.).

Dominic packs well; give him the pax to post.

pact, see packed.

1. pad: a mattress; a soft buffer (q.v.) between, for example, a pack-horse's back and the pack-saddle; a bed; a number of sheets of paper fixed at the edge so that one sheet after another may be used.

2. PAD: a paw; particularly of a tiger, wolf or other wild animal; the imprint of a wild animal's paw.

3. PAD: a tool-handle having an adjustment screw to take several kinds of bit (q.v.).

4. PAD: the floating leaf of an aqueous plant.

5. PAD: to tramp heavily along.

6. PAD: the sound of footsteps.

7. PAD: a gentle horse.

8. PAD: a dialect name for both a toad (q.v.) and a starfish. .

9. PAD: a basket, constructed from osiers; a measure of fish.

10. PAD: a path, track or road, hence a robber on the highway.

11. PAD: to fill out, or to cover, with a resilient material; to increase the length of a literary work by the interpolation of unnecessary material.

12. PUD: a childish form of No. 2 above.

Sitting in his Bloomsbury basement chamber, listening to the pad of footsteps on the pavement above, he tore the last sheet he had written from the pad and, realizing that he'd have to pad very considerably, recommenced work: in the morning he'd pad down to Fleet Street with it, and, with luck, pad his pocket, so what matter if he worked all night—the pud of the wolf was clearly marked at the door.

1. page: originally an attendant upon a knight, later, a male servant, hence, an office at Court; in modern usage, the boy employed at an hotel to run errands, and perform minor services for guests; to send a page-boy through the public rooms of an hotel calling for a person who is wanted.

2. PAGE: one side of a written or printed sheet; to arrange type and

pictorial matter in the form of a page.

Send that idle page to page the editor, we must page-up and go to press immediately.

1. **pail:** a vessel built up from wooden staves, or sewn together from leather, or rolled, riveted and galvanized in sheet metal, or moulded in plastic, usually the shape of a truncated cone open at the wide end and provided with a bow-handle, for carrying water or other liquid.

2. PALE: an upright stave; one unit of a fence (q.v.).

3. PALE: blanched; lacking in colour.

4. PALE: in heraldry, an upright ordinary, central of the shield.

The sign of a pail inverted on top of a pale caused him to turn pale.

1. **pain:** hurtfulness; distress; soreness; the opposite to pleasure; punishment; suffering; penalty.

2. PAIN: extreme care, and great patience expended in performing a task.

3. PANE: a panel; one section of the panelling lining a room; one side of a quadrangle; one side of any object having several sides; one section of cloth in a garment; a rectangular piece of land; one section out of a number of rectangular sections; a panel of glass set in a window; that part of a hammer-head extending in the opposite direction to the face (q.v.).

You can expect pain when father sees you've broken another pane in the greenhouse.

1. **pair:** two objects of a kind.

2. PARE: to cut away skin, or other outer surface.

3. PAYER: one who pays.

4. PEAR: fruit of trees of the genus *Pyrus.*

Give me a knife to pare this pear; a pair of scissors will not do.

1. **pal** (sl): a friend.

2. PALL: a vestment; a rich cloth; a cover for a coffin.

3. PALL: to make apathetic; to destroy the relish in, or appetite for; to surfeit, or sicken.

4. PAUL: a masculine personal name.

5. PAWL: a bar, hinged at one end, made to engage in a capstan, or a rachet, so as to prevent unwinding.

My pal Paul said that reversing the pawl would pall upon him, would put him under a pall, so he did not take part in the fire-escape pitching contest.

1. **pala:** the impala, a red African antelope distinguished by large black lyrate antlers; *Alpyceros melampus.*

2. PALAR: in heraldry, descriptive of a line from centre-chief to base-point, dividing a shield into two halves; descriptive of the orientation of any charge, or group of charges, occupying the central, upright, position.

3. PALEA: scales enclosing the stamens and pistil (q.v.) in the flower of grass; scales on the stems of some ferns; the wattles of a fowl (q.v.); of the nature of chaff.

4. PALER: a comparative term, to be more blanched, or pale, than another; to have less, or weaker colour than another.

5. PALLA: alternative spelling of No. 1 above.

6. PALLA: an outer garment, mantle or wrap, worn by Roman ladies.

7. PALLOR: to have, or to be in a state of paleness.

He was pallid when he entered the witness-box and his pallor increased when the judge demanded that the Coat of Arms, being exhibit number one, should be shown to him: upon his observing, to the sinister of the palar line, a pala head caboshed, sable, he turned even paler.

1. **palace:** the Palatine, one of the seven (q.v.) hills of Rome, the site (q.v.) of the home of the Caesars, hence, the official residence of a king or other royal ruler; extended to include any superior dwelling, and also a house of entertainment.

2. PALLAS: the Greek goddess, patroness of Athens, and goddess of wisdom.

In our travels we were shown the palace of Pallas.

palar, see **pala.**

1. **palate:** the roof of the mouth, hence, taste, or preference for certain foods.

2. PALETTE: a board, tile, or other surface on which an artist mixes colours; the combination of colours used in a particular picture.

3. PALLET: a bed of straw; any non-luxurious bed.

4. PALLET: the part in a watch (q.v.) or clock that engages with the teeth of the escapement wheel; any similar mechanism.

5. PALLET: in heraldry, a sub-ordinary, half the width of a pale (q.v.).

    The artist flung himself down on his humble pallet, satisfied with the unique palette he had employed in his latest masterpiece, but it did not appeal to the palate of his patron.

pale, see **pail.**

palea⎱ see **pala.**
paler⎰

palette, see **palate.**

pall, see **pal.**

palla, see **pala.**

Pallas, see **palace.**

pallet, see **palate.**

pallor, see **pala.**

1. **palm:** a tropical tree of the order *Palmae*; any non-tropical tree, as the willow, used in celebrating Palm Sunday.

2. **PALM:** the inner surface of the hand from wrist to fingers; to conceal in the palm of the hand, hence, to cheat.

    Keep a sixpenny piece conspicuous in the palm of your hand, and they will not palm you off with willow in place of the genuine palm.

1. **paltry:** insignificant; trifling; petty; contemptible.

2. **POULTRY:** domestic, edible birds; birds raised for food.

    I thought it very paltry when he banned poultry to the servants.

1. **pampa:** the treeless plains (q.v.) south of the River Amazon.

2. **PAMPER:** to indulge, to spoil, to make a mollycoddle.

In his study of the people of the pampa he indicates that mothers do not pamper their children.

pamper, see preceding group.

1. **Pan:** the ancient Greek goat-god.

2. PAN: a flat, open vessel used for cooking; a skillet; any vessel employed in a process involving the application of heat, particularly for evaporation.

3. PAN: betel-leaf, areca-nut and lime used as a masticatory.

4. PAN: to prospect for gold by washing river gravel.

5. PAN: to eventuate, to fit, to coincide.

6. PAN-: a prefix indicating exclusiveness, all.

7. PANNE: a kind of velvet.

    The pan - British population scheme did not pan out: you now see the streets stained red with expectorated pan, Chinamen pan gold on the river and Greeks, each the living image of Pan, sit by their market stalls, frying in a pan, a mixture reeking with onions, while rich American ladies, clad in panne-velvet gowns, leisurely parade the boulevards.

1. **panda:** a small tree-bear, or bear-cat, native of the South-Eastern Himalayas, *Aelurus fulgens.*

2. PANDER: a procurer; one who serves in bringing about clandestine sexual relationships, hence, to offer compliments, and act in a servile manner in order to attain an end.

    If we wish to secure a red panda for the zoo, we will have to pander to the local Grand Himitiman.

pander, see preceding group.

pane, see **pain.**

panne, see **Pan.**

1. **pants:** to be engaged in taking involuntary, short, rapid breaths.

2. PANTS: abbreviated form of 'pantaloon', masculine nether undergarment.

3. PANTS (Am.): trousers.

4. PANTS (Am. sl.): the buttocks.

    The American visitor still pants for breath having been giving the English valet a verbal kick in the pants for ironing his drawers when asked to press his pants.

1. **par:** pertaining to equality.
2. PARR: a young black codfish; a young salmon.
3. PAS: the right of taking precedence; a dance.

In the ballroom his execution of the pas is above par, but on the river his execution of parr makes him unpopular.

1. **parable:** an allegory; an example; an inference; a fiction to point a moral.
2. PARABLE: easily obtainable.

The Magistrate dismissed the case, but not without reciting the parable of the parable perquisites.

1. **parade:** a number of soldiers formed up for routine inspection; for drill, or for any other purpose; a march-past; a military display; of civilians, to promenade ostentatiously; a description of a street, road, square or row (q.v.) of houses or shops.
2. PRAYED: pst tns of 'pray' (q.v.).
3. PREYED: pst tns of 'prey' (q.v.).

The shopkeepers on Marine Parade, with an eye to business, prayed that the Ceremonial Parade would be held again, for they had always preyed upon the crowds of sightseers.

pare, see **pair.**

1. **Paris:** capital of France, on the river Seine between Seine-Oise and the Seine-Marne confluences.
2. PARIS: son of Priam King of Troy, who abducted Helen, and brought destruction to the city.
3. PARIS: surname of Matthew Paris, (–1259), monk of St. Albans, Chronicler of England, herald-painter of outstanding merit.
4. PARIS: surname of Bruno Paulin Gaston Paris (1839–1903), French scholar, Professor of Medieval French Literature at the Collège de France.
5. PARISH: an ecclesiastical division of territory, under the spiritual guidance of a Vicar or a Rector, having a church where Registers of Birth, Marriage and Death were (or

ought to have been) kept; a secular territory under the jurisdiction of the Guardians of the Poor (who no longer function); a civil parish.

6. PARISH: surname of Sir Woodbine Parish (1796–1882), diplomat, Chargé d'Affairs at Buenos Aires, 1825–1832.
7. PERISH: to be killed; to die; to disintegrate; to suffer destruction; to come to an untimely, or an unexpected end; to die without hope of hereafter.

When the parson spends weekends in Paris and neglects the parish Religion will perish.

parish, see preceding group.

1. **park:** the land, often largely woodland, surrounding a country house; a tract of land preserved in a built-up area, and ornamentally cultivated for the use and recreation of the public.
2. PARK: space reserved in a military encampment for artillery, and stores, hence, space in towns where vehicles may be left standing.
3. PARK: surname of Mungo Park (1771–1806), explorer of the River Niger.

The 'spouters' in Hyde Park are now protesting against the suggested establishment there of a public car-park.

1. **parky:** intensely cold weather (q.v.).
2. PARQUET: geometrical design in wood inlay.

It's too parky to polish the parquet.

parquet, see preceding group.

parr, see **par.**

1. **parse:** to make an analysis of a sentence, describing the words as parts of speech, their inflections, tense (q.v.) etc.
2. PASS: to move forward; to proceed; to refrain from stopping; a way through; a journey; a metamorphosis; a change of state or condition; a document giving authority to travel; to succeed in an examination.

Parse the sentence, pass the test, show your pass as you pass out of the hall, and pass rapidly back to school.

1. **parson:** a vicar or a rector; any clergyman; a Nonconformist pastor.
2. PERSON: a human being; inflection of words to conform with pronouns, 1st p. the person speaking; 2nd p. the person spoken to; 3rd p. the person spoken of; any one of the spiritual conceptions making the Holy Trinity.
   Our parson is a curious person.
1. **partition:** a more or less flimsy erection parting a room; the act of dividing into parts; separation of one part of a country from another; lines dividing the armorial shield; the separation of real estate out of joint ownership into individual holdings.
2. PETITION: a formal asking for favour, hearing, redress, etc, submitted to a person, or a body corporate, having power or jurisdiction; a supplication; a prayer.
   The Protestants will petition for partition.

pas, see par.
pass, see parse.

1. **passed:** having proceeded in space from one end, or from one side, to another; having proceeded in time from earlier to later; having succeeded to qualify in an examination.
2. PAST: belonging to former time; referred to a former ability; of behaviour at a prior period; gone by in time; above, or exceeding.
   As he passed by, one could see that he was past his prime, and to think that in the past no one passed an exam without his aid.

past, see preceding group.
paste, see paced.

1. **Pasteur:** surname of Louis Pasteur (1822–1895), French bacteriologist and discoverer of a method of sterilization.
2. PASTOR: a minister of religion.
3. PASTURE: grassland; meadow; grazing ground for cattle.
   The Pastor took the Sunday School up on the open, sunny pasture, and later told the children the story of the life of Pasteur.

Pastor ⎱ see preceding group.
pasture ⎰

1. **paten:** the dish on which the bread rests at the celebration of Eucharist.
2. PATTEN: an overshoe with projections on the sole (q.v.) used to keep the feet out of the mire.
3. PATTERN: an example; an object to be used as copy for the manufacture of similar objects; a shape against which material is to be cut; a dummy (q.v.) in wood on which a founder makes a sand-mould for casting in metal.
4. PATTERN: a design, or a decorative motif.
   The pattern was plain, but when the silversmith had cast the paten he engraved the rim with a pattern based on a conventionalized patern because it was for St Margaret Pattens Church.
1. **patience:** the ability to wait without suffering distress or becoming irritable; to endure without complaint; to perform minute and monotonous tasks; to suffer fools gladly.
2. PATIENTS: people in various states of ill-health under the care of a doctor, or undergoing treatment by a dentist.
   All the patients in the ward appreciated the patience of the nursing staff.

patients, see preceding group.

1. **patrol:** visiting rounds in camp, barracks or a garrison to check (q.v.) disorder; traversing a beat (q.v.) by civil police; a detachment of troops, or of police, engaged on a reconnoitre.
2. PETRAL: pertaining to rock; ossification; fossilization.
3. PETREL: any sea-bird of the order *Procellarii formes,* particularly stormy petrel.
4. PETROL: spirit of petroleum, separated from crude mineral oil by fractional distillation. It has a low flash-point and its chief use is as fuel for internal-combustion engines.
   His brains are so petral that when I mentioned the stormy

petrel he asked if I wanted somewhere to store my petrol, yet, in the army, he was a brilliant Officer of Patrol.

patten } see **paten.**
pattern }

Paul, see **pal.**

1. **pause:** hesitation; brief stoppage of activity.
2. PAWS: pl (') of 'paw' (q.v.).
3. PORES: pl of 'pore' (q.v.).

Pause before teasing that cat, for if he reveals to you the secret contents of his paws your pores will be working overtime.

1. **paw:** the foot of any animal having claws.
2. PAW: obscene; indecent; dirty; a term of disparagement, in which setting it is generally doubled.
3. POOR: pitiable, ill-supplied; lacking wealth or substance.
4. PORE: a minute aperture in the skin through which perspiration is exuded; to concentrate attention.
5. POUR: to cause the flow of a liquid from one vessel to another; a heavy descent of liquid, as a cascade, or excessive fall of rain.

The poor scholar will pore over his books till he sweats at every pore; his lecture on the anatomy of the paw was most enlightening, and thus will he pour out his knowledge free to all and remain poor.

1. **pawk:** trickery; cunning; slyness.
2. PORK: meat (q.v.) of the pig.

It took some pawk to take some pork.

pawl, see **pal.**
paws, see **pause.**
pax, see **packs.**
payer, see **pair.**
pea, see **P.**

1. **peace:** the period free from fighting between one war and the next; freedom from quarrels between one person and another; a state of inner calmness.
2. PEAS: pl of 'pea' (q.v.).
3. PIECE: a section or part of a whole; a selected and defined portion, particularly of land; a unit from a group constituting a whole.

There was no peace till each boy

had another piece of cake and an extra piece of sugar.

1. **peach:** the sweet, pulpy stoned fruit of the tree *Amygdalus persica.*
2. PEACH: to accuse; to inform against; to divulge; impeach, hence (sl) an informer, a detective (in which usage it is often mispronounced 'preach').
3. PEACH (sl): anything sweet, pleasing or satisfactory; a girl.

He got himself a peach of a girl, he did! He snatched a peach for her as they passed the fruit shop, and when the shopkeeper came after them she turned peach.

1. **peak:** the summit of a mountain; the top of a pointed hill; the highest point reached or reachable.
2. PEAK: to dwindle; to diminish; to become increasingly flaccid.
3. PEEK: look; peep; pry; observe.
4. PIQUE: to offend; to wound a person's pride; to stimulate a person to activity by disparaging his ability.
5. PIQUÉ: a hard, ribbed cotton cloth.

You take a peek while I pique him on his inability to scale the peak: he'll pull the peak of his piqué cap down over his eyes and peak and pine for an hour.

1. **peal:** a set of tuned bells; the ringing of changes on such a set of bells.
2. PEEL: the rind, skin, or outer covering of fruit, particularly of citrus fruits.

The peal they rang today was in celebration of the vicar's seventieth birthday, not, as was rumoured, because the local political agitator had slipped on a piece of orange peel and broken his neck.

pear, see **pair.**

1. **pearl:** a gem-stone formed within the shell of the oyster and other molluscs, being a concretion round some intrusive foreign body such as a grain of sand; to be of the yellowish-grey colour common to pearls; a ball of silver-gilt, usually one inch in diameter and set upon points on the upper rim of a coronet.

2. PURL: thread twisted with metal used in art-needlework; the looped threads along the edge of a braid (q.v.) or a ribbon; an inversion of plain knitted stitches.

3. PURL: a small, rapid, agitated stream.

4. PURL: a drink of hot beer with gin, sugar and spice.

The pearl-grey satin makes a fine argent field for the banner, but you will have to purl the edges; such braid as is required is not made; you've embroidered the pearl of the coronet very well, and I think a pint of purl will give you fresh courage: who knows, when the Grand Duke receives it, he may present you with a pearl necklace—or, perhaps, confer a title.

peas, see **peace.**

1. peck: a measure of capacity equal to two gallons.

2. PECK: the action of a bird in striking with its beak; to eat but little; to kiss hurriedly.

When I peck at my food I am off-colour, for normally I put away a peck.

1. peculiar: odd; strange; of a strong individual character; special; private; exclusive.

2. PECULIAR: a parish outside the jurisdiction of the Bishop of the diocese.

3. PIACULAR: sinful; wicked; any act calling for expiation or atonement.

When our vicar preached that cats, dogs and other animals have souls, we thought it peculiar, but the Bishop wrote saying it was piacular whereupon the Church Wardens reminded him that this parish is a Peculiar.

1. pedal: a lever worked by pressure of the foot.

2. PEDAL: pertaining to the foot; the foot of a mollusc.

3. PEDAL: the root end of a form of Italian straw used for plaiting; a plait (q.v.) of this straw.

4. PEDAL: to work a pedal, as the pedal keyboard of an organ, or the levers of a bicycle.

5. PEDDLE: to travel on foot from place to place and from door to door

offering goods for sale; to be engaged in selling.

We grew gaunt trying to peddle an improved bicycle pedal.

peddle, see **pedal.**

pee, see **P.**

peek, see **peak.**

peel, see **peal.**

1. peep: a small, shrill sound, as made by an infant bird.

2. PEEP: to look slyly; to look through a small opening; to make a first, unostentatious appearance.

At peep of dawn you hear the peep of the nestlings.

1. peer: an equal, either of persons or things; a fellow citizen; a member of the English nobility; a member of the House of Lords.

2. PEER: to stare; to look closely and searchingly.

3. PIER: a structure similar to a bridge extending from the shore (q.v.) into the sea (q.v.) used as a landing-stage by ship's passengers, and as a pleasure promenade by seaside visitors; one of the columns supporting an arch (q.v.); a solid mass of masonry sustaining pressure; a pier-glass, looking-glass or mirror.

The local press revealed that an impoverished Peer was employed by the Town Council to sweep up on the pier, and asked promenaders not to peer at him.

1. pelisse: a fur-lined outer garment; an enveloping garment for infants when out of doors.

2. POLICE: a body of men, trained, drilled and provided with uniform, whose duty is to assist the public in the maintenance of civic discipline and order, to detect crime, and to apprehend criminals, and perform similar services; any group of persons selected for oversight in private surroundings, as docks.

The local Police Force refer to the new regulation overcoat as a pelisse, it being hot, heavy, and far from waterproof.

1. pelt: the skin of a fur-bearing animal.

2. PELT: to attack by throwing stones or other missiles; to rain heavily.

He pegged the pelt in the sun to dry and had to pelt numerous rodents who came to eat it, and to add to his troulbes it began to pelt with sudden rain.

1. **pen:** a wing; a feather or quill, hence, a writing instrument that transfers ink.

2. PEN: a hill.

3. PEN: a female swan.

4. PEN: to enclose, or shut in; a small enclosure to confine an animal; an enclosure where a child can play freely without getting into danger, a play-pen.

5. PEN (Am. sl): a penitentiary.

Sitting in a sheep-pen on Mc Culloch pen he sketched with his pen a pen on the burn.

1. **pencil:** an artist's brush; a cylinder of graphite, or other marking material, contained in a wooden, or other, tube, for writing and drawing.

2. PENSIL: a small pennon flown from a lance.

3. PENSILE: hanging, drooping; built upon arches.

The artist, with a few strokes of his pencil, depicted the still heat of the day, and the trooper ambling past, his pensil pensile like every flag in the town.

1. **pendant:** an object that is hanging, particularly a jewel (q.v.) or other ornament worn at the neck or the wrist.

2. PENDANT: the word used in the Navy to describe a long, narrow, triangular flag the geometrical base of which is the hoist; a shape of pennant, or pennon.

3. PENDENT: to be hanging or suspended.

The ship in harbour was gay with bunting; the paying-off pendant floated on its bladders astern, but the captain and his officers were much concerned, for at the party last night the Duchess's diamond pendant, pendent from a platinum chain, had disappeared during the dance.

pendant, see preceding group.

1. **penis:** the male intromittent organ.

2. PINNACE: a man-o'-war's long boat, rowed by eight oars.

Jack, tell that Wrens Officer that her crew can have the pinnace 'sarternoon arter dinner: you're more edgercated nor what I am.

1. **perch:** a fresh-water fish, *Perca fluviatilis*.

2. PERCH: a measurement of 5½ yards used by surveyors; a twig or stick (q.v.) on which a bird rests, hence, facetiously, a chair.

Tom went fishing for perch but, with less than a perch of line unreeled, he sat sleeping while a sparrow used his rod for a perch.

pensil } see **pencil.**
pensile }

perish, see **Paris.**

person, see **parson.**

1. **pervade:** to pass through; to diffuse; to permeate; saturate, fill.

2. PURVEYED: pst tns of 'purvey', to provide; to plan beforehand; to estimate for supplies; to provide requirements; to cater; to make provision for another, or for others.

An awe-stricken silence seemed to pervade the air when I mentioned his name and revealed that he had purveyed the refreshments at the garden-party.

petition, see **partition.**

petral }
petrel } see **patrol.**
petrol }

1. **pettitoes:** pigs' trotters, particularly when prepared for food.

2. POTATOES: an edible tuber widely used for food.

Pettitoes and potatoes for supper.

phare, see **fair.**

phase, see **face.**

phial, see **file.**

philtre, see **filter.**

phiz, see **fizz.**

phlox, see **flocks.**

phonetic, see **fanatic.**

phrase, see **fraise.**

piacular, see **peculiar.**

1. **picaresque:** relating to rogues and vagabonds, and particularly to the literature of the activities of such.

2. PICTURESQUE: like a picture; a subject suitable for a picture; appealing to the imagination; vivid writing; strong description.

Crime fiction is always picaresque but seldom picturesque.

1. pick: a curved pointed steel bar with a central socket to hold a shaft, or haft, used for breaking hard ground, loosening stones, demolishing brickwork, and the like; any spike used for breaking, as an ice-pick.

2. PICK: to select; to gather; to separate.

3. PICK: the best; the choicest specimens from a batch.

4. PICK: to gather flowers, crops, etc.

5. PICK: one journey of the shuttle from one side of the loom to the other.

6. PICK: to steal.

He went out to pick apples, and put the pick of them aside for himself; he did not, however, pick a good hiding place, and I was able to mash them with a pick, hoping that the mess would persuade him not to pick and steal.

1. picks: the action of picking, to pick (q.v.).

2. PIX: a box or coffer (q.v.), the receptacle for the sacramental bread; a box in which gold and silver coins are placed at the Royal Mint, London, for assay.

3. PYX: alternative (and more usual) spelling of No. 2 above.

Father O'Donovan is getting very old, he always picks the wrong person to carry the pyx; but he carefully picks a good place from which to see the Worshipful Goldsmiths of the City of London, going to the Mint for the trial of the pyx.

picturesque, see picaresque.

1. pie: meat, or fruit, placed in a pan, covered with pastry, and baked.

2. PIE: a magpie.

3. PIE: a set of rules used in the Church before the Reformation.

4. PIE: a mass of mingled type.

5. PIE: an Indian coin of small value.

6. PYE: alternative spelling of No. 3 above.

The printer, having eaten too much steak pie, was sleepy, and made pie of an afternoon's work.

piece, see peace.

pier, see peer.

1. pig: a hog or a sow (q.v.), swine; animals of the genus *Sus*; extended to people of crude and dirty habits.

2. PIG: a rectangular block of base metal, pig-iron, pig-lead.

3. PIG: one of the natural segments of an orange.

4. PIG (sl): to live roughly, without ceremony.

I shall pig in the foundry tonight for we must execute the order for a thousand blocks of pig-iron by tomorrow. I shall fry a slice or two of pig for supper.

1. pike: a point or spike, particularly a spike or blade mounted at the end of a staff, being an archaic foot-soldier's thrusting weapon; any spike, prickle or thorn; a hedgehog's bristles.

2. PIKE: a pointed hill; a mountain peak; a pointed stack of hay or corn.

3. PIKE: a barrier across a road where toll (q.v.) is to be paid, hence, a turnpike, a main road.

4. PIKE: a voracious fresh-water fish with a pointed snout or beak, *Esox lucius*; the 'lucie' of heraldry.

The semi-savage tribesmen inhabiting the pike invaded the valley to fish for pike, but each man carried a pike, so the lowlanders hesitated to impose toll at the turnpike.

1. pile: a javelin, hence, a pointed blade of grass; a log pointed at one end driven into soft ground to form a foundation; any post or rod used for this purpose; in heraldry, a wedge-shaped sub-ordinary.

2. PILE: a heap, a mound, raised without organization; a collection of resinous logs or the like used in cremation; a pyre; a big building; a pillar (q.v.); a mole (q.v.); a large sum (q.v.) of money; a series of bi-metal plates arranged in a chemical solution to generate electricity; the reverse of a coin (q.v.).

3. PILE: the hair-like surface of certain kinds of cloth or carpet.

4. PILE: varicose veins of the anus.

In spite of his ugly habit of incessantly scratching at a pile with which he was afflicted, he made his pile out of his enterprise of erecting that pile of office buildings on a compound concrete pile: the officers of arms wittily granted him gules, on a pile Or a torteau, when he became a baronet.

1. pill: a small ball of, or containing, a form of medicine; something unpleasant that must be borne.

2. PILL: local name along the Bristol Channel for a tidal creek.

3. PILL: to rob; plunder; obtain by violence; pillage.

4. PILL: to lose either skin or bark (q.v.); to become bald.

'Tis a bitter pill to swallow that bandits from across the channel bring boats up every pill and pill our farms at night.

1. pillar: a vertical post (q.v.) or column, often built of stone which (q.v.) may (q.v.) stand in isolation, but is generally one of a row (q.v.) supporting some overhanging development of a building.

2. PILLER: one who commits pillage; a despoiler, robber or thief.

3. PILLOR: to condemn an offender to stand in the pillory.

4. PILLOW: (C) a cushion to rest the head.

He had been a pillar, and they made preparations to pillor him, and there he slept, the foot of a stone pillar his only pillow.

pillor ⎫
pillow ⎭ see pillar.

1. pine: any tree of the genus *Pinus*; the timber of such trees.

2. PINE: to experience intense desire; to languish; to suffer torment or distress.

3. PINEAPPLE: the cones of pine-trees, but more commonly the South American fruit *Ananassa sativa*, and the West Indian fruit *Bromelia pinguin*.

When Louis XI heard that his captive was known to pine for pineapple, he supplied a pine-wood bowl filled with pine-cones.

1. pink: a flower, *Dianthus plumarius*, and other varieties.

2. PINK: a pale, or diluted red (q.v.) colour; the crimson of a hunting coat.

3. PINK: a generic term for colours diluted with white.

4. PINK: to produce a pattern (q.v.) in cloth, or in leather, by a series of punch (q.v.) holes; to scallop, or invect, the edge of cloth or leather.

5. PINK: a subsidiary noise made by an internal-combustion engine when there is unbalance between piston and cylinder.

6. PINK: a sailing boat; a young salmon; to stab or be stabbed.

7. PINK: perfection.

That motor is not in the pink, do you hear it pink? They had it up to the axles in mud while fishing for pink, and I observed a pink hue in the exhaust fumes: they left it whilst they went picking pink in the woods and it slipped down into the river, and their maiden aunt, sitting in the back seat unconcernedly, continued to pink the seams of the frock she was making.

1. pinna: the pineapple; a fabric made from pineapple leaf fibre; a genus of bearded molluscs.

2. PINNA: the external ear; the fin of a fish, or the flipper of a seal (q.v.); each division of a fern-leaf.

Having gathered a goodly crop of pinna while walking on the beach he made a bag of pinna to carry them.

pinnace, see penis.

1. pip: a disease of the throat and tongue that attacks poultry and other birds; a non-medical description of various human ailments (q.v.); an irritable depressed state.

2. PIP: a seed, particularly of apple, pear (q.v.) and orange.

3. PIP: one of the shapes that appear on playing-cards; one of the spots on dice; any spot; particularly on fabric.

4. PIP: to emerge, break out of the shell as a bird; to utter sounds as a young bird.

5. PIP: to defeat; to fail in an examination.

6. PIP: signaller's term for the letter P (q.v.) to distinguish it from B (q.v.).

7. PIP: the star of rank (q.v.) on a military officer's uniform.

He was certain they would pip him in the oral exam and that he'd never pip into practice, so he had got the pip, and was trying to do a numerological prophecy by juggling with every pip in a pack of cards, and counting orange pips.

pique, see **peak.**

1. **pistil:** the female organ of a plant.

2. PISTLE: a story recounted verbally.

3. PISTOL: a pocket fire-arm designed to be used in one hand.

4. PISTOLE: an old Spanish gold coin.

When John said he had counted every pistil in the garden, Grandfather, a slightly deaf ex-seaman, shouted, 'What! What? You found a pistole? They've been at my chest! Give me my pistol!' and back at school John's account of it was voted the best pistle of the term.

pistle ⎫
pistol ⎬ see **pistil.**
pistole ⎭

1. **pit:** a hollow, or an indentation, either one formed by nature or delved out by man, in the ground; a hollow, or an indentation in any substance.

2. PIT: to strive against; to compete; to match.

The miners pit their wits against the pit-owners.

1. **pitch:** a black substance, plastic when hot and brittle when cold, being a residue of the distillation of turpentine, or of coal-tar.

2. PITCH: to throw, toss or bowl a ball or other object; to plunge forward or downward.

3. PITCH: a station or place; an allotted position for a salesman in a market; a place occupied by a vendor of newspapers, or flowers, or matches; the name given to the ground on which certain games are played.

4. PITCH: height; altitude; the highest point of an arch.

5. PITCH: the particular quality of a specific sound, or range of notes.

6. PITCH: slope; a declivity; an angle (q.v.); distance between the centres of the teeth of a cog or gear wheel; cutting angle of a tool.

7. PITCH: to select a place; erect a tent; to tell a story, particularly an improbable one; to fall; to gamble by throwing coins at a mark.

He selected a pitch at the fair to pitch a pitch-and-toss tent, but the local busybody pitched an aweful warning, at the full pitch of her voice, about those who touch pitch being soiled, and she advised the boys to go and pitch for coconuts: little did she dream that the pitch of the floor there made it impossible to win, she having been brought up in the tradition of the cricket pitch, and finally one or two boys decided to pitch mud at her.

1. **pitcher:** an earthenware jug of large size used for drawing and conveying water.

2. PITCHER: one who pitches, or throws, as the workman who throws hay up to the stacker, or the player who throws the ball.

When the stacker wanted water, the pitcher pitched the pitcher.

pix, see **picks.**

1. **place:** a particular location; an estate; a house; a building; position, social status; office or employment, particularly domestic service; to dispose of a literary or dramatic work to a publisher or a producer; to remember the setting and circumstances of last meeting a person; to recognize a person or a thing; a street, a square, an avenue; the site (q.v.) of a market; to assign to an object a position that shall be the right position, as a book on a shelf; of a horse attaining second or third position in a race (q.v.).

2. PLAICE: a flat-fish, *Pleuronectes platessa*.

To place plaice on my desk is very out of place: if the parlourmaid thus displays the manners of the market-place, she must find herself another place: when I saw the parcel there I was quite unable to place it.

plaice, see preceding group.

1. **plain**: a flat tract of open country; clear; without obstructions; a flat field.

2. PLAIN: simple; easily understood; not decorated; not highly flavoured; not coloured; not involved or elaborate.

3. PLAIN: outspoken; candid; frank; without pretence; humble; not distinguished in ability, achievement or appearance.

4. PLAIN: lament; to give utterance to distress; complain.

5. PLANE: a tree of the genus *Platinus*, misapplied to the sycamore, *Acer pseudoplatonus*.

6. PLANE: a perfectly flat surface; the facets of a crystal; the wings of a heavier than air flying machine.

7. PLANE: a woodworking tool used for securing a flat surface.

The tests on Salisbury Plain made plain that a plane could not be constructed from plane timber because the skill required to plane it would not be easy to find, and the colonel, in plain speech, told the politicians that they'd be guilty of plane murder if they went on with the scheme.

1. **plaister**: a dressing for a wound, or a medicated external application.

2. PLASTER: alternative (and more usual) spelling of No. 1 above.

3. PLASTER: a form of refined cement used in facing brickwork, and for other purposes; to daub, or coat as with plaster.

I think you would derive benefit from a mustard plaster which is easy to apply, and you will then have no need to plaster yourself with ointment: your broken leg is, however, not yet knit, and must remain in plaster.

1. **plait**: to form a braid (q.v.) by interlacing three strands; to fold cloth back upon itself, to pleat.

2. PLAT: a small, flat piece of land.

3. PLATE: a small, shallow dish-like vessel, usually round, and of earthenware, on which food is served for eating: a similar article used for other purposes.

4. PLATE: to cover one metal with another, usually a base with a precious, as copper, with silver; articles made from such a laminated sheet; a thin, flat sheet of base metal; such a sheet prepared for use, as a base-plate, back-plate, etc., or engraved, or otherwise treated for printing from; a railway line; a sheet of sensitized glass or other transparent matter used to make the negative in photography.

5. PLATE: in heraldry, a roundel argent, probably representing No. 6 below.

6. PLATE: an old Spanish silver coin, *real de plata*.

7. PLATE: the name of a major South American river.

8. PLATE: armour, and parts of armour, made from sheet steel instead of mail (q.v.).

9. PLATE: an upper set of false teeth.

Plait this copper wire for me. I will plate it with silver and attach it to the plate I am making for the offertory: the vicar wants to get a photographer to take the finished article and give him the plate so that he can use it for a plate in his book on Church Plate: the design is one I saw on a piece of antique plate excavated in the valley of the Plate.

1. **plaiter**: one who makes a plait (q.v.).

2. PLATTER: a large plate (q.v.) or a dish on which food is served.

The potter had a plaiter to make the edge for every platter he produced.

plane, see **plain**.

1. **plant**: an organism of the vegetable kingdom; to set seeds for the production of such organisms.

2. PLANT: machinery.

Amateur farmers pay more attention to their petrol-driven plant than to what they plant.

plaster, see **plaister.**

plat, see **plait.**

plate, see **plait.**

platter, see **plaiter.**

1. **pleas:** pl of 'plea', to bring an action into court (q.v.); a defence; a supplication.
2. PLEASE: a polite prefix or suffix to a request; to be pleasant; to gratify; to choose (q.v.) to give pleasure.

   Please pay attention to my incessant pleas to you to refrain from whistling: you are so utterly selfish that you can please only yourself, and so utterly foolish as not to realize the profits that accrue when we please others.

please, see preceding group.

1. **plight:** danger; distress; subject to forfeiture; under an obligation.
2. PLIGHT: to plait (q.v.) or fold; a manner of folding; a standard length of lawn-cloth (q.v.).
3. PLIGHT: condition; situation; state of health.

   He will be in sorry plight who will plight his troth on romance alone.

1. **plot:** a small portion of ground; a building site.
2. PLOT: a plan made between parties in secret to accomplish some lawless, revolutionary or criminal act.
3. PLOT: the course of the theme of a story or a play.
4. PLOT: to draw a plan; to construct a graphic representation of progress in time; to draw a curved line; to mark a ship's course on a chart.

   The plot of a novel called attention to the plot of the tycoons to convert the plot left in a will for building houses, to the erection of offices: they had already commissioned an architect to plot out the scheme on paper.

1. **pluck:** courage.
2. PLUCK: to pull, jerk or snatch; to tear something away from something else.

   A man needed more than pluck to pluck a mandrake.

1. **plum:** fruit of the *Prunus domestica* tree (see also 'prune').
2. PLUMB: a lead weight attached to a cord to gauge verticality.
3. PLUMB: to take a sounding: to test water for depth.

   With a plumb no larger than a plum he attempted to plumb the Atlantic.

plumb, see preceding group.

1. **plump:** a large number, or a compact mass, of persons, animals or objects.
2. PLUMP: to fall heavily.
3. PLUMP: well covered with flesh; chubby; full and round; blunt; forthright in speech.
4. PLUMP: to choose hurriedly; to show a strong preference for.

   I plump for a plump girl who will plunge plump into the river and drive a plump of fish into my nets.

1. **plumper:** comparative of 'plump' (q.v.); one who is more plump than another, or than formerly.
2. PLUMPER: a device for giving the appearance of plumpness.
3. PLUMPER: one who shows a heavy bias in favour of something.

   Jack will be a plumper for that slimming system—he's getting plumper, you know.

1. **poach:** to trespass; to steal game.
2. POACH: to cook eggs by boiling them without their shells.

   You poach on my preserves when you poach eggs.

pocket, see **packet.**

1. **pocks:** small ulcers, or pustules, developed during certain fevers; the pit-like scars left on the face by such eruptions.
2. POX: syphilis; the suffix in the compound names of fevers as mentioned in No. 1 above, small-pox, chicken-pox.

   In the eighteenth century the disfigurement of pocks was as common as the contraction of pox.

1. **pole:** a long cylinder of wood; a ship's mast (q.v.); the internal support for a tent; a mast from which a flag is flown; a standard of lineal measurement equal to five and a half yards (see also **perch**).

2. POLE: the points on a sphere at which a diameter, extended in two directions, would pierce the surface; such points about which a sphere revolves, hence, North Pole and South Pole of the earth; the points in an outer sphere where the extended diameter of an inner sphere would meet the surface, hence, the poles of the ecliptic in the celestial sphere, the centres round which the firmament seems to revolve.

3. POLE: either end of a bar of magnetized iron; either terminal of an electric battery; or generator of direct current (q.v.).

4. POLE: a flat-fish, *Pleuronectes cynogyossus.*

5. POLE: a person from Poland.

6. POLL: the human head, particularly the top, or crown of the head, hence a person.

7. POLL: to count people as heads for the purpose of taxation, or for recording votes, hence, an election.

8. POLL: shortened form of Polly, an altered shape of Molly, itself a diminutive of Mary; the name given to a parrot.

9. POLL: to cut a person's hair; to cut the horns of a beast; to cut straight as distinct from scalloped the top edge of a legal document; a document thus cut, hence, not an indenture; to cut a tree at the top; to behead.

10. POLL: to persecute, to fleece, to plunder by excessive taxation, as 'assessed' Income Tax.

He erected a pole to serve as a pointer to the celestial pole, and later he wired it to the positive pole of a flash-light battery under the delusion that it would incline to the North Pole. His next door neighbour, a Pole, thought it great fun to encourage such experimentation, but complained to all and singular that such a one had the right to go to the poll: he said a Poll-parrot had more right to vote.

police, see pelisse.

1. Polish: a person, or a thing, from Poland.

2. POLISH: a shining, glossy surface of either wood or metal; dressing employed in producing such a surface; the act of applying such dressing; politeness.

Beware of deceptive Polish polish.

poll, see pole.

1. pollack: a fish like a cod; a whiting; *Pollachius,* also called coal-fish.

2. POLLACK: a Yiddish word for a Pole (q.v.) adopted by London's underworld where it is employed as an expression of contempt for the Polish (q.v.) criminals operating in the West End.

This fried pollack has gone bad, give it to that Pollack ponce and poison him.

1. pollard: cut back; a tree lopped of all branches; an erstwhile great nation (as the British nation) that has abandoned its colonies and antagonized its friends.

2. POLLARD: an animal that has had its horns cut, or has cast (q.v.) them; a polled beast.

3. POLLARD: a rich, good-quality bran; barley and other grain that is without beard.

The stump of pollard oak may stand, for our pollard navy will not require it: from the branches they made a yoke for the pollard.

1. Polly: name for either a girl or a parrot; diminutive of Poll (q.v.).

2. POLY: a herb common to Southern Europe; *Teucrium.*

3. POLY: a prefix meaning many.

Since Polly has been at the Polytechnic she has made friends with some polyglot people who write to friends in foreign parts to send them poly in place of pepper.

poly, see preceding group.

1. pomade: a perfumed grease used for the hair.

2. POMMARD: a type of red wine named from a village in Côte d'Or, France.

The stench of his pomade ruins the flavour of my pommard.

pommard, see preceding group.

1. **pommel:** a ball-shaped terminal, particularly of a sword or a dagger hilt; the frontal, rising part of a saddle.
2. PUMMEL: to deliver repeated blows, particularly with the fist.

   If that bronc don't buck that guy over the pommel and break his doggorn neck, I guess it's up to me to pummel the ribs out o' his cayoute's hide.

poor, see **paw.**

1. **poplar:** a tree of the genus *Populus*, which includes the aspen.
2. POPULAR: open to all; suitable for all classes; finding acceptance by the masses.

   In the days of Queen Victoria poplar trees were popular at the end of long gardens.

1. **populace:** the mass of the population.
2. POPULOUS: densely inhabited; crowded; having many people.

   The entire populace of the industrial north goes to one holiday resort which, during the season, becomes so populous that one cannot move through the streets.

popular, see **poplar.**

populous, see **populace.**

pore, see **paw.**

pores, see **pause.**

pork, see **pawk.**

1. **port:** a place of refuge for a ship; a town having dock accommodation.
2. PORT: the side of a ship that is on the left hand when facing forward.
3. PORT: a gateway; a doorway; an opening.
4. PORT: an obsolete method of carrying a rifle (q.v.) on parade, sloping over the chest from left to right.
5. PORT: the red sweet wine of Portugal.
6. PORTE: the name of the Turkish government before the revolution.

   We were stove in on the port side and all portholes smashed, so we put into the nearest port and were immediately in trouble, not having received permission from the Porte, but the skipper squared the Turkish officer with a bottle of port, and put a guard, with a loaded carbine held at the port, on the gangway.

1. **porta:** a gate, hence, the opening in the liver (q.v.) through which the arteries and veins (q.v.) pass.
2. PORTER: one who serves at a door or a gate.
3. PORTER: one who serves by carrying, particularly at a railway station.
4. PORTER: a dark brown bitter beer.

   He manifests a chronic crust on the porta because, having been head porter at a big hotel, he was, during the war, drafted as a porter at a railway depot where his pay did not provide so much as porter.

Porte, see **port.**

porter, see **porta.**

1. **poser:** a searching, difficult question; one who sets questions in an examination paper.
2. POSEUR: one who behaves in an affected manner.

   She is an intellectual poseur, the simplest question put proves to be a poser to her.

poseur, see preceding group.

1. **post-:** prefix from Latin: after, or following.
2. POST: an established place or fixed position.
3. POST: carriage of letters and parcels from one place to another.
4. POST: to place a person or thing in position; to convey verbal or written information; to transfer accounts from one book to another.

   The post-war Post Office suspended service to the isolated forestry post and, deaf as a post to complaints, offered to post a telegraphist there.

potatoes, see **pettitoes.**

1. **potter:** to perform a task in an inefficient, slow, unorganized way; to walk about without purpose or direction; to be engaged without accomplishing an end.
2. POTTER: a craftsman who makes vessels of earthenware; pottery.

   The kindly potter lets the old man potter about in his workshop—he does no harm.

poultry, see **paltry.**

1. **pounce**: the claw or talon of a bird of prey.
2. POUNCE: a fine powdered resin, used as an absorbent medium on ink, and as a filler on parchment and vellum.
3. POUNCE: to seize in a rapid, avid manner.
4. POUNCE: to raise by hammering a design on sheet-metal.

The scribe made a pounce on the pounce to dry the hawk's pounce he had drawn as an ornamental capital letter, and it occurred to him that this would make him a good design-motif to pounce on the metal corner plates of the cover.

1. **pound**: a standard of weight; sixteen ounces avoirdupois, twelve ounces troy weight; 1 lb.
2. POUND: a standard of money; a sovereign; twenty shillings; £.
3. POUND: an enclosure into which strayed cattle are put pending their redemption.
4. POUND: to pulverize by repeated blows; to administer a sound beating.
5. POUND (sl): to apply one's strength, to assist in lifting.

When Farmer Parker's prize pig was put in the pound it cost him a pound to get it out, and since it weighs three hundredweight if it weighs a pound he could not get it into the cart and no one would give him a pound: now he says he'll pound the Parish Beadle.

pour, see paw.
1. **pout**: an alternative name for the bib (q.v.) and some other fish.
2. POUT: to inflate; to protrude the lips in an expression of sulkiness or annoyance.

If you pout over pout you'll make mows at mussels.

pox, see pocks.
1. **practice**: the business of a doctor, a lawyer, and certain other professional men.
2. PRACTISE: to repeat a performance, or an exercise, in order to improve one's execution; a habit; the repetition of an activity.

You must practise if you hope to qualify and set up in practice.

practise, see preceding group.
1. **praise**: laudation; approbation; commendation; eulogy; to set a price upon a thing.
2. PRAYS: the act of addressing the Deity, the Sovereign, Parliament, Court of Chancery; the act of supplicating.
3. PREYS: feeds upon; is a parasite on; steals from.

The fact of his having accepted unblushingly, when he was a Member of Parliament, the high praise for a book bearing his name, but which had been 'ghosted' for him, preys upon his mind, and he prays incessantly for forgiveness.

1. **pray**: to address the Deity; to supplicate; to beseech, ask earnestly; a form of address to the Sovereign, to Parliament, to the Court of Chancery; a sincere and forceful form of 'please' (q.v.).
2. PREY: the creatures hunted, killed and eaten by wild carnivorous beasts; the victims of aggression or pillage; to obtain by violence, deprive, destroy.

Pray, pray we do not prove their prey.

prayed, see parade.
prays, see praise.
1. **precede**: to go before, or ahead of.
2. PROCEED: to commence, or to continue doing.

Decide which part of the work must precede and you will be able to proceed.

1. **precedent**: that which goes before; an example from the past; an action taken that will in future be copied.
2. PRESIDENT: the elected first citizen in a State having no hereditary head; the head of an American company; the chairman of an organization or society.

If we hold our Annual General Meeting in the absence of our President we will be creating a precedent.

1. **prefer**: to put into office; to put in front of; to offer; to select; to hold

someone or something in higher esteem than some other person or thing.

2. PROFFER: to offer something; to put an idea forward for acceptance.

If you proffer that scheme to the committee I will move its acceptance: I prefer it to the other.

1. **premices:** first fruits.

2. PREMISES: the fact foregoing a logical deduction; the assumption on which an argument is based.

3. PREMISES: a building, or part of a building.

4. PREMISSES: alternative spelling of No. 1 above.

Your assertion that the premises are worth the rent charged is based on false premises.

1. **prescribe:** to write (q.v.) beforehand; to write a recipe for medicine; to lay down rules, laws or orders; to limit.

2. PROSCRIBE: to prohibit, forbid or prevent; to denounce; to interdict; to outlaw or banish; to condemn to death.

Hurry along to your panel doctor and get him to prescribe a bottle of brandy before the Minister can proscribe liquor.

1. **presence:** the fact of being present (q.v.); to possess a grand air, or an impressive personality.

2. PRESENTS: pl of 'present' (q.v.); the contents of a document.

3. PRESENTS (prèsents): the act of bestowing a gift.

He presents his compliments, and bids me inform you that your presence and your presents will both be expected at the wedding.

1. **present:** a free and unsolicited gift.

2. PRESENT (pre`zent): the act of bestowing a gift; of making an introduction.

3. PRESENT: now; at this time.

4. PRESENT: in attendance; in this, or in that place.

Well—no. He will not accept a bribe, but he does appreciate a present. When he is present in the room start a conversation about books. At present, I hear,

he is collecting old botany. If he rises to the bait you can present him with one.

presents, see presence.
President, see precedent.

1. **press:** a crowd; a large group of people gathered together without cohesion or discipline.

2. PRESS: a machine for squeezing, hence a wine-press, a printing-press.

3. PRESS: the product of the printing-press, hence, a newspaper.

4. PRESS: a large, built-in cupboard.

5. PRESS: to exert force, generally downward; to persuade; to influence.

The press on public transport during the rush hours is an evil the press does not expose although they receive numerous letters trying to press them to do so: in the office of *The Daily Dispute* there is a press-full.

1. **pressed:** pst tns and ppl of the v 'to press' (q.v.)

2. PREST: a payment in advance.

3. PREST: ready, alert, rapid, skilful.

He pressed for a prest which was refused him.

prest, see preceding group.
prey, see pray.
preyed, see parade.
preys, see praise.

1. **price:** the sum of money required to make a purchase; the equivalent, in terms of money, of the value of an article; the amount of money that would be expected to constitute an acceptable bribe; the monetary reward offered for the capture, or the death, of a miscreant; to gain a victory; to be preeminent.

2. PRIES: the act of prying, of enquiring too closely into other people's business.

3. PRISE: the seizure of a tenant's goods by a feudal landlord; customs and excise (q.v.).

4. PRIZE: the symbol of victory in a contest; a reward given to a schoolchild for excellent work; descriptive of a piece of work, or an exhibit, that has gained, or is likely to gain, a trophy.

5. PRIZE: property, particularly ships, taken in time of war from the enemy.

6. PRIZE: to wrench, lever, or by other means force open.

7. PRIZE: a wrench, lever or crowbar.

8. PRYCE: to take or capture.

9. PRYSE: alternative spelling of No. 8 above.

The price of clothing coupons rose steadily, and hitherto smart young men learned to prize old coats, and even when the navy prysed an enemy ship full of cloth it was sold as a prize overseas: school-boys were glad to receive a second-hand blazer as a prize, and cracksmen did better to prize open a clothing-store than a bank.

1. **pride:** a high opinion of one's own achievement, abilities and ancestry; pleasure and satisfaction experienced as a result of something well done, praiseworthy; honour; the most excellent.

2. PRIDE: a number of lions living and acting in a group.

3. PRIDE: a name for the fresh-water lamprey. *Petromyzon.*

4. PRIED: pst tns of 'pry' (q.v.).

That fellow's pride since he managed to escape from a pride of lions knows no restraint—he actually pried into my preparations for going on safari, and he pried open one of my boxes.

pried, see preceding group.

pries, see **price.**

1. **Prince:** the son and the grandson of a monarch; a male member of a royal, or a ruling family; a courtesy title used to describe a Grand Duke, or a Landgrave.

2. PRINTS: impressions made on paper with ink by contact with an engraved plate, a die, or set type; the impressions of feet, hooves or paws in a soft medium such as clay or sand.

The Prince is a collector of prints, hence dealers' footprints lead to his door, but his agent prints a monthly list of requirements.

1. **principal:** the man or woman in charge of, or having authority in, an institution such as a school or college.

2. PRINCIPIAL: something indicative of a beginning, such as a rubricated capital letter.

3. PRINCIPLE: rules influencing action; a high code of honour and morality; the basic laws of a science.

The principal insisted on every student indicating paragraphs with a principial on principle.

principial } see preceding group.
principle }

prints, see **Prince.**

prise } see **price.**
prize }

proffer, see **prefer.**

1. **profit:** gain; the difference between cost and selling price.

2. PROPHET: an inspired reformer; one who declares his denunciation of mankind to be the warnings of the Deity; one who claims to foretell future events.

Heed the prophet—profit thereby.

1. **project** (proh'ject): a plan; a purpose; a scheme or a proposition; a suggestion; a forecast of work to be done.

2. PROJECT (pro'ject): to obtrude; to jut out; to extend from; to cast an image from some form of lantern.

If that project is carried out they will demolish the buildings that project into the main road.

prophet, see **profit.**

1. **pros:** plural of 'pro', for, in favour of; often coupled with 'cons', against.

2. PROS: colloquial description of professional actors, athletes, and other entertainers.

3. PROSE: written language other than poetry.

Consider the pros and cons as carefully as you will, but you cannot deny that the persistent prose in praise of pros is preposterous.

proscribe, see **prescribe.**

prose, see **pros.**

1. **prune:** fruit of the plum (q.v.) tree, *Prunus domestica*; specifically, a dried plum.

2. PRUNE: to cut back; to trim a plant in order to control its growth.

3. PRUNE: to pay attention to one's personal appearance; to tidy oneself; to preen.

He will prune himself when he should prune his trees, and he will not harvest a single prune.

1. prunella: the name of a strong kind of cloth from which shoe uppers can be made.

2. PRUNELLA: name of a plant, self-heal, *Prunella vulgaris*.

3. PRUNELLA: a name given to camp-fever (typhus) in the sixteenth century; in later times, to quinsy, and other throat disorders.

4. PRUNELLE: salt used for gargling the throat.

5. PRUNELLO: a prune (q.v.) of the best quality.

While out picking prunella there came a heavy rainfall which soaked through her prunella shoes and gave her an excuse to go to bed with flannel round her neck, complaining of an attack of prunella, demanding a gargle of warm prunelle, and really simply playing-up for prunello and cream.

prunelle⎱ see prunella.
prunello⎰

1. pry: to enquire closely and impertinently into the affairs of other people; one who is prone (q.v.) to behave in such a manner.

2. PRY: to lever, wrench, or otherwise force open; an implement for effecting this; a crowbar.

I will not pry the lid off the packing-case till that poke-and-pry party has gone home.

pryce⎱ see price.
pryse⎰

1. psalter: a book containing the Psalms arranged for devotional reading.

2. SALTER: one who makes, or vends, salt; a vessel to contain salt.

3. SALTIRE: in heraldry, the name of the X-shaped cross; of charges conforming to such orientation.

The rustics thought her ladyship carried a psalter marked with a saltire, but it was actually

the leather case of a portable salter.

pud, see pad.

1. pulse: the throb, or beat, palpable in the arteries caused by the impulse given by the heart to the blood; any rhythmic beat.

2. PULSE: edible seeds such as peas, beans and lentils.

The constant diet of pulse increased his pulse rate before meals.

pummel, see pommel.

1. punch: to strike with the fist; to drive cattle by prodding with a stick.

2. PUNCH: to create a hole in a sheet of material by driving a rod through.

3. PUNCH: rods of various shapes for making holes, or for embossing a pattern (q.v.) or for marking a surface, or depressing a nail-head; such cutters mounted in pivoted handles.

4. PUNCH: a drink consisting of rum, or other spirit, mixed with hot water, lemon, sugar and spice.

5. PUNCH: a thick-set, powerfully-built man or beast.

6. PUNCH: short for Punchinello, a clown, a humorist; the protagonist in the Punch and Judy Show.

7. PUNCH: an old-established, dignified English humorous periodical.

You are a regular punch of a fellow so guard the door—here's the punch—punch all tickets, and if any of them try to punch their way in without one, give them a punch in the ribs and remind them this Punch and Judy Show is given for charity, and the punch-cup, to follow, has to show a profit.

purl, see pearl.

purveyed, see pervade.

1. puttee: a strip of cloth, about four inches wide and six feet long, wound about the leg from ankle to knee.

2. PUTTY: powdered abrasive used for polishing; a mixture of fine cement without aggregate; a paste made from powdered whitening and linseed oil used for fixing panes of

glass, or for covering irregularities
in woodwork.

The soldier on fatigue duty destroyed his puttee by stepping
knee-deep into a drum of putty.

putty, see preceding group.
pye, see **pie.**
pyx, see **picks.**

Q

Q, see **cue.**
1. **quad:** an abbreviation for several
words such as 'quadrangle', 'quad-
rat', 'quadruple'; a stationer's term
for paper of a certain size (q.v.); a
printer's term for a metal space.
2. QUOAD: to the extent of; as much as;
as far as.
3. QUOD: prison.

You must study the slang of the
underworld: when he says he is
a college-boy, and refers to the
quad, you think of a Public
School. He means prison.

1. **quail:** a migratory bird, allied to the
partridge, of the family *Perdici-
dae*; in U.S.A. birds resembling
the Old World quail, as Virginian
quail, *Ortyx virginianus*; Californian quail, *Lophortyx californicus*.
2. QUAIL: to manifest fear; to fail, be
daunted; to become faint (q.v.) to
lose heart.

The thought of a meal of American quail makes him quail.

1. **quarrel:** a bird-bolt; a broad arrow.
2. QUARREL: a lozenge-shaped piece of
glass as used in leaded lights; a
glazier's diamond.
3. QUARREL: to break a friendship; to
contend violently; a cause of contention; a state of hostility.

The quarrel commenced when
we were practising archery. I
misdirected a quarrel and
smashed a quarrel in his armorial window.

quart, see **cart.**
1. **quarts:** pl of 'quart' (q.v.).
2. QUARTZ: a mineral, forming hexagonal
crystals, and assuming divers (q.v.)
colours, but in the pure state consisting of silicon dioxide, SiO_2.

When he's had a few quarts he'll

tell any tenderfoot where to find
gold-bearing quartz.

quartz, see preceding group.
1. **quaver:** a musical note, in length
half a crotchet.
2. QUAVER: to tremble, or vibrate; to
quiver; to make use of trills in
singing.

The prima donna, temperamen-
tal about the quaver in the fourth
line, invariably sang it with a
quaver in her voice.

1. **quean:** a healthy, objective young
woman; a female cat, hence, a term
of abuse; an immoral, sexually
promiscuous woman.
2. QUEEN: female Sovereign head of a
State (q.v.); consort of a King.

The Queen of Siam, who developed a strain of emerald-
green Siamese cats, sold to an
American tycoon a quean for a
million dollars.

queen, see preceding group.
1. **queerest:** strangest; oldest; the most
puzzling.
2. QUERIST: one who asks questions.

That child is the queerest
querist.

querist, see preceding group.
queue, see **cue.**
1. **quick:** having life; growing; ani-
mate.
2. QUICK: any extra-sensitive part of the
body, hence, the flesh beneath the
nails.
3. QUICK: speedy; without pause or pro-
crastination; lively.

Push a pin into his quick quick
to test if he is quick.

1. **quicken:** to give life; to stimulate; to
induce vigour; an advanced state
of pregnancy.
2. QUICKEN: to add to, or to increase
speed or tempo.
3. QUICKEN: couch grass; the stems of
grass beneath the surface.
4. QUICKEN: the rowan, or mountain-ash
tree, *Pyrus aucuparia*.

You must quicken the rate of
eradication or quicken will in-
vade your pastures before the
cattle quicken.

1. **quid:** that which an object is; in the
U.S.A. the name given ca. 1805 to
a section of the Republican Party.

2. QUID: a piece of hard tobacco cut to a size and shape convenient for chewing.

3. QUID (sl): one pound sterling; a sovereign; £1; 20/-.

The quid of this quid is its nicotine content and I'd give a quid for a chew at times.

1. **quiver:** to tremble; to vibrate.

2. QUIVER: a tubular case to hold arrow

The enemy began to quiver as the English archer unstrapped his quiver.

quoad, see **quad.**

quod, see **quad.**

quoin, see **coign.**

R

R }
R } see **ah!**

1. **rabbet:** a recess, or a groove cut into wood or stone to accommodate a ridge cut into another piece; the cut-back part of a picture-frame into which the glass etc. fits.

2. RABBIT: a burrowing vegetarian quadruped, related to the hare (q.v.), *Lepus cuniculus.*

3. REBATE: discount on a cash payment; alternative spelling of No. 1 above.

The rabbet in the frame was too shallow to accommodate my picture of a rabbit, and I intend to demand of the supplier a rebate.

rabbit, see preceding group.

1. **race:** a group of people, animals or plants, each member of which possesses similar transmitted physical characteristics.

2. RACE: a competition in speed; the uncontrolled rapid running of an engine in the absence of a load (q.v.); pertaining to progress of any kind at speed.

3. RACE: a channel provided to create an artificial rush (q.v.) of water from a natural source (q.v.), a mill-race.

4. RACE: the entrails of a calf (q.v.).

5. RACE: a blaze (q.v.), or white mark on the head of cattle, or of dogs.

6. RACE: preserved root-ginger.

7. RACE: nodules of a calcium compound found in clay.

8. RACE: to shave; to scrape.

The black race, productive of offspring, is winning the race for domination while the white race is productive of good works for the benefit of their black brethren: in short, they race the social and intellectual engine.

1. **rack:** a perforated shelf, or trough, to hold cattle fodder; a frame, a series of bars or a net used to hold or support something; a straight (q.v.) strip of metal having teeth to engage in a cog or pinion; an ancient instrument of torture, hence, to cause, or to suffer, distress, anxiety or grief; to charge extortionate rental; a collision, impact or shock; a mass of wind-driven cloud.

2. WRACK: revenge; damage or injury inflicted; a state of ruin; goods lost in, and timbers from, shipwreck when washed ashore; seaweed; weed, twigs, grass and other matter cast by a river onto its banks; rubbish adrift on a pond; a shape of wreck (q.v.).

The estate has gone to wrack and ruin since it has been open to holiday crowds: I rack my brains for a means of keeping the ornamental waters free from wrack: I've erected a rack for litter, but the public ignore it.

1. **racket:** noise; confusion; a din; a large and unrestrained social gathering; a business transaction, particularly one on a large scale, that lacks the seal of commercial morality.

2. RACKET: alternative spelling of No. 4 below.

3. RACQUET: alternative spelling of No. 4 below.

4. RAQUETTE: a bat (q.v.) made from a net stretched over a frame, used in lawn-tennis and other games; a North American snow-shoe; a weight-distributing attachment to the feet to enable progress to be made over marsh-land.

That racket next door will continue, and they will kick up a racket into the small hours: the very wealthy host runs a racket whereby people who want a tennis-racquet repaired get caught.

racquet, see preceding group.

1. **rag:** a generic term for cloth; a fragment of cloth; a term of contempt when applied to clothes or flags or newspapers.

2. RAG: a form of coarse (q.v.) grained stone; a large roofing slate.

3. RAG: a form of hysteria that from time to time attacks University students resulting in disorderly conduct on a major scale.

4. RUG: a thick woollen square of fabric used as a wrap, or cover, when travelling in cold weather; an oblong mat, usually of carpet material.

The rug is a rag—throw it away.

1. **raid:** a military expedition; any sudden descent upon, or rush at an objective with a view to either plunder or destroy or both; the act of making such an attack.

2. RAYED: pst tns of 'ray' (q.v.), having rays or beams or emanations; being arranged in order.

The raid on the camp was accomplished by the attackers, who were rayed on each side of the field and were armed with rayed lanterns with which they dazzled their victims.

1. **rail:** one of a pair of rods laid parallel to each other along the ground, on which run fast-moving heavy vehicles drawn along by an engine; a railway track; a horizontal bar (q.v.) or rod, supported between posts, being a rack (q.v.) or a fence (q.v.); a horizontal bar set up as a boundary; an H-shaped length of metal set sideways in a pelmet on which curtains are hung.

2. RAIL: a bird of the family *Rallidae.*

3. RAIL: to express oneself loudly, forcibly and protestingly against something; to abuse; to assert authority.

4. RÂLE: an auxiliary sound, not caused by respiration, heard in unhealthy lungs.

I rail at those boys to keep out while the rail are nesting but they pay no attention, and with the râle in my lungs I ought not to shout: I shall have to go to the expense of erecting a rail.

1. **rain:** atmospheric moisture of condensation which, during the English summer, falls in copious quantities over prolonged periods, and is often accompanied by a cold wind.

2. REIGN: the period of a sovereign's authority; to be supreme.

3. REIN: the strap, or cord, attached to the bit (q.v.) that enables the rider, or the driver, to guide and control a horse.

He seized the rein and leapt to the saddle crying, 'So long as my Queen doth reign, I will do my devoir—in spite of the rain.'

1. **raise:** to lift up; to cause to stand; to erect; to stimulate; to cultivate; to improve in either quantity or quality.

2. RAYS: pl (') of 'ray' (a beam) (q.v.).

3. RAYS: pl ('), fish of the family *Raiidae.*

4. RAZE: to cut down; obliterate; destroy.

You'll never raise prize plants if you do not raze those old sheds and raise good glasshouses that that will admit the rays of the sun; and some people fertilize with rays from electrical apparatus.

1. **raiser:** one who, or that which, raises, lifts or elevates.

2. RAZOR: a knife of highly tempered steel, or a substitute, or any blade sharp enough to, and used for, the purpose of shaving.

He was a great cutler: a raiser of standards in razor grinding.

1. **raisin:** dried grapes.

2. RAISING: lifting; elevating; producing.

3. REASON: the guiding principle of human thought; a basis of argument; a goal (q.v.); to solve by a process of thought.

The reason for raising the price of the sun-dried raisin was said to be increased transport charges.

raising, see preceding group.

1. **rake:** a large iron or wooden comb (q.v.) set at right angles (q.v.) to the end of a pole (q.v.) used for

gathering cut grass or other crops, straw etc. in a stable; to use such an implement; to pull small coal together in a fire; to make a search.

2. RAKE: the extra length fore and aft of the deck of a ship over the length of the keel; the sternward slope of the masts of a ship.

3. RAKE: one who leads an immoral, dissipated life.

The wealthy rake who came to watch us work dropped a diamond ring, so the boy was set to rake with his fingers among the shavings, for we did not have a rake, and when it was not found he departed with less of a rake to his spine.

râle, see rail.

1. rally: to call together a scattered company; to revive or stimulate; to converge upon, to gather in; a place for the purpose of holding a reunion, a meeting or a conference.

2. RALLY: to tease in a good-natured manner; banter; ridicule.

Rally him on how he spent his time at the Old Comrades' rally.

1. rancour: bitterness; hatred; spleen.

2. RANKER: a military officer who began his army career as a private soldier; a private soldier, one in the ranks.

3. RANKER: comparative of 'rank' (q.v.), more sour, more rancid, more foul than something else.

The Colonel spoke sternly to the Sandhurst lieutenant who manifested rancour towards his ranker Captain: such behaviour, he said, was ranker than a mistake in Mess accounts.

1. range: a series of mountains, buildings or other things extending in line; the distance or area limited between points in either time or space during, or in, which an event could occur, or in, or over, which a breed of animal may wander, or plant grow; the distance a gun can throw a shot; a place set aside for the purpose of shooting at targets.

2. RANGE: a kitchen stove, or fire-grate with an oven attached.

The fittings range from electric stoves to refrigerators throughout the entire range of modern flats, but give me a good, old-fashioned kitchen range.

1. rank: a number of persons or things arranged in line abreast, hence, various grades in the social scale; the ranks, the private soldiers of a regiment.

2. RANK: large; coarse (q.v.); superabundant; overdeveloped; lustful; indecent; exuding a strong, offensive smell; rancid; corrupt; foul (q.v.).

Give me rich Gorgonzola cheese which, in a humbler rank of society, they rank rank.

ranker, see rancour.

1. rap: a sharp punitive blow (q.v.) with a stick, or with a ruler (q.v.) not intended to be severe.

2. RAP: a short, sharp knocking sound, particularly when supposed to be produced by discarnate spirits.

3. RAP: admonition, blame or punishment, often implying that one assumes, or is forced to assume, responsibility for the delinquency of another.

4. WRAP: a scarf, rug, shawl or other loose outer garment; to enclose, envelop, or entwine; to make a parcel or package; to disguise, conceal or cover.

There came a rap on the door which opened wide, leaving no time to wrap the cards in the wrap we had ready, and the Corporal, who had conscientiously enough given us all a rap on the knuckles for gambling, is to go before the Colonel and take the rap.

1. rape: to force a woman into sexual congress; to take by force; to violate; to tear (q.v.), rend, destroy, desecrate.

2. RAPE: the common turnip; a plant, *Brassica napus*, used as fodder for sheep; another plant, *Brassica campectris oleifera*, from the seeds of which oil is produced.

3. RAPE: the stalks and pulp left (q.v.) in the press after the juice is taken for wine; this residue used in

RAPPED

[140]

RATE

making both vinegar and low-grade wine, hence, the vessel in which vinegar is made.
4. RAPE: a form of snuff.
5. RAPE: any one of six districts into which the County of Sussex was divided for purposes of administration.
    Take a pinch of rape and a sup of rape; feed on fresh fish fried in rape-oil, and rape neither the kitchen nor the cook.
1. rapped: pst tns & ppl of 'rap' (q.v.), a light (q.v.) blow (q.v.).
2. RAPT: in a trance, or a trance-like state; in a state of deep concentration of attention; carried away; transported.
3. WRAPPED: in process of being, or having been, placed in a wrapper, enveloped, enclosed, packed (q.v.).
    The attackers rapped on the door with the hilts of their swords, but he stood rapt as his faithful clerk wrapped the secret document.
1. rapport: connection; sympathy; a mystical relationship between two minds resulting in thought-transference, hypnotism, and other items of extra-sensory perception.
2. REPORT: a formal account of an occurrence.
3. REPORT: to present onself to, or before another, particularly a senior.
4. REPORT: the sound of an explosion.
5. REPORT: a rumour.
    The Press report stated that the report, when the powder magazine blew up, was heard twenty miles away and that the Officer-in-Charge is expected to report to the Colonel in spite of the report that he had been killed: it seems there is rapport between them.
rapt, see rapped.
raquette, see racket.
1. rare: sparse; uncommon; infrequent.
2. RARE: of eggs or meat when lightly cooked.
    It is a rare treat to get a rare steak in a restaurant.
1. rash: a skin eruption consisting of red spots or areas, generally secondary to, and symptomatic of, various fevers.

2. RASH: incautious; headstrong; reckless; impetuous; with undue haste.
3. RASH: a form of fine silken fabric.
4. RASH: a rustling noise.
    He's very rash; he dived into, and swam across, what he thought was a lake, but it turned out to be a sewage pool, and now he is covered in a rash.
1. rasher: a slice of bacon.
2. RASHER: comparative of 'rash' (q.v.), more rash, more heedless.
    I can think of nothing rasher than to cook and eat a rasher that has curled up with old age.
1. ratan: a species of cane (q.v.) of the genus Calamus.
2. RATTAN: alternative spelling of No. 1 above.
3. RATTEEN: a form of woollen cloth, no longer made.
4. RATTEN: to destroy tools and machinery in order to bring harm to an employer.
5. RATTON: a dialect form of 'rat'.
6. RATTOON: alternative name for the racoon.
7. ROTTEN: in a state of decay; putrid; foul; corrupt.
8. ROTTON: alternative spelling of No. 5 above.
    They decided to ratten the ratteen mills, and the days had gone by when we might have saved the situation by the generous application of a rattan, but when men are rotten enough to act like ratton, the good Lord punishes them: the mill closed, and so they lost their living.
1. rate: the sum of the value of a number of things used as a basis of calculation of the value of one; value of individual pieces, or equal quantities; the basis of comparative value of currency between nations; a fixed payment for work executed based on a standard of value; payment, based on a standard of house property, made by the individual into the public funds of a Municipal Corporation.
2. RATE: comparative speed.
3. RATE: comparative quality, class, kind; classification of ships by size and the number of guns carried.

4. RATE: to chide, scold, nag (q.v.), abuse, rail (q.v.).

If you work at a quick rate they put you on a low rate of pay, therefore they supply third-rate goods for export. They blame the rate of exchange, and soundly rate everyone they employ.

1. rath: an earthworks; a fort.

2. RATH: premature; of fruit or flowers ripened early; the morning; early; the first part of any period of time.

3. RATHE: alternative spelling of No. 2 above.

4. RATHE: too quickly.

When the O'Toole lived in a rath they were rathe in hailing him High King of all Ireland.

rattan ⎫
ratteen ⎪
ratten ⎬ see ratan.
ratton ⎪
rattoon ⎭

1. raw: not cooked; not prepared for table; in a crude or a natural state; harsh; the material before being subjected to a manufacturing process; immature; uncultured; lacking experience or training; thin; skinned; undiluted.

2. ROAR: to make a loud grating cry as a lion; to shout boisterously; to behave in a loud offensive manner; any loud noise as of thunder, big guns, explosion; the sound of a wind storm.

The raw recruit fainted on hearing the sergeant roar.

1. ray: a straight line of light; a similar line of any emanated force; a line of vision.

2. RAY: in heraldry, a narrow triangle having wavy long sides.

3. RAY: to place in order, arrange.

4. RAY: to dress; to assume raiment.

5. RAY: a form of striped fabric.

6. RAY: diminutive of Rachael, a feminine personal name.

7. RAY: diminutive of both Raymond and Raphael, masculine personal names.

8. RAY: fish of the family *Raiidae*; a skate (q.v.).

9. RAY: one of the sections of a starfish.

10. RAY: one of the sounds of the tonic sol-fa system of musical notation.

Ray, cheering as a ray of sunshine, comes home: in her shopping-bag a large fresh ray and many other delicacies; all of these she will ray in order on the table, then ray herself in a sleeved apron made of ray, before she begins to sing 'doh, ray, me', as she cooks.

rayed, see raid.

rays ⎫
raze ⎭ see raise.

razor, see raiser.

1. reach: to stretch forth one's arm.

2. REACH: a section of a river between two bends: or of a canal between two locks.

3. REACH: to vomit.

4. RETCH: alternative spelling of No. 3 above.

5. WRETCH: a miserable, or a despicable person.

The poor wretch was forced to retch as we sailed up Greenwich reach and I had to reach out to prevent his falling overboard.

1. read (reed): to look at, and understand, what is conveyed by handwriting, printing, pictures or other cyphers.

2. READ (red): pst tns of No. 1 above.

3. RED: a primary colour, first in the spectrum; one who supports the Marxian political fallacy.

4. REDE: counsel; advice; to tell, relate or explain; a proverb.

5. REED: a plant, *Phragmite*; a flexible strip of metal which, by vibration, sets up a musical note.

He is a red, and a broken reed: if I read the signs aright: my rede to him is to read the Bible: I have myself read it from cover to cover nineteen times and I cherish the copy, bound in red morocco, presented to me by Aunt Priscilla when I was confirmed.

1. reading: looking at print, or writing, and understanding the meaning conveyed by the combination of cyphers.

2. READING (Redding): County town of Berkshire, situated in the Thames Valley and world famous for its biscuit making.

She lounged in a first-class compartment and passed through Reading reading a recipe for baking biscuits.

1. real: having objective existence.
2. REEL: a modified cylinder on which yarn and other products are wound.
3. REEL: to walk with a staggering gait.
4. REEL: a Scottish dance.

Sandy McQuich said he did not reel home after the reel, but that he was walking like that so as to step over the red rats and other things that infested his path: to prove it he instanced the cotton-reel which was real enough, and his ankle is still in plaster.

1. rear: the back part of anything; behind; last.
2. REAR: undercooked; an alternative for 'rare' (q.v.).
3. REAR: of a quadruped, to stand on the hind legs; to call oneself to attention, to stand rigid and erect; to stand an object up, to stand on end; to erect.
4. REAR: to nurture; to bring up; to provide for.

If you wish to rear chicks don't have the coop in the rear of the house, feed them twice a week on yolk of rear egg, and you'll see them rear themselves up like so many fighting cocks.

reason, see raisin.

1. reave: to pillage, plunder or rob; to seize, to deprive by force; to rend, tear (q.v.) or split.
2. REEVE: to pass a rope through a slot and over a pulley as a block, or truck (q.v.); to pass a rope or a chain through an aperture without obstruction.
3. REEVE: a mayor (q.v.) of a seaport— Portreeve; a minor official; an overseer of labour on an estate.
4. REEVE: a bird, female of the ruff (q.v.).
5. REIVE: alternative spelling of No. 1 above.

When the buccaneer came to reave the town our Portreeve

showed his mettle: we had to reeve no rope through the town-gallows, but hanged them all from their own yard-arms.

1. recede: fade away; become more distant; journey away from; to draw back; to decline.
2. RECEDE: to give again, as lands after sequestration.
3. RESEED: to plant again; cultivate anew.

When they recede your estate reseed the fallow fields and your troubles will recede after the harvest.

rebate, see rabbet.

1. reck: to heed; take care; be thoughtful; to value highly; to be aware of; to take an interest in; to regard as important, worthy of consideration.
2. WRECK: a ship, broken on rocks, or in shoal-water, or by some other means; anything broken, destroyed or fallen down; a person whose health, or whose spirit is undermined; of plans or intentions that are obstructed; to cause such disaster and destruction.

Little did he reck, when he in-insisted on taking the wheel, that in five minutes the car would be a total wreck.

1. recks: the act of taking careful heed, operative of 'to reck' (q.v.).
2. REX: the King's majesty.
3. WRECKS: (') the act of bringing to ruin and disaster.

He who recks not of his bounden duty towards Rex, strengthens the force of evil that wrecks Throne and State.

1. recourse: to flow back, hence, to have the right of returning; to return to some person, or thing, for safety, or for protection.
2. RESOURCE: a backing of money, raw material or goods on which to draw; aid; assistance; ability to adapt what is available in substitution of what is required.

He had recourse to his only resource and that failed.

red
rede } see read.
reed

1. **reef:** a horizontal section of a sail, marked by a row (q.v.) of points, or cords, that may be tied down to reduce the area of canvas exposed to the wind; to shorten sail; to tie a reef-knot.

2. **REEF:** a ridge of rock, or of sand, rising to near the surface of the sea; a lode (q.v.) of gold-bearing rock.

> We had discovered a rich reef, but we lost all our bullion when the shipmaster refused to take in a reef and was, in consequence, wrecked on a reef.

1. **reek:** dense, strong-smelling smoke, steam or other vapour; a foul (q.v.) odour (q.v.); an unclean atmosphere.

2. **RICK:** a stack of farm-produce, particularly of hay, or straw, built and thatched for storage.

3. **RICK:** to sprain, or wrench, a muscle, particularly in the back, or a joint.

4. **WREAK:** to express anger; to seek revenge.

> The reek of burning hay was carried on the wind, and the farmer realized that in this way poachers wreak vengeance, and in attempting to save the rick I gave my back a rick and was laid up for a month.

reel, see **real.**

1. **reflect:** to remember; to concentrate the attention.

2. **REFLECT:** to return an image by the rebound of light; to bend or refract light.

> Young man! Reflect upon what the mirror will reflect in the morning!

1. **refrain:** to abstain; to hold back; to check or stop; to forbear.

2. **REFRAIN:** a chorus; a phrase, or passage, repeated at intervals in a song or poem, generally marking the end of a verse or a stanza.

> I'll refrain from singing the refrain.

reign } see **rain.**
rein }

1. **rent:** money paid at regular periodic intervals by a tenant to a landlord for his occupancy of land, or a tenement, or both.

2. **RENT:** torn; split; shattered or broken open.

> He rent his garments at the thought of paying rent.

1. **repair:** mend; restore to condition; make good a breakage, or the result of wear.

2. **REPAIR:** to go somewhere, to make a journey; an influx of persons to a place.

> I will repair to my native village where they repair their old clothes and are not self-conscious.

report, see **rapport.**

reseed, see **recede.**

1. **residence:** to live, dwell or abide in, or at, a certain place; to be temporarily living at a place in fulfilment of a duty; a house, or other dwelling place.

2. **RESIDENTS:** those who live in a certain place; the population of a town or a borough.

> The local residents went in a deputation to the Town Hall in protest at the scheme to convert the residence, now vacant, in the High Street, into a hostel for coloured immigrants.

residents, see preceding group.

resource, see **recourse.**

1. **rest:** relaxation after work; to be still after movement; sleep; freedom from responsibility; quietness.

2. **REST:** a place set aside for persons to enjoy repose; a home.

3. **REST:** any object on which something may be set, or deposited.

4. **REST:** the remainder; those that are, or that which is, left (q.v.); the balance (q.v.).

5. **WREST:** to twist and pull; to acquire by vigorous action; to obtain by force, or by persecution; to force; to struggle.

> After the effort to wrest the rest of the lease of the Rest from the holder who knew better than to rest on his word, he needed a rest.

1. **resty:** sluggish; lacking energy; lazy; unproductive.

2. **RESTY:** rancid.

3. **RUSTY:** of iron (q.v.) or steel (q.v.),

covered with oxide; of persons, lacking culture; of intellect, dulled by want of use; of plants, affected by fungus or mould (q.v.); of clothing, old and faded; of horses, restive, hence, of persons displaying bad temper.

4. RUSTY: alternative spelling of No. 2 above.

He was a resty, sleepy character, wearing a rusty frock-coat with rusty steel buttons; he smelt resty, and when crossed, he cut up very rusty: he was a victim of a certain psychopathogenic condition the name of which eludes me: I am very rusty on the subject.

retch, see reach.

1. **retort:** to reply sharply and wittily to a verbal attack; to give a strong answer to a statement; to give such a reply.

2. RETORT: a vessel, or a chamber, in which substances for distillation are heated; an alembic.

Accused of firing the retort without filling it, he made the sharp retort that by the speaker's example he thought gas came off automatically.

1. **reveal:** make known; disclose; publish; tell.

2. REVEL: merrymaking; boisterous mirth; to enjoy without restraint.

3. REVEL: to draw back blood from some part of the system.

He is of the kind that will revel in a chance to reveal matters reflecting upon someone else.

revel, see preceding group.

1. **review:** to look again; to revise a literary production; an inspection of the armed forces of the Crown; a critical account of a book; a periodical that criticizes current (q.v.) events.

2. REVUE: a form of light entertainment, with sound-effect called music, consisting of unconnected, and generally pointless, scenes.

The Exposit Weekly Review published a perfectly sizzling review of *The Bunkum Bilge Revue* at The Palace.

1. **revolution:** the act of rotating; the

period of time in which a complete circuit is made.

2. REVOLUTION: sudden and unexpected change; complete change; the (often forcible) overthrow of a government by the governed.

That particular revolution of the Earth on its axis when the revolution and regicide occurred should remain unnumbered in the calendar of history.

revue, see review.

Rex, see recks.

1. **rheum:** a watery discharge from the eye, nose or mouth, any mucous discharge; catarrh.

2. RHEUM: the botanical name for rhubarb.

3. ROOM: a space within a building having a floor, a ceiling (q.v.) and bounded by four or more walls.

4. ROOM: to have space; to make space for something; to stand aside for a person to pass (q.v.); a space allocated to house a certain article or articles.

To alleviate your rheum take hot stewed rheum without sugar and stay in your room, thus making room for one whose nose does not drip to visit the yacht and collect the documents I pushed into the chartroom.

1. **Rhodes:** the largest island in the Dodecanese archipelago and the most easterly island in the Aegean Sea.

2. RHODES: the surname of Cecil John Rhodes (1853–1902), pioneer of African expansion, founder of Rhodesia.

3. ROADS: pl of 'road', a path (q.v.).

4. ROADS: pl, but also the usual form, of 'road', a strip of sheltered water; an anchorage.

Cecil Rhodes, sleeping on the deck of his yacht anchored in the roads off Rhodes during a vacation, was heard to mutter, 'All roads lead from the Cape to Cairo.'

1. **Rhône:** a European river flowing from the Rhône Glacier to the lake of Geneva, and onwards through France to the Mediterranean Sea, about 500 miles.

2. ROAN: archaic spelling of Rouen, France.
3. ROAN: of mixed colours; of an animal whose basic coat is speckled with another colour.
4. ROAN: an archaic shade of colour between chestnut-brown and red.
5 ROAN: a leather similar to morocco leather.
6. ROWAN: the mountain-ash tree, *Pyrus aucuparia.*

Riding a strawberry-roan mare and wearing top-boots made of roan, he set out to view the rowan-tree plantation, having in mind a plan to grow them on the banks of the Rhône.

1. **rhyme:** consonance of terminal words in metrical lines of poetry; two words in which the syllables preceding the last stressed vowels differ and those following are the same.
2. RIME: frost; freezing fog.

He sat on a stone with the rime on his beard and the rhyme that he wrote was most horribly weird. It's a rhyme of the time when the rime stopped the chime, and that was the reason they slept a whole season.

rick, see reek.
1. **ridden:** pst ppl of 'rid', to clear away, to dispose of; to disencumber; to kill or destroy.
2. RIDDEN: pst ppl of the v 'to ride', be conveyed, be a passenger in a vehicle; bestride and manage a horse.

I have ridden over with a load of poisoned bait which you must spread about if you are to be ridden of rats.

1. **riddle:** obscure English composition; a phrase or sentence containing a rebus or pun for the listener to discover, hence, a form of juvenile entertainment.
2. RIDDLE: a sieve, hence to pierce with many holes.

Fighting in Fuzzwuzzania is not fun: they ask each prisoner a riddle harder than that of the Sphinx and when he does not solve it they riddle him with bullets.

1. **rifle:** a groove, specifically one of

several cut spirally in the bore (q.v.) of a fire-arm; a fire-arm having such grooves.
2. RIFLE: to search very thorouglhy and rob on a broad basis; to strip; to pillage.
3. RIFLE: to play dice; to dispose of goods by a raffle; to gamble to one's detriment.

If you had the muzzle of a rifle pressed into your midriff you'd let 'em rifle your pockets without so much as a word.

1. **rig:** banter, or ridicule; a mischievous prank; a method of cheating on an organized basis, as in a fair (q.v.) or market.
2. RIG: the masts, spars, cordage and sails of a sailing-vessel; the combination of these that give the vessel a specialized name, as schooner, ketch, barque (q.v.), etc.; to erect masts and run cordage.

While they rig the schooner, the crew, sent ashore to purchase tropical rig, are stripped of every penny by a thimble-rig man.

1. **rigger:** one who erects masts and standing cordage on a ship, or pylons, or scaffolding, ashore.
2. RIGOR: stiffening of the limbs; temporary or permanent paralysis of the muscles.
3. RIGOUR: severity; sternness; hard weather (q.v.) conditions.

The rigour the rigger exercised in diet was to prevent rigor.

1. **right:** the side of the body that, when facing north, is to the east; that which is correct; an irrefutable claim; an angle (q.v.) of 90°.
2. RITE: a ceremony of a strongly established kind; ceremonies connected with religious observances.
3. WRIGHT: a constructional craftsman.
4. WRITE: to inscribe letters of the alphabet in such order as will make words.

None has the right to either enter or leave after the priest takes the wand in his right hand. and the rite has commenced: it is not right to make light of such solemnity, that is why the playwright was forbidden to write a play concerning it.

rigor ⎫ see **rigger.**
rigour ⎰

rime, see **rhyme.**

1. **ring:** to emit the sound of a bell; a rich resonance in the voice; to sound loud and clear.

2. **RING:** an enclosed space of any size or shape set aside for sports, generally of a brutal nature.

3. **RING:** an endless circular band of metal or other material.

4. **WRING:** to twist, or press strongly; to force juice out of fruit; to extract information; to knead (q.v.) and twist the hands together in grief; to cause distress.

They lead the bull by the ring through the nasal septum into the ring, and ring bells, and their voices ring with glee, and they wring the perspiration from their handkerchiefs while the poor beast is slowly and brutally slaughtered.

1. **ringer:** one who performs upon bells, particularly a member of the team who peal (q.v.) church bells.

2. **WRINGER:** a piece of domestic machinery used for squeezing the water out of garments and the like after washing.

Jack Triples, the ringer of our tenor bell, always turns his wife's wringer: he says it keeps his muscles in trim.

1. **riot:** disorder and violence by a group of citizens; lack of restraint; wastefulness; a wild party; abundance; exuberance; excess.

2. **RYOT:** an Indian tenant-farmer or smallholder.

There was a riot when a ryot set up a stall in the bazaar.

1. **ripe:** sufficiently developed to be edible, or nubile; to be of advanced age; to be sober in judgement.

2. **RYPE:** a ptarmigan; a mountain bird of the family *Lagopus.*

The rype you shot was not ripe.

rite, see **right.**

1. **road:** the metalled path from place to place along which journeys are made; the carriage-way as distinct from the pavement or footpath; a

route; the track along which the lines are set forming a railway.

2. **ROAD:** a sheltered strip of the sea where ships may rest at anchor, generally pronounced roads, (q.v.).

3. **RODE:** pst tns of 'ride'.

4. **ROED:** having roe (q.v.).

5. **ROWED:** pst tns of 'row' (q.v.).

He rode four miles along the road then rowed across the ferry to procure a soft-roed bloater for his tea.

roads, see **Rhodes.**

1. **roam:** to walk without cause and without pre-determined destination; to amble; to wander.

2. **ROME:** a city on the west coast of Italy; the Roman Empire; the jurisdiction of the Pope, hence, the Roman Catholic religion.

In his youth he would roam from creed to creed but now he is a staunch Son of Rome.

roan, see **Rhône.**

roar, see **raw.**

1. **roc:** a mythical gigantic bird in the actuality of which the Arabs believe, and the probable eggs of which explorers claim, from time to time, to have found.

2. **ROCK:** a mountain, or a cliff, or a reef of stone; a piece of this material; the fused foundation forming the earth's crust; any form of crystallized mineral; extended to describe any substance that is abnormally hard.

3. **ROCK:** a hard sweetmeat, generally cylindrical in form, having a red exterior and a white core impressed from end to end with the name of the town (seaside resort) in which it it is sold; any hard sweetmeat.

4. **ROCK:** pertaining to a gentle swaying movement that is calculated to induce slumber.

5. **ROCK:** a distaff.

I suck Southend rock, angels rock me gently to sleep, suddenly a roc swoops down and seizes me and I regain consciousness having been struck on the head by a falling rock.

rock, see preceding group.

1. **rocket:** a shell or a missile (q.v.)

self-propelled by means of a rearward discharge of products of combustion; a firework of this nature.

2. ROCKET: to rise upward at a high speed.

3. ROCKET: a form of edible leaf, used in Europe for salad, *Eruca sativa.*

When the International Committee for Universal Disaster decided to send a rocket to Mars, they set up a sub-committee to decide the nature of its head; the German delegate demanded an atom bomb, but the Frenchman said a bowl of rocket salad would be a pretty compliment.

rode, see road.

1. roe: a species of deer, *Capreolus Capraea.*

2. ROE: the egg packed ovarian cyst of a fish.

3. ROW: objects, or people, arranged in line.

4. ROW: a quarrel; a great deal of disturbing noise.

5. ROW: to use sweeps, or oars, to propel a boat.

There was such a row on the beach that he wished to go for a row but his father refused him a boat with the result there was a row, because a whole row were tied up at the jetty. He was so angry that he had to go into *The Roe-Buck and Heather* and have soft roe on toast.

roed, see road.

1. roes: pl of 'roe' (q.v.).

2. ROSE: a flower of the genus *Rosa;* the armorial badge of the English sovereign, hence, the emblem of the English Nation; the symbol of beauty, or perfection; a pale red colour; an optimistic outlook or appraisal of social facts.

3. ROSE: pst tns of 'rise'.

4. ROWS: pl of 'row' (q.v.), objects in line.

The prospective M.P. rose, took from the glass on the table a red rose and made pious patriotic remarks around it; then, assuring his audience that he took no rose-tinted view of current affairs; he made a dramatic

gesture and alas! out of his back pocket fell a tin of soft roes, and the dense packed rows of his would-be constituents laughed heartily.

1. roke: smoke; steam; fog; polluted air; a reek.

2. ROOK: a large black bird; a crow (q.v.) *Corvus frugilegus.*

3. ROOK: a piece used in the game of chess, the Castle.

4. ROOK: fleece (q.v.), cheat, overcharge.

He sits in the roke of a nightclub where he grows hoarse as a rook through drink, and the 'wide boys' rook him unmercifully: one of them sold him a boxwood chess-rook, guaranteed to be an antique Chinese ivory carving.

1. rôle: the part played by an actor; one's duty, or function or position in life.

2. ROLL: a length of flexible material wrapped about itself to form a cylinder.

3. ROLL: pastry or pudding in cylindrical form; a very small loaf (q.v.) of bread.

4. ROLL: to push a circular, cylindrical or a spherical object along.

5. ROLL: membranes of inscribed parchment sewn one below another and wrapped about itself, forming a cylinder; a register; a list of names.

Your rôle is to roll the cloth, mine to call the roll, his to roll the goods round to the customer, and if you put each roll back into the right place we'll have Swiss roll for tea.

roll, see preceding group.

Rome, see roam.

1. rondeau: a poem of thirteen lines, having only two rhymes and a repetition of the opening words.

2. RONDEL: alternative spelling of No. 1 above; a round tower.

3. ROUNDEL: in heraldry, a circle of either metal or of any tincture or fur; a round change; the round of a ladder.

4. ROUNDLE: a circle; a ring; a circular wooden trencher; a round shield; a round pane (q.v.) of glass in a window; a small round decorative

panel; alternative spelling of No. 1 above.

A carved roundle with the arms of the Medicis repeating the roundel six times set him to work trying to describe it in a rondel.

rondel, see preceding group.

1. **rood:** the cross of Christ; a crucifix.
2. ROOD: a measure, either lineal or superficial, allied to the rod (q.v.), pole (q.v.) or perch (q.v.) but lacking standardization.
3. RUDE: rough; lacking fine finish or polish (q.v.); crude; rugged.
4. RUDE: a display of bad manners; uneducated; lacking in refinement; uncultured; deficient.
5. RUDE: sexual inferences, conversation or behaviour.
6. RUED: pst ppl of 'rue' (q.v), to have suffered remorse.

He rued having been rude to the local squire, who claimed to have unearthed an ancient rood, when his application to rent a rood of land was rejected.

rook, see **roke.**
room, see **rheum.**

1. **root:** the nutriment and moisture absorbing ramifications of the stem of a plant beneath the soil; the basal part of a thing, or an organ, involved in another thing or organ; the cause of an event or of a complex of events; the place of origin of a thing or a person; a number that multiplies to a square or a cube.
2. ROTE: to learn by a process of repetition without complete understanding.
3. ROUT: absolute defeat; a disorganized rabble; to dig with the snout, hence, to turn a person out of bed.
4. ROUTE: predetermined direction; course; way, or road, for a journey.
5. WROTE: pst tns of the v 'to write' (q.v.).

A secret route over the hill enabled us to rout the enemy, and days later, stragglers, whom we watched rout for roots, were rounded up and made to learn by rote how to ask the route to

the prisoners' camp, but we also wrote it with charcoal on their backs.

rose, see **roes.**

1. **rota:** a political theory of rotation in government; a rotation; a list of people serving or doing a tour of duty in rotation.
2. ROTOR: the armature of an electric generator or motor; a wind-motor.

You are sixth on the rota, one to four a.m.: the rotor must be watched twenty-four hours a day.

rote, see **root.**
rotor, see **rota.**
rotten } see **ratan.**
rotton }

1. **rough:** not smooth; harsh, irregular surface; broken ground with thick undergrowth; lacking refinement; ill-mannered; a hairy skin; a shaggy coat; heavy-handed; not gentle; inclined to violence of both language and action; unfinished; crude.
2. RUFF: a sparoid sea fish; a freshwater fish, *Acerina cernua*; a male bird, *Tringa* or *Machetes pugnax*.
3. RUFF: a projecting, fluted, stiffened collar, as worn (q.v.) during the reigns of both Queen Elizabeth I, and King James VI and I.
4. RUFF: a state of elation or excitement, hence, swagger, bluster.
5. RUFF: in heraldry, of a ship in motion.

The boiled ruff gave him indigestion: he began to ruff at everyone, and pulled his neighbour's ruff, but he was among friends who had a rough idea of his disability and did not get rough with him.

roundel } see **rondeau.**
roundle }

1. **rouse:** to waken; to stir into activity; to set in motion; any disturbing event or circumstance.
2. ROUSE: the morning bugle-call in an infantry regiment.
3. ROUSE: of a bird, to shake the feathers; of an animal, the coat.
4. ROUSE: a bout of drunkenness; a carousel.
5. ROWS ('): pl of 'row' (q.v.), quarrels.

6. ROWS ('): pl of 'row', a line (q.v.).
  They are constantly having rows because nothing will ever rouse him in the morning, and in consequence of his neglect whole rows of plants are destroyed.

rout ⎫ see root.
route ⎭

1. rove: to wander aimlessly.
2. ROVE: to sail the seas with no particular destination in mind; to be engaged in piracy.
3. ROVE: a thread of wool, or of cotton, drawn out and twisted.
4. ROVE: a washer, or ring over which nails are clinched in shipbuilding.
5. ROVE: a special method of ploughing.
6. ROVE: pst tns of 'reeve' (q.v.), through.
  He would rove about the countryside, watching the ploughman rove; his fingers incessantly at play upon a copper rove rove upon a tarred string about his neck; the local rustics believed he had rove upon the high seas in his time, and they envied him his suit of woollen rove.

row, see roe.
rowan, see Rhône.
rowed, see road.
rows (ranks), see roes.
rows (quarrels), see rouse.
1. Royalty: Kings, Queens, Princes and Princesses individually and collectively; any member of a Royal Family; Sovereignty.
2. ROYALTY: a percentage of the retail price of a book, or of the box-office takings at a theatre, paid by respectively a publisher or a producer to an author; similar payments made by a commercial enterprise to a landowner for the privilege of working a mine, or by a manufacturing organization to an inventor.
  When the author, upon acceptance of his first book, excitedly told his wife that they would now receive royalty, she replied that they could not entertain even foreign Royalty unless they had a new carpet.

rude, see rood.

1. rue: sorrow; distress of mind; repentance; to regret, to be contrite; to suffer remorse.
2. RUE: a medicinal bitter herb, being leaves of the evergreen shrub, *Ruta graveolens*.
  You may yet rue the day you decided that rue is the panacea.

rued, see rood.
1. rues: to actively rue (q.v.), to be regretting.
2. RUSE: a stratagem; a trick; a pretence; a hunted animal's sudden turn to confuse its scent (q.v.).
  He rues the day he tried that ruse.

ruff, see rough.
rug, see rag.
1. rule: a standard of behaviour, imposed upon a group of people, but having less authority than a bye-law; a customary set of compulsions and prohibitions.
2. RULE: a strip of type-metal from which a line is printed.
3. RULE: a lath (q.v.) or a tape, graduated in either inches and fractions, or millimetres and multiples, or both, used for measuring, and for guiding a scribing tool.
  By the Trade Union's new rule, the employer must supply every workman with a steel-rule.
1. ruler: one having authority; a sovereign, or the president of a republic: the head of a state, or other community; the chief, or headman, among primitive people.
2. RULER: a lath (q.v.) or a cylinder, used for guiding the pen or pencil in drawing straight lines.
  Armed with nothing more formidable than an eighteen-inch ruler, he established himself ruler over twenty thousand savage warriors.
1. rum: abbreviation of 'rubullion', or 'rumbustion', a strong spirituous drink distilled from by-products of sugar-cane, chiefly in the West Indies.
2. RUM: strange of manner; unsociable; abnormal in dress or habit.
3. RUM: in Ireland, a poor country parson.
  The local Rum is a rum fellow

when he has a drop taken: it's rum he's been at now.

1. **rung:** one of the horizontal footholds between the strings of a ladder; a strong round stick (q.v.) used as a rail (q.v.).
2. RUNG: of a bull or an ox having a ring (q.v.) inserted in the nasal septum.
3. RUNG: pst ppl of the v 'to ring' a bell.
4. WRUNG: pst ppl of the v to wring (q.v.) to twist a cloth for the purpose of expressing water or other liquid; to have been deeply distressed.

It wrung my heart to hear the bellow of the bull-calf when it was rung; the sound has rung in my ears for days and it pleased me to learn that he had broken more than one rung of the farmer's cart-rail.

ruse, see **rues.**

1. **rush:** a plant, *Juncaceae*, used in the past (q.v.) for floor covering, and also as an illuminant; a thing of no value.
2. RUSH: to move with speed; to cause a thing, or a person, to move with speed; to induce a person to reach a decision without due consideration; to cheat by over-charging; a sudden migration of numerous people to a specific place for a particular purpose.

You rush to join the gold-rush, and the store men will rush you for a shovel or a billy-can, and you will return, if you survive, worth not a rush.

rusty, see **resty.**

1. **rut:** a state of sexual excitement in animals.
2. RUT: a furrow, track or trench depressed deeply in a road (q.v.) by the passage of wheels: an unchanged procession of habits, or way of life.

He is in so deep a rut that were a stag in rut to attack him he could not deviate to save his life.

1. **Ruth:** a Biblical character, the symbol of faithfulness; a feminine personal name.
2. RUTH: the quality of pity, compassion, mercy; sorrow, mournfulness.

Ruth had ruth for Naomi, and Naomi, ruth for Ruth.

1. **rye:** a form of grain used extensively in Central and Eastern Europe for making bread, *Secale cereale.*
2. RYE-GRASS: alternative spelling of ray-grass, wild rye; grass of the genus *Elymus.*
3. WRY: twisted; contorted; a contortion of the features expressive of disgust, distaste, dislike, disapproval; ill-temper; injustice; deviation; awry.

He made a wry face at rye bread.

ryot, see **riot.**
rype, see **ripe.**
ryper, see **riper.**

S

1. **Sabbath:** the seventh day, to be kept Holy by order of the Fourth Commandment; a period of rest (q.v.) and religious observance; a witches' frolic
2. SABOATH: an army; a host (q.v.).

Lord God of Saboath, bless Thy Holy Sabbath.

saboath, see preceding group.

1. **sac:** one of the rights of jurisdiction vested in the Lord of the Manor in the feudal period, sac and soc.
2. SAC: a tubular cavity, closed at one end.
3. SACK: a bag, usually large, of canvas or other coarse (q.v.) material.
4. SACK: to destroy.
5. SACK: white wine.
6. SACK (sl): to give or to receive dismissal from employment.

He was proved to be drinking the master's sack, a sack full of empty bottles being under his bed, and he got the sack without notice for fear he would sack the place, hence, he set up a soap box on the corner of the cul-de-sac off the High Street in our local town, and publicly denounced our good master whom he declared to be worse than a feudal baron with powers of sac, soc and infangethef.

sack, see preceding group.

1. **sage:** wisdom; a person possessed of wisdom.
2. SAGE: a plant, *Salvia Officinalis*.
   The cook gave some sage advice about sage.
1. **sail:** a sheet of spread canvas by means of which the wind pressure is used to propel a ship; any device to catch the wind and convert it into power for grinding corn, or for pumping water; a device to catch the wind and drive a dynamo to supply electrical power.
2. SAIL: of a ship propelled by the wind; to control such a ship; to make a voyage in such a ship
3. SALE: the act of exchanging goods for money; to offer goods in exchange for money; a seasonal disposal of large quantities of inferior goods on the pretence that they are remainders, offered at a loss.
   On our way to the jetty where one could arrange not only to go for a sail, but to be taught to sail, we passed a draper's shop with an 'end of season' sale in progress, and Mary stopped dead. I fingered the 'Trip Round the Bay' tickets in my pocket meditating that I might as well offer them for sale at a cut price to the passers by.
1. **sailer:** of a sailing ship with reference to her performance when under way (q.v.).
2. SAILOR: a mariner; one whose occupation is that of working a ship.
   The 'Torrens', as every sailor knew, was a good sailer, so she never lacked a crew.
sailor, see preceding group.
1. **saim:** obsolete spelling of seam (q.v.) a cooking fat.
2. SAME: identical with another; unchanged; in agreement.
   The fried egg will be flavoured with onion—I used the same saim.
1. **sain:** to make the Sign of the Cross on, or over, a thing or a person as a protection from witchcraft.
2. SANE: rational; mentally balanced; not mad.

Oh Father! Sain me: for though they say my neighbour is sane, she is most surely possessed of an evil spirit!
1. **salaam:** Peace; an Oriental form of greeting, often accompanied by a low bow (q.v).
2. SLALOM: a ski (q.v.) race with obstacles on the track.
3. SLAM: to close doors, books, windows, boxes and the like with violence and noise; to speak to a person in a rude and aggressive manner.
   He'll salaam the master and slam the servant.
salary, see celery.
sale, see sail.
1. **sallow:** a plant of the genus *Salex*; a willow.
2. SALLOW: a moth of the genus *Xanthia*.
3. SALLOW: a skin of a dark hue (q.v.); yellow or brown complexion.
   The fellow with the sallow complexion took a colour-photograph of a sallow moth feeding on a sallow bush.
1. **salon:** a reception room in a mansion; the room of a Parisian lady, hence, a gathering of artists and writers as guests; the Exhibition of Art held annually in Paris.
2. SALOON: a large room, or a hall, where exhibitions may be held; a large cabin where first-class passengers gather on a ship; a railway car furnished like a drawing-room; a hall, open to the public, for dancing, playing at billiards and the like; a barber's shop; the more expensive bar of a public-house.
   London lacks culture: there is no salon as in Paris, and in Paris there is no saloon bar.
saloon, see preceding group.
1. **salt:** Sodium chloride, NaCl; to preserve with salt; a sailor; the end product of a chemical union of an acid and a base.
2. SALT: the condition of rut (q.v.) in a bitch.
3. SAUGHT: an agreement; to be in agreement, reconciled, at peace.
4. SAULT: an assault, or attack.

5. SAULT: a jump or leap.
6. SAULT: a waterfall; rapids.
7. SAUT: ransom for murder.
8. SAUTE: fried, particularly in butter; cold boiled potatoes fried rapidly in butter.
9. SORT: a particular kind or type of person or thing.
10. SORT: to separate one type of thing from among other types of things.
11. SOUGHT: pst ppl of 'seek', to have been searched for, or desired.

> He is not worth his salt: he is the sort that has never sought an honest living, and is not suitable even to sort rags.

salter ⎱ see psalter.
saltire ⎰

1. salvage: payment made to persons who save a ship, or its cargo, from loss; the saving of goods and other property from loss by fire, flood or other disaster; the goods so saved.
2. SELVAGE: either edge of a length of cloth.
3. SELVEDGE: alternative spelling of No. 2 above.

> In the sale of salvage were rolls of cloth only slightly scorched on the selvage.

same, see saim.
sane, see sain.
sank, see cinq.

1. sap: the vital fluid that carries the life force of plants.
2. SAP: a cut-and-cover tunnel used to make a concealed attack; to dig a cavity under defences.
3. SAP (sl): one who takes pleasures in books and learning.
4. SAP (sl): a simpleton.

> The twins were identical of form but opposite of mind: John was a sap who could not close a book, James a sap that could not open one: John received the O.B.E. for making synthetic sap to increase crops at home, John won the D.S.O. for drilling a sap under the Hun's main line of defence.

1. sari: the exquisitely beautiful, simple and becoming costume habitually worn by Indian women.
2. SURREY: a South Eastern county of England.

3. SORRY: an apology; an expression of sympathy; distress; a lamentation; to feel grief or sadness; in poor condition; of inferior quality.

> The male natives, in a certain Surrey vilage, still discuss, with enthusiasm, the sari worn by an Indian lady who visited there more than ten years ago, and the females are sorry they did not give the garment more attention.

1. satire: a written, or a spoken, denunciation of vice or folly by means of wit, sarcasm or irony.
2. SATYR: in ancient Greek mythology, a being, human to the waist (q.v.) (though horned on the brow) and goat from the waist down; a spirit of the woods.
3. SATYR: the ape, orang-utan, *Simia satyrus*.
4. SATYR: a butterfly of the *Satyridae* type.

> The new play is a satire in which a Satyr, playing sweetly on a shepherd's pipe, is supressed by a satyr escaped from the orang-utan cage at the Zoo, who blows discordantly down a saxophone, and stops only to snatch at the satyr as they flutter near, and eat them.

satyr, see preceding group.

1. sauce: a liquid prepared for the purpose of adding a relish to an otherwise plain (q.v.) dish.
2. SAUCE (sl): impertinence.
3. SOURCE: place of origin; cause of a chain of events; a spring (q.v.); the starting point of a stream or river.

> Sauce from tomatoes for men, but the source of the average boy's sauce is the Youth Club.

saught ⎫
sault ⎬ see salt.
saut   ⎪
saute ⎭

1. savant: a scholar; a man of learning.
2. SAVANTE: French boxing in which kicking is as legitimate as punching.
3. SERVANT: one who works for an employer; one who serves.

> The savant lives in the slums and has for his servant a former savante champion.

savante, see preceding group.

1. saver: one who, or that which, conserves; a thrifty person; a device to assist in economic consumption of a commodity.
2. savor: flavour and aroma; to enjoy a flavour or aroma; to have especial tastiness; to detect a background flavour.
3. savour: alternative, and usual British spelling, of No. 2 above.

The soup is greatly improved, it now has a pleasant and warming savour due to the cook having installed an asbestos saucepan saver.

savor }
savour } see preceding group.

1. saw: a maxim, or proverb.
2. saw: a plate of thin steel cut into triangular teeth along one edge and fitted at one end into a handle, used for cutting wood, metal, stone or other substances.
3. saw: pst tns of 'see' (q.v.).
4. soar: to rise to a great height, or to glide upon the wing.
5. sore: an eruption of the skin; in a painful condition; grieved; angry; of a serious or distressing character.

I saw upon Victoria Embankment, where sea-gulls soar above Cleopatra's Needle, a man with red, watering, sore sightless eyes, who produced on an old steel saw, dulcet melody as from a vlolin, and reflected on a saw or two concerning patience, and meek submission to fate.

1. sawed: pst tns of the v 'to saw'; to have cut with a saw (q.v.).
2. soared: pst tns of the v 'to soar' (q.v.).
3. sword: a weapon consisting of a long slender blade mounted in a handle, or hilt, suitable for either cutting or thrusting; this weapon used as a symbol.

His rectitude and his achievement had sawed through all social barriers, and his heart soared with emotion as the sword of the accolade rested upon him.

1. scald: to immerse in, to treat with, to subject to, water or other liquid, at a very high temperature.
2. scald: ringworm, and other affections of the scalp.
3. scalled: alternative spelling of No. 2 above.
4. skald: a poet in ancient Scandinavia who sang the fights and victories of the Norsemen.

To cure his scald-head, scald linseed, and lay it on hot enough to scald; the patient will give you a blood-curdling recitation like a skald of old.

1. scale: a balanced beam provided with a pan, or holder, at each end, used for weighing.
2. scale: a graduated rod, or dial; a standard of measurement; a comparative pertaining to magnitude, or extent.
3. scale: a series of musical notes arranged in ascending or descending order at fixed intervals.
4. scale: flakes of horny epidermis growing in laminations and protecting the skin of fish, reptiles and some insects, hence, any crust or hard deposit.
5. scale: to mount; to climb; to climb over; a ladder; a staircase.

The scale of pay the men get for removing scale from boilers is so-much a hundredweight: each man shovels his own cuttings onto the scale, and as the scale turns they scale the heights of Parnassus, and sing lustily up and down the scale.

scalled, see scald.
scallop, see escallop.

1. scar: a rocky face on a mountain; a cliff; a rock formation in the sea bed.
2. scar: a superficial blemish or mark on the skin, being the site (q.v.) of a previous wound, burn, or other injury.

The scar on my head commemorates a fall down a scar when a boy.

1. scene: the place and time of an occurrence; the registration of strong disapproval in a quarrelsome manner; the aspect of objects in their setting as cognized either objec-

tively by the eye, or subjectively by the mind; the setting of either action or dialogue in fiction; a division of an act in a stage-play; the painted canvas used to create stage-effect; the environment.

2. SEEN: pst ppl of the v 'to see' (q.v.). You can't have seen it, you were not on the scene.

scent, see cent.

1. **sceptic:** one who doubts; a disciple of Pyrrho who doubted the possibility of real knowledge; one who reserves judgement, or acceptance, pending proof.

2. SEPTIC: putrefying, hence poisoned by the product of putrefaction; festered; unclean; invaded by bacteria.

The fat district medical officer said septic tanks right themselves: the thin district sanitary engineer—a sceptic if there ever was one—ordered them to be cleaned nevertheless.

1. **Scilly:** the name of a group of small islands, being outliers of the granite highlands of Cornwall.

2. SILLERY: a wine of champagne type.

3. SILLY: foolish; unwise; mentally deficient.

The clerk, having had a glass of sillery with his mid-day sandwich, made a spelling mistake that sent a party of mentally retarded children to the Scilly Islands instead of the Silly School.

scion, see cion.

scollop, see escallop.

1. **Scot:** an ancient Gallic-speaking people who, ca. eleventh century, migrated from Ireland and settled in the northern part of Britain. They subsequently gave their name to the area, hence a person of Scottish blood.

2. SCOT: a payment; a share of the cost of entertainment; a tax levied on inhabitants of the marshes of Kent and Sussex.

McTavish insisted, being a true Scot, on making payment scot and lot but not a single bawbee more.

1. **Scotch:** pertaining to any product that is a speciality of Scotland, as whisky, shortbread, tweed, etc.; applied to persons from Scotland.

2. SCOTCH: scratch; incision; groove; to scratch out; destroy.

3. SCOTCH: a block, or a wedge, placed under a wheel to prevent a vehicle running downhill under its own volition; to obstruct, or prevent; to hesitate.

MacTavish says that only a Scotchman can drink a pint of neat Scotch and then enter a game of hop-scotch. He declares it a test that will scotch any Sasunnach.

1. **screed:** a long letter (q.v.); a long and tedious report.

2. SCREED: a straight-edged board used for levelling plaster (q.v.) or concrete; plaster or concrete so levelled.

I have received another screed from the contractor complaining about the screed.

1. **scrub:** stunted trees and dense bushes; land so overgrown.

2. SCRUB: a small breed of cattle, hence, a person of no account.

3. SCRUB: to clean by means of a stiff bristled brush applied vigorously.

4. SCRUB (sl): to delete.

Scrub that scrub off our list of guides; he took a party through scrub and bog and they had to scrub their clothes to get them clean.

1. **scull:** to propel a boat with one oar (q.v.) worked over the stern (q.v.).

2. SCULL: a small size oar, a pair of which can be manipulated by one person rowing a boat.

3. SKULL: the bony structure of the head.

They dared him to scull across the harbour and paint a black skull and cross-bones on the white luxury yacht.

sea, see C.

seal, see ceil.

sealing, see ceiling.

1. **seam:** a joining, edge to edge, of any material by any process; the visible line left (q.v.) by such a joint.

2. SEAM: an old standard of weight for a horse load; 3 cwt.

3. SEAM: fat (q.v.) lard.
4. SEEM: to appear to be; to exist in imagination; expressive of uncertainty.
5. XEME: a forked-tailed gull, genus *Xema.*

It would seem that the seam in the cylinder is binding the piston: dress it with a good layer of seam.

1. **seamen:** sailors, mariners, particularly good and competent sailors.
2. SEMEN: the impregnating fluid; the seed of male animals.

British semen made British seamen.

sear, see cere.
1. **seas:** pl (') of sea (q.v.) the ocean as a whole; the high seas.
2. SEES: the act of seeing.
3. SEISE: to put a person in possession of an estate; to bestow or convey a land holding.
4. SEIZE: alternative spelling of No. 3 above; to take possession of goods etc. either by process of law, or by violence; to take hold quickly and avidly of anything; to grasp with hands, teeth or claws (q.v.); to avail oneself of an opportunity; to take in mentally; to splice ropes; of a piston, or other working parts of a machine, rigidly held and prevented from moving by another part; to bind.

If he sees a chance to seize other people's property he will seize it, and the waters of all the seas will not prevent him.

1. **season:** one of the four natural divisions of the year; an appropriate time for an activity, or for consuming certain kinds of food.
2. SEASON: to mature; to become mature.
3. SEASON: to flavour plain food with spices or other pungent essences.

In a good hot season oak will season in a year, and the smell of tannin is strong enough to season a stew.

1. **second:** a measurement of time being one sixtieth part of a minute; a three-thousand-six-hundredth part of an hour.
2. SECOND: following the first; indicated by the ordinal 'nd' following the figure 2—2nd; not the chief; a voice, lower in pitch than the chief voice in a part song; of goods imperfect in manufacture; of goods part used.
3. SECOND: to be the friend, supporter, and the attendant upon a belligerent, either in a duel or a boxing match.

The heavyweight boxer's second declared his man second to none, and asserted that on the night of the match he'd fell his opponent in half a second.

1. **secret:** not patent; not generally revealed; concealed; known to but a few; unknown.
2. SECRETA: a prayer repeated in hushed tones by the celebrant after the Offertory.
3. SECRETA: the products of secretion.
4. SECRETE: to produce matter by glandular, or by similar action; to produce and void waste tissue and matter.
5. SECRETE: to hide (q.v.) to conceal; to convey an object into, or out of, a place by stealth.
6. SECRETE: the process of treating fur with a chemical substance.

While in church, during the murmuring of the Secreta, the secret of the walled garden was suddenly revealed to me, and the secreta of my adrenal glands made my flesh creep and my hair stand on end: I decided, then and there, to secrete myself in a gardener's cart and, with my own eyes, from a secret place, watch them secrete the furs.

secreta ⎫
secrete ⎭ see preceding group.

seder, see cedar.
see, see C.
seed, see cede.
seel, see ceil.
seem, see seam.
seen, see scene.
seer, see cere.
sees ⎫
seise ⎬ see seas.
seize ⎭

1. **sejant:** heraldic term for sitting.

2. SERGEANT: a non-commissioned officer's rank in both the army and the police force.
3. SERJEANT: a lawyer of high degree; a senior barrister-at-law.
   When the drill-sergeant described a member of the school's O.T.C. as a monkey sejant, the Headmaster said it might be slander, and dangerous, because the boy's uncle was a serjeant-at-law.

sell, see cell.
seller, see cellar.
selvage } see salvage.
selvedge }
semen, see seamen.
sense, see cense.
sensual, see censual.
sent, see cent.
sentry, see centaury.
septic, see sceptic.
sere, see cere.

1. serf: a slave; a peasant whose freedom of travel is, or may be, restricted by the landlord.
2. SURF: the turbulent breaking of the waves of the sea (q.v.) on a shallow beach (q.v.).
   Ivan, who listened to agitators, decided he would not be a serf, but would run away to England: however, when he saw the surf he thought he'd rather return home.

1. serge: a fabric of wool and cotton mixture.
2. SURGE: an onrushing wave, hence, of a rope or chain slipping away, a crowd running, or any irresistible progress.
   The women will surge to the sale of serge.

sergeant, see sejant.
serial, see sejant.
serjeant, see sejant.
servant, see savant.
session, see cession.

1. set: a number of objects, or of persons, constituting a unified group.
2. SET: to place in order; to arrange in position; to sharpen; to start a person, or an animal, upon a certain course (q.v.); to commence an activity; to place young plants in the open ground to continue their

growth; to place a trap in position; to harden; to fix; a tool for guiding another tool.
   The weather being set fair, he set out for the village to get his saw set, hoping that when he returned the glue in the joint would be set: on the way he saw the sporting set set dogs at rabbits, and in the next field a set of traps set by the farmer who set the saplings by the roadside, and he reflected that the entire set-up was aimed at the extermination of the cony.

1. seven: the number after six and before eight; 7; VII; vij.
2. SEVERN: the name of the major estuarine river in the West of England.
   Ships from the seven seas anchor in the Severn.

Severn, see preceding group.

1. sew: to join with stitches using either needle or awl (q.v.); to execute decorative work with needle and thread.
2. SO: in that manner (q.v.); similar to; identical with; because of; to a certain extent; in order that; with what effect (q.v.) or result.
3. SOH: one of the sounds of the tonic sol-fa notation.
4. SOUGH: the soothing murmur of gentle winds or of running streams.
5. SOUGH: a bog or a pool; a drain or a sewer (q.v.).
6. SOW: a female pig (q.v.); an ingot of metal (q.v.).
7. SOW: to place seeds in the ground (q.v.); to create discord; to disseminate.
   What, pray, is so attractive about the country? The sough of the wind is drowned by the grunting of the sow; one has but to step out of doors to sink knee-deep in a sough: I find there is nothing to do save sit and sew so, for distraction, I sow discontent among the rustics.

1. sewer: one who sews; who executes needlework; one who joins, or who decorates fabric with stitches.
2. SEWER: a server; a waiter; an attendant at a meal (q.v.).

3. SEWER: the main drain of an urban centre; a cloaca.

4. SOUR: not sweet; of sharp, or acid flavour; fermented; a smell akin to that of acetic acid; peevish, unfriendly; disagreeable.

5. SOWER: one who sows; who places seeds in the ground.

6. SUER: one who sues; who institutes legal proceedings; who litigates.

Penelope was a brilliant woman: not merely a sewer who won medals for art-needlework, but a socially active person. She took the Chair at the Local Ladies' Superintendance Society in which capacity she proved a sower of discord. In addition to their reaching, and publishing, a resolution, 'that this town's sewer is both inadequate and dirty', they circulated an adverse criticism of the Vicar's sermon on 'The Parable of the Sower', and the reverend gentleman, sour at the best of times, was put into a fury and consulted his lawyer who advised him not to fill the role of a suer.

1. shackle: each ring of a pair of manacles or handcuffs; the corresponding parts of fetters; a ring (q.v.) or a loop of iron (q.v.) or steel (q.v.) which can be opened and closed, used for coupling as, for example, the vehicles of a railway train (q.v.); the hinged, U-shaped hook of a padlock.

2. SHEKEL: a Babylonian unit of weight whereby the coinage of antiquity was standardized; used colloquially, generally in the plural, for money.

If you haven't a shekel you haven't a shackle.

shagreen, see chagrin.

1. shake: oscillatory movement; tremor; vibration; to quake or shiver; to move a person roughly to and fro; to agitate the body in order to throw something off; a split in a boat's planking; a rift, or a cleft, in rock or other geological formation.

2. SHEIKH: the chief of an Arab clan or family; the chief, headman or leader of an Arabian settlement, or of a caravan; a general title of respect; an Islamic term for a saint; in India a title of contempt applied to Hindu converts to Mohammedanism; in the English-speaking world a female's term of admiration of the male.

Sure, I guess it'll shake him when he hears Sadie refer to that goggle-eyed giggling guy as a sheikh.

shanty, see chanty.

1. share: the part or fraction due to one when something is divided between a number of persons; one unit of the capital of a Limited Company; to possess property jointly with others; to contribute one's part in work; to apportion.

2. SHARE: the blade of a plough.

I think you share my opinion of the poor quality of the new plough-share, and I assume you will accept your share of the blame for buying it—I think that the high-pressure salesman must have had a share in the firm supplying them.

1. shaw: a small thicket; a common surname.

2. SHORE: where land and water meet; the beach (q.v.).

3. SHORE: a drain.

4. SHORE: a temporary buttress, usually of timber (q.v.) placed against a building or other structure.

5. SHORE: pst tns of 'to shear' or cut.

6. SURE: convinced; satisfied as to the accuracy of a statement; reliable; having certainty.

I am sure that Farmer Shaw shore the sheep too close since they graze along the windy shore with no slight shore to protect them: recently some fell in the shore and were drowned, and ten were killed when the wall collapsed for want of a shore.

1. she: third person feminine pronoun.

2. SKI (she): strips of wood strapped to the feet and used in an Alpine sport of sliding downhill on snow.

Gee! can she ski!

1. shear: a cutting instrument the action of which is on the principle (q.v.) of scissors, hence, to cut.

2. SHEER: precipitous, steep; pure, absolute; of thin fine fabric; unadulterated.

3. SHEER: the line, or curvature upward of the forepart of a ship.

4. SHEER: to drift athwart an anchorage, or, when under way, to make excessive leeway.

To shear off half her bowsprit would be an act of vandalism, spoiling the line of her sheer for no purpose for she'd still sheer off course.

1. shed: a range (q.v.) of high ground between two tracts of flat country; a range of mountains or hills from which a tract of country receives its water supplies.

2. SHED: a light (q.v.) building used for storage or for shelter; a lean-to; a hut.

3. SHED: to drop, exude or discard; to throw off, scatter; part; to fall; to relinquish.

4. SHE'D: contraction of 'she would'.

He shed tears at the thought of the peasant's large family living in a small shed, but the mother said she'd shed blood before they would leave it, and even at midsummer they shed no garments.

sheer, see shear.

1. sheet: a superficial expanse of any material that is thin; the large rectangles of linen used on a bed; a rectangle of paper; a tarpaulin.

2. SHEET: the rope on which a sail is paid out and hauled in.

3. SHEET: the great anchor used in an emergency.

The main sheet carried away and the schooner, riding to her sheet anchor, was in danger of losing her mast when the skipper, who was on watch below, came on deck clad in his cot-sheet like a kilt, and took the matter in hand.

sheikh, see shake.

shekel, see shackle.

1. shift: to move, to change place or position.

2. SHIFT: rotation, especially of workmen; one gang, team or crew following another on a tour (q.v.) of duty; the time of change-over, and the duration of, such a company.

3. SHIFT: a cunning device, stratagem, dodge or trick; to evade an issue; to equivocate.

4. SHIFT: to substitute; to accept cheerfully, something inferior, particularly a meal.

5. SHIFT: a woman's intimate undergarment; a chemise.

Come on! shift yourself. You know I am on the one o'clock shift, so if dinner is not ready I'll have to make shift with bread and cheese—and get that child dressed! Poor little thing, standing shivering in nothing but her shift.

1. shoal: a shallow; a spit (q.v.) or sandbank; a bar.

2. SHOAL: a school, group, or large number of animals, particularly marine mammals and fish; to swarm; to assemble.

They sailed boldly through shoal water to net a shoal of herrings.

1. shoe: a covering, not extending above the ankle, for the human foot; a U-shape steel (q.v.) protector secured under a horse's hoof; a metal socket to receive the lower end of a pole (q.v.) or a mast (q.v.); the outward turned bottom segment of a rainwater fall-pipe; an iron trough to go under a cart wheel when descending a sharp gradient; the face-plate of a brake (q.v.); a metal brush that slides along the conductor rail (q.v.) and picks up current (q.v.) driving an electric train.

2. SHOO!: an exclamation used to drive away cats and other inquisitive creatures.

I went out to shoo the fowls into their coop, and lost my shoe in the mud.

shoo!, see preceding group.

shoot, see chute.

shop, see chop.

shore, see shaw.

shute, see chute.

Sicily, see Cecily.

1. sick: illness; weakness; to vomit; pertaining to ill-health.

2. SICK: to encourage a dog to attack.
3. SIKE: a sigh.
4. SIKE: a stream; a rill; in heraldry, a roundel barry-wavy argent and azure.
5. SIKH: a Punjab warrior.
6. SYKE: alternative spelling of No. 4 above.

A sikh who fell sick refused medicine and, heaving a deep sike asked to be led to a syke in order to say prayers.

1. side: either the left-hand, or the right-hand half of the body from the centre of the spine; the surface of the body from armpit to thigh; the long measurements of a rectangle; the half of anything on either aspect of a median line; near to; the bank, or verge, of an expanse of water; the spin imparted to a billiard ball; support given to one faction or another, or to one of two contrary, or opposing, points of view.
2. SIDE: ostentation; assumption of superiority.
3. SIGHED: pst tns of 'sigh', to express grief by a deep intake of breath.

She settled down by his side at the side of the brook in the shade of the side of the barn and pulled the side out of the cardboard box containing the sandwiches: 'I cannot side with you in your quarrel with the vicar,' she sighed.

sighed, see preceding group.

1. sighs: pl of 'sigh', an involuntary, deep, sobbing breath, expressive of grief.
2. SIZE: magnitude.
3. SIZE: a glutenous substance boiled down from horns, hooves and bones which, in solution, is used to seal (q.v.) the pores of an abosrbent surface.

He sighs that he must size walls of that size.

sight, see cite.
sighted, see cited.

1. sign: to attach one's signature, or one's seal, to a document; to make a significant gesture; to indicate; a mark or a symbol; a board projecting from a building on which appears the owner's name, or his recognizable mark, badge, or cognizance.
2. SIGN: a trace; a vestige; an indicator; an unusual appearance of the sky, or some cataclysm accepted as indicative of divine wrath.
3. SIGN: one of the twelve sections of the Zodiac.
4. SIGN: to make the Sign of the Cross.
5. SINE: one of the terms used in trigonometry; a curve or bend; a gulf (q.v.) or bay (q.v.); the bosom of a garment.

He gives no sign of understanding, sine remains a mystery: he may as well sign on the dotted line and withdraw from the navigator's examination: his sign of the Zodiac must be down; he'd best go and seek solace at the sign of the 'Sextant and Chart'.

signet, see cygnet.

sike⎫
sikh⎭ see sick.

sillery⎫
silly ⎭ see Scilly.

silt, see celt.

1. simulate: to pretend; to pose; to assume an appearance.
2. STIMULATE: to inspire into activity; to imbue with energy; to renew vitality.

The speaker on politics said his party would endeavour to stimulate interest in the welfare of the aged, whereupon a heckler cried out that they simulate interest in everything except their own personal welfare.

sine, see sign.
sinical, see cynical.

1. sink: to submerge; to go down; to recline on a seat or bed; to fall into ill health; to suppress; a stone, or porcelain, or wood, or metal trough, having a drain pipe set in the bottom, built into a kitchen for the disposal of water.
2. ZINC: a blue-grey metal, used chiefly for covering roofs, plating iron, and, in its perforated form, filling ventilation apertures; Zn.

We have our kitchen sink made out of zinc.

sirkar, see **circa.**
sist, see **cist.**
1. **sisterly:** in the manner of a sister; kindly; with genuine solicitude.
2. SYSTOLE: contraction, particularly periodic contraction opposed to dilation, as of the heart.

> When at the heart hospital he learned that he possessed a murmuring systole, his distress became manifest and the sympathetic nurse was most sisterly.

site, see **cite.**
sited, see **cited.**
size, see **sighs.**
skald, see **scald.**
1. **skate:** a large flat fish, *Raia batis.*
2. SKATE: a long narrow thin steel (q.v.) plate (q.v.) secured under the sole (q.v.) of the boots, to enable a gliding progress to be made over ice; a flat plate mounted on four small wheels used for gliding on a flat, but not a frozen surface; to make use of such implements; to proceed, or progress smoothly, quickly and easily in any occupation.
3. SKITE: a sharp, oblique blow.
4. SKITE: a person held in contempt.
5. SKITE: to void excrement.

> You can skate over the repair to the skate that skite brought in, by giving it a good skite with a heavy hammer, then we'll go out and get some skate and chips for lunch.

1. **skep:** a basket, usually rectangular; a bee-hive of wicker-work; a measure of grain (q.v.).
2. SKIP: to spring, or jump, from the ground; to jump over a rope maintained in motion over the head and under the feet; to move with alacrity; to omit, either a portion of reading matter, or a task.

> I want you to skip along to Uncle Tom and borrow his skep: if you do that you can skip lessons this afternoon, and go and skip with the children next door.

1. **skewer:** a dowel stick with a point at one end, or a length of stiff wire pointed at one end and bent into a ring at the other, used for securing rolled meat.

2. SKUA: a predatory gull native of the northern latitudes, *Stercorarius catarrhactes.*

> That old skua has gathered so much meat that I expect him to come in and borrow a skewer.

ski, see **she.**
skip, see **skep.**
skite, see **skate.**
skua, see **skewer.**
skull, see **scull.**
1. **sky:** the firmament; the upper stratum of the atmosphere; the ceiling (q.v.) of clouds.
2. SKYE: the largest island of the Inner Hebrides; the name given to a breed of terrier.

> My Skye-terrier is better than a barometer; he sits and whines at the sky when it's going to rain.

Skye, see preceding group.
1. **slab:** a flat, broad, solid, generally rectangular piece of timber, stone or metal; such a piece of material set up as a bench or counter; a temporary table, hinged to the wall outside a dining-room door, whereon servants can rest trays and the like.
2. SLAB: mud; slimy matter in a mass; viscous.
3. SLAB: a length of wood flat on one side and rounded on the other, being the first cuts from a tree-log to square it for cutting planks.

> The fishmonger, using the edge of a piece cut from a deal slab, scraped the slab of scales and slime from his marble slab.

slalom ⎫
slam ⎬ see **salaam.**

1. **slay:** to kill with a weapon; to bring about the death of a number of persons or animals.
2. SLEIGH: a sledge (q.v.).
3. SLEY: an instrument used in weaving.

> Sure, if he lets that party of kids play with his rickety old sleigh it will slay the lot of 'em.

1. **sleave:** silken fibre that is separated from a thicker fibre; silken thread made for splitting, used by embroiderers.
2. SLEEVE: tubular extensions from a body-garment for the purpose of covering the arms.

3. SLEEVE: any tubular part of a machine, or of an instrument, that houses, or protects, another part.

Did you observe his left sleeve embroidered with his armorial badge executed in multi-colour sleave?

1. sledge: a truck (q.v.) provided with ridges at each side in place of wheels (q.v.) and used for travel and transport of goods over snow and ice.

2. SLEDGE: a heavy, long-handled hammer, as wielded by the blacksmith's striker.

Ivan travelled ten versts by sledge to swing the sledge for Boris the Smith.

1. sleeper: one who slumbers.

2. SLEEPER: a beam (q.v.) or a log of timber placed to support and distribute a heavy load; such logs, transverse to the rails, occurring at regular intervals along a railway track.

3. SLEEPER: a compartment on a railway train fitted with bunks to enable a passenger to sleep through a night journey.

Many a sleeper in many a sleeper mumbles of rails on many a sleeper.

sleeve, see sleave.

sleigh, see slay.

1. sleight: skill; cunning; speed, dexterity; jugglery.

2. SLIGHT: small in quantity; a mere (q.v.) trace; of very little effect; unsubstantial; a person of small build.

3. SLIGHT: an insult; to treat with contempt; to ignore, omit, pass over; treat with disrespect.

Do not slight him! A man of such sleight with the sword might consider the using of it but a slight thing.

1. sleugh: alternative spelling of slough (q.v.) a marshy place.

2. SLEW: alternative spelling of No. 1 above.

3. SLEW: pst tns of 'slay' (q.v.), to have slaughtered.

4. SLEWED: to turn about sharply; to turn an object round on its own axis.

5. SLEW (sl): to make drunk; to cause intoxication.

It near slew me when the oldtimer told me to slew around and beat it before the fumes off the sleugh slew me, like as if I were some tenderfoot dude.

slew, see preceding group.

sley, see slay.

slight, see sleight.

1. slip: to slide; lose one's footing; to fall; an error; to make an error; a false move.

2. SLIP: an article of feminine attire worn as a foundation to lace or some other transparent material; an undergarment.

3. SLIP: anything long and narrow as, for example, the paper on which a printer pulls proofs from a galley of type; a thin, young person.

4. SLIP: a twig, or a cutting from a plant.

5. SLIP: a mixture of fine clay and water used in pottery making.

Slip into your slip and slip along to my study and bring me the galley-slip on my desk, but mind you do not slip on the polished floor, you are only a slip of a girl and we want no broken bones.

1. sloe: the fruit of the blackthorn, *Prunus spinosa*.

2. SLOW: at a low speed; lacking vigour; dull.

He found life slow till he found sloe-gin.

1. slop: a loose garment; an ill-fitting garment; clothing supplied to seamen; any inferior garment.

2. SLOP: liquid or semi-liquid forms of food; refuse of liquids; mud; slime; sentiment.

3. SLOP (sl): a police-constable.

Though he was disguised in a slop rigout from the ship's store, the crew knew he was a slop, so they made it a point of honour to slop every bucket of bilge-water over him.

1. slot: an opening in some form of machine or apparatus for the insertion of a coin.

2. SLOT: a groove or opening cut in wood or in other material.

3. SLOT: a rod or bar; a cross-piece; a bolt (q.v.).

4. SLOT: a deer's hoof, hence, the track of a deer, extended to that of any animal; a trail; a scent (q.v.).
We had to cut a slot in the post to fix the new fool-proof slot the master bought in town, and while working, all the prize deer escaped into the woods and we had to follow their slot. When we emerged on a main road we got chocolate out of a slot-machine.

1. smack: a slap; a resounding blow from the flat hand; the sound of parting the lips, of kissing noisily; the crack of a whip.

2. SMACK: a flavour; a distinctive taste; a suggestion of such taste; a sample, or to sample.

3. SMACK: a fore-and-aft rigged vessel of light burden (q.v.) often used for fishing.
I'd like to smack him in the eye—with that smack of salt about him he convinced me he had a commission to sell a racing yacht, and when I went to view it I found a smack, stinking of fish, and without standing gear.

1. smart: a peripheral pricking or stinging sensation; any form of pain, either physical or mental.

2. SMART: fashionable; neat; tidy; well groomed.

3. SMART: witty; clever; quick in perception; apt at repartee.
I'll make that boy smart for his smart remarks to my smart customers.

1. smelt: to melt; to extract metal from its ore (q.v.) by subjecting it to heat.

2. SMELT: a fish, *Osmerus eparlanus*, also the related *Osmerus mordax*.

3. SMELT: to have cognized by the sense peculiar to the olfactory organ; to have investigated by inhaling sharply through the nose to have exuded an odour (q.v.).
We had put the crucible in the furnace to smelt when Jack said he smelt gas, but Bob retorted that what was smelt was the fried smelt Jack had in his dinner basket.

1. snarl: to emit an angry growling sound and lay bare the teeth prior to making an attack; a disagreeable quarrelsome tone of voice.

2. SNARL: to tangle; to make an incorrect knot (q.v.); to involve, or to become involved, in a complex situation; a trap made from crossing cords, a net; to catch in a net; to strangle.
You do-gooders who poke into other people's affairs find yourselves in a snarl, and you earn a snarl from everyone concerned.

so, see sew.

1. soak: to immerse in liquid for a prolonged period; to absorb liquid; a drunkard.

2. SOKE: a city and its environs, or a rural area having a right of local jurisdiction.
They soak clay-pipes in mead in the Soke of Snailhurst.

soar, see saw.

soared, see sawed.

soh, see sew.

soke, see soak.

1. sold: pst ppl of 'sell' (q.v.); exchanged for money.

2. SOLD: money paid in wages particularly to soldiers.

3. SOLED: provided with a sole.

4. SOULDED: qualitative of the soul (q.v.).
He is a generous souled fellow, he sold a book to raise money to get his friend's shoes soled.

1. soil: earth; an area or a district, one's native place.

2. SOIL: to make dirty; to tarnish.

3. SOIL: excrement; dung.

4. SOIL: a muddy place where animals wallow.

5. SOIL: to feed cattle on fresh cut green vegetables; to fatten fowls.
Heed that you soil not your fair fame and name in this tournament lest you receive a shovelful of soil on your shield to abide there in the symbol of a delve tenné, even after you retire to your native soil.

1. sola: a plant found in swamps in India, *Aeschynomena aspena*, from

the pith of which sun-proof helmets are made.

2. SOLA: a single hill, not a member of a range of hills.
3. SOLA!: a shout; a cry to attract attention.
4. SOLAH: alternative spelling of No. 1 above.
5. SOLAR: pertaining to the sun; of time measured by the sun; of religion, or worship directed to the sun.
6. SOLAR: an upper room, or attic, originally open to the sun. (Sometimes confused with 'cellar', q.v.).
7. SOLARE: alternative spelling of No. 6 above.
8. SOLEA: a raised floor.
9. SOLLAR: alternative spelling of No. 6 above: alternative spelling of sallow (q.v.) the *Salix*.
10. SOLLER: further alternative spelling of No. 6 above.
11. SOWLA: alternative spelling of No. 3 above.

Manning the solar observation post on the top of a sola in Equatorial Africa, he was thankful for the protection afforded him by his sola hemet, wondered how the huntsmen at home had energy to shout 'Sola!' and decided that when he retired he would not buy a house having a solar.

solah ⎫
solar ⎬ see preceding group.
solare ⎭

1. solder: an alloy of comparatively low melting point used for uniting two pieces of metal; the act of so joining.
2. SORDOR: the condition of sordidness.
A man living in such sordor cannot be permitted to solder cooking vessels in his own home.
1. sole: the under-surface of the foot; the forward part of the under-surface of a boot or shoe; the under-surface of anything in contact with the ground.
2. SOLE: a delicately flavoured flat-fish, *solea vulgaris*.
3. SOLE: alone; the only person to hold office; without competitors; exclusive.
4. SOUL: seat of the higher faculties and

emotions; an abstract essence regarded as immortal; the spirit; the seat of mystical awareness; enthusiasm.

He wore his sole down to the upper trying to sell 'Sammy's Tinned Sole', but when he secured the sole agency for 'Slobber's Sparkling Soft Soda', he put his soul into his work—he went so far as to make it his sole drink.

solea, see sola.
soled, see sold.
sollar ⎫ see sola.
soller ⎭

1. some: a certain, but unspecified, number of persons or things; a quantity.
2. SOME: a specific, but unknown, or unspecified person.
3. SUM: the total amount, quantity or number; any problem in arithmetic.
Some boy put some calcium-carbide in the ink, so the master made us all do a sum.
1. son: male offspring, particularly of human beings.
2. SUN: the day-star; centre of the planetary system; the source (q.v.) of heat and light.
Let your son sun himself.
1. Sonny: a familiar, or affectionate, form of address to a boy; a sarcastic form of address by a sober mature man, to a noisy, or a brash, young man.
2. SUNNY: brilliant sunshine.
It's sunny, Sonny, let us go out.
sordor, see solder.
sore, see saw.
sorry, see sari.
sort, see salt.
sough, see sew.
sought, see salt.
soul, see sole.
souled, see sold.
1. sound: vibration of air causing the sensation of hearing.
2. SOUND: healthy; in good repair; of good quality.
3. SOUND: a narrow sea-channel.
4. SOUND: to dive; to probe.
5. SOUND: to emit a note from a musical or other instrument.

Without uttering a sound he accepted the task of navigation through the sound in spite of the fog: he intended to sound with the lead every inch of the way and sound the siren every fifth minute: his hearing being sound he knew he'd catch the slightest sound from the shore: this seemed to him a sound method of making headway, and he realized that even if he ran aground the vessel was sound.

1. **sounder:** comparative of 'sound' (q.v.), that which is in better repair than, better condition than, or more reliable than something else.
2. SOUNDER: one who sounds, either by making, through an instrument, a vibration in the air, or one who tests the depth of water.

His theory is no sounder than yours, we must await the return of the exploration ship and study the figures of the sounder.

sour, see **sewer.**
source, see **sauce.**
sow, see **sew.**
sower, see **sewer.**
sowla, see **sola.**

1. **spacious:** wide; roomy; extensive.
2. SPECIOUS: false; not of a quality commensurate with appearance; imitation; gaudy but valueless.

The rooms are spacious but the house is specious.

1. **span:** the measurement from the tip of the thumb to the tip of the little finger when the hand is expanded, standardized as nine inches; any short distance or space of time; the distance between walls, or columns, or piers; a bridge; an arch.
2. SPAN: a pair of horses, or a team of two yokes of oxen.
3. SPAN: to harness draught (q.v.) animals to a vehicle; to fasten; to tighten.
4. SPAN: neat; smart; new (see also 'spick').
5. SPAN: pst tns of 'spin'.

To span the rift they felled tall trees, but the first span of oxen to cross side-slipped and span like a falling leaf into the depth

of the ravine; now, however, there is a bridge, and all is spick and span.

1. **spar:** a rounded log of wood; the masts, booms and yards (q.v.) of a sailing ship.
2. SPAR: a crystalline mineral, varying in its chemical nature, but having a lustre.
3. SPAR: to secure a door or a gate with a log of wood.
4. SPAR: to engage in fisticuffs; to practise boxing; to give a display of boxing.

While they spar they spar the door; the spar they use is decorated with pieces of local spar.

1. **spat:** pst tns & ppl of the v 'to spit' (q.v.).
2. SPAT: the spawn of shell-fish, particularly of oyster; the eggs of the bee (q.v.).
3. SPAT: a sharp smack (q.v.).
4. SPAT: short form of spatterdash, a shoe cover; a short gaiter.
5. SPAT: a splash of, for example, mud.

That dandy wanted to see the oyster spat; on the way down he got one spat covered with mud, and there was a spat or two of it on his grey jacket, and he spat venom at me as though I'd planned it.

1. **spear:** a lance; any weapon consisting of a head, or blade extending from a shaft.
2. SPEAR: a church spire.
3. SPEAR: a blade of grass.
4. SPEAR: the rudimentary shoot of grain, or any other seed that is germinating.
5. SPEAR: a young oak-tree; any sapling.
6. SPEER: a branch, or tyne, of an antler.
7. SPEER: to ask a question.
8. SPEER: to look; to peer.

He cut down a spear to make a shaft for his spear with its blade like a deer's speer, and I wondered greatly but could only speer fit to cross my eyes. I dared not speer upon it for fear of his answer.

1. **spec** (sl): an abbreviation of either speculation, or expectation.

2. SPECK: a minute (q.v.) blemish; a small spot; a particle; anything that is small by comparison; a distant object as a cloud in the sky (q.v.) or a ship at sea (q.v.).
3. SPECK: whale (q.v.) blubber; hippopotamus fat; bacon, or pork (q.v.) fat; the fat of any butcher's meat (q.v.).
4. SPECK: fruit that is sub-standard in either quality or appearance.
5. SPICK: smart; new; neat and tidy—generally followed by 'and span' (q.v.).
6. SPICK (Am. sl): a native of Mexico.
I bought, just on spec, some speck peaches from a Spick who, though he might have been boiled down for speck, kept a very spick and span shop, and to my surprise I found not a speck on them.
1. specie: minted coin.
2. SPECIES: a physical form common to a group; of a kind (q.v.).
Money of divers metal makes all species of specie.
specious, see spacious.
speck, see spec.
speer, see spear.
1. spell: to construct words by placing letters in consecutive order; to read slowly, letter by letter.
2. SPELL: a turn of work in relief of the present worker.
3. SPELL: a cantrip; an incantation; a magical formula of words.
4. SPELL: an occult influence.
5. SPELL: a splinter.
6. SPELL: a fit (q.v.).
He had a spell when a child, and did no work until he was forced to do a spell during the war, but in a few minutes he ran a spell into his finger and began to act as if he was under a spell: the doctor gave the condition a name that the welfare officer could not spell.
spick, see spec.
1. spike: a cut, as distinct from a wire, nail; any short, sharp-pointed piece of metal or wood.
2. SPIKE: a form of lavender, *Lavendula spica*, from which the essential oil is obtained.

He made a hole with a spike and knew from the smell that the canister contained oil of spike.
1. spill: a splinter or strip of wood or bone; a length of paper, folded close, used for carrying a light from a burning object to one to be ignited.
2. SPILL: a rod of wood or of metal forming a spindle.
3. SPILL: an outpouring of liquid; an upsetting of a vessel or a container.
4. SPILL: a fall or tumble.
5. SPILL: to destroy; to kill.
He asks for a spill to light his pipe, and he and his mate between them spill the entire jarful into the fire so we let down their bicycle tyres hoping they have a spill on the way home.
1. spirit: the soul; vital force; a refinement of overt meaning; a ghost; courage; to lure.
2. SPIRIT: alcohol; any liquid of a volatile nature; essence obtained by distillation; liquor (q.v.) with a high alcoholic content distilled for drinking.
'The spirit is abstinent but the flesh is bibulous' he replied with spirit when offered spirit, yet he acknowledges having seen a spirit who warned him to observe both the spirit and the letter of the law of abstinence.
1. spit: saliva; to eject saliva; to eject from the mouth something in the manner of ejecting saliva; to make the sound and movement of ejecting saliva without doing so; a similar sound and motion made by cats and other animals, in expressing anger; to eject semen; to lay eggs or spawn; very light rain.
2. SPIT: a long pointed metal rod used for pushing through meat (q.v.), or poultry (q.v.) in order to suspend it before the fire and keep it turning while roasting; a skewer, used either for meat or fish; to cook meat by this method.
3. SPIT: a long narrow tongue of land projecting into the sea, sometimes uncovered at low tide; a shoal (q.v.); a sand- or mud-bank.
4. SPIT: a spadeful of earth; the depth

to which a spade can be thrust when digging.

A netful of small-fry, taken on the spit, were placed in a tub of sea-water with a spit or two of sand at the bottom: the cat jumped onto the rim, and began to spit; the cook called out that they'd be eaten tomorrow, to-day there were fowls on the spit.

1. **spoke:** pst tns of 'speak'.
2. SPOKE: one of the rods radiating from the hub, and supporting the rim, of a wheel (q.v.).

A spoke broke, the cart col-lapsed, and the driver spoke his mind fluently.

1. **sport:** the unnecessary, often brutal, generally safe occupation of killing harmless animals.
2. SPORT: organized games and athletic exercises.
3. SPORT: fun; amusement; often, mis-chief.
4. SPORT: an unexpected and inexplic-able deviation from type that breeds true.
5. SPORT (sl): a good-natured, broad-minded, generous and obliging person.

I am poor at sport, hence my father regards me as a sport on our family tree: be a sport and explain to him what sport work is.

1. **spray:** a bunch of flowers; a cutting from a tree, shrub, or other plant (q.v.); twigs used in thatching.
2. SPRAY: water, or other liquid atom-ized and blown in the form of a mist; small particles of water thrown up by violence, as by the stroke of an oar (q.v.); the act of creating such a mist; an instru-ment, or a machine, for producing and blowing minute (q.v.) particles of liquid.

Spray that spray of fading flowers.

1. **spring:** that part of a year between the vernal equinox and the sum-mer solstice.
2. SPRING: the place where a flow of water issues from the ground; the source of a stream or a river; a well (q.v.).
3. SPRING: a shoot, small branch or twig; a sucker (q.v.); a wood of young trees.
4. SPRING: of a tide, following a new, or a full moon, that rises and falls respectively higher and lower than other tides.
5. SPRING: to leap or jump.
6. SPRING: a strip of steel, or other metal, having enough elasticity to return to its previous shape after having been forced from it by winding, bending, compressing or extending; the motive force of (spring loaded) clockwork.
7. SPRING: the beginning, or lower ends of an arch.
8. SPRINGE: a trap, or snare.

Last Spring, grandfather, when on a visit to a mineral spring, began to spring about like a buck; he broke his watch-spring by vigorously over-winding, and would actually have gone swim-ming had he not feared the depth of the spring-tide: all this benefit was, however, negated when he trod in a springe and broke his ankle.

springe, see preceding group.

1. **spruce:** a special type of fir (q.v.) tree; timber cut from such trees; a name for Prussia, and for goods obtained therefrom.
2. SPRUCE: neat and tidy; of smart appearance; to make neat and tidy.
3. SPRUCE (sl): deception of a more or less playful character.

He said he would spruce his house up by having all wood-work made from spruce: they believed him, because he is him-self always spruce, but I knew it to be a spruce.

1. **sprue:** a disturbance of the digestive tract; *psilosis*.
2. SPRUE: the opening in a founder's mould (q.v.) into which the metal (q.v.) is poured.
3. SPRUE: inferior asparagus.

Asparagus appeared on the menu, sprue was served—such stuff might have come into ex-istence through the sprue—one can't eat cast iron, it causes sprue.

1. **squall:** to cry in a loud, high-pitched discordant voice.
2. SQUALL: a short, sharp burst of violent weather (q.v.).

   An onshore squall carried away the roof, and the fisherman's family began to squall.

1. **squib:** a firework; an explosive missile; a smart (q.v.) retort (q.v.); an insignificant person.
2. SQUID: to utter or write witty, sarcastic attacks; to fire blank cartridges.
3. SQUID: a cuttlefish; any cephalopod of the family *Loliginidae, Teuthididae,* or *Sepiidae.*

   That little squid, apeing the author, has produced a misleading monograph on the history of the squib and other fireworks: his ink, like that of a squid, darkens the scene.

squid, see preceding group.

1. **stabile:** firmly established; permanent.
2. STABLE: reliable; well-balanced; fixed securely; not likely to weaken, or to deviate; not likely to decompose or to decrepitate.
3. STABLE: a building, or a range of buildings, fitted with stalls for the housing of cattle particularly horses; the horses belonging to a breeding and training establishment; the staff and property of such an establishment.

   The chief trainer was of stable character, and insisted on transferring the entire stable into stabile buildings.

stable, see preceding group.

1. **staff:** a walking-stick of between five and six feet (q.v.) in length; a shepherd's crook; a pole (q.v.) erected to carry a flag (q.v.); that which acts as a support, hence, an essential form of food; a baton of office; the gnomon of a sundial.
2. STAFF: a system of notation written on and between five horizontal parallel lines.
3. STAFF: persons employed by a company, or by an organization, for the purpose of transacting its business.

   The proprietor of the printing firm who, having a withered leg, had to support himself with a staff, addressed the entire staff, from manager to errand boy, on the importance of their reading staff notation.

1. **stage:** a platform; the theatrical profession *per se*; a station, or place, or position; a gangway erected to enable passengers to disembark.
2. STAGE: a definite point in progress; a place where travellers board or alight from a regularly running vehicle; a period in development; the various parts of, or manifestations of, a disease.

   At that stage of her career she wanted to go on the stage, but they took her abroad and during the third stage of the tour she ran away with a foreigner and in the last stage of the romance was glad to stage a 'prodigal returns' act.

1. **staid:** reliable; of restrained and sober character; reserved; proper; polite; sedate.
2. STAYED: pst tns & ppl of 'stay', to stop, remain in one place; to support, hold up.

   It was when he stayed with me for a holiday that I discovered how staid he is.

1. **stair:** one of a series of shelves or platforms rising one above another on an inclined plane, to enable ascent and descent to be made; a step (q.v.); a flight of steps leading down into the water along the Thames water front.
2. STARE: to gaze fixedly, and often rudely, for a prolonged period; to open the eyes abnormally wide; to express surprise, or amazement, by widely opened eyes; wide open eyes indicative of mental vacuity.
3. STARE: to stand on end, hence descriptive of an animal's coat when out of condition.

   The lodgers sit on the stair and stare.

1. **stake:** a post, pointed at the lower end, for driving into the ground, hence, the place of execution by burning; any similar post driven into the ground for numerous uses.

2. STAKE: a bolster, or small anvil for use on a bench; the foundation rods in a basket; a Mormon Bishop's See (q.v.).
3. STAKE: a sum of money placed in support of a dog or a horse in a race in which the owner of the winning animal receives cash instead of a cup, etc.; to place money as a bet on the result of a race; to hazard.
4. STEAK: a thick slice of meat (q.v.) particularly from the rump of an ox; a thick slice of fish, particularly of cod, salmon, or halibut, etc.
   I'll stake my reputation on the assertion that the cook who ruined this steak would, in the Middle Ages, have been sent to the stake.
1. stalk: the stem of a plant.
2. STALK: to advance slowly, cautiously and silently in pursuit of an animal.
3. STALK: to stride forward haughtily and aggressively.
4. STORK: a large bird with long beak and long legs, frequenting watercourses, *Ciconia*.
   You stalk along tramping down every stalk and think you can stalk stork.
1. staple: any article, or substance, that is paramount among articles or substances of the same nature; chief; leading; of outstanding importance.
2. STAPLE: a U-shaped piece of stiff wire, with pointed ends, used, for example, to secure electrical wire to a wall; any similar loop acting as a hold for some object, or device as for example, a gate-hook.
   The manufacture of the Belwar insulated staple has become a staple industry.
stare, see stair.
1. start: to begin.
2. START: an advantage granted to a competitor in a race (q.v.).
3. START: a sudden spasmodic movement, hence, a fright or a surprise.
   It gave me a start when I heard he's to have a start of six feet in the race, but let him look out when I really start to run.

1. state: condition either physical or mental.
2. STATE: to announce.
3. STATE: a territory, its population and their government as an organic whole (q.v.).
   The agitators state that State ownership will bring benefit to all, but look at the state of the already nationalized items.
1. stationary: at a fixed place; standing still.
2. STATIONERY: all kinds of writing material.
   The stationary van is a stationery van.
stationery, see preceding group.
1. statuary: a group of statues; works of sculpture.
2. STATUTORY: according to law, passed (q.v.) and recorded.
   There is a statutory obligation upon the tenants for the time being to preserve the statuary in the grounds.
1. statue: a portrait in the round; a likeness moulded in a plastic medium, carved, or cast (q.v.) in three dimensions.
2. STATURE: height of a person, or of an animal when standing.
3. STATUTE: an Act of Parliament; a Law.
   There should be a statute enacted against the erection of a statue deceptive of stature.
stature }
statute } see preceding group.
statutory, see statuary.
1. stave: each of the shaped wooden boards that go to the construction of a barrel; a cross-bar supporting the legs of a chair or a table; any similar cross-bar; one section, or verse, of a poem; the five parallel lines on which music is written.
2. STAVE: to reduce to staves; to break up; to break a hole in or through; to burst in or to crush inwards; to fend off.
   Stave him off while I stave this in; we can do with a stave or two for firewood.
stayed, see staid.
1. stays: of a ship turning to windward; in stays.

2. STAYS: objects to support other objects.
3. STAYS: the act of stopping, or delaying.

This ship stays in stays as long as a fashionable lady trying on new stays.

steak, see stake.

1. steal: to dishonestly take; an act of theft; to plagiarize; to take without permission; to contrive for extras.
2. STEEL: a form of iron to which has been imparted increased hardness and flexibility; the properties of steel as an attribute hence, strong nerves, great physical endurance; fearlessness; sword, lance, bayonet, dagger or other edged weapon; a suit (q.v.) of plate armour.
3. STELE: a monolithic monument; an incised standing stone.

With nerves and sinews of steel he went alone to steal the sacred stele of the tribesmen.

steel, see preceding group.

1. steep: to immerse in liquid for a prolonged period; to soak (q.v.).
2. STEEP: having a very strong gradient, hence, of an excessive price, or of a story that is incredible.

His story of the primitive people who steep their babies in brine is too steep; and what steep prices he asks for his curios.

1. steer: a young bullock.
2. STEER: to guide or direct; to manipulate the rudder of a ship, the handle-bars of a bicycle, the wheel of a motor-vehicle; to influence a person into a course of action; to direct a business; to govern a State (q.v.).
3. STERE: a cubic metre.

Round up that steer, steer him into the paddock, he's been at that water long enough to have swallowed a stere.

stele, see steal.

1. stem: that part of a plant that rises from the seed, and out of which branch leaves and flowers; a basic ethnic group to which variations may be traced; the main line of descent from which collateral branches of a family trace their ancestry; a slender cylinder sup-

porting a cup, glass, or other vessel; the central quill of a feather; the upright stroke of a letter of the alphabet or other cypher (q.v.); the mouthpiece of a tobacco-pipe; the part of a word that is not changed by inflexion.

2. STEM: the upright timber carrying a ship's planks, hence, the prow, or forward part of a ship.
3. STEM: to stop, check, or dam up; to prevent the flow.
4. STEM: to proceed against, particularly against wind and tide, hence, to make headway, to sail or navigate up stream.

We had to stem the tide of adversity, for the jungle grass had a stem as stiff as steel and when we cut ourselves on it we had nothing but leaves to stem the flow of blood, and the local inhospitable natives were descended from a man-eating stem.

1. step: to place one foot before another in the act of walking; to progress by walking; to place the feet in various positions constituting a dance; the distance between one foot and another when walking; any short distance; an action leading to a train (q.v.) of actions directed to a result; advancement.
2. STEP: a rise from one level to another; each of a series of flat platforms protruding from an inclined plane, for the purpose of ascending and descending; each rung or round of a ladder.
3. STEP: prefix to a term of relationship indicating that the association arises from the remarriage of a parent.
4. STEPPE: a section of the very extensive area covering much of both Russia and Siberia, where no trees grow; similar tracts of land in other parts of Europe.

My stepbrother who always walked with a brisk military step, took the first step in influencing my father to have a step cut in the steep garden path, although it was but a step from one end to the other; he contended that such an improvement was a step in the right direction: he had said before that our garden, though as wide as a steppe, and as wild as a wilderness, was only one step from a desert.

steppe, see preceding group.

stere, see **steer**.

1. **stern**: hard; exacting; rigid in rectitude; relentless in punishment; firm in discipline; stubborn in argument.
2. STERN: the aft-most part of a ship, hence, the buttocks, the hind quarters of an animal; the tail of a wolf or a shaggy dog; the steering gear of a ship, the rudder.
3. STERN: the sea bird, black tern, *Hydrochelidon nigra.*
   As stern a ship-master as ever sailed, he had the crew over the stern to paint with a following sea running.

1. **stick**: a long slender piece of wood, either of natural growth, or shaped; anything having the form of such a wand; the club (q.v.) used for impelling the ball in certain games as golf, hockey; the ribs that carry the mount of a fan; a violin bow; a musical conductor's baton; the control lever of an aircraft.
2. STICK: to pierce, stab with a knife or other sharp, pointed instrument.
3. STICK: to adhere; to stay in position; to come to a halt (q.v.), to maintain an attitude of mind or a point of view; to be adamant; to persist.
   That boy will stick at nothing: he carries a big pin to stick in his next neighbour: if the modern school-master dared to use the stick he might stick at his lessons.

1. **stile**: a gate provided with footholds so that human beings can, but cattle cannot, pass.
2. STYLE: a distinctive manner or way.
   In merely climbing a stile he displays style.

1. **still**: to be stationary; without way (q.v.) or motion; at rest; to subdue; to stop.

2. STILL: an ordinary photograph as distinct from a cinematograph film.
3. STILL: a distillatory; an apparatus consisting of a boiler and a condenser in which liquids are refined, cleansed or created; a retort (q.v.); an alembic.
4. STILL: continuing.
   It seemed time had stood still when, visiting the scene of my childhood, I found old Angus, apparently no older, and still cannily operating his secret still.

stimulate, see **simulate**.

1. **stock**: the trunk of a tree; in heraldry, the stump, the lower end of a tree-trunk; a line of descent, ancestry; a race (q.v.) or a family; a framework or a support for a ship during building; the cross-beam of an anchor; the wooden part of a gun; the head of a carpenter's or a draughtsman's square; the lever in which screw-cutting dies are held; the section of an exchequer tally kept in the possession of the person making the payment.
2. STOCK: a form of neckwear; the black front that is visible between a clergyman's collar and his waistcoat.
3. STOCK: the gilliflower, any plant of the genus *Matthiola.*
4. STOCK: the goods held by a shopkeeper, or other trader, from which he makes sales in the course of his business; any form of property that yields an income, hence, money invested, the vehicles of a transport organization; the animals on a farm.
   Though his name is Woodstock he has no claim to the rebus of 'a stock eradicated' for he is no scion of that exalted stock: his stock-phrase is that he comes of a very good family, and he implies that they own the Stock Exchange: my private opinion is that he is the son of a shopkeeper, too poor to lay in adequate stock, and making ends meet by selling bunches of sweet-scented stock that grows profusely in his garden—when

in his company be conscious of livestock!

1. **stole:** an item of the ecclesiastical vestments; a long narrow scarf; a garment.
2. STOLE: pst tns & ppl of 'steal' (q.v.).
    Someone stole the bishop's stole.
1. **stoop:** to bend the body forward and downward; to abandon one's dignity, or moral standards; to lower one's self.
2. STOOP: a platform projecting from the front of a house.
3. STOUP: a drinking vessel; a stone font set in the wall of a church, to contain holy water.
4. STUPE: a pad of wadding wrung out in hot water and used to foment a septic focus.
    I would not stoop to ascend the stoop and take a stoup of beer with him.
1. **storey:** each of the superimposed floors of which a building consists.
2. STORY: alternative spelling of No. 1 above.
3. STORY: a history; a work of fiction; a recital of events; legend; a newspaper report; a lie (q.v.); any work of art depicting either real or imaginary events.
    The story of the art of architecture was closed when the modern multi-storey building was evolved.
story, see preceding group.
stoup, see **stoop.**
1. **stout:** corpulent, fat; physically strong; robust.
2. STOUT: courageous; enduring; determined; resolute.
3. STOUT: of good quality; strongly constructed; reliable; hard; resistant.
4. STOUT: a strong, dark coloured beer; a form of porter (q.v.).
5. STOUT: a gnat, a gad-fly or a horse-fly.
    A stout flew into his eye and he dropped his pint of stout; the glass, being stout, did not break but the landlord, a stout, lazy man, made as much fuss as if it had: the victim of the accident, being stout of limb and fearing no man, put up a very stout verbal counter-attack.

1. **stove:** an apparatus for containing a fire, or for consuming coal-gas or electricity; a space artificially heated.
2. STOVE: pst tns of 'stave' (q.v.); to break open.
    He got drunk and stove in the stove.
1. **straight:** without bends, angles or curves.
2. STRAIGHT: honest.
3. STRAIT: narrow, difficult; distressing; a long narrow area (q.v.) of the sea (q.v.).
    Straight is the path and strait the gate, but the straight man need fear not.
1. **strain:** overload; bend, distort or damage by overloading; activity or responsibility that overloads a person's strength.
2. STRAIN: a passage of music; the emotional quality of speech; the general tendency of a statement.
3. STRAIN: ancestry; pedigree; lineal descent.
4. STRAIN: to press; crush; seize (q.v.); grip.
5. STRAIN: to purify or to clarify, by passing through a sieve or filter.
    He will strain his ears to catch that strain of music, for it recalls the days of his youth, when life exerted no strain on him, but he never mentions his distress, for a strain of fighting blood from his feudal ancestors is strong in him.
strait, see **straight.**
1. **strand:** a beach, variously of sea, river or lake.
2. STRAND: the elements of a rope or cord; a thread; a lock (q.v.) of hair.
3. STRAND: to leave isolated on the beach; to be in a strange place; to be without means.
4. STRAND: a main thoroughfare in central London, at one time the Thames bank.
    He strolled bare-footed on the driftwood covered strand, his fingers absently unravelling a strand from a rope end, his mind's eye watching the passing throng under the bright lights of

the Strand, and his thoughts occupied with the callousness of his relations to strand him thus.

1. **stroke:** a blow (q.v.) with the hand, a weapon or a tool; an impact; an attack of illness; a paralytic seizure.

2. STROKE: the sound of a clock actuating a bell to call attention to the hour; a tune or a rhythm; the movement, either up or down, of a piston in a cylinder; any one pull on an oar (q.v.) when rowing; the title of a boat's leading oarsman.

3. STROKE: a brilliant sally of wit; to receive or to achieve by luck; a mark of the pen or pencil; to achieve by bluff.

4. STROKE: to pass the hand over an animal in caress, or a human being in healing.

Since he had his stroke he will every day at the stroke of twelve, stroke the cat, and then, with a stroke of the pen, cancel an imaginary will, and say what a brilliant stroke it is on his part to deprive his relations of such a stroke of luck as coming into his money would be.

1. **strut:** a beam of wood, or a wooden construction, or a rod of iron or steel, or a construction of such metal, applied to an edifice, or to works in progress, to take a strain (q.v.), support, or to strengthen.

2. STRUT: to walk with an exaggerated bearing of importance; to walk with an air of superiority.

Don't strut about like a turkey-cock! Give a hand to erect that strut.

1. **stud:** a form of button used, chiefly for attaching collars to shirts; a rivet; a nail-head; a projecting knob; a strengthening bar welded across each link of a chain.

2. STUD: a farm, or a stable, stocked with stallions and mares, where horses are bred (q.v.); the collection of horses belonging to such an establishment.

3. STUD: an upright post or prop; upright laths in a wall or partition.

He was invited by Lord Eckween to visit that nobleman's famous racing stud, but he lost his back-stud, lost his train, and lost his opportunity.

1. **stuff:** fabric; raw material used in a manufacturing process.

2. STUFF: any unspecified material; a medicinal mixture; an accumulation of objects.

3. STUFF: to fill; to pack tightly; to over-eat; to placate by untruths.

I have enough stuff to make a frock, and from the cuttings I will make rag-dolls and stuff them with saw-dust: such stuff will sell at the bazaar, and if father raises any objection I'll stuff him up with some sad story.

stupe, see stoop.

1. **sty:** an enclosure to house pigs.

2. STY: an inflamed and swollen eyelid.

3. STYE: misspelling of No. 2 above.

The sty on his eye made it painful to bend, but he had to clean the pig-sty.

style, see stile.

1. **subtile:** mobile; fluid; tenuous; delicate; acute; keen.

2. SUBTLE: slender; not easily apprehended; abstruse; spiritlike; insidious.

3. SUTTLE: nett weight.

4. SUTTLE: to sell provisions to soldiers; to keep a cook's-shop in a garrison town; to be a sutler; to keep a suttling house.

I couldn't suttle while the Blankshires were here, but now the Blobshires have taken over I'm doing all right. It's a very subtle business.

subtle, see preceding group.

1. **succour:** aid, help, assistance; to provide such aid.

2. SUCKER: an infant mammal still dependent on its mother's milk for sustenance; unweaned; a shoot springing from a root, and growing beside the original stem, an organ adapted for holding by suction; the piston of a pump.

3. SUCKER (sl): something to suck, a sweet.

4. SUCKER (Am. sl): a gullible person, one easily taken in or imposed upon.

Someone ought to succour that

sucker, they've just sold him a plantation and counted a trunk and a sucker as two trees.

sucker, see preceding group.

1. **suede:** leather finished with a nap (q.v.) surface; fabric woven in imitation of such leather.

2. **SWAYED:** moved from side to side; caused to oscillate, or to deviate; to be influenced by oratory.

Swayed by his enthusiastic praise of suede shoes I bought a pair.

suer, see sewer.

1. **suite:** a series; a collection; rooms adjoining; a number of pieces of matching furniture; one of the four divisions of a set of playing-cards; related tunes; a company of servants and other attendants accompanying a person of high importance.

2. **SWEET:** pleasing; a gratifying odour; a sugary flavour; dulcet to the ear; stimulating to the affections; applied to a kind, good-natured peaceful gentle person; fit to eat; wholesome; not sour or putrescent; a pudding; a pie, any form of confection; a confectionery course (q.v.) closing a meal (q.v.).

It was sweet of the Duchess to provide a sweet for the whole of the Prince's suite, particularly as their spurs had damaged her drawing-room suite.

1. **suitor:** a follower; an adherent; one who seeks a woman in marriage.

2. **SUTURE:** stitching or sewing a wound together; the gut or wire used for this purpose.

The suitor said his heart was broken and he was told to hurry off for a suture.

sum, see some.

sun, see son.

sunny, see sonny.

1. **super-:** a prefix indicating superiority; high in quality, or in quantity; greater in rank or degree; better than; above; over.

2. **SUPRA-:** a prefix indicating a position or place at the top of, over or above; higher than; earlier than.

He is a man of super intellect,

note his broad domed brow and the prominence of his supra-orbital ridges; his superabundant writings have all been published, and his monograph on the supra-renal body has been translated into every European language.

supra, see preceding group.

suppress, see cypre.

sure, see shaw.

surf, see serf.

surge, see serge.

1. **surplice:** a loose white vestment with wide sleeves worn by clergymen and others engaged in conducting a church service.

2. **SURPLUS:** a remainder; the quantity of anything that is left (q.v.) when the amount required has been used; more than is necessary.

The curate's wife bought some Government surplus nylon to make him a surplice and herself a frock.

surplus, see preceding group.

Surrey, see sari.

suture, see suitor.

1. **swallo:** a name for the trepang (q.v.) or sea-slug, *Holothuria edulis*, also called sea-cucumber, and bêche-de mer.

2. **SWALLOW:** a migratory bird, *Hirundo rustica*, visiting the British Isles in summer.

3. **SWALLOW:** to effect a spasm of the gullet that conveys food from the mouth to the stomach; to make such a motion in the absence of food; to take food and drink; to absorb or to assimilate, as a large Company a small one, a strong nation a weak one; to accept information that is improbable; to believe.

I had accompanied my host to the beach where we gathered swallo, and on the return journey to the village we saw a swallow darting in and out of a barn window: these birds, the countryman declared, have no claws on which to perch, but this townee did not swallow that.

swallow, see swallo.

swayed, see suede.

1. **Swede:** a native of Sweden.
2. SWEDE: a form of turnip, having a strong flavour and yellow colour, *Brassica campestris*.

   My next-door neighbour, who is a Swede, complains that he cannot get a good swede at any greengrocers.

sweet, see **suite.**

1. **swift:** at a high speed; fast; without delay.
2. SWIFT: a bird, *Cypselus apus*, visiting the British Isles during the summer.
3. SWIFT: a moth of the genus *Hepialus*, or of the family *Hepialidae*.
4. SWIFT: a newt; in heraldry, a newt or a lizard; an eft.

   You'll need to be swift with your butterfly net to collect swift: if the swift doesn't get them on the wing, the swift darts out from behind a stone and gets them when they're at rest.

1. **swish:** the hissing sound made by the rapid transit of a solid body through the air.
2. SWISH (sl): expensive; attractive; luxurious.
3. SWISS: a person, or a thing from, the manners and customs (q.v.) of, Switzerland.
4. SWITCH: a slender rod, stick (q.v.) or cane (q.v.).
5. SWITCH: a hank of false hair.
6. SWITCH: a mechanical device to divert a railway train (q.v.) from one track (q.v.) to another; to bring about such a diversion.
7. SWITCH: an instrument for interrupting and re-establishing an electrical circuit.

   The train will swish by and the passengers will switch the lights on as they enter the tunnel where a swish looking Swiss woman lost her switch, and attacked with a switch a little boy who laughed.

Swiss } see preceding group.
switch }

sword, see **sawed.**
syke, see **sick.**
symbol, see **cymbal.**
symmetry, see **cemetery.**
sypher, see **cipher.**

T

1. **T:** the twentieth letter of the alphabet between S and U; t; a prefix descriptive of objects resembling the letter in their shape.
2. TE: the seventh note in the tonic sol-fa scale; when hyphenated to 'he' or 'hee', it expresses vapid laughter.
3. TEA: the prepared leaves of the shrub, *Thea*; the drink brewed from such leaves; the late afternoon meal at which such a drink takes first place.
4. TEE: a mound of earth or of sand, or a peg of wood or other material used in the game of golf (q.v.) to elevate the ball for convenience of striking.

   Come with me while I buy a T-square, and examine a patent golf-tee, then I'll take you to the Grand Hotel for tea—why do you Te-hee?

1. **ta:** a colloquial—perhaps slang—form of 'thank you', used almost exclusively by Cockneys.
2. TAHA: a South African bird, *Pyromelana taha*.
3. TAR: a black, viscous, strong-smelling liquid, a mixture of resin, various other hydrocarbons, and free carbon, being a residue in the destructive distillation of coal, wood, and other organic substances, strongly water proof, hence, used on ship's bottoms, or other timber, on cordage and on roofs.

   'Arf a pint o' tar—Ta!

1. **table:** a board (q.v.) supported on legs, or on a central leg, whereat one may sit for a purpose, such as to eat, or to write, or to play a game.
2. TABLE: a flat, more or less thin, slab of wood, stone or metal which carries an inscription, as, for example, the ten Hebraic Commandments, some Greek, some Roman Law, hence, the Laws so inscribed.
3. TABLE: the arrangement of facts and figures in columns and rows to summarize information, as a Railway time-table; a multiplication

table; a logarithm table; a tide table.

Uncle John, who was a Colonel in the Guards, has laid down a table of holiday behaviour for the children: they must repeat one multiplication table, and trace one cross-country journey by means of the time-table before they go to the table to play snakes and ladders.

1. **tack:** a small nail; a temporary stitch; a pipe bracket; a means of securing lightly or temporarily; to fasten with a tack or with a number of tacks (q.v.).

2. TACK: to sail a zig-zag course (q.v.) to windward; certain ropes, lines or cords used for making fast (q.v.) a sail (q.v.).

3. TACK: food, particularly unappetizing food, more particularly, ship's biscuits—hard tack.

As we came over on the windward tack a ship's lamp, hanging from a tack, fell into the cask of hard tack.

1. **tacked:** lightly secured, as with small nails, or long, loose stitches; to have sailed a zig-zag course.

2. TACT: a sense of touch, hence, a delicate perception and understanding of people's emotions and reactions, and the ability to avoid giving offence, or shock.

It might be lack of tact to point out that one can see where the frock had been tacked.

1. **tacks:** pl of 'tack' (q.v.).

2. TAX: compulsory payments made by the citizen for the upkeep of the State; a strain, or a burden on a person or a thing; to accuse; to charge a person with the responsibility for something.

Tax him with culpable negligence—he should have known that such a weight of books would tax a shelf secured only with tacks.

tact, see **tacked.**

1. **tail:** a continuation of the spine, forming a flexible posterior appendage in most vertebrate animals; the organ (q.v.) at the opposite extremity of the trunk (q.v.) to the head; any posterior appendage, as, for example, the train (q.v.) of a dress, or the hanging backpart of a coat, or in birds, feathers, in fish, fin-material; the hindmost, or lowest extremity of anything; the least active members of a group or a party; the buttocks; any appendage in the rear (q.v.); the reverse of a coin (q.v.).

2. TAIL: pertaining to real (q.v.) estate limited in inheritability; entailed.

3. TAIL (sl): a detective, one who follows a person.

4. TAILLE: a form of taxation.

5. TALE: a narrative; a discourse; a romance, or other work of fiction; a malicious report; a breach of confidence; a speech calculated to arouse sympathy; a lie (q.v.).

6. TALE: to enumerate; to record by numbers; to distribute by numbers.

7. TOWEL (C): an absorbent cloth used for wiping that which is wet.

Take tail of the stragglers as they come in; they are the tail of the defeated force: ignore their tale, and let them tail on in the rear of our Labour Company. They look like monkeys—I suspect each of them of having a tail—but still, issue each with soap and a towel, and make sure that they use them, we want no epidemics.

1. **talc:** a name applied to flaked translucent minerals such as mica.

2. TALK: conversation; the expression of thought by vocal delivery; to speak; gossip; to promise without performing.

3. TORC: an antique neck or wrist ornament made of a twisted strip of metal.

4. TORQUE: twisting; a unit of measurement of the force or strain (q.v.) of twisting; an alternative spelling of No. 3 above.

I have tested the torque in the torc you unearthed so now you have something to talk about that will be more to the popular taste than the fact of its being found in a bed of talc.

tale, see **tail.**

1. **'Talian:** sloven form of 'Italian'.

2. TALION: retaliation; retribution; the justice of revenge; 'an eye for an eye'.

The law of talion falls on both individuals and nations—look at the 'Talian plight for following fascism!

1. talisman: a gem, or a trinket, to which occult power is attributed, that can avert evil and induce good.

2. TALLYMAN: one who does a door to door business on a hire-purchase basis.

The tallyman carried a talisman.

talk, see talc.

tallyman, see talisman.

1. tambourin: a tabor; a form of drum used in Provence; a dance; music to accompany such a dance.

2. TAMBOURINE: a circular frame fitted with cymbals (q.v.), or jingles, and closed on one side with a stretched skin forming a miniature drumhead.

3. TANGERINE: a small orange grown in Tangier; a native of Tangier; pertaining to Tangier.

The street performer manipulated a tambourine with one hand, peeled a tangerine with the other, danced a tambourin, and 'took the hat round' with his teeth.

tambourine ⎫
tangerine ⎬ see preceding group.

1. tap: a tube embodying an opening and closing mechanism, used for drawing liquid, as required, from a source of supply; a cock, a valve, a faucet.

2. TAP: a light, audible blow; the sound produced on a drum; to attract attention by a light blow (q.v.).

3. TAP: a form of dance in which rhythms are produced by means of beating with metal-clad toes and heels onto a hard surface.

4. TAP: a tool for cutting a female screw thread.

5. TAP (sl): to borrow money.

Tap him on the shoulder, and send him back to turn off the tap.

1. tapa: a kind of cloth made by the natives of Polynesia.

2. TAPER: to diminish in size from one end to the other, as a cone.

3. TAPER: a candle; a wick impregnated with wax used for carrying a light from a fire, or a flame, to something that requires ignition.

4. TAPIA: mud or clay used for building walls.

5. TAPIR: a mammal indigenous to Central America, ungulate, and posessing a prehensile probosis, of the family *Tapiridae*.

6. TAPPA: alternative spelling of No. 1 above.

When we were hunting tapir we built a 'hide' of tapia and covered it with tapa; we made it taper upward, and we fixed, at the apex, a lighted taper.

taper ⎫
tapia ⎬ see preceding group.
tapir ⎭

1. tare: vetch, particularly when growing among corn (q.v.).

2. TARE: the weight of the container of goods.

3. TEAR: to rend. Reduce to pieces by pulling.

4. TEAR: to proceed with excessive speed.

5. TEAR: a drop of water from the eye; any drop of liquid.

6. TIER: a row out of several rows placed closely one above another.

Tear a piece from the packet, it will reduce the tare, but in it wrap a sample of the grain which is more than half tare, then tear away to the Inspector of weights and measures who will put the dishonest supplier in the first tier of the court-room and we'll see him shed a tear.

1. tarry: delay; sojourn; procrastinate; waste time.

2. TARRY: treated with tar (q.v.) flavoured as with tar; black in colour; of a viscous, or a sticky, nature.

Do not tarry; the tarry blocks must be laid before the rains begin.

1. tarse: a rich cloth, imported from the Orient, and popular in the fourteenth and fifteenth centuries.

2. TERCE: a measurement of capacity; a cask of such a size (q.v.).

3. TERSE: neat and tidy; concise; a piece of literature free of redundant verbiage and compact in meaning; polished; burnished.

4. TIERCE: one third; alternative spelling of No. 2 above; in Scots Law, a special provision for a widow; the third hour of the canonical day; interval of a major (q.v.) or a minor (q.v.) third in music; a company of soldiers; in British Heraldry, one third of a shield's area (q.v.), in French Heraldry, a charge.

He wrote a terse monograph on marshalling Arms on a field parted per tierce.

1. tart: a crust of pastry, either covering, or itself containing some form of food, as meat, fruit, jam.

2. TART: sharp; painful; cutting; offensive; of a sharp, sour, or acrid flavour.

3. TART: a female, particularly a young female, and more particularly a fast (q.v.) or immoral one.

See that tart eating a fruit tart—well, she's got a tart tongue, too!

1. tartan: a hard-wearing woollen fabric having bands of varying colour crossing each other and forming a repeat pattern of multicolour rectangles; the pattern itself, being the insignia of a clan, or the uniform of a Highland Regiment; any cloth, fabric, or other material having a tartan pattern.

2. TARTAN: the title of the Commander of the Ancient Assyrian host (q.v.).

3. TARTAN: a vessel having a lanteen and a foresail, common in the Eastern Mediterranean.

4. TARTANE: alternative spelling of No. 3 above.

The Tartan of Assyria, being himself a Scot, always wore his tartan, and flew a tartan ensign from the masthead of his tartan.

tartane, see preceding group.

1. Tartar: ethnologically, a member of the Turkic branch of the Ural-Altaic family: colloquially, any native of Central Asia east of the Caspian Sea; the host of Jenghiz Khan, hence, the inhabitants of Eastern Europe.

2. TARTAR: a violent, overbearing person; a thief; a beggar.

3. TARTAR: Potassium bi-tartarate, deposited on wine-casks, hence, any incrustation deposited from a liquid, particularly calcium phosphate, deposited from saliva onto the teeth.

The Housemaster, a regular tartar, made the boys clean their teeth with sand which, he asserted, would remove the tartar.

1. tartareous: of the nature of, or pertaining to tartar (q.v.).

2. TATAREOUS: of, or pertaining to, Tartarus (see No. 4 under), hence, wicked, infernal.

3. TARTAROUS: of a substance derived from, or containing, tartar (q.v.); of morbid conditions formerly thought to be caused by tartar in the body.

4. TARTARUS: the lowest part of the infernal regions in ancient Greek mythology, hence, hell (q.v.); used to describe any dismal, unpleasant place or circumstance.

The servant girl emerged by way of the area steps from the depressing Tartarus of the scullery and visited the doctor who said she was infested with inspissated tartarous fluids, and he prescribed a bottle of tartareous-antimonate, remarking that the girl's Tartareous occupation caused her condition.

tartarous ⎫
Tartarus ⎬ see preceding group.

1. taught: pst tns & ppl of the v 'to teach'.

2. TAUT: tight; stretched; under tension or strain (q.v.); neat and tidy.

3. TORT: a misdemeanour consisting of breach of duty that involves another person in loss or damage; an injury.

They had been taught to keep taut and avoid tort.

taut, see preceding group.

1. taw: a marble; a specific game of marbles; the line on which players stand in the game.

2. TAW: to tan hides by a specific process.

3. TAW: to abuse, to flog a person.

4. TOR: a cone-shaped, lofty hill; a pile of rocks.
5. TOR: tor-ouzel, a name for the ring-ouzel, *Turdus torquatus*.
6. TORE: pst tns of 'tear' (q.v.), to rend.
7. TOUR: a journey undertaken for the purpose of visiting numerous famous places in sequence; a period of activity, or duty, in sequence with others.
8. TWOER: a marble with two coloured rings round the 'equator', having the value of two larger, plain tinted marbles.

> Tom tore my taw-bag and took my lucky twoer, Now he is on tour round the back street shouting he'll play anyone on Saturday on top of the tor, but wait till I catch him, I'll taw him black and blue.

tax, see tacks.
1. taxes: large sums of money forced from the citizen to balance wasteful and wanton State spending.
2. TAXIS: movements made by organisms in response to stimuli.
3. TAXIS: hackney carriages fitted with a meter (q.v.) that converts mileage to cash value and shows on the dial the amount of fare due.

> After paying taxes we cannot ride in taxis.

taxis, see preceding group.
te } see T.
tea }
1. teal: fresh-water birds, *Querquedula crecca* and other related kinds; any small duck (q.v.).
2. TEIL: the linden, or lime (q.v.) tree, *Tilia europaea*.

> There is a teil thicket right down to the water's edge and the stream is crowded with teal.

3. team: a number of persons acting in concert; a group associated in playing a game, or in executing work.
2. TEAM: a pair (q.v.) or a greater number of horses, oxen, or other beasts of burden, harnessed to a cart, waggon, or other load.
3. TEAM: a number of young produced at a birth; a litter; a family; a brood (q.v.).
4. TEAM: a number of wild birds flying in line ahead.

5. TEAM: an Anglo-Samon law process for recovery of goods stolen.
6. TEEM: of water, flowing copiously; to rain heavily; to pour out; to empty; to remove or discharge contents.
7. TEEM: to be pregnant; to give birth; to be prolific, fertile, full.

> The village football-team was conveyed in high style to the scene of the match by a team of oxen; supporters of the home team said the visitors looked like a team of sucking pigs and as it had begun to teem with rain they replied that they would go straight to victory like a team of wild ducks on the wing —'Us teem wi' goals'! cried the captain.

tear, see tare.
1. teas: pl of 'tea' (q.v.).
2. TEASE: to pull fibres apart; to form a nap (q.v.) on cloth; to worry and annoy in a petty way.
3. TEES: pl of 'tee' (q.v.).

> They tease him about the occasion on which, when asked to pay for the tees, he paid for the teas of the entire golf club.

tease, see preceding group.
tee, see T.
teem, see team.
1. teen: harm; damage; spite; malice; grief.
2. -TEEN: a form of ten, used as a suffix for numbers from three to nine: 'in one's 'teens', the years of life from thirteen to nineteen.

> He had suffered much teen by the age of eighteen.

tees, see teas.
teil, see teal.
1. temper: mental or emotional balance, particularly when under strain (q.v.); to lose control of oneself when angered; to be inclined to violence.
2. TEMPER: to bring a substance to a state of finish, or to make useable, by admixture with some other substance, or by the application of heat, or both.

> When the steel is not of the correct temper, the foreman flies into a temper.

1. **tender:** one who attends; a waiter; one in charge of a machine, or of a business, or of one section of a business.
2. TENDER: something constructed and used for the purpose of serving something else, as the coal and water truck attached to a steam locomotive; a small ship that carries passengers and their luggage from a great liner to a landing stage.
3. TENDER: to offer, as for example, arrangements in settlement of a debt, or to supply goods at a fixed price; the coin (q.v.) of the realm which may be used in payment.
4. TENDER: young; soft; gentle; fragile; frail; easily hurt, or injured.
5. TENDER: affectionate; kind; gentle with, or careful towards; considerate; thoughtful for; fond of.
   The bar-tender on the tender serving the trans-Atlantic liners, put in a tender to run the booze business on his own account, but the Directors, observing him to be a youth of tender years, thought it best to tender his apologies and reject the offer, which they did, surprising enough, in a quite tender manner.
1. **tenner:** a number, or amount, or value of ten; a ten-pound note, £10; a ten-dollar bill, $10.
2. TENOR: an adult male voice between bass (q.v.) and alto; the songs etc. written to suit such a voice; a vocalist possessing such a voice; descriptive of any musical instrument of a certain pitch (q.v.); the heaviest bell in a peal (q.v.).
3. TENOR: the purpose, or the meaning, of a speech or writing; the face-value of paper money; continuance; quality.
4. TENURE: tenancy; rights and duties between tenant and landlord; a holding.
   I'll bet a tenner that the tenor, in spite of his long tenure of the part, has not grasped its tenor.
tenor, see preceding group.
1. **tense:** the form of word or phrase that indicates time, past, present and future, in the construction of a sentence.
2. TENSE: tight; stretched; under strain; nervous excitement.
3. TENTS: pl of 'tent' (q.v.).
   I noticed that John was very tense when they referred in the past tense to the tents he had lent them.
1. **tent:** a spread of canvas, supported on a pole or poles and secured with guy-ropes, used as a portable dwelling, or as an enclosure for an exhibition or a social function.
2. TENT: a pad of cotton-wool used in surgery and in dentistry to keep an incision open, or hold the cheek away from the teeth.
3. TENT: an adhesive, hard-setting medium, used in mounting precious stones.
4. TENT: a Spanish wine, high in colour and low in alcoholic content.
5. TENT: an embroidery frame.
   A tramp found dead in a tent had a half-healed wound in which a surgical tent was imbedded, a bottle of tent laced with methylated spirit, a fragment of glass cemented with tent into a brass finger-ring, and on a piece of canvas stretched in a tent he had worked his name and age.
tents, see **tense.**
tenure, see **tenner.**
terce, see **tarse.**
1. **term:** a specified length of time; a period of time in which a court sits, or a scholastic establishment gives instruction; the duration of pregnancy.
2. TERM: a limiting condition; a limit to the relationship between persons.
3. TERM: an expression in words of a descriptive character; a way or style of speaking.
4. TURM: a troop of cavalry; a band of thirty-two horsemen.
   The term the Sergeant-Major used to describe the performance of a turm of cavalry recruits in the riding-school does not come on the curriculum of the advanced English course at the

High School this term or any term.

1. **tern:** sea-birds of the genus *Sterna;* sea-swallow (q.v.).
2. TERN: relating to a group of three; a trio or triplet; to be placed in groups of three, column of three marching order; a double-three in the game of dice; three winning numbers in a lottery.
3. TURN: to revolve, go round; to twist, to bend; to deviate or to cause deviation; to change; a crisis; a shock; to follow others in sequence in performing an action or in executing a task; to give shape, or form, to a piece of metal, wood or other material in a lathe (q.v.); to reverse; to move pages of a book from right to left when reading; to advance past a point in one's age; to change from friendship to enmity; to change one's mind; to change sides in a contest; to spoil the edge of a knife; to become curdled, sour, tainted, unfit for food.

If you take your turn at feeding the tern in this hard weather, no one can turn an accusing finger at you: come with me when I turn out for the job, and I will point out to you the dangerous turn in the cliff-path: when you turn fifty you, too, will turn away from dizzy heights: now I must turn back to my work—help me turn the boat over, and then take a round-turn of this line on that post: but if the weather takes a turn for the worse, I shall turn it in.

1. **ternary:** pertaining to three; groups of three; arrangement in threes; having, or consisting of, three elements or sections.
2. TURNERY: articles made by turning on a lathe (q.v.) particularly woodware.

The wood-turnery industry of Jura has a ternary disposal system through collector, factor and exporter.

terse, see **tarse.**

1. **thaw:** the end of a frost; the melting of snow and ice; warming after severe cold.
2. THOR: Scandinavian god of war, of thunder, and of agriculture.

During the storm it was as though Thor was hammering on the roof, but thanks to him the thaw has set in.

1. **the:** reference to a thing, a place or an idea; indicating a particular object.
2. THEE: objective case of 'thou'; you, yourself.

Thee and me do not serve the devil.

thee, see preceding group.

1. **their:** possessive of them.
2. THERE: relative to a particular place.
3. THEY'RE: contraction of 'they are'.

They're there; their hats are in the hall.

Thor, see **thaw.**

1. **thorn:** a sharp-pointed, hard spike, numbers of which protrude from the stem (q.v.) and other parts of certain plants as a means of protection; a collective term for all plants that produce thorns.
2. THORN: an Old English (Anglo-Saxon) letter of the alphabet, being a fused th, þ, later represented by lower-case (sometimes upper-case) y, hence, ye = 'the', yᵗ = 'that'.

1. **threw:** pst tns of the v 'to throw' (q.v.).
2. THROUGH: from the beginning to the end; from one side (q.v.) to another; to penetrate; to traverse; to proceed from end to end; to complete a task; progress in time; because of; due to; as a result of.

Through ignorance he threw away proof of his innocence; they threw him into prison from whence he escaped through a drain for which they threw the blame upon the turnkey, but he was able to prove that he threw the bolt, and the escaped prisoner, all through life, sent him a pension through the post which generous act threw the authorities into such a rage that one threw a fit.

1. **thrift:** economy; saving; prosperity; frugality; meanness.
2. THRIFT: a flowering plant, sea-gilliflower, *Armeria maritima vulgaris,*

including other, similar plants of coastal and alpine growth.

1. **throe:** a violent, intense pain; a paroxysm; agony of mind; the struggle of parturition, hence, the irritable, nervous state of an author during the period in which he is engaged on a book.

2. THROW: to propel an object from the hand through the air; to spill, over-set, cause an animal or a person to fall, especially in wrestling; of a horse that shakes the rider from his back; to turn wood in a lathe (q.v.) or clay on a potter's wheel; to cast a shadow; to project a beam (q.v.) of light (q.v.) or an image; turn a key in a lock; to handle carelessly; to construct a bridge; to put troops into action; to direct blame onto a person; to move the points on a railway; to move a lever.

He was not the man to throw his country to the wolves yet they throw the blame for the disaster upon him although, when the evil deed was in progress, he was in his death-throe.

1. **throne:** a chair of state, or dignity; the seat of the Sovereign, the Pope, a Bishop; the assumed seat of a deity; a seat set on a platform where a portrait painter's model sits; the Sovereign.

2. THROWN: pst tns of 'throw' (q.v.).

A throne is not thrown down without dire consequences.

through, see **threw.**

throw, see **throe.**

thrown, see **throne.**

1. **thrush:** birds of the genus *Turdus*, particularly *Turdus musicus*, the song-thrush; the Mavis and the Throstle.

2. THRUSH: a child's disease of the mouth and throat, *parasitic stoma-titis,* or *aphtha,* caused by a fungus; a horse's disease of the hoof.

Before the poor child had thrush he would sing like a thrush all day.

1. **thwart:** to oppose; prevent; to cross, go against.

2. THWART: the seats across a boat.

He lowered himself over the side into the dinghy, sat firmly on the thwart, and taking the oars in determined hands he murmured savagely, 'They shall not thwart me', and pulled for the shore.

1. **thyme:** an aromatic plant, *Thymus labiatae.*

2. TIME: a measurement relative to motion through space; the procession of days and months and years; the particular point at which we now exist in the procession of hours.

3. TIME (sl): a term of imprisonment.

I assume, if I diligently apply the watering-can, that the wild thyme planted on my garden bank will grow in time.

1. **tiar:** a jewelled head ornament; a tiara.

2. TIRE: to become sleepy, or drowsy; to cause to become sleepy.

3. TIRE: clothing; to provide with clothing; attire.

4. TYRE: a protective outer covering for the rim of a wheel.

In the nineteenth century they attended Court, glittering with diamonds from tiar to shoe-buckle, and the rattle of the iron-tyre on the granite road did not tire them as much as later did the vibration and exhaust-fumes of motor-vehicles, notwithstanding the soft rubber tyre.

1. **tic:** a spasmodic twitching of a muscle; *tic douloureux,* painful twitching of the face occasioned by severe neuralgia.

2. TICK: a parasite of the family *Ixodidae,* which infests the fur, or the hair of animals; extended to include flies of the families *Hippoboscidae* and *Nycteribiidae.*

3. TICK: a bag containing feathers, or kapok, used for a pillow; the tight woven impenetrable fabric of which such bags are made.

4. TICK: a quick, light tapping sound as produced by the escapement mechanism of clock-work, or by certain wood-boring beetles; any light throb, or rhythmic beat (q.v.); a short interval of time.

5. TICK: a mark like a letter V with the

right-hand stroke extended upward employed to check items on a list. √

6. TICK: debt; credit; hire-purchase.

Lured by the hire-purchase firms' advertisements he had acquired so many articles on tick, that he made a list and put a tick beside what he thought he'd finished paying for but nonetheless he was driven to depressive insanity, dressed himself in tick, developed a tic in his eyelids, carried with him ten clocks that had long ceased to tick, and slept in a sheep-fold where he got a tick in his hair.

1. tical: a Burmese coin equal to an Indian rupee.

2. TICKLE: to touch a person in the vicinity of certain sensitive nerves which induce hysterical laughter; the sensation so experienced; to cause an agreeable excitement; to appeal pleasantly to one or another of the senses; to amuse; to proceed without vigour in a matter that needs vigour.

You tickle my fancy by your story of the Burmese brassware obtained for a tical or two, but one would need to buy big: it is useless to tickle the surface of such a trade.

1. ticca: the Indian term for hired, employed, engaged on contract; a fixed fare, or a nett price.

2. TICKER: something that emits a tick, as clock-work, telegraphic apparatus, tape-machines.

He is ticca to the Colonial Office: the news has just come over the ticker.

tick, see tic.
ticker, see ticca.
tickle, see tical.

1. tide: the rising and falling, the flooding and ebbing of the ocean; a similar periodicity in media other than the sea; the period of time between high-water and low-water; any large moving body of water; a flood.

2. TIDE: to help a person in difficulties by bringing about a temporary rise of fortune.

3. TIDE: a periodic occurrence in time, Christmas-tide, Easter-tide; the propitious time for an activity; a space of time, a period, season or age.

4. TIED: secured by a cord; restricted in liberty by a length of cord; to be fastened or drawn together with a cord, tape or thong; to have made a knot (q.v.); to be restricted in either commercial, or industrial, freedom; to be joined legally or morally; to be strongly attached.

Were he not tied by his employment he'd be off to sea next tide, ashore he is a misfit: I lent him £10 to tide him over last Whitsuntide and he repaid with work: he tied canvas covers over my timber-stacks. Woe betide his employer if the tide of his troubles rises too high: I trust I shall not be tied up with it.

tier, see tare.
tierce, see tarse.

1. till: a drawer, or a box in which money is kept.

2. TILL: expressive of a limit in time; onward to the time specified; before a certain time.

3. TILL: to prepare land and raise (q.v.) farm produce.

4. TILL: a name for boulder clay.

You will not fill your till till you till efficiently.

1. tiller: one who tills the soil.

2. TILLLER: a long handle or lever by means of which the rudder of a boat is moved.

3. TILLER: a shoot, or a sucker from a root or a stalk; a shoot from a felled tree; a sapling.

4. TILLER: the groove or socket that held the arrow in a cross bow.

He was an industrious tiller of the soil when ashore, and an intrepid seaman when afloat, the tiller of his fishing-boat he had himself made from a tiller that had grown through the fence of his little farm.

1. tilt: to incline from the vertical or horizontal; to tip up; to pour out.

2. TILT: the bar or barrier at each side of which the contestants in a tournament rode (q.v.), hence, a

trial of skill between lances; a tournament.

3. TILT: a large, generally waterproof, cover for a cart or a boat; any protective covering of coarse (q.v.) cloth, hence, a tent.

4. TILT: an American sea-bird of the plover family.

The Curate put a prayer book under the Magic Lantern to tilt it into focus: he was aware that his display of slides depicting a tilt, and the banners borne in a tournament, to a party of schoolchildren, seated uncomfortably on forms, and protected from the heavy rain only by a tilt, was a failure from the start.

1. timber: wood, generally of large dimensions.

2. TIMBRE: tone, pitch or quality of sound.

The bells swinging upon the stage were of timber; the peal was produced by the orchestra who faithfully imitated the timbre.

timbre, see preceding group.

time, see thyme.

1. tip: the attenuated end of a slender object; a piece of metal used to strengthen, or to protect such an end.

2. TIP: an item of private valuable information.

3. TIP: a small sum of money given as a present to a servant, or to a young person.

4. TIP: incline; tilt (q.v.); put out of balance; to empty; to overthrow.

5. TIP: a form of hopper, or funnel for loading coal, sand, gravel and like materials into trucks; a place where refuse is deposited.

I gave him a tip when he gave me the tip that the stolen goods were hidden in the refuse tip, but it was on the tip of my tongue to ask him how he knew.

tire, see tiar.

1. to: progression; arrival; limitation; attachment.

2. TOO: in addition; abundance.

3. TWO: the sum of one and one; 2, II; ij.

The two of you had better go to

bed; you are too tired to stay up to supper.

1. toad: an amphibious quadruped, Bufonidae.

2. TOED: having toes; to impel an object, ball or pebble, with the toes.

3. TOWED: pst tns of 'tow' (q.v.); drawn along.

As the footballer toed the ball into the net, a witty supporter of the opposing team enlikened him to the six-toed toad, preserved in spirit, in the local museum, nevertheless, he was friendly, and towed home the player's car which had broken down.

1. tocsin: an alarm bell; the tune played by a clock before striking the hour.

2. TOXIN: poison; bacterial contamination.

Civilization has bereft mankind of the sensitivity that sounds a tocsin when in danger from a toxin.

1. toe: one of the terminal digits of the foot.

2. TOW: fibres in a mass.

3. TOW: to haul, drag or draw a vehicle or a vessel behind another.

The lorry, loaded with three tons of tow, broke down and was taken in tow by another, the driver of which sprained his toe.

toed, see toad.

1. toil: contention; strife; warfare, severe struggle; heavy gruelling labour.

2. TOIL: a trap; a snare.

3. TOILE: a fabric; linen and silk mixture.

The dressmaker will toil with the toile, and when you wear it it will prove a toil for some poor, unsuspecting young man.

toile, see preceding group.

1. told: confessed to; related; recounted; imparted verbally.

2. TOLLED: pst tns of 'toll' (q.v.), to ring a bell.

As his passing bell was tolled the village elders told of his virtuous life.

1. toll: a tax (q.v.); a fee paid for right of way on a road or over a bridge;

charges for transport by railway or by canal; port (q.v.) dues; market dues.

2. TOLL: the rhythmic repetition of a single stroke on a great bell; to produce this effect.

3. TOLL: a forced payment in either cash or kind.

4. TOLL: to pull or drag; to entice or allure; to decoy wild animals into traps.

5. TOLL: to defeat; obstruct; to bar entry.

They toll the bell again for the dead; motor traffic is taking its toll; they'd go slower if we had toll gates protecting the roads, and those who objected could pay their toll and travel by train.

tolled, see **told.**

1. **ton:** a standard of weight; twenty hundredweight; two thousand, two hundred and forty pounds; a unit of a ship's carrying capacity equal to one hundred cubic feet; a capacity measure for timber, forty cubic feet hewn, fifty cubic feet rough; any large weight.

2. TON: the mode; the latest fashion; the people who live up to fashion.

3. TUN: a wine barrel.

His sole concern was the dictates of the ton: he was so corpulent that he must have weighed a ton, and it was said he drank a tun of wine at one sitting.

too, see **to.**

1. **tool:** any implement by means of which raw material is worked, or by which repairs are executed; to put a design on leather with a shaped punch (q.v.).

2. TULE: a Californian bull-rush, either *Scirpus locustris,* or *Scirpus tatora.*

3. TULLE: a fine silken net used in women's dresses, and for veils (q.v.).

Tilda looked so sweet in her tulle frock that when she asked me to pick tule for her I could not refuse although, having no tool to cut them, I just had to use my teeth.

1. **top:** the apex; the highest point; a cover; a tent (q.v.).

2. TOP: a toy that spins; a cone of wood with a metal peg in the apex; an all-metal development of the foregoing.

He threw his top up in the air and lost it on top of a shed.

tor } see **taw.**
tore }

torc } see **talc.**
torque }

1. **torse:** a theoretical surface created by a straight line in motion through more than one plane (q.v.).

2. TORSE: the trunk; the body without limbs or head; a piece of statuary without limbs and head; the trunk of a tree; the stem of a plant; a torso.

3. TORSE: in heraldry, a band of two or more strips of fabric twisted together, and placed on the crown of the helmet of rank; a wreath of the colours.

For Crest he bore, issuant of a torse argent and sable, a human torse proper.

1. **tot:** an addition sum; the process of adding.

2. TOT: a young child.

3. TOT: a small, unspecified measure of volume; a short drink, usually of spirit.

Everyone in the village, including young George who is a mere tot, you might say, takes a tot of rum during the evening, and it must take the landlord an hour to tot up, after closing.

1. **totter:** to walk with unsteady footsteps as if about to fall; to push, or to shake an object so as to cause it to nearly fall.

2. TOTTER: one who completes an addition sum; a cashier; an accountant.

The auditor's totter revealed that the business was on the totter.

tour, see **taw.**
tow, see **toe.**
towed, see **toad.**
towel, see **tail.**
toxin, see **tocsin.**

1. **trace:** a track, spoor, or other indication of the passage of a person, animal or object; to follow such an indication, hence, to find that which is lost, by careful and

methodical searching; to find among the archives or other documents the record of someone, or of something, belonging to the past.

2. TRACE: a minute quantity the existence of which can be deduced.

3. TRACE: to copy a drawing or a diagram by covering it with translucent paper or cloth, and following with pen or pencil the semi-visible lines.

4. TRACE: one of the pair (q.v.) of chains, straps or ropes by means of which a vehicle is attached to the collar or the yoke (q.v.) of a draught (q.v.) animal.

5. TRACE: to find the way (q.v.); to follow the course (q.v.) of a road, or of a river, by studying a map; to go; to make a journey.

Dr. Dimnut asserts that he can trace all the prehistoric migrations because each left a recognizable trace; his opponents declare that there is not the minutest trace. I will try to trace my copy of the printed report on the controversy and, if I succeed, I will trace for you the sketch-map that accompanies it. The most amusing incident of the Dimnut Expedition was their being stranded for three months due to a broken trace, and a mule who decided to trace his footsteps home.

1. tracked: followed by the observation of clues; provided with a path.

2. TRACT: a pamphlet dealing with either religion or politics used for propaganda; a monograph; an area or extent of territory; to tow (q.v.) haul or draw along, to subject to traction.

The juvenile's delinquency was tracked to a pious tract he had read in infancy, and his offences were re-labelled 'compensation behaviour'.

tract, see preceding group.

1. train: to teach or instruct; to direct.

2. TRAIN: anything that is drawn along, as part of a dress, or a barge on a canal, hence, the persons following a prince or a nobleman.

3. TRAIN: military apparatus and vehicles; a line of gunpowder or fuse; to direct gunfire.

4. TRAIN: a number of objects interdependent for motion, as carriages and trucks coupled behind an engine, or cogwheels in a clock or a watch (q.v.).

Put the recruits in a train for Aldershot and we will train them so that they can go on a ceremonial parade before a visiting Prince and his train, and go on guard at a state function without getting mixed up with a lady's train.

1. trait (trae): a characteristic.

2. TRAY: a board, or a sheet of metal having raised edges used for containing, or transporting small objects.

3. TREY: the number three, applied particularly to a playing-card of that value.

Every time he is dealt a trey he reaches for the tray and pours a stiff drink; is that not a curious trait?

1. trapan: to lure, or trap; to cheat or swindle; one who decoys others into acts profitable to himself, but dangerous to the victim.

2. TREPAN: alternative spelling of No. 1 above.

3. TREPAN: a saw used in cutting small sections of bone from the skull.

4. TREPAN: the operation on the skull in which such a saw is employed.

5. TREPAN: formerly an engine used in sieges; a machine employed in sinking bore holes.

6. TREPANG: a sea-slug, *holothuria edulis*, sea-swallow (q.v.); beche-de-mer.

7. TRIPANG: alternative spelling of No. 6 above.

He was a trapan if ever there was one, and he put several likely lads away, but when he tried to cheat a Chinese merchant over a consignment of trepang he got a crack on the head, and a Chinese doctor gave a certificate of death due to a trepan.

tray, see trait.

1. **treaties:** agreements, particularly between nations.
2. TREATISE: a formal exposition of a subject in an essay or a book.
3. TREATY'S: possessive case of 'treaty'.
4. TRISTESSE: an atmosphere of sadness, depression, hopelessness.
   In the latest treatise on treaties one discerns a certain tristesse.

treatise ⎱
treaty's ⎰ see preceding group.

trepan ⎱
trepang ⎰ see **trapan.**

trey, see **trait.**
tripang, see **trapan.**
tristesse, see **treatise.**

1. **trompe:** a machine for creating a blast which is produced by collecting air compressed and carried in a turbulent stream of falling water.
2. TRUMP: a blast upon a trumpet; loud acclaim.
3. TRUMP: a playing-card in the suite that for the time being is accepted as superior in power, or in value, to the rest (q.v.) of the pack, hence, an obliging, helpful, good-natured person.
4. TRUMP: to make a false accusation; to bring a false charge; to unscrupulously and falsely attribute to an innocent person reprehensible acts or motives.
   You trump up this charge against me; but my brother, who is a perfect trump, has spent time and money looking into your past, and has supplied me with a trump-card which I have yet to play; when I do so, you will deflate like a trompe with the water turned off, and I will trump my victory all over the town.

1. **tronk:** a prison, hence, a closed, inaccessible place, hence, a system installed in some hotels, restaurants and other establishments engaged in public services, whereunder all tips are paid into a fund which, periodically, is distributed in proportionate shares to the whole staff, including those who have no direct contact with the customers.

2. TRUNK: the body or main part; the bole (q.v.) of a tree; the body, without limbs and head, a torse (q.v.); a main road, railway or canal, having minor branches; the major arteries, veins and nerves; a main telephone line between towns.
3. TRUNK: a large box, or case, to contain clothes and other goods when travelling; a chamber, or cage afloat on a river or a lake, in which special fish are isolated; a unit of fish-marketing, being an open box holding between 80 and 90 lb. of fresh fish.
4. TRUNK: a tube or pipe, hence, the elongated, prehensile proboscis of the elephant, the tapir (q.v.), some other animals, fish and insects.
5. TRUNK: short tight-fitting drawers or underpants.
   The circus elephant went with his master to market and brought home, on his back, more than one trunk of fish for the sea-lions, and in his trunk several bags of vegetables and nuts for the monkeys; on the journey they overtook the Equestrienne returning from holiday, and added her trunk to the load: they were traversing a trunk road, and the hooting, and whizzing past of motors annoyed the laden animal who, tossing aside his multiple burden, lay reclined at his ease across the full width of the carriage-way, and a trunk-call had to be sent through to order on a breakdown crane the driver of which, disapproving of the tronk system installed at his firm, was in no hurry to arrive on the scene.

1. **Troy:** a town of antiquity, home of fair Helen, besieged, and ultimately taken by the Greeks who concealed a task-force inside a wooden horse which they permitted the Trojans to capture.
2. TROY: a system of weight used for precious metals and gem stones, named from Troyes, France.
   She occupied a back-room in Soho, but she considered her-

TRUCK [187] TUBA

TRUCK [187] TUBA

self a veritable Helen of Troy, and carried several pounds weight troy in jewellery about her so that it should not be left behind when her Paris came to carry her off.

1. **truck:** a platform set upon wheels for the purpose of transporting goods.
2. TRUCK: barter; dealings or transactions.
3. TRUCK: the round-edged disc that roofs a mast (q.v.).

When we offered our truckdrivers luncheon vouchers, the chief agitator said it was a violation of the Truck Act, and they'd have no truck with it.

trump, see trompe.
trunk, see tronk.

1. **truss:** a bundle, particularly a bundle of hay or of straw.
2. TRUSS: a line by which a yard-arm is secured to the mast; an iron ring serving the same purpose.
3. TRUSS: an appliance consisting of a pad and spring worn to support a rupture.
4. TRUSS: a framework supporting some part of a building; a bracket or corbel; one of the timbers supporting a hull during ship-building.
5. TRUSS: to tie the carcase of a bird for cooking; to make a bundle; to furl sails; to make fast (q.v.); to bind or tie; to secure in a strait- (q.v.) jacket; to confine.

That man must not lift so much as a truss of straw, he wears a truss; he ruptured himself when at sea by hauling in a truss, and double-ruptured himself in the shipyard when fixing a truss: I employ him to truss fowls, and to truss up the light parcels for post.

1. **trussed:** supported by a truss (q.v.); of a bird prepared for roasting; tied up in a bundle.
2. TRUST: to rely upon; to have confidence in a person; to give credence to a statement; belief in; hope of; to give credit.
3. TRUST: to bear a moral responsibility; to be responsible for adminis-

tering, or managing affairs or estate on behalf of another; to receive credit.

4. TRUST: a commercial misnomer for a combine of companies who ruthlessly kill all small competitors and, having secured a monopoly, proceed to advance prices and to reduce quality; a totally mercenary body of businessmen.

The Trust trussed up their victims, arranged for raw material suppliers not to trust them, destroyed the bank's trust in them, and having trussed up the trade betrayed the public's trust in them.

trust, see trussed.

1. **trustee:** a person, or a body of persons in whom is vested the temporary ownership of money or property, with the duty of using and administering on behalf of another, for example, a minor (q.v.).
2. TRUSTY: a person, or an organization of high integrity in whom trust (q.v.) may safely be put; an object that can be relied upon to serve its purpose with minimum risk of breakdown or failure; in the U.S.A., a mild-mannered wellbehaved superior sort of convict who is granted numerous privileges.

After the big-time gangster had been sprung from the Pen, everyone knew it was the trusty (who had been a defaulting trustee) who had supplied a trusty rope ladder, but the screws dared not try their trusty tricks to make him come clean.

trusty, see preceding group.

1. **tuba:** a straight, bronze trumpet; the war-trumpet employed by the ancient Romans; an 8 ft. pressure reed (q.v.) stop in an organ (q.v.).
2. TUBA: a mythical tree; one of the plants believed to be growing in the Mohammedan heaven.
3. TUBER: a thickening on a root having buds out of which new growth may arise.

No son of Islam will accept the tuber and reject the tuba; he would as soon sound the tuba on the Sabbath day.

tuber, see preceding group.

1. **tuck:** a fold, or pleat generally in the bottom of a garment.
2. TUCK: a light blow, as on a drum.
3. TUCK: confectionery; a feast of delicacies.
4. TUCK: conceal.

If mother thinks I will wear her left-off frocks with a tuck in the bottom, and let her tuck me away in the country to serve in a Girls' School tuck shop, she'll be alarmed by the tuck of rebellion's drum.

tule } tulle } see **tool.**

tun, see **ton.**

turm, see **term.**

turn, see **tern.**

turnery, see **ternery.**

1. **tweel:** a form of fabric having diagonal lines woven in.
2. TWILL: alternative (and more usual) spelling of No. 1 above.
3. 'TWILL: contracted form of 'it will'.
   'Twill look well in twill.

twill, see preceding group.

two, see **to.**

twoer, see **taw.**

1. **type:** an accepted standard against which other similar objects, or people, are measured.
2. TYPE: letters of the alphabet raised and reversed for printing.
3. TYPE: to use a typewriter.
   She is the type of girl who will type accurately enough for her work to be set up in type.

tyre, see **tiar.**

U

U, see **ewe.**

upbraid, see **abrade.**

ure, see **ewer.**

urn, see **earn.**

U's } use } see **ewes.**

1. **used:** of an object that is being employed for the purpose for which it was designed.
2. USED: pertaining to habits and customs of the past.

That tool looks as though it has never been used: how careful, how patient and how skilful craftsmen used to be.

1. **utter:** speak; to express verbally; to reveal.
2. UTTER: to sell or offer for sale; to circulate forged (q.v.) currency.
3. UTTER: extreme; exterior; total; decisive.
   It is utter nonsense to suppose that he did not utter a word when warned not to vend or utter his wares in that market-place.

V

1. **vail:** to lower, or haul down, to let fall, to doff the hat, either as a token of respect, or to symbolize submission.
2. VAIL: sunset.
3. VAIL: a side-profit; a secondary income; a gratuity or tip (q.v.).
4. VALE: a valley (q.v.).
5. VEIL: a cloth, curtain or piece of drapery hanging so as to cover, or to conceal something; to provide a covering or means of concealment; the life lived by a nun (q.v.); to hide, or divert attention from a true meaning.
   The custodian of the Vale of Phallic Monuments is constantly vigilant to veil his vail.
1. **vain:** without effect; without value; sense of one's prowess or attractiveness.
2. VANE: an ornamental flag-like revolving metal plate pivoted on a building at a high altitude to indicate the direction of the wind.
3. VEIN: a blood-vessel; a marking suggestive of the appearance of blood-vessels; a crack or channel in the earth's crust; such a fissure when filled up with matter differing from the surrounding matter, as metal ore (q.v.); a quality discernible in a person's character; a special ability; a talent; a mood.
   He made the armorial vane in vain, for being vain, and having

in him a strong vein of contempt he distorted the lion, and the squire rejected the work.

vale, see vail.

1. **valet:** the masculine equivalent of a lady's maid; a gentleman's personal servant.
2. VALLEY: a long and comparatively narrow tract (q.v.) of country between heights; the country through which a river flows; any trough, as between waves, or two planes meeting at an angle.
3. VOLET: one of the side wings of a triptych.
4. VOLLEY: a flight of numerous missiles in concert; an outpouring of numerous and violent words.

I presented the local museum with a valuable volet, but when I claimed to have the best valet in the valley I received a volley of abuse from the entire committee.

valley, see preceding group.

1. **van:** a vehicle for the transport of goods, generally permanently enclosed, but sometimes merely provided with a tilt (q.v.); the abode of a gypsy.
2. VAN: the front rank, or the foremost group of advancing troops.
3. VAN: a winnowing fan.

In the van went the big guns each served by a van loaded with shells, and the enemy scattered like chaff before the van.

vane, see vain.

1. **vault:** an arched roof; the space under an arched roof; a crypt; a cellar (q.v.) particularly when used for housing wine in bulk.
2. VAULT: to leap, spring or jump particularly over an obstruction.
3. VOLT: the Anglicized form of the surname of Allesandro Volta, Italian physicist (1745–1827), and used to express a unit of electromotive force.
4. VOLT: a sharp turn to avoid a thrust in fencing; a circular movement in equestrianism.
5. VOLTE: alternative spelling of No. 4 above.

The boys playing with a medical magneto in the wine-vault found that at half-speed they made a complete involuntary volt, and another volt or two caused them to vault over a hogshead.

veer, see fear.

veil, see vail.

vein, see vain.

1. **verdure:** greenery; vegetation in general; flourishing grass or other plants; freshness of flavour in fruits; taste or smell.
2. VERGER: a garden.
3. VERGER: an official who, carrying a rod as his symbol (q.v.) of office, walks before the dignitaries of a university or a church; one who takes care of the interior of a church.
4. VIRGER: alternative spelling of No. 3 above.

The last notes of the organ died away as the virger, knowing the Archbishop's love of verdure, led the way into the shady, scented verger.

verger, see preceding group.

vial, see file.

1. **vertu:** a love of, or a knowledge of fine art, or of antiques; objects of art, or of antiquity.
2. VIRTU: alternative spelling of No. 1 above.
3. VIRTUE: rectitude; morality; excellence; special ability; authority; high value either in money or utility.

His only virtue is that he will buy an article of vertu to save it from the melting pot.

1. **vice:** depravity; corruption; evil habits and occupations.
2. VICE: a tool consisting of two jaws that can be brought into apposition (q.v.) by a screw, used for holding an object while working upon it.
3. VICE: deputy.

The vice-chairman of the Anti-Vice League said Satan grips youth in a vice.

vile ⎫
viol ⎭ see file.

virger, see verdure.

virtu ⎫
virtue ⎭ see vertu.

volet, see **valet.**

1. **Volga:** the great Russian river; the longest river in Europe.
2. VULGAR: general; plebian; common; crude, impolite.
   The Volga Boat-Song, at the apex of its popularity, was in danger of becoming vulgar.

volley, see **valet.**

volt } see **vault.**
volte }

W

1. **wade:** to walk through water deep enough to impede progress; to execute a large accumulation of work.
2. WEIGHED: pst tns & ppl of 'weigh' (q.v.).
   He couldn't swim—he had to wade, his boots weighed a ton!
1. **wae:** a form of 'way' (q.v.) or 'wo' (q.v.) the call used to a horse to stop, and extended to any circumstance as a warning to stop; an obsolete form of woe (q.v.).
2. WAY: a path, track or road; a route (q.v.) by which a destination may be reached; a person's manner, or characteristics; at a great distance in either space or time.
3. WEIGH: to lift; to set against a known weight in a balance; to estimate the importance of, and possible effect (q.v.) of, a person or a circumstance; to ponder, consider carefully.
4. WHEY: the liquid part of curdled milk.
   Wae! You are going the wrong way: if you want to see the crew of the schooner weigh anchor and get under way, you must go the short way, and not stop at every farm on the way and drink whey. Way back in the nineteenth century you'd have had no paved way to walk on, and modern boots do not weigh so much—weigh my words carefully.
1. **wag:** a humorist.
2. WAG: to shake, or oscillate.
   That cat is quite a wag, just

look how he will wag his tail when you talk to him.

1. **wage:** a weekly payment for services rendered.
2. WAGE: to make war.
   The Trades Unions still wage war over the wage question.
1. **wail:** a long drawn-out cry; a mournful cry; lamentation.
2. WALE: one of the broad horizontal planks running from stem (q.v.) to stern (q.v.) of a boat or a ship, forming the gunwale; bracing timbers between the piles (q.v.) of a dam (q.v.); the woven top edge of a basket.
3. WHALE: a fishlike marine mammal of the order *Cetacae.*
   Did Jonah wail as they tossed him over the gunwale? He was silenced only by being swallowed by the whale.
1. **wails:** pl of 'wail' (q.v.); the act of wailing.
2. WALES: pl of 'wale' (q.v.).
3. WALES: a Principality occupying the mid-western extremity of Great Britain; Cambria.
4. WHALES: pl (') of 'whale' (q.v.).
   Who wails in Wales when cast sprats catch no whales?
1. **wain:** an open wagon, a hay cart.
2. WANE: decrease; decline; shrinkage; the moon's phases after the full.
   He sprawled, half somnulent, on a hay wain, and reflected that his popularity had begun to wane.
1. **waist:** the narrow section of the body above the hips (q.v.) and below the ribs, hence a narrowing between the parts of anything.
2. WASTE: unused; misused; made use-
   less.
   That woman will waste more pounds a week on clothes than she has inches in her ample waist measurement.
1. **wait:** a period of time spent in anticipation of an expected event; to tarry, delay or postpone action; to attend; to keep an appointment.
2. WAIT: one who sings Christmas hymns for alms.
3. WEIGHT: comparative mass, or heaviness; a standard against which

goods can be balanced; comparative seriousness.

Wait till the lads of the village hear of your plan to be a Christmas wait: you will be crushed by the weight of their sarcasm.

1. **waive:** to give up; relinquish or abandon.

2. WAVE: an undulatory movement; oscillation in an elastic medium; movement to and fro or up and down; to bend in the form of a wave; to oscillate the hand in a gesture of farewell.

A wave of anger shook me on learning that I must waive my right to wave my hair, but I had to wave good-bye to it.

1. **wake:** to emerge from sleep; to emerge from a state of lethargy.

2. WAKE: the depression, or track left upon the water behind a ship under way (q.v.), hence, a trace (q.v.) left behind.

3. WAKE: the watch (q.v.) kept by the living over the dead, frequently accompanied by drinking.

4. WAKE: the eve of a religious festival.

Ahoy! there, helmsman; if you don't wake up and stop signing your name in the wake your relations will be getting drunk at your wake.

wale, see **wail.**

Wales, see **wails.**

1. **wall:** one of the four outer surfaces of a building; an erection of brick or stone considerably longer than it is thick, to enclose a space, or act as a barrier, across territory; an embankment on the coast, or along a river frontage, to hold back floods.

2. WAUL: a loud penetrating unpleasant cry emitted by tom-cats and young babies.

3. WHORL: a spiral; a spiral shell; petals or leaves surrounding a stem, a speed regulator in a spinning-wheel.

He threw a whorl-shell over someone's garden wall, and there came a blood-curdling waul.

wane, see **wain.**

1. **war:** a state of armed combat between nations, or between opposing parties or factions in the same nation; conflict between any living beings; opposition between forces; competition between commercial and industrial organizations when carried to indecent excess.

2. WORE: pst tns of 'wear' (q.v.).

During the war men wore either khaki or blue.

1. **ward:** to guard; a minor (q.v.) under guardianship; the place where sick persons are under the guardianship of doctors and nurses; a sector of a town or city under the jurisdiction of an alderman, or one that elects a councillor; each of the ridges on the inside of the faceplate of a lock that guard against the turning of a wrong key, hence, each of the grooves and slots in the bit (q.v.) of a key that admit the passage of the lock's ridges; to act as guard; to fend or turn aside attack.

2. -WARD: a suffix indicating direction of movement.

3. WARRED: pst tns of 'war' (q.v.).

When the rebels from the North warred against the City, the aldermen of each Ward rallied their train-band, and sent a man to swell the ranks of the Castle Ward: at the Guildhall a chamber was set aside as a ward for the wounded, and the Court of Chancery ordered every ward it had, who resided in the city, to travel a day's journey southward.

1. **ware:** an article of merchandise.

2. WARE: cautious; prudent; to bear in mind, beware of.

3. WEAR: to bear upon one's body, hence, clothing.

4. WEAR: to use; to decrease efficiency or to destroy by use; to endure or to be enduring; to tire.

5. WEAR: to bring a ship's head across the wind.

6. WEIR: a dam (q.v.) an artificial waterfall.

7. WHERE: pertaining to place; the place from which a person or a thing comes, or to whence he or it goes.

Where do you think you will

sell your ware if you wear clothes showing signs of wear? Really—you wear me out! Throw those rags over the weir and wear a smile with your Sunday suit: and 'ware moths when you open the wardrobe.

1. **warn:** to give notice; to caution.
2. WORN: used; damaged or diminished by use; weakened, or exhausted by use.

I warn you, the spiral staircase is worn.

warred, see ward.

1. **washer:** one who washes; a machine for washing raw material in some industries.
2. WASHER: a name for the wagtail, *Motacilla lugubris*.
3. WASHER: a disc of metal with a central hole through which a screw or a bolt passes to increase the bearing area of the head; a similar drilled disc used to pack loose fitting parts of a machine; such discs cut out of materials other than metal used for numerous purposes; a spongy, compressible disc or hemisphere, used to prevent leakage in a water tap (q.v.) faucet or bibcock.

'The average washer does not turn the tap off', wrote the lavatory attendant in his Annual Report; and 'fit new washer' the Borough Engineer scrawled in the margin, but the Municipal Psychologist wrote, 'Hot or Cold?'

1. **watch:** a part of the night; wakefulness; religious exercise during the night; to be vigilant, on guard; a sailor's tour of duty; to observe.
2. WATCH: a small time-piece, suitable for carrying in the pocket or wearing strapped upon the wrist.

The noise and confusion on deck during the first dog-watch was occasioned by the old man dropping his gold watch overboard.

1. **watt:** a unit of electrical energy.
2. WHAT: interrogative; of time, of number, of purpose, of identity, etc.
3. WOT: to know, be aware of.

What switches there are to be pressed, what networks of wires behind them, press what you will, and consume a watt or two more than you wot of, what does it matter? What can you do about it, what alternative have you?

waul, see wall.

wave, see waive.

1. **wax:** a fusible, plastic, homogenous substance secreted by bees and used by them to form cells which, charged with honey, house their eggs and larvae; any substance either vegetable or mineral, having a similar nature and chemical composition.
2. WAX: to grow in size; to increase in strength; to accumulate power.
3. WHACKS: pl of 'whack', a smack (q.v.) with hand or stick; the clap of sound so created; a portion or share; to proceed vigorously; to put, or deposit.

Who whacks out the cash for wax candles that light may wax round his bier?

way, see wae.

1. **we:** the speaker and another associated with him; the speaker and his audience; the Sovereign's reference to himself; an editor's reference to himself as identified with his periodical; reference to a company or other industrial or commercial undertaking or enterprise.
2. WEE: small; of small size, or to a small extent; of minor importance.

He has a wee shop in a back street and does all the work single-handed but loftily refers to his enterprise as 'we' when talking business.

1. **weak:** short of either physical or moral strength; likely to bend or break under strain (q.v.); unhealthy; heavy diluted; having a minimum of effect (q.v.).
2. WEEK: a period of seven (q.v.) days (q.v.).
3. WEEK: a form of squeak; imitation of the cry of a mouse or a bat.

His mother thought he was weak and drenched him with weak barley-water, and he dared not say week to a mouse, but he ran away to sea and in about a week complained that the issue rum was too weak, and he offered to fight any weak-kneed swab who argued.

1. **weakly:** in a weak (q.v.) manner; in a manner lacking vigour, or vitality; with minimal effect.
2. WEEKLY: at recurring intervals of seven days; once a week (q.v.).
He protested weakly, weekly.

1. **weal:** well-being; welfare.
2. WEAL: a ridge-shaped inflamed swelling caused by the stroke of a rod or whip on bare (q.v.) flesh.
3. WEEL: a fish-trap.
4. WE'LL: contraction of 'we will.'
5. WELL: a spring, particularly one having reputed medicinal properties; a brick- or stone-lined shaft sunk to make underground water available; a bore-hole sunk to obtain mineral oil; open shafts, in buildings covering an extensive area, to admit light and air to internal windows; the floor-space of a court of law; any pit designed to receive, or that contains, droppings; any prolific source (q.v.) of information.
6. WELL: in good health; of that which is favourable or satisfactory; in good or sound condition; on good terms with; pleasing; in good order.
7. WELL: to boil; to boil over, hence, any liquid arising or seeping out of any place.
8. WELL: in addition to; one thing, or circumstance, added to another.
9. WHEAL: an alternative spelling of No. 2 above.
10. WHEEL: a circumferential frame joined to spokes (q.v.) radiating from a central cylinder one or more of which, supporting a vehicle, enables it to advance smoothly.
We'll first look in the weel and if it's full, wheel the fish down to the village hall as our contribution to the local public weal; and after that, buy some cooling lotion to treat the weal on your arm raised when the fishing line snapped; it will be well to give it some proper attention, and

not just bathe it in water from the village well as the local rustics, having faith, do for everything, and get well.

1. **weald:** a tract (q.v.) of land between the North and South Downs (q.v.); part of Kent, Sussex and Surrey.
2. WHEELED: of a vehicle or a chair, being provided with wheels (q.v.); to have been transported in a vehicle or chair having wheels.
3. WIELD: to govern or command; to direct movements; to use or handle (particularly (of) a weapon) with skill; to use tools skilfully.
Although I am but an invalid, I wield power here, and I insist on being wheeled over the weald every day.

1. **weam:** a Scottish prehistoric underground dwelling.
2. WEAN: to induce an infant animal to take nourishment other than mother's milk; to induce a person to abandon a habit or custom.
3. WEAN: a young child.
4. WEEN: to suppose; to think; likely; to guess.
I ween they did no' wean a wean soon when they lived in a weem.

wean, see preceding group.

wear, see ware.

1. **weather:** condition of the atmosphere controlled by barometric pressure, temperature, humidity, etc.
2. WETHER: a castrated male sheep.
3. WHETHER: a distinction, or a selection, between two.
4. WHITHER: to what place.
5. WITHER: to shrivel.
Wither goes the wether, weather like this? Whether his horns wither in the frost or not, he goes.

wee, see we.

week, see weak.

weel, see weal.

1. **weld:** to join two pieces of iron or steel by heating to near melting point in the forge (q.v.) and hammering; to join ferrous or other metals by fusing the closely abutted edges before the blowpipe: the joint so made.

2. WELD: a dye (q.v.) and the plant from which it is made (q.v.), *Roseda luteola.*

3. WELLED: pst tns of 'well' (q.v.), of water, or other liquids that have bubbled or seeped upward from the earth or elsewhere.

Tears welled up in his eyes when he learned that the fatal accident had been caused by the severance of a weld he had guaranteed.

we'll } see **weal.**
well

welled, see **weld.**

ween, see **weam.**

weigh, see **wae.**

weighed, see **wade.**

weight, see **wait.**

weir, see **ware.**

1. **wen:** a wart, or other excrescence on the skin.

2. **WHEN:** at a certain time; on a certain occasion.

Do you remember when Gertrude went to the hospital to be rid of a wen on her nose?

1. **were:** pst subjunctive of 'be' (q.v.).

2. **WE'RE:** contracted form of 'we are'.

3. **WHIRR:** a buzzing sound, as of insects' wings.

We're safe now, but we were in danger then, did you not hear the whirr of the missiles?

1. **wet:** carrying a quantity of water; moist; soggy; in a liquid condition prior to solidification; to sprinkle with water; to become so sprinkled; of molten solder when it runs.

2. **WHET:** to sharpen; to stimulate; to clear the voice by drinking.

You have no need to whet my appetite after my adventures: first I stepped knee-deep in wet cement, seized a rail covered with wet paint, and so spilled a water-tank and I'm wet through.

wether, see **weather.**

whacks, see **wax.**

whale, see **wail.**

whales, see **wails.**

what, see **watt.**

wheal } see **weal,**
wheel

wheeled, see **weald.**

where, see **ware.**

whet, see **wet.**

whether, see **weather.**

whey, see **wae.**

1. **which:** indicative of selection; one of many.

2. **WITCH:** a woman supposed to be in league (q.v.) with evil spirits in order to cast spells, and to bring destruction and death to her neighbours.

3. **WYCH:** of a tree with pliant branches, particularly the elm, and the hazel.

Which witch wych-hazel philtres makes?

1. **whig:** a political term for opponents to the Tory party.

2. **WIG:** a head-covering of hair used to supply a natural deficiency, or as part of the ceremonial costume of barristers and judges; jocularly to the natural hair.

No need to tear your wig out at the mere thought of a Whig.

1. **while:** a period of time; an evaluation of time spent; at the same time as; to engage in a light, or an amusing occupation to cover a period of otherwise idle time.

2. **WILE:** a ruse; a means of deceiving an opponent; cunning, artfulness.

In a little while he will be employing a wile to go and while away his time while the rest of us work; to complain is not worth while.

1. **whiled:** pst tns of 'while' (q.v.); to pass time.

2. **WILD:** savage; untamed; uncultivated; uninhabited; undeveloped territory; uncivilized; not amenable to discipline; bad-tempered; cruel; violent; angry.

3. **WILED:** pst tns of 'wile' (q.v.).

Having wiled his way into a sinecure he whiled away his time reading paper-back books about wild Indians and thus made many people wild.

1. **whin:** heath, furze or gorse; the bush *Ulex europaeus*; any form of thorn or prickly shrub.

2. **WIN:** to conquer, prevail, gain ascendancy; to get or obtain by hard labour; to get the best of a bar-

gain; to succeed in a game or a competition; to receive money in a lottery; to secure affection or loyalty.

The obstacle race is to be through a mile of dense whin: if you possess a suit of plate armour you will win.

1. **whine:** a shrill, mournful and protracted cry; a complaint.
2. WINE: fermented juice of the grape.

The child, having belly-ache, will continue to whine, give him some wine to soothe him.

whined, see **wind.**

1. **whirled:** revolved rapidly; at a high speed.
2. WHIRRED: pst tns of 'whirr' (q.v.).
3. WHORLED: of a shell developed about a central spindle.
4. WHURLED: alternative spelling of No. 3 above.
5. WORD: an element of speech; a guarantee of truth.
6. WORLD: the earth; mundane interests.

I give you my word, there is no word to express the poet's contempt of the world of fashion; he gazed upon a whorled shell, the wings whirred around him, he identified himself with the world of nature and he could not be whirled away.

whirr, see **were.**
whirred, see **whirled.**

1. **whisht:** an exclamation demanding silence.
2. WHIST: a game of cards.
3. WHIST: alternative spelling of No. 1 above.
4. WIST: to know.

Whisht! They are playing whist, and I wist they will want no noise.

whist, see preceding group.

1. **whit:** a small amount; a negligible matter.
2. WIT: apt and amusing expression, particularly unpremeditated and fitting the occasion; one who habitually makes such remarks.
3. WIT: wisdom; intellect; the faculty of thought; mental ability.

That he was a wit served him not a whit when he fell into unpopularity, and he had to exer-

cise much wit to re-establish himself.

1. **white:** colourless; of the quality of light in the spectrum; of colourless substances, or articles.
2. WIGHT: name of an island, off the south coast of England.
3. WIGHT: a person, particularly one who is strong, agile, full of energy; a bold fighter.
4. WITE: culpability; pain; punishment or torture.
5. WYTE: alternative spelling of No. 4 above.

What wyte might turn that wight white?

whiter, see **weather.**

1. **whitlow:** a septic condition of the finger end, involving the nail, *paronychia.*
2. WICKLOW: a mountainous district in Leinster, Ireland.

I didn't enjoy the holiday in Wicklow, I was nursing a whitlow.

1. **whoa:** a call to a horse to stop.
2. WO: a form of No. 1 above.
3. WOA: a further form of No. 1 above (see also 'wae').
4. WOE: grief, misery; lamentation.
5. WOW: an expression of surprise, or of aversion; the cry of a dog.

He expected woe when, having called 'whoa', and 'wo' and 'woa' as well as 'wae' the horse simply sped faster, leaving him speechless but for 'wow'!

whole, see **hole.**
wholly, see **holey.**
whoop, see **hoop.**
whore, see **haw.**
whored, see **hoard.**
whores, see **hause.**
whorl, see **wall.**
whorled } see **whirled.**
whurled }

1. **why:** a question, demanding for what reason or purpose; suggesting opposition or negative; because of; an expression of surprise, or of protest.
2. WYE: the name of a river rising on Plynlymmon and flowing through Wales (q.v.) and Herefordshire where it enters a world-famous gorge; the name of a tributary of

the Derbyshire Derwent; the name of a tributary of the River Thames.

3. Y: the twenty-fifth letter of the alphabet between X and Z; y; anything of that shape, a biforcation rising out of a stem.

Why do you suggest that after we have seen the Wye Valley you go north-west and I go north-east, thus making a Y-shaped tour?

1. whys: pl of 'why' (q.v.).

2. WISE: the ability to exercise sound (q.v.) judgement, or perception; a manner (q.v.) or a way (q.v.) of approach.

3. Y'S: pl of 'Y' (q.v.).

Why all these whys and wherefores? Were you wise you'd reach the Xs, Ys and Zs by starting with the As and Bs and Cs.

1. wicket: a small door fitted into a large one to give access to premises without difficulty.

2. WICKET: an erection of three stumps, or sticks topped with bails (q.v.) at which the bowler (q.v.) aims in the game of cricket.

The team came onto the pitch through the wicket and went straight to the wicket.

Wicklow, see whitlow.

wield, see weald.

wig, see whig.

wight, see white.

wile, see while.

wiled, see wild.

1. will: desire; wish; inclination; determination; purpose.

2. WILL: a document setting forth the manner in which property is to be distributed or disposed of, after death.

3. WILL: a verb expressing determination, to do.

4. WILL: in dialect, to be astray, lost.

5. WILL: diminutive of the masculine personal name, William.

It is my will that Will Shakespeare's will is published in facsimile: I will provide the money.

1. wilt: to become limp; to dry up, wither (q.v.); to become dispirited, lacking in energy.

2. WILT: second person singular present indicative of 'will' (q.v.).

Wilt thou go for water ere the plants wilt and die?

win, see whin.

1. wind: air in motion; breathing; light talk; promise without fulfilment; flatus (q.v.); to sound a horn or trumpet.

2. WIND (wynd): to twist, turn or roll; to go one's way; to follow a circuitous route (q.v.); to enwrap; to put thread, yarn, wire or the like on a reel (q.v.) or to turn it about itself, forming a ball; to tighten the spring in a clockwork mechanism; to turn the crank-handle of a winch.

3. WHINED: pst tns of 'whine' (q.v.).

4. WYND: a narrow street, or alleyway.

The wind whined over the rooftops in the wynd, I heard the watchman wind his horn and I was reminded to wind the clock.

wine, see whine.

wist, see whisht.

wit, see whit.

wite, see white.

wither, see weather.

wo ⎫
woa ⎬ see whoa.
woe ⎭

won, see one.

1. wont: habit; manner; custom; usual manner of proceeding.

2. WON'T: contraction of 'will not'.

It was his wont to obstruct the doorway and snap 'won't!' when asked to move.

1. wood: timber (q.v.); the substance of the trunk and branches of a tree; objects made of wood; a tract of land on which trees grow densely.

2. WOULD: desire or intention.

When I have sold this cart-load of firewood, I would like to laze in a shady wood, and make music on a whistle of wood.

word, see whirled.

wore, see war.

world, see whirled.

1. worms: pl of 'worm', a more or less long, cylindrical limbless segmented organism that burrows in the earth, *Lumbricus*; any member of the class *Annelida*, having rings; an internal parasite infesting either

the stomach or the bowels of man and beast; any grub (q.v.), maggot or caterpillar; a snake; a dragon.

2. WORMS: an ancient city on the left bank of the Rhine.

> In Teutonic story the lind-worms attacked the city of Worms.

worn, see warn.

1. worst: the least desirable; the super-lative of 'bad'.

2. WURST: German sausage.

> Germans enjoy even the worst wurst.

wot, see watt.

would, see wood.

1. wound (woond): damage inflicted on either the body or the mind; to in-flict such damage.

2. WOUND (wownd): pst ppl of v 'to wind'.

> As he wound the cross-bow the cord snapped and he received a severe wound.

wow, see whoa.
wrack, see rack.
wrap, see rap.
wrapped, see rapped.
wreak, see reek.
wreck, see reck.
wrecks, see recks.
wrest, see rest.
wretch, see reach.
wright, see right.
wring, see ring.
wringer, see ringer.
write, see right.
wrote, see root.
wrung, see rung.
wry, see rye.
wurst, see worst.
wych, see which,
Wye, see why.
wynd, see wind.
wyte, see white.

X

Xeme, see seam.

Y

Y, see why.
Y's, see whys.

1. yale: one of the fictitious creatures of Heraldry which attracted a great deal of public attention as one of the Queen's Beasts, at the time of the Coronation of Her Majesty, Queen Elizabeth II.

2. YALE: a cylinder-lock, named after the manufacturer.

3. YALL: alternative spelling of No. 1 above.

4. YELL: a shout; a strident cry.

> There is a huge crowd outside the Abbey annexe, and they yell like wild animals at the sight of the yale among the models of the Queen's Beasts: you'd better fit an extra yale lock on the door, in case of accidents.

yall, see preceding group.

1. Yank: abbreviated form of 'Yankee', applied to any American citizen.

2. YANK: to pull or haul; to jerk or twitch.

> Yank that drunken Yank out by his collar.

1. yap: the shrill concussive bark of a lap-dog.

2. YAPP: a style of bookbinding having limp leather covers with turn-down flaps top, bottom and fore-edge.

> Victorian Sunday, yap of pug-dog, yapp-bound Bible, church bells ringing, and muffins for tea!

yapp, see preceding group.

1. yard: an enclosed space, generally paved; a back-garden; parallel sets of connected rails used for assem-bling a railway train (q.v.).

2. YARD: a unit of lineal measure con-taining three feet (q.v.); thirty-six inches; 3'; 36".

3. YARD: a weighing machine in which the principle (q.v.) of leverage is applied.

> The yard was a yard too short for the long lorry to rest on the steelyard.

1. yarn: thread (q.v.); spun fibres; cot-ton, wool or silk in lengths for knitting, weaving or sewing.

2. YARN: a story, particularly a long in-incredible story.

> The ex-seaman spun his yarn while his industrious wife spun her yarn.

1. **yaud:** an old mare (q.v.); a decrepit horse.
2. YAWED: a jolt occasioned by a sudden deviation from course (q.v.); due to bad steering when under sail (q.v.).
3. YAWED: infected with yaws (q.v.).
   The schooner yawed again, and the skipper described the helmsman as a cross between a yaud and a yawed Negro-sea-cook.

yaw, see **ewer.**

yawed, see **yaud.**

1. **yawl:** a ship's boat smaller than a pinnace (q.v.); a small sailing-boat, cutter rigged.
2. YAWL: to weep vociferously; to howl; the challenge cry of tom-cats about to fight.
   The yawl sailed well in dirty weather with the yawl of the wind like fifty cats.

1. **yaws:** a contagious tropical disease involving a skin-affection contracted by negroes.
2. YAWS: jolts and shocks sustained by a sailing-ship under way (q.v.) occasioned by bad steering.
3. YOURS: possessive of 'you' (q.v.).
   The little ship of my domestic establishment yaws dangerously: both my house-boys have yaws, have yours?

1. **yeah:** a sloven pronunciation of 'yes', employed in higher social circles in U.S.A. than in Britain.
2. YEAR: the period of time (q.v.) occupied by the earth in one circumgyration of the sun (q.v.).

So youse wanna ye
little thing, yeah?
hire me a guy to do

year, see preceding group.

1. **yeld:** of barren cows, yielding milk.
2. YELLED: pst tns of 'yell
   'Yon cow is yeld,'
   Giles.

yell, see **yale.**

yelled, see **yeld.**

yew, see **ewe.**

yews, see **ewes.**

1. **yoke:** a shaped board
   shoulders; of an
   harness, or of a
   support two bucke
   duty.
2. YOLK: the inner, yell
   tion of an egg.
3. YOLK: lanoline.
   Having broke
   china milkmaid
   she would stick
   egg but, of cou
   white.

yolk, see preceding gr

yore, see **ewer.**

you, see **ewe.**

your }
you're } see **ewer.**

yours, see **yaws.**

zinc, see **sink.**